THE ANDAMAN STORY

Audrey,

The Andaman Story

*with love for
you are the bestest of friends*

N Iqbal Singh

May 1978.

VIKAS PUBLISHING HOUSE PVT LTD
New Delhi Bombay Bangalore Calcutta Kanpur

VIKAS PUBLISHING HOUSE PVT LTD
5 Ansari Road, New Delhi 110002
Savoy Chambers, 5 Wallace Street, Bombay 400001
10 First Main Road, Gandhi Nagar, Bangalore 560009
8/1-B Chowringhee Lane, Calcutta 700016
80 Canning Road, Kanpur 208004

Copyright © N Iqbal Singh, 1978

ISBN 0 7069 0632 2

1V02I0501

The illustration used on each chapter-opening page, as well as at the back of the jacket, is that of a *lenta* (magic board). *Lenta* are made during an epidemic or serious illness to fight evil spirits. The human figure in the *lenta* is that of the Creator—Deuse. (The height of this board is 61.5 inches; the colours are brown, white, green and black.)

Printed at Ashoka Printers, Sri Nagar Colony, Delhi 110052

to

*the winsome Ongé damsel
I met in Little Andaman:
may her tribe
increase!*

Preface

If he only had a sum of £250 to his credit in all the world and nothing else, and was asked to choose a place where he would like to settle for the rest of his days, which one would it be? Sir Compton Mackenzie, the distinguished writer, was asked this question in a BBC quiz programme broadcast shortly after the end of the second world war. Pat came the answer—Car Nicobar. (Sir Compton had just been there.) I am not surprised. I would say the same because, to borrow Robert Louis Stephenson's picturesque phrase, Car Nicobar is like "a grove of palms, perpetually rustling fan". But I would perhaps not restrict my choice to Car Nicobar alone. I would go further and may even plump for one of the many other islands in the Andaman and Nicobar chain, for they have a unique beauty and scenic grandeur: not only the islands, but also the seas around them.

Speaking for myself, it was a case of *veni vidi vici* in reverse. I went, I saw, and I was conquered. And the spell lasted for all the four years that I spent in the islands. Not only that, I went back again in 1975, after a lapse of five years. The enchantment still held.

It would be an exercise in futility to try and write about all those who have, in the past, fallen for the charm of these mysteriously beautiful islands, for there have been so many—Arabs, Chinese, Europeans and others, both from the Orient and Occident. Some came as travellers, others as adventurers. But even among the administrators, who came after the British occupation of the islands after the Great Mutiny, there have been some remarkable characters.

The pride of place among those who came as adjuncts of the British administration must go to Edward Horace Man. Edward was the son of Captain (later Lieutenant-Colonel and eventually General) Henry Man, who had originally raised the British flag and formally occupied the islands after Blair's settlement had ended in a fiasco more than half a century earlier. Edward Horace Man could be described as a child of the islands. He belongs to that unusual breed who really tried to identify themselves with the "locals", in this case the aborigines. He travelled extensively and got to know the islands and its people. He studied the life-style, the mores, the customs and the language of both the Andamanese and the Nicobarese. And his studies were in depth. His works on these people are definitive. He even compiled a dictionary of the Central Nicobarese language, which to this day stands as the most authentic work in that genre.

One of the earlier chief commissioners in the 1870s was the colourful Major-General (eventually Field Marshal) Sir Donald Martin Stewart, Bart., who came to the Andamans as chief commissioner after having fought with distinction in Qandahar during the Afghan War, and in the Mutiny. He was to end up eventually as the Indian commander-in-chief. It was said of him that he was "strong, brave, genial, eminently wise and just, forgetful of self and modest, [he] did with his might and whatever his hand found to do".

Lieutenant-Colonel Sir Richard Temple, Bart., is another chief commissioner who deserves a place in this roll of honour. He conducted the first ever general census in 1901. His census report is undoubtedly perhaps the ablest ever written so far. What is remarkable about Temple is that he did not confine his writing to the islands alone. He compiled, along with someone by the name of Mrs Steele, a selection of tales known as *Wide Awake Stories*. Before coming to the Andamans, he had already published a two-volume work—*Legends of the Punjab*. He was also editor of Fallon's *Hindustani Proverbs* and Barnett's *Devil Worship of the Tuluvas*. Temple edited and owned *The Indian Antiquary*.

Nearer our times, we had Lieutenant-Colonel M L Ferrar between the years 1923 and 1931. He had been a contemporary of Sir Winston Churchill at Sandhurst and, in an interview broadcast from the Port Blair station of All India Radio in 1969, then in his nineties, he recalled his days at Sandhurst and, with a great deal of nostalgia, the years he spent in the Andamans. Ferrar was not only popular with the "locals" but he is among the few who could claim to have had friends among the convicts, because he used to go and play hockey with them in the Cellular Jail compound. Ferrar's hobby, while in the Andamans, was collecting butterflies. And in his broadcast he said that, modesty aside, he considered his to be the best collection of butterflies of the islands ever made. He added that he had made a present of it to the British Museum, where it can still be seen. When I asked an officer of the Andaman and Nicobar administration, who had served it for 41 years and under 16 different chief commissioners, both British and Indian, who in his opinion was the best and most outstanding chief commissioner, his reply was categorical—it was Ferrar. Ferrar also had the doubtful distinction of having been an aide to General Dyer of Jallianwala Bagh fame!

The Andamans also attracted some eccentric characters who came there obviously to escape the hard and bitter realities of life. One among them was the Honourable Athelstan Alcock in 1909. His is a sad story. While at Simla he had fallen in love with a planter's wife. Not being the type who would indulge lightly in an affair, he was so conscience-stricken that, instead of continuing to go about it in a discreet manner, which then was the norm, he and his love went to her husband and announced their love. Everyone knew that she had been desperately unhappy, but sanctimonious Victorianism took over. A scandal followed, and there was a divorce. To run away from it all, he asked for a posting to the Andamans. But, within a week of their marriage, Alcock's wife died. He arrived in Port Blair a shattered man, fully convinced that he had been punished by Providence for his adultery. Consequently, he spent most of his time writing letters to his wife, which bore the legend—*Mrs Athelstan Alcock, Heaven*. When a contemporary wag was told that the local post master had a sackful of all those letters addressed to Mrs Alcock in Heaven, his wry, albeit cruel, comment was: "Anyway they are unstamped, and they don't pay postage dues where she's gone."

Be that as it may, the fact of the matter is that whoever has lived in the islands of Andaman and Nicobar, despite their being termed *Kale Pani*—the black waters—has come back completely charmed, and one keeps on hoping that one will go back there yet again. I do hope that for me this will not turn out, to quote T S Eliot, a hope "without hope of the lost thing".

And now it is my pleasure and privilege to express my thanks and gratitude to all those persons and institutions who have, in one way or another, helped me in writing this book.

It all began with a telephone call, one evening some three years ago, from my friend Uma Vasudev, to say that she and her husband, L K Malhotra, an old colleague and friend, were at the Press Club, and would I meet them there for a drink? And it was there that I met someone who has since become a very close friend. During the course of our conversation, it was he who suggested that I write a book on the islands, since I had lived there. So my thanks to all three of them—particularly to the one who has chosen to remain anonymous; I owe him a special debt of gratitude.

Uma Anand has been, to use a cliché, a tower of strength, and at every stage has proved the proverbial friend, philosopher and guide. I am grateful to her for the enormous help she has rendered. Satindra Singh is another person to whom I owe gratitude. Although he did occasionally drive me round the bend, he not only helped with the loan of many books but also looked at some pages of the script, with a toothcomb as it were, and gave me valuable suggestions. My thanks are due to Trevi Sen for going through the script.

Among the institutions I must thank are the National Archives of India, the Sangeet Natak Akademi Library, the Nehru Memorial Library, the Census Commissioner's Office Library, the Historical Division of the Ministry of Defence, the United Services Institution, and lastly, the India Office Library and Records in London. Here I must add that the material I was able to get from London was entirely due to my old friend, Len Allinson, the then British deputy high commissioner in Delhi and thanks to him I received every assistance from Joan Lancaster and Martin Moir of the India Office Library and Records, who were able to put me in touch with Major Denis McCarthy and Colonel Christopher Hodson. Major McCarthy has been good enough to allow me to quote from his unpublished account of *Operation Baldhead I*, which he had conducted during the Japanese occupation of the islands in the second world war. Similarly, Colonel Hodson wrote and gave me details of the part he played in the logistics of organizing various intelligence operations code-named Baldhead. It was also due to Len Allinson that I was able to write to Lord Mountbatten, who very generously sent me a photostat copy of the entry he had made in his personal diary about his one-day visit to Port Blair. He also gave me permission to quote from it, for which indeed I am duly obliged.

The chief commissioner of the islands in 1975, Har Mander Singh, was personally most helpful. I wish I could say the same of some other members of his staff, an exception of course being the then harbour master, Commander K P Nair. He and his wife, Lakshmi, not only extended to me their warm hospitality, but Commander Nair went out of his way to help me visit some of the islands I wanted to visit, notably Strait Island, where live the two dozen remnants of the Great Andamanese tribe. T N Pandit, the superintending anthropologist of the Anthropological Survey of India, was another person who proved of great help. He and his wife, Roshi, were also very generous in their hospitality. I thank them. And also Captain Johnson Boaz, the ebbulient master of *M V Ongé*, who made the one-week cruise of the Nicobars one long picnic.

My thanks to Billie Ahmed and Dr K M Ganapathy for the loan of some out-of-print books, and also to L P Mathur, whom I have never met, for providing such an exhaustive bibliography in his *History of the Andaman and Nicobar Islands (1756-1966)*.

I am also most grateful to Dr Simon Kooijman of Riskmuseum Voor Volkenkunde, Leiden, for supplying me with a transparency (and a black and white photograph) of the rare Nicobarese *lenta* ("magic board", acquired by the museum in 1881 from the Giglioli collection) and to the Anthropological Survey of India for the transparency of the Ongés: they are on two sides of the dust-jacket. The other photographs—Rami Chhabra has contributed *Ruins at Ross, Great Andamanese on Strait Island, Timber afloat in a creek* and *A Jarawa comes aboard*; Prem Kapur: *Corbyn's Cove, the Andamanese raja, The pig is their wealth, Nicobari devils, Port Blair* and *Seas and skies*; and the Armed Forces Film and Photo Division of the Ministry of Defence, government of India: *I N S Narbudda*. Most of the other photographs were taken either by S Dorai Rajan of All India Radio, Port Blair, who accompanied me during my peregrination of the islands in 1975, or by P C Philip, official photographer of the Andaman and Nicobar administration. To all of them, my many thanks.

One solitary individual was rudely non-cooperative. He was Chief Commissioner S M Krishnatry. So if some of the statistics (or other present-day information) be out of date, it is due to him.

Two of the institutions that I have not mentioned so far, which I would single out for special gratitude, are the Indian Airlines (and its Public Relations Manager, Ajit Gopal) for giving me a complimentary air ticket to enable me to visit the islands once again, and All India Radio (and P C Chatterji, its director-general, in particular) for the help and assistance rendered to me by All India Radio, which took many forms.

I must not forget to express my appreciation of what my very dear friend, Fred Burn (who is now no more), and his hospitable wife, Jean, did for me during my early days in Port Blair. In fact, they were the ones who first exposed me to the beauty of the Andamanese hinterland by taking me out on what he used to describe jokingly as "Cook's Guided Tours"; he also unrolled for me the magic carpet that lies under the Andaman waters, by letting me sail with him in his motor-boats.

One word of personal explanation: readers would notice that I have refrained from giving any footnotes or references at the end of the text. It is a personal quirk with me—I find them both irritating and distracting. The responsibility for this omission, if it is to be termed as one, is therefore entirely mine. I must, however, hasten to add that whatever material I have used has full documentary support.

My last word of thanks—to all those, some, in particular, who added to the enchantment of the islands during my stay there.

New Delhi, 1978 N IQBAL SINGH

Contents

1 THE DARK BACKWARD   1

2 THE LIE OF THE LAND   8

3 GOD-GIVEN GIFTS   13

4 THE BRITISH DEBUT   20

5 SPORADIC FORAYS AND AN INCREDIBLE SHIPWRECK   31

6 MORE SHIPWRECKS   41

Contents

7 RETURN OF THE BRITISH   49

8 THE ABORIGINES: NEGRITOS, NOT NEGROES   57

9 THE ONGÉS   67

10 THE BIRTH OF THE PENAL SETTLEMENT   73

11 TEETHING TROUBLES   83

12 THE NICOBARS AND NICOBARESE   87

13 A NICOBARESE FOLK-TALE   104

14 PENAL SETTLEMENT GROWS AND A VICEROY IS KILLED   107

15 TAMING THE ANDAMANESE   124

16 BEFRIENDING THE ONGÉS   142

17 THE UNTAMED JARAWAS   153

18 PENAL SETTLEMENT—TO BE OR NOT TO BE   165

19 THE EARLY "POLITICOS"   182

20 COME THE POLITICAL PRISONERS   188

21 DURING THE GREAT WAR AND AFTER   205

22 THE MIKADO'S SHADOW   229

23 JAPANESE "SPHERE OF CO-PROSPERITY"   237

24 JAPANESE REIGN OF TERROR, NETAJI'S VISIT AND THEIR ULTIMATE DOOM   246

25 THE NICOBARS DURING THE OCCUPATION   266

26 LIBERATION ... AND HORRORS RECALLED   269

27 INDEPENDENCE—AND AFTER   279

   Bibliography   307

   Index   313

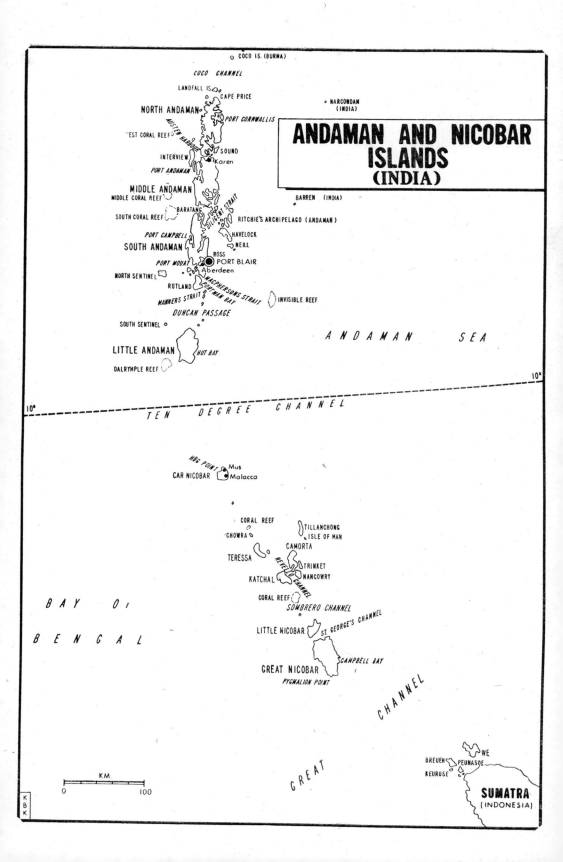

1

The Dark Backward

A Hindu legend, perhaps apocryphal, has it that when Lord Rama wanted to bridge the sea, in order to recover Sita, his consort, who had been abducted by King Ravana of Lanka, he first considered the possibility of using the Andaman and Nicobar range of islands for the purpose. Subsequently, of course, he abandoned this enterprise, and built the bridge at the more practicable point known as Adam's Bridge. This is perhaps the first reference in history or legend to the two groups of islands now known as the Andamans and Nicobars.

Claudius Ptolemaeus, popularly known as Ptolemy, the great geographer of the Roman Empire, located these islands in his maps in the 2nd century. Ptolemy, who lived in Alexandria, however, described these islands as "Islands of the Cannibals". The next reference to these islands is found in the writings of I'Tsing, the Chinese traveller who, sailing on a Persian ship, started on a voyage to India in AD 671. He studied Buddhism in Sumatra, and then took another ship, which is supposed to have anchored somewhere in the Nicobars, and finally landed in India in AD 673. He referred to the islands as *Andaban* and described the inhabitants as cannibals. Obviously, he had based this description on hearsay. Then came two Arab travellers who, also it would seem, did not actually visit any of the Andaman group of islands. Their account was translated in the 18th century by Abbe Renaudot, the French priest. The Arabs had perhaps actually undertaken their travels some time in the 870s. Describing these islands and their people they wrote:

The people who inhabit the coast eat human flesh, absolutely raw. They are dark, have fuzzy hair, frightful faces and eyes, enormous feet, almost elbow-length, and they go about naked. They have no boats and, if they had, they would be eating all passers-by they could get hold of.

Another traveller who passed by these islands during the course of his travels, but perhaps did not visit them, was Marco Polo, a citizen of Venice. He started on his odyssey in AD 1260. It extended to China and practically the whole of Asia. In an account of his travels, he spoke of Andaman as a "very big island". He went on to say:

The people have no king. They are idolaters and live like wild beasts. Now let me tell you of a race of men well worth describing in our book. You may take it for a fact that all the men of this island have heads like dogs, and teeth and eyes like dogs: for I assure you that the whole aspect of their faces is that of big mastiffs. They are a very cruel race: whenever they can get hold of a man who is not one of their kind, they devour him. They have abundance of spices of every kind. Their food is rice and milk, and every sort of flesh. They also have coconuts, apples of paradise, and many other fruits different from ours. The island lies in a sea so turbulent and so deep that ships cannot anchor there or sail away from it, because it sweeps them into a gulf from which they can never escape. This is because the sea there is so tempestuous, that it is continually eating away the land, scooping out trees at the root and toppling them into this gulf. It is truly marvellous how many trees are driven into the gulf without ever coming out again. Hence it happens that ships that enter the gulf are jammed in such a mess of these trees that they cannot move from the spot and so are stuck there for good.

Friar Odoric, a passer-by in 1322, described the people of the Andamans as "dog-faced and cannibals". In the early 15th century, Nicolodra Conti "visited" the Andamans. He had followed the roads and routes of the east from Damascus to Indo-China during the years 1414-39. He too repeated the same myth when he said that "the inhabitants of these islands tear strangers to pieces and devour them". The myth continued till even as late as in 1625, because Master Caesar Frederike, who published his *Eighteen Yeere's Indian Observations* in that year, wrote:

> From Nicubar to Pegu is, as it were, a row or chain of an infinite number of islands, of which many are inhabited with wild people; and they call those islands the islands of Andemaon, and they call their people savage or wild, because they eat one another: also, these islands have war with one another; and if by evil chance any ship be lost on those islands, as many have been, there is not one man of those ships lost there that escapeth uneaten or unslain. These people have not any acquaintance with any other people, neither have they trade with any, but live only of such fruits as those islands yield.

It was not till the East India Company started taking a certain amount of interest in these islands that the world, for the first time, began to learn with a certain amount of accuracy about the Andaman islands and its people. In 1788 Lord Cornwallis, the then governor-general of India, commissioned the great surveyor, Lieutenant Archibald Blair of the Indian Navy, to conduct a survey of these islands. But more of that later.

According to one theory, the name *Andaman* owes its origin to the Malays, who have known the islands from time immemorial, since the islands provided them with slaves. They used to sail across the seas, capture some of the aborigines and give them away as slaves in trade. The Malays called them the islands of *Handuman*, because that is how they pronounced the name of Hanuman in the *Ramayana*, our great classic. And Handuman eventually became Andaman.

Sir Henry Yule, who wrote a commentary on Marco Polo, has suggested that *Angamanian*, the name Marco Polo used, is an Arabic dual indicating the two Andamans, the Great one and the Little one. And some trace the origin of the word *Angman* to Ptolemy, who described them as the islands of good fortune, and hence the forms *Angaman*, *Agdaman*, and ultimately *Andaman*. In the first millennium AD, the Chinese and the Japanese knew the islands as *Yang-t'amang* and *Andaban*.

Nicolo Conti, in an attempt to give the word Andaman a meaning, called it "The Island of Gold", whereas in the great Tanjore Inscriptions of AD 1050, the islands appear to be mentioned under the translated name *Timaittivu*, which means the islands of impurity—perhaps because they were considered the abode of cannibals. Similarly, as a result of the possible influence of the Malays, they are referred to as the land of the

Rakshas in the Chinese history of the T'ang Dynasty, which ruled in China from AD 618 to 906. This would appear to confirm the ancient derivative of Andaman being from Hanuman, the monkey god, through the Malay Handuman.

There is less mystery about the name *Nicobar*, because through the centuries the Nicobar islands have often been referred to as the land of "the naked people". I'Tsing described them as *Lo-Jen-Kuo*, which means land of the naked people. The Arab travellers called them *Lakhabalus* or *Najabulus*, which was perhaps a mistranscription of some form of Nicobar, because it also means land of the naked. In the Tanjore Inscriptions they are mentioned as *Nakkavaram*, which translates as "Land of the Naked". Marco Polo's *Necuveran* (AD 1292), Rashiduddin's *Nakawaram* (AD 1300) and Friar Odoric's *Nicoveran* (AD 1322) are obviously lineal ancestors of the 15th and 16th century Portuguese *Nacabar* and *Nicubar*, and the modern *Nicobar*.

Very little is known about the early history of the Nicobar islands. If there is a reference to these islands in the Tanjore Inscriptions, it is likely that Rajendra I, the Chola king of South India, either conquered them, or at least sent a military expedition to these islands, because there is no doubt that he extended his hegemony over many countries of South-east Asia.

Before the discovery of the Cape of Good Hope, there does not appear to have been much contact between Europe and the Nicobars. But, once the sea route was open, European expeditions to the Far East became quite frequent, and the Nicobar chain of islands fell *en route*, as it were. The Portuguese pioneers tried to spread the Christian faith, but there are few records of their activities.

In 1556, Captain Fredrick touched the shores of one of the Nicobar islands. After him, many years later in 1601 (during the reign of Queen Elizabeth I), Sir James Lancaster, who was on his way to the Spice islands in command of an East India Company ship, paid a visit to these islands. He was followed by a Spanish missionary, Father Dominic Fernandes, while on a voyage from Malacca to Madras. Captain Alexander Dampier, on a voyage round the world, was on board the privateer *Cygnet of London* when she touched the coast of Great Nicobar Island. It was after some kind of mutiny against the behaviour of the ship's captain, Read, that Dampier and some of his other companions managed to land on the island. They spent a few days there before they could acquire a canoe from the local people, and then set sail for Sumatra. In *Voyages*, his journal, Dampier has written of a Captain Weldon having been there about the same time in one of the islands of the Nicobar group, possibly Nancowry. About the Nicobarese, he recorded that they lived "under no Government, equal without any distinction; every man ruling in his own house". He also mentions that Weldon had found on the island he visited, two "fryers" who had been "sent thither to convert the heathens".

In 1695, John Francis Gommeli, an Italian doctor, also landed somewhere in the Nicobars, while voyaging round the world. He wrote:

The island pays an annual tribute of a certain number of human bodies to the island of Andaemon, to be eaten by the natives of it. These brutes, rather than men... when they have wounded an enemy... run greedily to suck the blood that runs.

Another obvious case of hearsay!

The first organized attempt to convert the "natives" took place when, in January 1711, Faurè and Taillandiers, two French Jesuits who belonged to the French Society of Jesus, landed in Great Nicobar. We have their letters (in *Letters Edifiantes*) that testify to their being there for two and a half years. They then moved to other islands and ended up spending ten months in Car Nicobar. During this period, however, they were only able to convert one or two of their servants. A few years later arrived Father Charles de Montalembart from Pondicherry to spread the word, as also to explore the possibility of establishing a mission in the Nicobars. He had also been asked to select a site for setting up a factory by the French East India Company. He returned in 1742, after a year's stay, without accomplishing anything substantial. Next came the Danes—the Danish East India Company also wanted colonies in the Nicobars. They renamed the islands as Fredrick islands and set up a commercial mission. This was in 1756. Within a year, however, all members of the expedition had died of fever. The Danish East India Company came again in 1769—a few officers, accompanied by six missionaries and a few soldiers. They settled down in Nancowry. But they suffered the same fate, because in a couple of years most of them were dead due to climatic conditions. It was the turn of the Moravian priests now. Two of them, Haensal and Wangeman, when they reached Nancowry, found to their dismay that of the four missionaries who had preceded them, one had died already and three were seriously ill. By 1787, 11 Moravian missionaries had come to the Nicobars. All but one had died. While the Danish missionaries were still in the Nicobars, a Dutch adventurer named William Bolts appeared on the scene. He duly raised the Austrian flag and took possession of the islands in the name of the Austrian empress, Maria Theresa, and her successors. He had been able to persuade the Austrian government to trade with the East Indies and set up a partnership with Baron Von Prote of the Netherlands and two Dutch merchants. But it all ended in a fiasco.

In the meanwhile, in 1778, Car Nicobar was visited by a Swede, Dr I G Koenig, who had been a doctor to the missionaries at Tranquebar and a naturalist to the *Nabob* of Arcot. In his journal, he described what he called "Kare Nequebar" as being "agreeable" to the eye "on account of the pleasant change of wood with green fields, and trees standing in thin rows between them".

The entry of the adventurer Bolt in the affairs of the Nicobars, which the Danes had obviously begun to consider as their special preserve, put up the back of the Danes. They, therefore, sent another expedition in 1784. This too met with little success, mainly, again, due to adverse climatic conditions. Nevertheless, they did manage to keep "a wretched little guard", as Sir Richard Temple was later to describe him, at the Nancowry harbour. He was there from 1793 to 1807. During this period the Moravian missionaries made two isolated attempts, in 1790 and 1804, to stage a comeback. Taking advantage of the Napoleonic wars, which raged in Europe between 1807 and 1814, the British took over the control of the islands. But they handed them back to the Danes once the wars were over.

The evangelists, however, had not let up even during the Napoleonic wars—an Italian Jesuit had come over for a while from Rangoon, only to make a hasty retreat due to ill health. The Danes continued to be incorrigible. Rosen, a Danish missionary, arrived in 1827 to establish yet another colony. He met with the same fate, and had to leave in 1834, having fallen ill. His small colony, though, lasted for another two years. It was now the turn of the French Jesuits, Supries and Galabert. They came in 1836 and, after suffering for two years, abandoned their mission without having converted anyone. They were followed by two more French missionaries, Chopard and Beaury, in 1842. Beaury died due to sickness after a stay of less than two months. Chopard had never remained in a state of good health either. In 1843, Father Renier came to join him. After a while, he was able to persuade Chopard to go back with him to Moulmein for treatment. Chopard returned, but had to go again to Moulmein. He was back soon after; and this time with two other French missionaries—Plaisant and Lacrampe—who left shortly afterwards. Chopard stayed on, only to die eventually in a hut at Teressa on 25 June 1845. He had succeeded in converting only one woman, who had come to him to be tended while sick.

The Danes made yet another attempt, their last one, to colonize the Nicobars in 1845. This time they chose as their representative a person named Busch, who arrived on board *L' Espiegle*, a British ship which had sailed from Calcutta. He hoisted the Danish flag, both in Great Nicobar and Little Nicobar, in the name of King Christian VIII of Denmark. Soon after, he was joined by Captain Steen Bille. Bille had been sent with a new scheme to help Busch in his efforts at colonization. Finally, however, it seems as though it suddenly dawned on the Danish government that all their efforts at colonization of the Nicobars had not been worth their while. So, in 1848, they finally withdrew.

In 1858, the Austrians appeared again with their own scheme of settlement, which came to nothing. In 1868, Franz Mauer, a Prussian officer, advised the Prussian government to take over the Nicobars. Nothing came of that either. Eventually, it is the British who stepped in, in 1869. And their stay lasted till the year 1947, when India achieved independence. They were there right through, except for a brief period during the second world war, when the islands were under Japanese occupation.

The Nicobarese themselves believe that there was once a great cataclysm which flooded the entire land. According to this legend, one of them, a man, was able to swim across to a big tree and clamber on to it. He managed to live on the branches of the tree until the rains stopped and the flood waters receded. When he climbed down from this tree, he saw a bitch atop the branches of another one. The ears of this bitch were spiked by the great thorns of the *kun-hiol*, a thorny palm. He rescued the bitch, took her with him and made her his wife. They lived together and begat children which were human. The Nicobarese are supposed to have descended from them. No wonder that even till today they wear the *kisat*, a scanty loin cloth which has a tail like a dog's. They also wear a band round their head which has ears pricked up like that of a dog.

There is yet another legend about the origin of the Nicobari people. According to this, a Burmese princess was sent into exile by her father because she had developed an unnatural relationship with a dog. She was expecting a child when she landed on the shores of the Nicobars. But before the birth of her child she killed the dog to wipe out any evidence of her shame. She, however, felt a compulsive urge to procreate. So she married her son. And the Nicobarese are the result of that union.

The aborigines of the Andaman islands also trace their genesis to a cataclysm. According to this legend, there was once a great cataclysm in their land, which caused a subsidence of many parts of their great island. The big island became fragmented into the many islands that today comprise the Andaman chain of islands. And it was also because of this great flood that Maia Tomola, the ancestral chief of the nation from whom all the Andamanese have sprung, dispersed them. A large number of the then inhabitants were drowned, according to this belief; so were many large and fierce beasts that have since disappeared. Of course, it was all due to *Puluga*, the anthropomorphic deity. *Puluga* brought about this cataclysm which engulfed the islands and separated the people!

2

The Lie of the Land

The Andaman islands, large and small, number 204 in all. They lie 590 miles away from the mouth of the river Hoogly, and are at a distance of 120 miles from Cape Negrais in Burma; Cape Negrais is the nearest point on the Burmese mainland. The Andaman group of islands is 219 miles in length; its extreme width, however, is nowhere more than 32 miles. The most important islands in the group are the three Andaman islands—North, Middle and South Andaman—popularly known as Great Andaman. These three islands are separated from one another by narrow straits. On the extreme north, some distance away from North Andaman, lies Landfall Island; the Labyrinth islands are off the south-west coast of South

Andaman; off the east coast of the same island lies Ritchie's Archipelago, also known as the Archipelago islands. Then there is Baratang, lying in between, but somewhat to the east of the Middle and South Andamans, and Rutland Island near the southern end of South Andaman. At the southern extremity of the southern group of Andaman islands, 31 miles away from Rutland Island, is situated Little Andaman, covering an area of roughly 26 by 16 miles. This island, which is more or less completely flat, is separated from Rutland Island by what is known as Duncan Passage, in which lies Cinque Island, and a few other tiny ones.

The Andaman islands lie between the 10th and 14th parallels of north latitude and between the 22nd and 24th meridians of east longitude. South of Little Andaman is the treacherous Ten Degree Channel, 90 miles wide. The Nicobars lie beyond. On the east of Great Andaman lie two volcanic islands—Narcondam and Barren.

Narcondom Island, which is 71 miles east of North Andaman, is like a high and lofty, flat peak rising out of the deep waters of the sea. It is arid and barren, with hardly any vegetation; nor has it any potable water. It is two and a half by one and a half miles in area and is 2,300 feet above sea level. Some trace the origin of its name to the word *narak* which, in Hindi, means hell. Barren Island is nothing but the crater of a volcano rising abruptly out of the sea. It lies 71 miles to the north-east of Port Blair, the capital of the Andaman and Nicobar group of islands. Its diameter is about two miles and the ground all round slopes gently from the sea to the base of the crater, which is about 50 feet above the sea level. The cone, in perfect symmetry, is about 2,000 feet in circumference and 100 feet high.

The volcano has been quiescent for a long time, though when Lieutenant Archibald Blair passed by it in 1795 he saw it in a state of eruption. A few years later, another passer-by by the name of Horsburgh, recorded an explosion every ten minutes and found a fire burning on the eastern side of the crater. Dr Fedrick J Mouat and Dr Von Liebig, who visited the island in 1857, though separately, also found "volumes of dark smoke, and clouds of hot, watery vapour".

When C Boden Kloss visited the island in January 1901, he found no volcanic activity. But, he says: "The scene was one of striking beauty. Against a background of bright blue sky the little island rose from a sea of lapis-lazuli, which ceaselessly dashed white breakers on the rocky shores. The steep brown slopes, part clothed in brilliant green, framed in the cone—a black and solid mass, round which a pair of eagles circled slowly." Besides the pair of eagles he also found, inside the cone, the little bird, white-eye (*zosterops palpebrosa*), and the Indian cuckoo. He was obviously thrilled by the cuckoo's loud cries of *ko-el, ko-el*, which resounded in all directions.

Great Andaman, which comprises North, Middle and South Andaman Islands, consists of a number of hills interspersed with narrow valleys.

The entire area is covered with thick tropical jungle. Some of the hills, particularly those on the east coast, are quite high. The highest hill, which is in North Andaman, is known as Saddle Peak. It is 2,400 feet high. An interesting feature of the Andamans is the absence of rivers in this group of islands. However, there are some perennial streams.

The scenery everywhere on the Andamans is beautiful, at times breathtakingly so. While flying in an aeroplane the multiple range of hills look as though daubed by a brush dipped in lavender; the sea glistens in all the shades of blue and green, and some of the coral beds in the innumerable bays that are a prominent feature of the landscape shimmer in all the colours of the rainbow. The coastline is heavily indented, thus providing many a natural harbour. There are tidal creeks aplenty.

The Nicobar group of islands has 19 islands in all, a dozen of which are inhabited. The total area of the Nicobars is 635 square miles, of which one island alone, Great Nicobar, covers 333 square miles. The length of the entire Nicobar chain from the northern tip of Car Nicobar to the southernmost end of Great Nicobar is 160 miles. The distance between Little Andaman Island and Car Nicobar is 60 miles and between Pygmalion Point, which is on the southern tip of Great Nicobar, and Achin Head, at the northern end of Sumatra in Indonesia, is about 91 miles.

The two most important islands in the Nicobar group are Great Nicobar and Car Nicobar. Great Nicobar is 30 miles long, but its breadth varies between seven and fourteen miles. There is a range of hills running along the east coast, but the highest point is in the north where lies Mount Thuillier, 2105 feet high. Near the centre of the island there is another range of hills, with a maximum height of 1333 feet. There are also irregular hills on the western side. And at the base of the foothills, as also between the hills and the sea, lie some vast alluvial plains. Great Nicobar is the only island in the Andaman and Nicobar chain of islands which can also boast of having what could become navigable rivers. The rivers known as Dagmar and Alexandra are on the west, and the one called the Galathea river runs to the south.

The other important island, in fact the most important island in the Nicobars, is Car Nicobar, which has an area of only 49 square miles. Shaped somewhat like Australia, it has an almost flat surface rising gently to about 200 feet in the north-west. The soil is very fertile and is covered with coconut trees. The people living in Car Nicobar tell a story about the genesis of the tree. Once upon a time, they say, there was a great scarcity of water on the island. From somewhere a man appeared—a devil man—who through sheer magic produced water from his elbow. The people, thinking him to be a devil incarnate, chopped off his head. But a tree sprouted where the head fell. And the tree grew big and began to bear fruit, and it resembled the head of the beheaded man. The people were afraid to touch the tree or eat the fruit, because it had grown out of the head of a man. So the ripe fruit continued to fall, and many trees grew, resulting in a dense coconut grove. An old man lay dying; he was therefore persuaded by some wise men to taste the fruit of the coconut tree to test its quality. The old man not only ate one, but he found it so delicious that he continued to eat the nuts, which were growing in such abundance. He regained his strength and began to look like a young man. Thereafter, the people began to eat the coconut and to grow this lush palm tree!

Apart from the Great Nicobar and Car Nicobar islands, other populated islands in this chain are Teressa, Tompuka, Camorta, Nancowry, Trinket, Katchal, Pullomillo, Kondul and, of course, Chowra. Incidentally, Chowra is the only island which, till today, has a living tradition of witch-doctors. Another remarkable feature of this chain of islands is the most perfect natural harbour at Nancowry. It lies in the midst of Camorta, Noncowry and Trinket and provides an almost perfect land-locked shelter.

According to one belief, the Andaman and Nicobar group of islands, also known as the Bay islands, which lie in the Bay of Bengal, once formed part of a continuous mountain range, stretching in a curve from Cape Negrais in Burma to Achin Head in Sumatra; Cape Negrais was itself in the nature of an extension of the Arakan Hills range which, in turn, is one of a series of ranges that run down the eastern Himalayas. C Boden Kloss, who examined this hypothesis in depth, does not agree. According to him:

> Although they form a chain that seems to indicate a past union of Sumatra and Burma, investigation proves that this is far from being the case. For soundings in this part of the ocean show that between Nicobars and the group of islands adjacent to the North-east point of Sumatra—entering from the open sea to the west, and thence tending north between the Andamans and Malay Peninsula almost as far as the latitude of Narkondam—there runs a long tongue of depressed ocean bed with depths everywhere of 1,000 fathoms. This fact, together with the shallowness of the sea-bottom around and connecting the Andamans with the Arakan Yoma Peninsula, suggest the inference that the former were at one time past the termination of a seaward extension from Cape Negrais of the Arakan Yoma Range—a conclusion that is in some degree emphasized by the zoological and botanical conditions common to the two.

To reinforce his point further, Kloss quotes A D Hume who, with a number of collectors, made a cruise around the Bay islands in 1873 to study the avifauna there. In Hume's opinion, this theory of "connection" does not derive, *"prima facie*, much support from a consideration of their fauna". He continues to say that:

If they ever were in uninterrupted communication with the Arakan Hills it must apparently have been at an immensely distant period, for not only are the most characteristic species of the Arakan Hills, as we now find them, absent from the islands, but the latter exhibit a greater number of distinct and peculiar forms, constituting, where the ornis is concerned, considerably more than one-third the number known.

Therefore, except perhaps in the very remote past, these islands have not formed part of the South-east Asian land mass. This theory is also borne out by the localized nature of the fauna because, again according to Kloss, "nearly every island possesses its own peculiar species of terrestrial mammals".

The Bay islands are exposed to both monsoons, the north-east and the south-west. The average annual rainfall is 127.35 inches. Of the total land area, more than three-fourths is covered with a thick and heavily luxuriant growth of tropical jungle.

3
God-Given Gifts

The vegetation in the Andaman islands can be divided into five distinct forest growths. According to C E Parkinson, whose book *A Forest Flora of Andaman Islands* is the only definitive study of the flora of the Andaman islands so far, they are:

(1) Mangrove forest, which confines itself to sea-washed soil, and which according to the formation of the seashores, forms belts varying from a few yards to a mile or more in width; (2) Littoral forest influenced by, but out of the reach of the sea, occupying flat strips of land along the coast varying from a few yards to several chains in width; (3) Evergreen forest found growing on the low alluvial damp strips

of land in the valleys or on the moist loamy fertile hills; (4) Forests of a more or less deciduous or leafshedding character usually found growing on undulating land of a somewhat poor-looking and comparatively dry soil; and (5) The type of forest found growing on the parched and shallow-soiled slopes of high hills.

Parkinson found that "from the water's edge to the tops of the highest hills, they [the islands] are nearly everywhere densely wooded". He went on to add that "the effect of the luxuriant and varied foliage is bewildering".

There is a preponderance of evergreen trees in the Andaman forests, but they are generally heavily laden with climbers. Occasionally, one also finds glades of bamboo. There are creepers all over. The timber is plentiful and of many varieties. According to the *Imperial Gazetteers* (1908), the timber could, for commercial purposes, be divided into three classes:

First class, *padauk, kokko, chuglam,* marble wood and satin wood; second class, *pyinma, bombway, chai, lakuch, lalchini, pongyet, thitmin, mowha, khaya, gangaw, thingan*; third class, *didu, ywegyi, toungpeingyi* and *gurjan.*

Padauk is best known of them all, and at one stage it was exported to Europe and America. According to Parkinson: "This well-known tree, often with large buttresses and stout spreading branches, form, with the crowns of other giants of these forests, the roof or upper canopy, which in these islands averages about 140 feet in height." (Incidentally, it was padauk wood that was used for the entire woodwork of the schooner *Lonely Lady,* in which Sir Elec Rose, the lone seaman, sailed round the world in record time in 1968.) Padauk is also unique inasmuch as it exhibits a variety of colours, ranging from light brown to dark crimson. Marble wood and satin wood are decorative and specially used for making ornamental furniture. Gurjan is mainly used for making sleepers and wood-paving; it also yields oil. Another kind of wood, perhaps found nowhere else, is *burr*. It is a kind of diseased wood, but the disease only results in a knotty outgrowth on the stem, producing beautifully figured timber. Anything made in *burr* is today a collector's item.

The variety and wealth of the flora found in the Andaman islands is evident from the fact that Parkinson deals with as many as 650 plants in his book. Of them 540, he thinks, are indigenous to the islands, and the rest perhaps introduced from outside at some stage. In the opinion of Sulpiz Kurz, another eminent botanist who also made a study of the Andaman flora in 1866, the number of indigenous phanerogamic plants may range between 1,500 and 1,800 species. Along the coastline, and also in the vegetation that borders it, there is a great variety of flora. Just behind some of the white sandy beaches, which dazzle when the sun shines bright, the growth is often luxuriant. Where there is no foreshore, the mangroves grow thick and in great profusion. And when the tide is high they get submerged in the sea, looking as though they are growing out of it. In areas which line the top of the beaches, there grows a kind of tree which has fleshy leaves and fan-like flowers in shape. There are hibiscus shrubs also, with branches stretching right into the sea. Another shrub has flowers like white lilies. Then there are thickets of Pandanus, the fragrant screw-pine. When the Pandanus is in bloom, it is really a sight for the gods. A little further back and above the beaches grow twining plants like the Goat's foot creeper, with lobed leaves and large purple flowers, or creepers with yellow flowers, like those of the pea. There is one that is spoon-shaped and has deep blue and white flowers.

Just behind the fringe, where the shrubs grow, there are trees—some tall, others not so tall. There is a tree with hibiscus-like flowers, yellow in colour, that blooms only at night. Another one has rings of leaves, with fruit that is open at the top, with a dark-coloured seed inside. Others include a tree with glossy leaves and a delicate, though quite large, pale pink flower (which Parkinson has likened to a powder-puff) and trees that grow scarlet and orange flowers, some very fragrant. But there is nothing to beat the awe-inspiring grandeur of the evergreen forests covering the myriad high hills in the islands.

There is also an abundance of orchids all over the islands.

In the Nicobars, according to the *Imperial Gazetteers:*

In economic value the forests of Nicobars are quite inferior to the Andaman forests; and, so far as is known, the commercially valuable trees, besides fruit-trees, such as the coco-nut, betel-nut, and *mallori* [*pandanus larum*], are a thatching palm and a few timber trees, of which only that known as the black *chuglam* in the Andamans would be there classed in the Andamans as a first class timber.

The other varieties of timber found in the Nicobars are not of much value.

But the palm-trees are a different story. They are not only economically valuable but exceedingly beautiful. In addition, there are large clumps of casuarina, and great fern trees. All along the coast grows a shrub known in botanical terms as *barringtonia speciosa*. Its leaves are large and shiny, and it has a crimson-tipped tassel-like blossom. Here also is a profusion of *pandanus larum*, the tall screw-pine, the fruit of which is the main item of diet of the Nicobarese. There are some climbing species of the bamboo, but hardly any of the tall variety. Mangosteen, cinnamon and pepper grow wild. And so does the betel palm, which provides the areca-nut. There are a large number of milky climbers to be seen everywhere and, in the southern forest, the rattan. The orchids are also found here.

Strange as it may seem, before they were planted there, there were no palm-trees in the Andamans. And consequently no coconut!

In the animal kingdom, there are none that are of a dangerous variety. The Andamans have the pig, the wild cat and the iguana. But strangely enough the pig found in these islands is related to the Chinese pig! There is a large variety of deer, but they are, comparatively speaking, a recent import. They have multiplied quickly. There are plenty of snakes, some of them poisonous. They include the cobra, the hamadryad, the blue krait, the sea snakes and two species of pit-vipers. In the Andamans is also found the green lizard (*phelfuma andamans*). Incredibly enough, the only other place where this green lizard is found is Madagascar!

South Sentinel Island, which is uninhabited, is the home of the coconut crab. It is also known as the rubber crab. Deep blue in colour, this kind of crab, as its name implies, lives generally on coconut. But in South Sentinel Island there are no coconuts. Obviously, it has learnt to live there on other plants and perhaps some animal food.

Then we have in the Andamans the green turtle, a gourmet's delight. (Who has not heard of turtle soup?) The local people, however, only kill the turtle for its flesh and also enjoy eating turtle's eggs, which it lays in great number.

In the field of zoology, there are the coral reefs, which are very extensive. There is also the sea-cucumber (*trepang*) and, of course, the birds'-nests (another gourmet's delight), which are of a very fine quality.

Lieutenant Archibald Blair, who surveyed the islands, has described one of the birds'-nest caves which he saw. He wrote:

> The principal cave is situated at the south point of Strait Island [in Diligent Strait], which is rocky, but not exceeding forty feet in height. The entrance, which is washed by the tide, is an irregular aperture, of about six feet wide, and the same height. On advancing thirty or forty feet, the height diminishes to four feet, and the breadth increases to twenty. Here it is rather dark, and very warm, and the top and sides of the cave are covered with nests; an astonishing number of birds twittering and on the wing, whisking past the ears and eyes. This, contrasting with the melancholy noise of the waves resounding through the gloomy cavern, formed a very uncommon and interesting scene. The birds are probably induced to choose this situation from the caves being inaccessible either to snakes or quadrupeds, and probably defensible against birds of prey. The nests in general are in form the quarter of a sphere, of two and a half inches diameter; one of the sections being firmly fixed to the rock, the other section leaves the nest open above.

The substance that comprises the bird's-nest, Lieutenant Blair goes on to say, "is glutinous... a mucilage exuding from the rock, moistened by exhalations from the sea, which washes the lower part of these caves. This mucilage, on being dried, has both texture, colour and taste of the nest...."

The nests are neither of animal nor vegetable, but of a mineral substance".

There are also any number of cattle bones, ornamental shells and tortoise shells in the Andaman islands.

The Nicobars have no wild animals that could be described as indigenous. They have a large number of pigs, but these are not dangerous at all. Most Nicobarese treat them as pets and consider them a form of wealth. At one time there were a few wild buffaloes and cattle on the island of Camorta—left behind by missionaries. On Great and Little Nicobar, and also in certain other places in that group of islands, particularly in the rivers in Great Nicobar and on the coast, there is an enormous number of crocodiles. There are also any number of monkeys on Great and Little Nicobar and on Katchal Island, but none elsewhere. They are dark, have long tails, and are of the crab-eating variety. Strictly speaking, one should describe them as crab-eating macaques.

Marine zoology in the Nicobars is very similar to that of the Andamans, except that pearl and pearl oysters are known to exist there. The Nicobars have birds'-nests too, and in addition, an inferior quality of the sponge.

Another notable feature of these islands is the preponderance of bats—of which 16 species are known—and rats, which are of 13 different kinds. There is a general, albeit mistaken, impression that there is a paucity of fauna on these islands. When, in 1872, Allan Octavian Hume (who also fathered the Indian National Congress), sent his collectors to these islands, they were able to collect as many as 2,000 birds in the course of their six-month stay. In February next year, Hume himself paid a month's visit to the islands, obviously to check up and see for himself the avifauna wealth of these islands. Humayun Abdulali, a well-known Indian ornithologist, visited the Andaman and Nicobar islands in 1964 because, as he put it, he had felt that there was "absolute lack of ornithological material from the Andaman and Nicobar Islands, where no work had been done in the [previous] fifty years". According to him, about the same time as Hume gave "an interesting account of this trip (1874) followed by a report on the collection", other "collections were made by Captain Ramsay Wardlaw and Wimberley, which were reported by Viscount Walden". After this, he goes on to tell us, "there was considerable activity for some time, which lapsed until revived by Butler [1899, 1900], Abbott and Kloss [Richmond 1903], and Osmaston [1905-08]". After that, apparently, there was nothing for many decades. Humayun Abdulali himself obtained 312 specimens of birds, 35 of which were from Car Nicobar and Nancowry.

Of the birds most commonly seen are two kinds of pigeons—the Nicobar pigeon and the Pied Imperial pigeon. The Nicobar pigeon, although named as such, is also found in the Andaman islands. A very pretty bird, its feet are plum-coloured, its head and neck a shade of delicate grey, and the tail, which is somewhat stumpy and hidden by the wings, absolutely snow-white. Its hackle and the rest of the plumage is a metallic green, which glistens in the sunshine. The Pied Imperial pigeon is arboreal and lives on fruit. Its overall colour is creamy white, but its flying feathers and the tip of the tail, which is broad, is of a jet-black tint. It is found both in the Nicobars and the Andamans, particularly in the two volcanic islands of the Andamans—Barren and Narcondam. Wild goats can also be seen in these two islands. The Andamanese fauna also include among its birds the Andaman Teal. It is a species of the duck and looks something like the whistling teal. Found generally in the creeks, its colour is grey but, while in flight, some white patches are visible on its wings and on the nape of its neck.

One of the most remarkable—and rare—birds found in Great Nicobar is the *megapode*. Amazingly enough, it is an Australian bird, and the only other regions where it is found are the Philippines and North-west Borneo, the nearest being Lombok Island, off Bali, 1800 miles away. It is no bigger than a domestic fowl. It lays eggs as large as that of a goose, but on a hillock fashioned out of alluvial soil. C Boden Kloss has described his own experience vis-à-vis the megapode:

> Just as I was entering the jungle by the mound, I noticed that earth was being thrown in a continuous shower from the top. Soon a bird ran out from a depression there; I shot it, and at the noise another jumped out for a moment and then went on digging, but appearing again a few seconds later, I got it also. It was about to lay, but the shot had unfortunately broken the egg: there is no external difference in the appearance of the sexes, but these were a pair, and it is therefore evident that when the hen is about to deposit the egg, the male assists in excavating the hole in which it is to be buried for incubation. The mound on which they were busy was between 7 and 8 feet high, and rather more than 100 feet in circumference, and had a large coco palm growing through the centre. It would certainly be the work of a number of birds, and must have taken many years to build.

The climate of the islands is very similar to that of most tropical islands. The normal rainfall in Port Blair can be anything from 105 to nearly 149 inches in a year; in the Nicobars it is about the same—occasionally more, but sometimes less. It is hot, but very pleasant when raining, and generally a sea breeze blows. It is very humid, though.

As far as the sea around the islands is concerned, a geodetic survey conducted by an international team of scientists some years ago revealed:

> A vast undersea valley, 600 miles long, 25 miles wide, and surrounded by towering mountain peaks... lies buried one to three miles under the sea. The valley, far larger in places than the Grand Canyon of the Colorado, extends from the northern tip of Sumatra in the Indonesian Archipelago to Narcondam Island, about 250 miles southwest of Rangoon, Burma. The width of the valley averages 20 to 25 miles bet-

ween peaks. The valley floor is about five to ten miles across. The deepest point found was estimated to be 15,000 feet, or almost three miles, under the sea. The floor of the valley is covered with more than a half-mile of muck and ooze. It is doubtful if man will ever tread its surface, regardless of the equipment he wears. The valley probably continues from Narcondam Island through the Irrawaddy River Valley in Burma. If so, it has been filled in by sand and mud deposited by the river over hundreds of thousands of years. The proven length of the valley is approximately 1,700 miles, equivalent to the distance between Washington and Denver, Colorado. The valley is part of the volcanic arc which includes Karkatoa, famous for its catastrophic explosion in the last century.

That is what lies some thousands of fathoms below the surface of the sea. Above it, lapping the shores of these many islands, is what not only the islanders but we too, in the rest of the country, could eat by way of sea food. Apart from tuna, the varieties of fish that are to be found all around include sardines, anchovies, barracuda, beaked fish, seer fish, mullet, the sea perch and other perches, mackerel, silver bellies, catfish, pomfret and hilsa. Besides, there are the sharks and the rays. There is also a plenitude of prawns, but what is available in plenty, though not often seen at anyone's table since the departure of the British, are lobsters, crabs and oysters. And for the aquariums—angels, damsels, emperors, surgeons, clowns, scorpions and many others in iridescent and dazzling colours.

4

The British Debut

The British government, or the honourable East India Company for that matter, had had very little contact with the Andaman group of islands or people there, barring once in a while, when an occasional lone vessel used to seek shelter in one of its many natural harbours to escape the fury of the monsoon, or when in distress. But after the Company had succeeded in establishing its hegemony over the Deccan plateau, the necessity to have a harbour east of the Coromandel coast became rather urgent.

In any case, some British maritime officers and surveyors had, for some time, been urging the Company to take a greater interest in these islands because, as one of them, John Ritchie, who had been busy conducting a survey of the Bay of Bengal in 1717, put it: "In whatever light these islands are considered a thorough knowledge of them will appear to be a matter of great utility." He was reporting to Warren Hastings, the then governor-general of India. In 1783, Captain Thomas Forrest wanted to visit the islands, his purpose being the establishment of some contact with the aborigines. Five years later Captain Buchanan, who had had an opportunity of seeing something of the coast of Great Andaman, also brought these islands to the notice of the Company.

Ultimately, the honourable East India Company took notice of these islands because it was greatly worried over the increasing number of piracies and the ill-treatment meted out to the shipwrecked crew that had sought shelter in some of the harbours of these islands. It therefore decided to commission Lieutenant Archibald Blair of the Indian Navy to survey the islands. Blair was given command of two ships—*Elizabeth* and *Viper*. In a letter dated 19 December 1788, the governor-general, Lord Cornwallis, while briefing Lieutenant Blair on the object of the survey, stated *inter alia* that: "The material object of the survey is to ascertain in which part of the Island there are good harbours and which it would be most for the Company's advantage to project one." It went on to add that:

the primary view of this research being, as already stated, the organization of an Harbour where fleets in time of war, can refit by any means on leaving the Coast of Coromondol upon the approach of the Stormy Monsoon, or to which any part or the whole may retire in the Event of a disastrous conflict with an Enemy, and so attain a Central position in the Bay, whence the ships may return to the Scene of Action as soon as possible.

Blair was also asked to report on the adjacent heights and the general surface of the ground, the quality of the soil, natural vegetation, vegetable production, climatic changes, the availability of fish, wood, water, clay, lime, stone, seashells, sulphur, tin and other metals. Besides, he was to make drawings, along with their detailed descriptions, of animals and birds extant on these islands.

Lieutenant Blair's instructions on the subject of the aborigines were:

With respect to the best method of opening an Intercourse with the people in the Rude State in which they have hitherto been described to be, much may be collected from the attempts made by the Modern Navigators on Discovery; and it would appear from their Relations that it would be most advisable for you at first to refrain from Landing, unless in the case of positive necessity, except at such places on the Coast as you may judge from their appearances will successfully answer the object of your Survey; for Grounds open Contentions are to be avoided, as far as possible, with the Natives, whose Indisposition to

> every kind of Intercourse, Mr Ritchie's instance excepted, has been attended with acts of Hostility to those who have heretofore visited the Islands, and in an attempt to offer them a Social Communication, which shall afford them the Comforts and advantages of more Civilised Life, the Dictates of Humanity no less than of Policy require that they should be effected as much as possible by conciliatory means, certainly without Bloodshed, it is therefore recommended to you to endeavour by Persuasion, Presents, and other allurements, but not by force or deceit, to prevail upon some of the Natives to come on Board . . . where kind and attentive treatment to them may remove the apprehensions of the Inhabitants in general and promote an easy intercourse while at the same time, an useful object may be gained in acquiring knowledge of their Manners and Customs, and of such Words and Expressions in their language as would facilitate the Communication between us.

Lieutenant Blair's instructions also included a directive that he was to be under the orders of Commodore Cornwallis, commander-in-chief of His Majesty's squadron in India, who was a brother of the governor-general. Lieutenant Blair was accompanied by Lieutenant Robert Hyde Colebrook of the Bengal Engineers.

Blair, on board the *Eliza*, accompanied by another ship, the *Viper*, sailed from Calcutta on 20 December 1788 and headed straight for Interview Island, which is on the east of Great Andaman, lying somewhere between North and Middle Andaman. Blair surveyed Port Andaman, the main port on this island. Then he sailed to South Andaman and surveyed Port Campbell, a harbour on its west coast. But it was not until he had his first glimpse of Port Cornwallis, now known as Port Blair, that he was able to tell himself that that was it. In his report to Lord Cornwallis, he said:

> It is hardly possible to conceive a more secure and perfect harbour. It is large enough to contain about fifty sails of the Line where they would lay perfectly sheltered from all winds and sea and though there is seven feet rise of tide there is no stream to incommode ships under repair. Its situation renders it easy of access in either Monsoon, and ships may quit it at all seasons, and here it is proper to observe that the harbours of this island are better situated for holding a constant intercourse with Calcutta than any other whatever.

Blair completed the survey of Port Cornwallis on 15 March 1789. He then surveyed the rest of the western coast of South Andaman and the shore of Baratang Island, which lies somewhere between Middle and South Andaman. He then set sail for Barren Island, the volcanic island situaed on the east of Middle Andaman; he found Barren in a state of eruption. He wrote in his report:

The Volcano was in a violent state of eruption, bursting out immense volumes of smoke, and frequently showers of red hot stones. Some were of a size to weight three or four tons, and had been thrown some hundred yards past the foot of the cone. There were two or three eruptions while we were close to it: several of the red hot stones rolled down the side of the cone and bounded a considerable way beyond us. The base of the cone is the lowest part of the island, and very little higher than the level of the sea. It arises with an activity of 32° 17′ to the height of 1,800 feet nearly, which is also the elevation of the other parts of the island .... From the present figure it may be conjectured that the Volcano broke out near the centre of the Island, or rather towards the northwest; and in a long process of time, by discharging, consuming, and undermining, has brought it to the present very extraordinary form.

Blair concluded that "those parts of the island that are distant from the Volcano are thinly covered with withered shrubs and blasted trees".

Barren Island was the last of the islands of the Andaman group he visited. He returned to Calcutta via Prince of Wales Island, which lies near Sumatra, and via Achin, a harbour at the northern end of Sumatra. Blair stayed in the Prince of Wales Island for nearly three weeks, mainly to gather supplies and do some essential repairs to the ship. He arrived in Calcutta in the first week of June 1789 and submitted his report to Lord Cornwallis, the governor-general, on 9 June 1789.

Blair's report mentions some incidents about his contacts with the aborigines. The first one was on 11 January 1789, when they were on a small, flat island "just in sight from Port Andaman". According to Blair:

In the morning we . . . had a visit from the Natives, after some hesitation they came close under the stern; they accepted some Knives and Looking Glasses, but seemed very indifferent about them. On showing them bottles they expressed a great desire for them and made signs that they wanted them to shave with, one of them very expressively putting his hand to his head which was only shaved at one side and when a bottle was held up he opened his hands to receive it and called out *Kee Kee* which probably signifies, give, in their language. They were peacable but extremely suspicious, and would not venture themselves on board even for bottles. Like those we have seen on Interview Island they were perfectly naked, their features, colour and hair resembling those of the natives of Africa.

He mentions another instance when he and his companions suffered "many unprovoked insults . . . from the Natives", as a result of which they were frequently "obliged to quit the shore to avoid a conflict". He wrote further:

But my peacable intentions would not avail. While watering the Party was suddenly attacked, and a *Naque* was wounded in the neck with an arrow; the party was obliged to defend themselves with Musquetry and wounded one of the Savages. This little incident had one good effect, for the two succeeding days the waters of both vessels was filled up without interruption.

The last incident occurred when they were in the vicinity of Peterie Island. While describing it, Blair wrote:

I met two Canoes, and gave the people which were in them, some bottles with which they were highly pleased, or seemed to be so, but to my astonishment one of them suddenly jumped out of his canoe, run within twenty yards of the boat and shoot all his arrows at us, which luckily did not hurt though most struck the boat; to punish the villain, I took, and carried his canoe on board, and set her on fire next morning, with a wind which would drive her to the place where we had been insulted.

The report submitted by Lieutenant Archibald Blair created a deep impression, and Lord Cornwallis' satisfaction was conveyed to Blair in these words:

The Governor-General in Council having had before him your report of your Proceeding while upon Service in the Bay of Bengal, I have orders to acquaint you that his Lordship is highly satisfied with the Investigation you have made of the Lands committed to your Survey of the Andaman Islands.

Events followed quickly. On 12 June 1789, barely a few days after the submission of Blair's report, the governor-general in council held a meeting, with Blair present, at which it was decided to colonize the Andaman islands, the main purpose of which would be to have a properly fortified harbour providing shelter to the British naval fleet; this would be particularly helpful in the event of a war, when ships were in distress due to the fury of the monsoons. It was also hoped that by their very presence the massacres at the hands of the aborigines of those seeking refuge would cease; also, the predatory activities of the pirates from Malay would be minimized. It was not the intention of the East India Company at that time to turn the Andamans into a penal settlement, but, as in the case of settlements in Penang and Sumatra, some convicts were sent, at a later stage, to clear the jungles and render assistance as labourers.

Blair left Calcutta along with some artificers, labourers and soldiers on 17 September 1789 and arrived in Port Cornwallis on the 28th, after a voyage which he described as "tedious and tempestuous", during which he lost "a great part of [his] stock" when "a small portion of the provisions were also damaged". On 25 October 1789 the British colours were hoisted on the redoubt which, by then, in the opinion of Lieutenant Blair, had become "tenable against any incursions which the Natives might make". It was a simple ceremony, the colours being saluted by the *Ranger* (the Company's ship which had carried Blair and his party), and the salute was returned with three volleys by the garrison.

Blair began his sojourn on Chatham Island by clearing the jungle, and planting it with vegetables and fruit trees. Grass was sown in some parts of the island. Living accommodation for as many as 119 men was constructed; even a hospital was built. Though most of the provisions were imported from Penang and Calcutta, in one instance the *Ranger* was sent to the island of Car Nicobar for "Plants, Coconuts, Stock and such vegetables as the Island affords". Not only did the ship return, according to Blair, "with an abundant supply of most of the articles" that he had been expecting, she also brought on board two Chinese gardeners, who were straightaway commissioned to cultivate a spot for a second garden.

The settlement made quick progress. By February 1790 a wooden wharf had been constructed, which exists to this day. In course of time, those who went on leave to Calcutta were even allowed to bring their families back with them. In March 1792, Blair reported that the settlement had been so healthy that even the absence of the surgeon, who had gone on leave, had made no difference to the general health of the settlers. What is more, Blair had also succeeded, to an extent, in establishing friendly relations with the aborigines, although there had been some trouble and bloodshed in the early stages.

M V Portman, officer in charge of the Andamanese at the turn of the last century, who published an authoritative history of the relations of the British with the Andamanese in 1899, has written:

> Although from the fact that Lieutenant Blair was ignorant that he had more than one tribe of savages to deal with in the Harbour, and that the two tribes were mutually hostile and ignorant of each other's languages . . . it would appear that he, very soon after his arrival, established friendly relations with the Jarawa tribe who occupied the Southern half of the Harbour.

This was obviously no mean achievement, considering that the Jarawas have been implacably hostile to any form of civilization—even till the present day. The other tribe, the Aka-Bea-da, who had then occupied the northern half of the island, did not give Blair any trouble at first, though they did so later, according to Portman. But then, in the opinion of Blair, this was due to the bad treatment they had received at the hands of the Malays, who had indulged in fierce depredations and had often been responsible for capturing them forcibly and carrying them away with the intention of making them slaves.

The success of the settlement notwithstanding, the government, as Portman put it, were "unable to let well alone", and it was decided to shift the settlement to the north-east harbour in North Andaman, now known as Port Cornwallis. This was to prove a disaster. It all began when, on 13 April 1790, Blair brought it to the notice of the governor-general that the north-east harbour deserved "the attention of the Governor-General". Thereupon the harbour was visited by Commodore Cornwallis who, as stated already, was a brother of the governor-general. Having formed a very good impression, the commodore directed Blair to conduct a special survey of the harbour. Blair did so in March 1791. On receipt of the report on this survey, the commodore wrote to the governor-general:

> I think North-East Harbour vastly superior for a fleet of Man-of-war to Port Cornwallis; this latter, I consider, too confined and liable to accidents, as well as being more subject—from being surrounded with high hills—to sudden violent squalls. They are alike in respect to fresh water, the rills being occasioned by the rains, and in regard to defence, the island is not near a gunshot from the farthest shore, which I tried by throwing shot across when working out. And though the Island is small, there is a great deal dry at the lowest tides.... I should apprehend, fully sufficient for the batteries.

He recommended that the settlement be moved to this new north-east harbour on North Andaman Island.

The recommendation was accepted, and in September 1791 Blair was informed that it had been decided to move the settlement to the north-east harbour. The final orders were issued on 16 October 1792. And soon after, the governor-general recorded a minute wherein detailed instruction regarding the method of the transfer were given. What is more, Captain Alexander Kyd of the Bengal Engineers, who had been surveyor-general in 1790, was named as the new superintendent. But the operation for the removal of the old settlement, as also the setting up of the new one, was placed under the charge of Lieutenant Blair, till such time as he was relieved by Captain Kyd. Lieutenant Blair happened to be in Calcutta at the time. He received his sailing orders on 12 November 1792. He was told that the new settlement was to be given the name of Port Cornwallis and that it had to be set up on the same lines as the old one. Four ships—*Union, Juno, Cornwallis* and *Seahorse*—were placed at his disposal. Lieutenant Blair on board the *Union*, set sail once again for the Andamans. He had with him stores and provisions for six months—and 360 settlers. They left Calcutta on 4 December 1792. While on the high seas they encountered violent storms, so the ships parted company. The *Union*, carrying Blair, arrived at the site of the new settlement on 30 December 1792. Lieutenant Wales had already preceded him on the *Ranger* and had taken up the work of clearing the site and making watering arrangements. Of the three other ships that had parted company with Blair, *Seahorse* and *Cornwallis* were quite safe, but *Juno*, which had obviously been exposed to the full fury of the cyclone, was never heard of again. It had gone down with its crew and a vast quantity of provisions and stores, along with as many as 90 settlers.

Work in the new colony made steady and rapid progress. Coincidentally enough, the new harbour also had its Chatham Island, where huts were built immediately, tanks and wells dug and even three bungalows erected. A smithy and kiln were installed, and also a kitchen garden and nursery. Captain Kyd arrived to take up his new assignment on 5 March 1793. Luckily for Kyd, dry weather had preceded his arrival and, since it was not the monsoon season in any case, there had not been much illness among the settlers, except for occasional cases of jungle sores aggravated by scurvy. He therefore wrote in the most optimistic terms about the future of the settlement. Soon after, more artificers and labourers arrived, as also, for the first time, 200 convicts. A couple of months later, 113 additional sepoys and settlers came, and, in May 1793, 72 labourers.

Kyd's optimism was short-lived because, during the two months following his arrival, as many as 21 settlers died; the cause of their death was the chronic complaint of jungle sores, brought on, of course, and accentuated, as usual, by scurvy. And when the monsoon broke there was an enormous increase in sickness. To jungle sores and scurvy were added fever and a disease of the spleen, perhaps due to a general state of debility among the settlers.

For the new settlement, the only event of significance that had occurred in 1793 was the news of the outbreak of war with France, which had resulted in Port Cornwallis being placed in a state of defence. Captain Kyd chose a hill on Chatham Island as a site where a fort would be constructed, which would provide protection to the vessels in the harbour and also house the women and children of the settlement. Major Kyd made all the preliminary arrangements and then departed for Calcutta to secure armament and men to reinforce the garrison. Though the government fully approved of Kyd's proposals, the reinforcement did not arrive, somehow, for several months.

The first batch of European convicts, which was also to be the last, arrived in 1794, but Kyd declined to have them. They were therefore sent back to Bombay. On a reference to the governor-general, it was decided that no European convict was to be transported to the Andamans. Indian convicts, however, did continue to arrive; one batch of 50 came in November 1794.

But the health of the settlement continued to cause anxiety to the governor-general in council. In a communication dated 14 May 1794, the governor-general in council remarked that "the situation at Port Cornwallis has of late proved very unfavourable to the health of the settlers".

He, however, entertained the hope that "the place will become more salubrious in proportion as it is cleared". It turned out to be a hope forlorn because, during the rainy season in the next year, 50 people died. The gravity of the situation was brought home to the governor-general in council when even Surgeon Raddich, the surgeon in charge of the settlement, died of sickness brought on by the unhealthy climate, and Lieutenant Ramsay, another officer, had to be removed to Penang due to extreme ill health.

The governor-general could now see the writing on the wall. Eventually, on 8 February 1796, the board of the honourable East India Company recorded a minute. It said:

> Considering the great sickness and mortality of the Settlement formed at the Andamans, which, it is feared, is likely to continue, and the great expense and embarrassment to the Government in maintaining it, and in conveying to it supplies at the present period, it appears to the Governor-General in Council, both with a view to humanity and economy, prudent to withdraw it. He observes that if, at the termination of the present war, it should be thought expedient to carry on the plan with vigour, it could be renewed with very little disadvantage, no permanent or valuable buildings having yet been erected, and there being few stores of value to remove. The expediency of withdrawing the Settlement admitted, no time should be lost, so that it may be done before the change of the Monsoon. The Board further observes that if it could be conceived that temporary removal from the Andamans could invalidate our claim to those Islands, were any foreign nation in the meantime to settle there [a circumstance, however, which is highly improbable], the objection may be obviated by keeping a small vessel at Port Cornwallis, to be relieved every six months. Resolved, therefore, that the Marine Board be instructed to take immediate measures for the removal of the convicts to the Prince of Wales's Island, and for bringing back the stores and settlers to Bengal; that they be further instructed to make provisions for keeping a small vessel at Port Cornwallis, to be relieved every six months.

At the time of the abolition, the settlement in Port Cornwallis had 270 convicts on its rolls, besides 550 men, women and children, including those belonging to the European artillery. In May 1796, the curtain was finally rung down on the settlement in Port Cornwallis in North Andaman Island. The convicts, along with their provisions and stores, were sent to Penang; the others returned to Calcutta. There is no record of any vessel having been left behind in Port Cornwallis.

Thus ended the first British occupation of the Andaman islands. It was, however, during this occupation that the world got to know, for the first time, something about the people who had been inhabiting these islands since time immemorial, perhaps since the days of the Stone Age. Lieutenant R H Colebrook, who had accompanied Blair on his first survey of the Andaman islands (conducted in 1788-89), published a monograph in the *Journal of the Asiatic Society of Bengal* in 1794:

> The Andaman Islands are inhabited by a race of man the least civilised, perhaps, in the world; being nearer to a state of nature than any people we read of. Their colour is of the darkest hue, their stature in general small, and their aspect uncouth. Their limbs are ill-formed and slender, their bellies prominent, and, like Africans, they have woolly heads, thick lips, and flat noses. They go quite naked, the women wearing only at times a kind of tassel, or fringe, round the middle; which is intended merely for ornament, as they do not betray any signs of bashfulness when seen without it. The men are cunning, crafty and revengeful; and frequently express their aversion to strangers in a loud and threatening tone of voice, exhibiting various signs of defiance, and expressing their contempt by the most indecent gestures. At other times they appear quiet and docile, with the most insidious intent. They will affect to enter into a friendly conference when, after receiving with a show of humility whatever articles may be presented to them, they set up a shout, and discharge their arrows at the donors. On the appearance of a vessel or a boat, they frequently lie in ambush among the trees, and send one of their gang, who is generally the oldest among them, to the water's edge, to endeavour by friendly signs to allure the strangers on shore. Should the crew venture to land without arms, they instantly rush out from their lurking places, and attack them. In these skirmishes they display much resolution, and will sometimes plunge into the water to seize the boat; and they have been known even to discharge their arrows while in the act of swimming. Their mode of life is degrading to human nature, and, like brutes, their whole time is spent in search of food. They have yet made no attempts to cultivate their lands, but live entirely upon what they can pick up, or kill. In the morning they rub their skins with mud, and wallow in it like buffaloes, to prevent the annoyance of insects, and daub their woolly heads with red ochre, or cinnibar. Thus attired, they walk forth to their different occupations. The women bear the greatest part of the drudgery in collecting food, repairing to the reefs at the recess of the tide, to pick up shell-fish, while the men are hunting in the woods, or wading in the water to shoot fish with their bows and arrows. They are very dexterous at this extraordinary mode of fishing; which they practice also at night, by the light of a torch. In their excursions through the woods, a wild hog sometimes rewards their toil, and affords them a more ample repast. They broil their meat or fish over a kind of grid, made of bamboos; but use no salt, or any other seasoning.

Colebrook also wrote about their singing and dancing:

> The Andamanese display at times such colloquial vivacity, and are fond of singing and dancing; in which amusements the women equally participate. Their melodies are in the nature of recitative and chorus, not unpleasing. In dancing, they may be said to have improved on the strange republican dance asserted by Voltaire to have been exhibited in England: *Ou dansant a la ronde, chacon donne des coupes de pieds a son voisin, et an receit autant.* The Andamanese likewise dance in a ring, each alternately kicking and slapping his own breech, *ad libitum.* Their salutation is performed by lifting up a leg and smacking with their hand the lower part of the thigh.

Colebrook, in addition, described their dwellings, their canoes, their bows and arrows, their weapons, their fishing nets, and other implements they use in their daily lives. He also gave a fairly exhaustive list of specimens of the Andamanese language. The earlier part of the monograph gives some details of the geography and topography of the islands, as also something about its climate and its flora and fauna.

That Colebrook's account is highly subjective is quite apparent. For instance, according to Colebrook, the Andamanese are ugly people and "their limbs are ill-formed and slender, their bellies prominent... they have woolly hair, thick lips, and flat noses". Whereas in the words of Dr Fredrick John Mouat, who was to head the Andaman Committee in 1858 (before the second British occupation), the Andamanese "are the most perfectly formed beings in existence. In proportion to their size, their general framework is well constructed, and their limbs present a remarkably good muscular development, and the whole form as elegant as that of any European".

Colebrook's account of the Andamanese bristles with inaccuracies. This was proved beyond doubt by later writers and anthropologists when they conducted more detailed and systematic studies of the life and habits of the Andamanese aborigines. Obviously, he had relied much on hearsay, or obtained his information second-hand, but, as Portman put it, "the remarkable point about Colebrook's paper is that it should contain so much that is reliable and correct".

5

Sporadic Forays and an Incredible Shipwreck

During the six decades following the abandonment of the first settlement in the Andaman islands by the British, there were some isolated visits by odd travellers to the islands. The Malays, however, lost no time in resuming their trade of capturing the aborigines and selling them as slaves in the various countries of South-east Asia. Apart from that, there were a number of shipwrecks.

About the year 1819, a party of Chinese and Burmese came across to the Andamans in search of trepang, which is a kind of sea slug eaten by the Chinese with great delight. One day, while they were busy collecting trepang just off the shore of one of the islands, a few aborigines swam towards them and suddenly shot off a number of arrows. The Chinese were taken by surprise, and four of them were wounded. The Burmese gave chase; most of the aborigines swam away, but two of them, an elderly man and a boy, were captured. While on board the ship, the man contracted cholera and died. The boy survived and lived for quite a few years in Penang in the service of a certain Captain Anderson of the Bengal Army, and later on with his son, who was in the Penang Civil Service. Ultimately, however, he took to drinking, and died of it.

There was another instance of an Andamanese family which was taken to live in Penang. This happened about two decades later. J B D Rodyk, an old pensioner of the Penang settlement, wrote about this:

> A family consisting of a man, woman, and two children, were brought over from there [Andamans] to this [Penang], whether as slaves or not I could not say, but they were left in the custody of the Police. The children were sent to the Boys' and Girls' Free School; the girl was called Mary Andaman, and the boy Friday Andaman. The man and the boy, a few years later died of cholera, and the woman soon after died of small-pox. When the girl came to the age of fourteen she was removed from the school by T.G. Mitchel, Head Clerk of the Police Court and Court of Requests, to serve in his family as an *ayah*, where she remained for many years. When she left the family I was told she went to Malacca and served a lady there as an *ayah*, and when she left her she went down to Singapore and settled there, and opened a girls school for native children but whether she is still living I don't know.

Rodyk wrote this in 1895. But from what he could remember, the Andamanese family had been brought to Penang some time during the years 1838 and 1841.

The British fleet also visited the islands once. This was in 1824, when the British vessels had foregathered in Port Cornwallis, mainly for collecting water, before proceeding to Burma to participate in the first Burmese war.

Next, there is, on record, an account of a visit to Little Andaman Island by James Edward Alexander in November 1825. He was a lieutenant in the "late His Majesty's 13th Light Dragoons, and attached to the suite of Colonel Macdonald Kinner, K.L.S. Envoy Extraordinary to the Court of Teheran".

Alexander had his first glimpse of the Andamanese when, early at daylight, the day after his arrival, he and his chief mate left their vessel in a cutter in search of water. He has written:

> We had six Bengal Lascars on board, armed with muskets, besides the tyndal or coxswain, who was a Malay. In pulling towards the shore, we observed on the beach a woman and child, who appeared to be

collecting shell-fish: on perceiving the boat approaching they ran into the jungle.

After they had landed—they had not yet gone very far—they suddenly came upon a party of Andamanese who were, in Alexander's words, "lying on their bellies behind the bushes, armed with spears, arrows, and long bows, which they bent at us in a threatening manner". He goes on to describe the incident that followed:

The Lascars as soon as they saw them, fell back in great consternation, levelling their muskets, and running into the sea towards the boat. It was with great difficulty we could prevent the cowardly rascals from firing: the *tyndal* was the only one who stood by the chief mate and myself. We advanced within a few paces of the natives, and made signs of drinking, to intimate the purpose of our visit. The *tyndal salam*ed to them, according to the different Oriental modes of salutation; he spoke to them in Malay, and other languages; they returned no answer, but continued crouching in their menacing attitude, pointing their weapons at us wherever we turned. I held out my handkerchief towards them, but they would not come from behind the bushes to take it. I placed it on the ground, and we retired in order to allow them to pick it up: still they did not move.

Alexander counted their number. They were 22 in all. They were strong, able-bodied and lusty. And, according to him:

They were very different in appearance from what the natives of the Great Andamans are described to be, namely, a puny race. The whole party was completely naked, with the exception of a stout man, nearly six feet in height, who was standing along with two or three women in the rear; he wore on his head a red cloth with white spots. They were the most ferocious and wild-looking beings I ever saw. Their hair was frizzled or woolly; they had flat noses, with small red eyes. Those parts of their skin which were not besmeared with mud [to defend them probably from the attacks of insects] were of a sooty black colour; their hideous faces seemed to be painted with red ochre.

Another attempt at communication was made. The *tyndal* was asked to strip, to prove that he was not carrying any arms. He approached within 50 paces of them and "offered them handkerchiefs, making at the same time signs of drinking, but upon his attempting to advance closer they drew their bows in a menacing manner". So he was asked to call it a day.

But later the same afternoon they paid another visit. They found no one, but discovered a hut, which was "about fifteen feet in height, of a conical shape, and thatched with rattan leaves to within a foot and half of the ground, leaving just room to crawl in underneath". Inside,

> the floor was strewn with leaves, and there were several cots, or raised sleeping-places, consisting of four stakes driven into the ground, on which was fixed a bamboo grating. Ranged round the walls were the smoked skulls of a diminutive species of pig. From the roof was suspended a piece of red and white chequered cloth, which seemed to be of Madras manufacture. In conical baskets there were pieces of jack fruit, with a nut resembling a chestnut, and several roots.

He also noticed their weapons which included a bow from six to seven feet in length and arrows from three to four feet long.

Alexander and his party had two more encounters with the Andamanse that day. They were still looking for water when, as Alexander recorded:

> We discovered a party of sixty or seventy of the natives waiting in ambush our approach. We went towards them in order to induce them to shew us another pool. So little intention had we of molesting or injuring them, that we had brought with us several looking glasses, cloth, and baubles to give them. However, we had no sooner got within fifteen yards of them than we were assailed with a shower of arrows, which struck several of us. I received a scratch in the leg which lamed me for several days after. We immediately extended the files to skirmishing order, and returned with a round of musketry, which killed and wounded several of them. Fixing bayonets, we then charged them; but they, well knowing the intricacies of the jungle, and being extremely nimble, succeeded in not only affecting their escape, but also in carrying off the disabled of their party.

The next encounter also proved unfortunate because that too resulted in casualties among the Andamanese. They had discovered a pool. And before starting to fill their casks, while they were busily engaged in their repast, Alexander records that:

> A strong party of the natives stole down upon us, and threw in a shower of arrows, which killed one and severely wounded three of the soldiers. We quickly formed, charged them, killed and wounded several, and continued skirmishing with them till sunset; for they made several desperate attempts to cut off the pioneers engaged in filling, and it required the greatest alertness to keep them off. At last, the pioneers having completed their task, we gave them a parting volley.

And that in effect was the end of Lieutenant James Edward Alexander's encounter with the Andamanese.

Two other travellers visited the islands in the 1830s. One was a gentleman by the name of Peddington, whose visit probably took place roundabout the year 1830. He landed on Landfall Island, which is at the northern end of the Andamans, and saw some aborigines around a fire which, on subsequent examination, looked like a badly charred human body.

The other traveller was Sir John Malcolm (sometime governor of Bombay) who, according to his *Travels in Southern Asia,* passed through Coco Channel, which is to the north of Landfall Island. He merely mentions having passed by the islands on 12 February 1836, and confines his account to repeating some old stories about the Andamanese.

Apart from these brief visits by travellers, something which created a minor stir among the official circles in the Company was the murder by the aborigines, near Port Cornwallis, of a Russian geologist named Dr Helfer in 1839. Dr Helfer was on a visit to the islands in search of gold — almost alone. Very courageous perhaps, but nonetheless foolhardy.

However, what will go down as the most remarkable event in maritime history are the shipwrecks of the two vessels *Briton* and *Runnymede*, within about a quarter of a mile of each other, on what is now known as John Lawrence Island. This took place in 1844 on the night of the 11th day of November.

The shipwrecks are an incredible coincidence, worthy of being cited as one of those fairy tales which have a happy ending. The two ships, sailing from two different ends of the globe—the *Runnymede* from Gravesend in England and the *Briton* from Sydney in Australia—separated by thousands of miles, were shipwrecked very close to each other. They could thus help in the survival of the people on board the ill-fated vessels. Had it not been for the fact that the ships were able to provide mutual help, it is difficult to imagine how anyone on board either of them could have survived the ordeal of being stranded on a strange island, inhabited by unknown and not-very-friendly aborigines, during a sojourn which lasted 55 days!

It is a fascinating story. On the morning of 12 August 1844, the men of Her Majesty's 80th regiment marched out of Sydney Barracks and embarked for Calcutta in four ships—*Royal Saxon, Lloyds, Enmore* and *Briton*—after seven years' service. Some were accompanied by their wives and children.

From the very beginning, they were plagued by hostile winds and a weather that could only be described as dirty. The four ships kept company part of the way, but eventually separated. When the *Briton* arrived in Singapore, she was all alone. She was commanded by Captain Bell with a crew of 34, and in all he had a complement of 431, which included 35 women and 43 children.

It all began on Saturday, 9 November, when they woke up to find the weather both cloudy and threatening. By nightfall it was rainy, with heavy, gusty winds. It was much worse by the afternoon of the next day, the gale having increased in intensity. The weather continued to worsen, and the ship suffered some damage. By 11.30 A M the next morning, the gale had turned into a hurricane. And the ship suffered a lot more damage. But by afternoon, it had become quite calm. And all on board heaved a sigh of relief and turned to repairing the ship's damage. But, suddenly, the ship was invaded by thousands of birds. They, too, had been completely exhausted by the storm and wanted to rest, for the moment forgetting the danger they faced from the human beings on board! Some hawks and golden kingfishers and goatsuckers were caught by soldiers and children.

The respite turned out to be much too brief. Back came the squall, with rain and thunder and lightning—and then another gale, followed by a hurricane. The ship began to roll. She lost two quarter-boats and much besides. The night was much worse.

The gale increased the next day, and the ship continued to labour and roll heavily. The soldiers were helping the crew in working the pumps and in rendering every other assistance. Some were hurt; one broke his leg. But the weather gods seemed to have gone berserk. By 2 P M that day the gale had already been blowing for 38 hours. (It had not been possible to light any fires, so those on board the ship were only given biscuits and a glass of rum each.) At about 4 P M the gale again turned into a hurricane. The ship rolled heavily. At 10 P M there was once again a brief lull, but it turned out to be the proverbial lull before the storm, because by midnight the storm had become awfully squally with thunder and lightning.

At midnight, according to the journal compiled by some of the survivors:

The hurricane still raged furiously, the ship making much water and labouring heavily; squall succeeded squall almost without intermission, with thunder and lightning.... About 12.30 the ship struck, and the sea breaking over her at the same moment threw her on beam ends; the larboard poop after cabin was swamped and raised from the deck, the Master's cabin was also floated. The cuddy door was jammed so that it could not be opened, and one of the windows, and steward's pantry, were stove in. Both the mates were washed out of their cabins.... The Spanker boom was broken in three pieces.... These were moments of awful suspense, the ship on her beam ends, and we clinging to whatever we could for support, expecting every moment that the next would dash her to atoms and seal our fate. The boatswain cried out for all hands to scramble up to windward, in order that perhaps she might right. Shortly after she appeared to be forced over into smooth waters, when she righted. At this time the leak between decks had so much increased that one of the soldiers came to report that they feared that the ship was breaking up; the water poured in so fast that it defied all their exertions to stop it.... The night was extremely dark and the decks so lumbered up it was impossible to find the pumps, but the attempt was made from between decks with better success, the party ascending the hatchway and contriving to reach them. After working for some time it was ascertained that the ship was ashore. The wind continued raging, and the sprays to break over her. The night was so dark it was impossible to see a yard before us, excepting during the flashes of lightning, when trees could be clearly discerned close on board the larboard side.

The compilers of the journal go on to say: "To describe this awful hurricane which had lasted some fifty hours ... would be impossible.... The ship was an utter wreck, crowded with upwards of 400 souls, and without a single boat on board. Such was our situation when it pleased God to come to our assistance." And God really came to their assistance when the next morning—Tuesday, 12 November—they discovered, to their delight and great astonishment, that they were on shore in the midst of a mangrove swamp and that about a quarter of a mile away from them lay a barque, which they soon found out was the *Runnymede*.

The *Runnymede* had sailed from Gravesend on 20 June 1844 with detachments from Her Majesty's 10th and 50th regiments. The ship was under the command of Captain Doughty, and had four officers, 105 privates, 13 women and 14 children on board. The army personnel was under the command of Captain Stapleton of the 50th regiment. The ship also had a surgeon, Dr Bell, who was the medical officer in charge.

The *Runnymede*'s voyage had been far from smooth, as she had all along met with winds which were either too light or simply contrary, which meant that the voyage had prolonged beyond all expectation. As the water and other supplies were near exhaustion, the *Runnymede* decided to head for Penang rather than chart a straight course to Calcutta. She anchored there, after over four months of hazardous travel on 29 October. After filling up her water casks and obtaining all necessary supplies, she set sail for her destination on 3 November. The weather continued to vary from fine to moderate till 8 November.

Then trouble started; it was becoming obvious that a squall was in the offing. The next day the wind was variable and squally and the barque split some of her sails. But the worst had yet to come. On Sunday, 10 November, the barometer fell and they experienced a strong gale and a heavy squall. The ship suffered many losses—sails, masts and other gear. The men had to be employed to bail water from between decks. But, according to Captain Doughty, commander of the ship: "The ship was still tight and proved herself an excellent seaboat." On Monday, 11 November, again according to Captain Doughty, "the hurricane continued with equal severity". At noon, as the hurricane raged, the ship became unmanageable because of its crippled state, but she "rode like a bird over a confused sea running from every point of the compass". At 4 P M the hurricane began blowing with terrific force, but by 8 P M there was some let-up. This proved to be short-lived, as by midnight it was again raging with severity. At 1.30 A M on Tuesday the 12th, in the words of Captain Doughty:

> They felt the ship strike, and considered the destruction of the vessel and their lives certain. But it pleased Almighty God to decree otherwise, for although the ship filled up to her lower beams with water, she was thrown so high on a reef that all the force of the water was broken and smoothened, and the bilge pieces keeping her upright, she lay comparatively quiet. Not knowing their position, the ship being bilged, and fearful of her beating over the reef into deep water again, they let go the larboard bower anchor, and the water shortly after leaving her, all hands fell asleep.

The people aboard this ship, too, had been reduced to living on a biscuit and a glass of rum ever since the storm had broken out.

When the men and women aboard the *Runnymede* woke up in the morning, imagine their wonder and surprise to see, up in the midst of the trees, another barque. *And it was the Briton!* Communication was soon established. As the weather was again threatening and, as the *Runnymede* was in poor shape, all men, women and children, and the crew left their ship before nightfall and were accommodated on board the *Briton*, where they were received with kindness and hospitality, notwithstanding their own misery. However, they were delighted to hear that the *Runnymede* had a fair stock of provisions on board.

Major Bunbury of Her Majesty's 80th regiment, who was on board the *Briton*, became the supreme commander of all troops and seamen, and it was decided that they should all be made subject to military law during what was, undoubtedly, an emergency.

On Wednesday, 13 November, which was the second day after their arrival, Captain Doughty, accompanied by the crew of both the ships, returned to the *Runnymede* to try and bring back as many stores as possible. This they did, successfully.

The total number of those shipwrecked was 618. The two problems which needed urgent and immediate attention were (a) to make a sea-going craft ready to summon help and (b) to find fresh water and food.

They found both food and water. Fatigue-parties were employed in building a causeway through the swamp to the shore; the causeway was ready by the afternoon of the next day and, once on shore, men were able to bring back prawns and shoot a few pigeons. They also saw the havoc that the hurricane had wrought over the entire island. Not a leaf remained on the trees, nor was any tree left unbroken. They lay all over— some crushed down by the fury of the squall, others torn up by the roots. Some trees were so large that they must have been over a hundred years old.

On Saturday, the 16th, all married soldiers were sent ashore to rig tents for themselves and their families. And more fatigue-parties were employed to bring stores from the *Runnymede*. As some officers and men were suffering from swollen feet, and the ship's surgeon, Dr Bell, feared that due to overcrowding on board the *Briton* there may be an epidemic, detachments of the 10th and 50th regiments were directed to make encampments for themselves on shore.

Next day, which was Sunday, there was a Divine Service by the entire company to celebrate their survival.

The main objective was now to establish, as soon as possible, some contact with civilization. The only boat that had survived the ravage of the hurricane was a longboat on board the *Runnymede*. Carpenters were detailed to put it into proper shape, and within a week it was ready to set sail. On Monday, 25 November, within a fortnight of the shipwreck, they were able to launch the boat from the deck of the *Runnymede*. Captain Hall and Lieutenant Leslie of the 80th regiment, along with a boatswain and five sailors, embarked on her and within an hour, at about 1 in the afternoon, she set out amidst much cheering. The boat, appropriately enough, had been christened the *Hope*.

There had been some contact with the aborigines. In fact the day the causeway had been completed, a fatigue-party had found bodies of two Andamanese, and parts of the wreckage of their country boat. The Andamanese were duly buried. Another day, when two soldiers were collecting shellfish, some aborigines appeared on the shore and tried to surround them. But they soon disappeared in their canoe when they saw an officer coming after them. Later the same night, another canoe, with a few Andamanese in it, tried to approach the *Runnymede*. They made off when a few shots were fired in their direction. The commanding officer, however, showed his displeasure because the Andamanese had been fired at; he had given orders earlier that every attempt was to be made to conciliate them.

Some days later, another party of men searching for shellfish was attacked by the Andamanese; this resulted in four men being wounded, one quite seriously. A party of men was sent in pursuit, but to no avail, as they had already escaped into the jungle. On another occasion, two canoes of the aborigines were seen. Two men were sent, along with a jacket, to see if they would be tempted with this present. They took the jacket off the broken stump of the tree, where it had been placed, trampled on it and tried to attack the two men. But they fled and hid in the bushes when they saw the cover party behind the two men raise firearms.

Meanwhile, the shipwrecked men, women and children tried to carry on as best as they could. Because of the poor quality of the water, there were a number of cases of dysentery, perhaps also because the shellfish disagreed with them. One man died. There were also cases of fever and affection of the head. Short rations and heavy fatigue was beginning to affect the health of the people.

The position regarding food was becoming increasingly difficult. Even at a reduced scale, the food was not going to last for more than 36 days, that is till 27 December. It was also becoming difficult to supplement the food with some from the island, because the supply of sea food had also more or less ceased. There were a few wild pigs around but very little edible fruit or vegetable.

Fifteenth December, a Sunday, dawned as usual. Divine Service was held. But 20 days had already passed since the *Hope* had left. It was on the cards that from next day onwards the rations would have to be halved. At about 11 A M, the island experienced two heavy tremors of earthquake. According to the journal:

> The last shock had barely subsided, when a shout was heard from the look-out tree on the right of the camp where the men had of their own accord established a sentry, relieving each other every hour. "A sail! A sail!" was quickly echoed from one end of the encampment to the other. The *Runnymede* hoisted her ensign and fired a gun . . . . The camp was in a regular commotion, shout following shout with little intermission, and everyone was on the look-out, asking "Where? Where?" and straining their eyes to get a glimpse of the stranger. Within a quarter of an hour she had rounded and was visible to all.

They were delighted to see that at the stern of the ship was being towed the *Hope*. The ship, *George Swinton*, named after the secretary to the government of India, came laden with food and other supplies. All talk of reducing the ration was abandoned straightaway. It was also the beginning of the end of the ordeal of the shipwrecked men, women and children.

Beginning with Saturday, 28 December, ships of Her Majesty's navy started coming in quick succession—Her Majesty's ship, the *Pilot*, then the *Ayershire*, the *Elizabeth Ainsalie*, and finally the *Agnes Lee*.

The last detachment of the 50th regiment embarked on the *Agnes Lee*. It was 5 January 1845. They had been on what was described by them as the most inhospitable island for 55 days. During this stay only seven adults and a few children had died.

6
More Shipwrecks

Before the second occupation of the Andaman islands by the British, two more shipwrecks took place: those of the *Flying Fish* and the *Emily*, both in 1849. The brig *Flying Fish* was commanded by Captain Shaw, and had two passengers, Birch and McKnight, on board. They were emigrating to Australia. With a view to obtaining water, they landed on Coco Island, situated at the northern end of the Andamans. Coco Island appeared so charming to the two emigrants that, instead of proceeding to Australia, they decided to make it their home. Captain Shaw heartily agreed with them and promised that he would return with a supply of goats, fowl, geese, ducks and also plants and seed which could grow in the particular climate obtaining in Coco Island.

On arrival in Moulmein, which was the destination of the *Flying Fish*, Captain Shaw gave such a glowing account of Coco Island that it induced quite a few of those living there to go to the island and try their fortune. Some time in mid-July 1849, the *Flying Fish* sailed back to Coco Island with her emigrants. In the words of the journal kept by one of the emigrants, they found "Mr McKnight sick, and heard that Mr Birch had gone over to Turtle Place to get turtles and eggs", but in Birch's house "every thing presented a gloomy appearance". Those on the island, after the departure of Captain Shaw and his brig, consisted, in the words of the journal again, of "Stewart, his wife and child, Birch and McNight, self, wife and three children. Ma Mentha, and son, and her sister". There were several other Burmans there besides, who had come to the island to gather coconuts. But the going was far from good. The few months that the settlers spent on the island would appear to be full of misery. There was a lot of sickness and want, which amounted to near starvation.

A few months later, in October 1849, Captain Shaw was in the Nicobars collecting a cargo of coconuts. His intention was to sail to Moulmein, discharge the cargo and then revisit the settlement which, in a way, he was responsible for having founded. But the stars decreed otherwise. The *Flying Fish* had hardly set sail when she encountered bad weather. The brig started making water and despite pumping she was waterlogged in a few days. Things became worse, and on the morning of 15 October came the catastrophe. The *Flying Fish* gave a lurch and turned over. Captain Shaw made every effort to make the ship seaworthy again, but with little success. Along with his crew, he ultimately abandoned the ship. In a boat they headed towards the island of Narcondam; a more inhospitable place was difficult to imagine. They went through great privation. Captain Shaw, who had not been well even before the accident, fell seriously ill, due mainly to exposure and for want of proper food.

However, after an 18-day stay at Narcondam, accompanied by a few of his crew, Captain Shaw took off in a sampan for Coco Island. It was a hazardous voyage. They were in great danger and the sampan got very nearly swamped on more than one occasion. But they did make it to the island. However, instead of being greeted by a flourishing settlement on arrival, he found there only the schooner *Sea Serpent*, on the point of departure. He and his men went on board the *Sea Serpent* and eventually arrived in Moulmein a few days later.

A report submitted by Captain Forsyth of the ship *Manchester*, on arrival at Calcutta, stated:

On the 27th November, close in with the North side of Narcondam Island, I picked up a boat with one seacunnie and four lascars belonging to the brig *Fyling Fish* of Moulemin; they reported there were six men on the island—sent a boat on shore and brought them off.

The ship *Emily* was in the Andaman seas; it became a total loss on the night of 1 September 1849, on one of the small islands lying to the west of North Andaman. It was under the command of Captain F Anderson. In a letter addressed to the owners of the ship, Anderson wrote:

> The night was dark and rainy, with heavy passing squalls, and had been so for three days previous, so that no observation could be obtained by either sun, moon, or stars, during that time.... The sad disaster took place at 4 A M, on the 1st of September; notwithstanding two look-outs on the forecastle, and one on each gangway at the time, still the low island was not seen until the ship was just amongst the breakers.

Despite every effort being made by the captain and his crew, the ship "bilged and filled forward almost immediately, her head being down in deeper waters". Those on board tried to save their lives by getting into one pinnace and another longboat with "a few pieces of pork and beef". The skipper was in the pinnace with 12 others, although it was small and very leaky. Eventually, they

> pulled along the shore inside the breaker looking for an opening to get out of, but did not succeed in finding one that night. At about two o'clock in the morning the tide fell, and left both boats dry on a coral reef.

They were there all night. In the morning, fortunately, they found a small opening. And here the two boats parted company. That was the last which those in the pinnace saw of the longboat.

Anderson and his companions found themselves, for the next four days, among small islands trying to find a landing place; this they did at long last, when they had only one pint of water left. They found some water on the island, and had just made for themselves a resting place under the trees for the night, when they were overjoyed to discover a brig coming round the island. They immediately launched their pinnace. But their joy was short-lived. In the words of Captain Alexander:

> We pulled and sailed after her for upwards of an hour and got within a mile of her when they saw us and hove to, which was a joyful sight for us all, but this was only for a short period as after she had laid for about ten minutes, sad was our disappointment when we saw her square her yards, set her fore-topsail and lower studding sails and go away and leave us, although only half a mile distant.

Captain Anderson believed they did so because they perhaps thought that the boat in which Anderson and his companions were sailing consisted of "pirates coming from one of the cannibal island".

They had no alternative left now except to try and make for the coast of Burma. Nine or ten days since after they had sighted the brig, they at last made land. They were suffering a great deal by now from hunger. Anyway, they now discovered some huts, but found them deserted. Taking possession of them, they went in search of food and soon found pumpkins, cucumbers and a few shellfish. They left the huts on the third day and, the same afternoon, saw an entrance into a small river. After pulling up for a few miles in the river, they found an inhabited village. Captain Anderson concluded his report with these words:

We landed and found the people very kind, they gave us fish and rice to eat, and made us two large fires to dry our clothes, it having been raining in torrents the whole day: we rested here for three days. We abandoned our boat, she being too leaky to venture to sea again, and agreed with these people to bring us on to Rangoon for the sum of Rs 120, as they told us we were still about 40 miles to the westward of the latter place; we made on in inland passage through rivers and creeks, and arrived there twenty-two days from the wreck.

It was as a result of the report submitted by Captain F Anderson that the *Sea Serpent* made two trips to recover what she could from the wrecked *Emily*; that was how she was able to pick up Captain Shaw and his companions from Coco Island after it had been deserted by its settlers.

Captain Anderson and his companions had also an encounter with the aborigines while on the first island, where they had sought shelter. Wrote Captain Anderson:

We had not been many hours on the island before the native savages came down upon us with their bows and arrows, one of the arrows passed within three inches of the boy Moffat. We had nothing to defend ourselves with, but we all got large sticks and held them up like arms, which I suppose the savages took them for, as they returned to the bush shortly after. We, at the time, being about thirty of us on the beach, making the best show of our number.

In the early months of the year 1854, a ship known as the *Lady Nugent* disappeared somewhere in the Andaman Sea. The *Sesostris*, under the command of G I Neblett, was sent in search of her. This ship, according to the report submitted by its commander, steered towards Teressa Island (one of the Nicobar group), saw several of the inhabitants and hailed them to come alongside, which they did. Neblett tried to gain from them some tidings about the *Lady Nugent*, but to no avail. He was, however, able to gather information about others who had previously been shipwrecked on the islands. The information was horrifying. The commander of the *Sesostris* reported:

> At Terrissa Island... there is an intelligent native known to Europeans by the name of Gold-Mohur. He speaks English but very badly. This man informed me that, within the last two years, six vessels [had] been cut off, and their crews murdered, by the inhabitants of Nancowry and Camorta [both islands in the Nicobar Group]—four of them, native vessels, during the South West Monsoon; and two other vessels during the North East Monsoon; one of the latter commanded by an Englishman, and two others by an Arab. On board the former were a Frenchman, an Arab, and a native merchant. On board the latter three females—one supposed to be the mother of the other two, was killed, and the youngest female, a child, was killed also. The other was reserved for a worse fate, but did not long survive. Gold-Mohur says that these women had a great number of gold ornaments on their arms and legs.

The *Sesostris* was careering round Teressa Island for three days, and the meeting with Gold-Mohur took place on 25 July 1854. The *Sesostris*, however, had to abandon its mission of looking for the remains, or the survivors, of the *Lady Nugent*; she returned to Calcutta due to some trouble with her engine. The government did not give up. It commissioned the *Pluto*, under the command of Captain S G Boon, to go ahead and conduct a thorough search. The *Pluto* set sail on 7 November 1854 but, despite a really thorough search, she too came back disappointed, without having found any trace of the *Lady Nugent*. In a letter addressed to Sir H C Montgomery, Bart, who was then chief secretary to the government of Bengal at Fort St George, the secretary in the marine department stated that it was "his painful duty to represent that there are no longer hopes of learning anything regarding that vessel's fate". It was a pity, though, because the *Lady Nugent* was reputed to be a most eligible vessel, standing in the highest class in Lloyd's Register.

Early next year, on 13 January 1855 to be precise, appeared a report that three seamen of the ship *Fyze Bakhsh* of Moulmein had been murdered and four others wounded by the Andamanese. In addition to that, from time to time, the crew of Chinese junks had often fallen in within the seas of the Andaman and Nicobar group of islands, through having either adopted an erroneous course or because of faulty navigation. No one had a clue as to how many lives were lost that way during the course of the years. However, there had been that one incident of the junk *Fuen Gren*, a report of which had been submitted by J C Haughton, magistrate in Moulmein, to Colonel Sir A Bogle, commissioner of the Tenasserin and Martaban provinces. This report carried, among other depositions, one by "Ali Meu, Chinese, son of Ah Saing, aged 20 years, native of Surveng in China, by profession a shipmaster". Ali Meu told Haughton:

> We made an island on which were two mountains, nine days after our departure; this we decided was not our destination, so . . . we came to another island five days after . . . . This island was one of the Huckmesau [The Negro Mountains] or Andaman Islands; coasting we saw some five or six men on the shore, and being short of water, concluded that it must be obtainable where men were; we therefore let down our boat and sent it on shore with eight men. When the people on shore saw our men coming to the shore, they fled to their mountains. Our men landed, and leaving six men with the boat on the beach, the remaining two went in search of water. Immediately we saw our two men fleeing back, following by twenty or so of the natives, who began attacking our men; the latter struggled to get off the boat from the beach on which they had hauled it up, but could not do so. We saw them kill all our men and drag them in the jungle. They also broke up the boat.

Houghton's comment was that to him it appeared "highly discreditable in a civilized government to allow such a state of things to exist within a sea, one may say, bounded by its own territories and on the high road to many of its emporia". This report was dated 3 March 1856. A few days earlier, Captain Henry Hopkinson, commissioner of Arracan, had also submitted a comprehensive report on the measures he "would propose for the protection of such British subjects as may unfortunately be cast away on the Andamans". He suggested that "the only effective remedy would be the occupation of the island", but went on to add that, should that not be practicable, he would suggest the "establishment of a British settlement on one of the islands, which might extend hereafter as circumstances allowed". In an interesting aside, Captain Hopkinson remarked:

> Looking on the map at the magnificent situation of these islands, their proximity to such seats of trade as Madras, Calcutta, Akyab, Rangoon, Moulmein, Penang, Singapore, considering their extent, which must comprise an area of not much under two thousand square miles, their many fine harbours, and the prospect, reasoning from analogy, of the abundant fertility of their soil, it does seem astonishing that their condition on the present day should be such as to make us wish that they could be blotted from the face of the ocean or sunk a thousand fathoms deep below its surface. That instead of offering a refuge to the miserable storm-driven vessel, they should be a snare in her path leading to utter destruction, and in place of engaging the enterprise, and furnishing subsistence to thousands of colonists, they should be left in the possession of a handful of degenerate negroes, degraded in habits

and intelligence to a level little above the beasts of forest with which they dwell.

Captain Henry Hopkinson went on to state that the reasons that led the Board of Administration to have a harbour in the Andamans in 1788 had rather gained in force in 1856. And if it was conceded that some sort of settlement was to be set up, his suggestion would be to "found a Penal Settlement, but so constituted that it might form a nucleus for a colony or that a colony might grow up side by side with it, into which it would hereafter merge".

He also went into the question of where the settlement should be located. His conclusion was that it should be where the occupation had "lasted for about six years and half, or from October or November 1789 to the middle of 1796" and where, according to Lieutenant Blair's report, the climate had been favourable all along. (He was referring to the original Port Cornwallis in South Andaman.) Captain Hopkinson concluded his report with the suggestion: "Any project for the reoccupation of the Andamans should also comprehend arrangements for exercising from them a surveillance over the neighbouring group of Nicobars".

Hopkinson's recommendations, although acceptable to the lieutenant-governor of Bengal, were not acceptable to the governor-general of India, firstly "because he thought there was no need of a new penal settlement," and secondly because, in the opinion of the governor-general, it was "impossible to carry out one of the objects of the occupation, viz. making the Islands a secure landing place for those who may be cast away upon them". This, he thought, would be possible only if they were prepared to defend the entire sea coast of the islands. And that, he concluded, could not be done "except at very considerable cost".

The honourable court of the East India Company, to whom the matter was referred to for consideration and orders, reserved their judgement on the desirability or otherwise of establishing a penal settlement on the Andaman islands. But meanwhile, they asked for more information about the islands. They, therefore, directed that

> steps be taken in the first instance to explore them and to report upon the sites which they [the islands] may offer both for the construction of harbours of refuge on the coast for the establishment of penal or other settlements, not only on the shores, but also on the inland parts of the islands.

In fact they wanted to know all that could be ascertained "without incurring great risks on the score of health, or heavy expenditure".

As regards the Nicobars, the honourable court were in agreement with the view that "the contemplated object would be very imperfectly obtained without the occupation of these islands also". They further observed that "as it is possible that the apprehension which deterred the Danish Government from continuing to occupy the islands may have been unfounded or exaggerated", they wanted information on the reputed insalubrity of the Nicobars. They wanted this information so that they could form, on the basis of such a report, an opinion "respecting the expediency of taking formal possession of the [Nicobar] Islands". This was in the autumn of the year 1856.

7

Return of the British

While the Indian government were cogitating and deliberating about what they should do, the march of events in India overtook them. The Great Mutiny, which we now describe as the first war of independence, broke out all over the country in 1857. There were thousands sentenced to life imprisonment on charges of "mutineering" against the government; once the mutiny had been suppressed, the question of what to do with them assumed tremendous importance. A submission was made once again to the governor-general in council that a penal settlement be established in the Andamans and the mutineers transported there.

This time the action taken was quick and fast. On 20 November 1857, the government of India appointed a committee, which subsequently came to be known as the Andaman Committee. It was presided over by Dr Frederic John Mouat, surgeon of the Bengal Army at the time. Other members of the committee were Dr G R Playfair and Lieutenant J A Heathcote of the Indian Navy. Their instructions were "to examine the shores of the Islands and select the best site which may be found there for the establishment of a Penal Settlement".

The members of the committee set sail from Calcutta on board the steam frigate *Semiramis* on 23 November 1857. They arrived in Moulmein on 1 December. At Moulmein they changed ship and boarded the steam vessel *Pluto*.

To protect the members of the committee while exploring the Andaman islands, Captain Campbell, commander of the *Semiramis*, placed at the disposal of the party one European officer and 20 European seamen. Further, to enable the committee to penetrate the thick jungles obtaining on the Andaman islands, the commissioner of Moulmein ordered that 12 short-term Burmese convicts and three convict peons accompany the party.

The *Pluto* left Moulmein on the morning of 8 November and anchored at Port Cornwallis (which had been the seat of the first British administration before it was abandoned) on the morning of 11 November at 8.30 A M. After examining Port Cornwallis, the *Pluto* was steered towards Craggy Islands because the committee hoped to climb to the top of Saddle Hill (the highest hill in the entire Andaman group of islands). To their dismay, they found this impracticable. So from there they proceeded to Sound Island, at the northern end of North Andaman, to explore the possibility of its eligibility or otherwise as a site for the new settlement.

The idea was soon abandoned because not only was it deficient in water but also in forest wealth. They explored the entire Andaman archipelago, found Barren Island still smouldering, and eventually on the morning of 19 December, in the words of the report as submitted finally by the committee, "anchored abreast of Chatham Island in Old Harbour, the site of Blair's first settlement. And as its original occupation had proved continuously healthy, we devoted four days to a very minute and careful exploration of islands in and at the mouth of the harbour, and of the adjacent mainland". Dr Mouat and his two other colleagues found that,

> nearly every tree of the original settlement has been effected.... The island is small ... with undulating ground, and a good soil, covered with vegetation, in which are a few large forest trees. There was no indication of water anywhere, but on boring near the foot of the mound, it was found in a clay bed at the depth of twelve feet, and it instantly rose to within five feet of the surface of the artesian well.

They discovered that the small strait which intervened between the islet (Chatham) and the southern shore (of what is now Port Blair) was "shallow, with a rocky bottom, being a continuation of Blair's reef. The water evidently came therefore from that side where it was subsequently discovered in abundance". The report continued:

> The North Shore is high, rising abruptly nearly 300 feet, with ledges of cultivable land on its southern aspect. The ridges are formed of sandstone, which was found to contain several water courses.... and to abound in bamboo, cane, rattan, and a sufficiency of large forest trees for building purposes. Good clay for bricks is abundant, and the supply of sandstone for building inexhaustible for piers, jetties, the metalling of roads.... The coral reefs in the more exposed bays would furnish an unlimited stock of fine lime.... The luxuriance of the vegetation, and its great variety may be assumed to be good proof of the fertility of the soil. The rocks bordering it abound in oysters and shell fish, and the harbour itself being open to the East with a strong influx and efflux, will doubtless prove a rich fishery.... The land at the Western end of the bay is elevated, supplied with fresh water.... The land on the Southern aspect of the harbour is lower, even more plentifully supplied with water, and from the character of its dense and multiform vegetation seems to possess a richer and more promising soil.... The Committee are not aware of any physical indications by which the healthiness of an uncleared locality can be absolutely predicted—but, so far as ordinary experience can be accepted as a safe guide, Old Harbour seems to afford fair promise of proving as healthy as any locality similarly situated in a tropical region.

Expressing their opinion on the suitability of the old site from the health point of view, they added: "We are, therefore, of the opinion that as a small portion of it—Chatham Island—proved continuously healthy during the time it was occupied sixty years since, that with ordinary care in the constructions of buildings, and strict conservancy arrangements, a more extended and permanent settlement will prove equally salubrious." The conclusion they arrived at was obvious—that the old harbour was the only suitable site for founding a new settlement. They said: "The Committee are of opinion that Old Harbour is the only place that possesses the greater number of requisites for a Penal Settlement, and accordingly recommend its occupation for the purpose, in preference to any other localities visited and examined." They paid high tribute to the judgement and perspicacity of Lieutenant Archibald Blair: "They [the Committee] cannot refrain from taking advantage of this opportunity to record their admiration of the great judgement of Lt. Blair in originally selecting that spot, and of his accuracy as Hydrographer." They thus suggested: "The name of Old Harbour may be changed to Port Blair, in honour of the distinguished officer".

Dr Mouat had obviously fallen under the spell of the enchanting Chatham Island and the island across the narrow strait where now lies the town named after Blair because, in a subsequently written book entitled *Adventures and Researches Among The Andaman Islanders,* he gives a lyrical description of his first glimpse of the islands:

> The land presented a series of low undulatory hills, the character, arrangement, and colouring of which formed a spectacle of the most lovely description. The lower parts of the various eminences were of a dark purple shade, gradually brightening towards the top, which reflected with dazzling brilliancy the golden tints of the morning. The vegetation with which they were profusely covered was of the usually brilliant and gorgeous character seen only in tropical regions. Every hill, from its summit down to the water's edge, looked like a neglected but beautiful garden, in which nature, left to its own resources, had scattered abroad and vivified the seeds of vegetable life with prodigality of which our poor sluggish soil, even in the most favoured parts of Europe, is altogether incapable. The shore was indented with numerous bays, in some of which the waters, shaded by overhanging hills, and the abundant foliage of the trees, presented cool spots on which the eye could rest with a sense of pleasure and relief; while in others they shone with all the brightness of a mirror, flashing back the dazzling rays of the ascending morning sun. The belts of pure white sand, with which the bays were edged, had a silvery radiance that contrasted beautifully with the rich colouring of the vegetation and trees by which they were immediately surmounted. The face and summit of the wildest cliffs were softened and adorned by patches of rich velvet moss, over which, like glancing lines of crystal, pure rills of fresh water, making music with their soft murmur before they reached the descent over which they fell, precipitated themselves with a loud crash, throwing glistening showers of spray in all directions.

Although, by the time of the Mouat Committee's visit to the Andaman islands, some knowledge of the original inhabitants had been gained by isolated encounters, it did not amount to very much. And the little that was known was so mixed with "fable and fiction" that it induced the committee, as the report put it, "to pay more than ordinary attention to all measures calculated to open an amicable intercourse with them, and throw light on their habits and customs".

However, according to their own admission, they do not seem to have succeeded in that objective to a significant extent. The committee reported:

> The first contact with them occurred in Craggy Island. On rounding that place to anchor under the shelter, a large party of them were sur-

prised fishing on a reef running from the mainland, with a few separated from them on a sandy pit of the Island. The latter we conjecture to have been women, and they had a small canoe lying on the beach. As soon as the Steamer had anchored, the Committee landed in two well-armed boats. The people who had been seen on the Island disappeared in the dense jungles which covered the Islet. In the canoe, which with its contents was left exactly as it was found, beads and looking glasses were placed, and the party immediately re-embarked to show the natives that their intentions were friendly, and free from even the semblance of hostility. During and previous to the time occupied by the proceedings, the men of the reef—ten or twelve in number—exhibited every sign of the most implacable hostility. They gesticulated violently, vociferated, waved their bows and arrows, and one of them brandished a spear, with a metallic head, which gleemed brightly in the rays of the setting sun. Another of them waded to his waist in the sea, howled defiance, and shot a couple of arrows in the direction of the Steamer.... They were all naked, and intensely black. They appeared strong, well built, sturdy men of middle size and did not exhibit the smallest fear of us.

They went on to state:

We approached to them as close as the surf on the reef permitted, waving handkerchiefs, and shouting the word *"Padoo"* which is given in a vocabulary published in the Asiatic Researches by Colebrook as signifying *"Friend"* in the language of the natives of the Andamans. All was in vain, and as the Committee were most desirous to avoid collision with them in their angry mood, which might have been caused by a belief that their women were in danger, the boats were withdrawn and pulled to the Southward to seek a safe place preparatory to searching for signs of fresh water. Five of the savages ran along the beach for more than a mile, and then disappeared in the jungle.... Sentries were posted near the boats to prevent surprise.... The advance guard had scarcely walked a hundred yards, when arrows were fired at them from an open patch of jungle. The attack was immediately repelled by a volley of musketry, which did no damage, but frightened away the savages, who were not again seen that evening. On the following morning... as the Steamer was leaving they reappeared and repeated their pantomime of hostility and defiance.

After this first contact, they had seven more. On four occasions the aborigines attacked but were repelled, fortunately, without any bloodshed. Twice, on seeing Dr Mouat's party, they just disappeared; they even left their fires burning, and their canoes. The last encounter proved to be the least happy. It occurred on South Reef Island, which lies at the southern extremity of Interview Island:

> After steaming round Interview Island to ascertain its general physical characters, the *Pluto* passed to the Southward of South Reef Island, and had turned against to the North, when a large group of natives, about thirty in number, were observed assembled together on the beach, gazing quietly at the Steamer as she passed. There were seven canoes lying on the beach, and the party were evidently waiting for low tide to fish upon the reef. The Committee left the Steamer in the first cutter. The second Cutter followed in case of need . . . . On approaching the island natives had taken to their canoes, the boats followed and soon gained upon them. All arms were carefully concealed and all gestures calculated to alarm the natives were avoided. When within a hundred yards of them they exhibited bows and arrows and began the usual gestures of hostility exactly as witnessed on the East Coast. Three of their canoes were isolated from the rest. The man in the first Cutter ceased rowing, and the boat drifted quietly towards them. Handkerchiefs were waved; presents were held up and shown, the shibboleth *Padoo* was shouted, and no act of hostility was committed by any one in the Cutter. The leading canoe was seen to be gradually edging away and when within about fifteen yards of us, the men in all canoes simultaneously started up, and discharged a flight of arrows at the first Cutter, with considerable force and precision. Lieutenant Heathcote, a seaman, and Dr Mouat's *Jemadar* were struck with arrows in the first Cutter, which had come up by this time. As the savages were well supplied with arrows and were about to repeat their aggression, the Committee opened fire upon them. Two of them were shot dead, the rest abandoned their canoe to swim to the shore, which the greater number were seen to reach in safety . . . .One of the natives, when in water, seized a strap thrown to him from the second Cutter, and was taken on board. The Committee deliberated anxiously as to the disposal of this man—whether to release, or to carry him to Calcutta. They ultimately decided on the latter course as the one acquired by the interest of humanity, although attended by hardship to the individual, until he can be instructed sufficiently to know the reason which led to his removal, from his country and his kindred.

This would turn out to be a great mistake.

In Calcutta, the presence of the Andamanese attracted a great deal of attention; he was the first one to be seen there since Blair and Kyd had taken one during the 1790s. He was unable to pick up any of the local languages; he pined for his home and his people. Ultimately, he fell sick; first he had an attack of cholera, from which he recovered, but then went down with bronchitis, which threatened to turn into a kind of typhoid inflammation of the lungs. It was, therefore, decided to send him back to the Andamans. He was taken back and landed on the southern end of Interview Island. He was given some presents, but was never seen or heard of again.

It must, however, be said to Dr Mouat's credit that he seemed to bear no ill-will towards the aborigines, despite the committee's far from happy encounters with them. In his book, published in 1863, he quotes with approval Lieutenant Blair's view that:

> The inveterate, deep-rooted hostility with which they regarded all strangers who approached their coasts, had its origin in the fact that they had once been in a state of slavery, and that the remembrance of their sufferings, which nothing could efface, was so vivid as to produce those feelings of enmity which nothing but the blood of all whom they regarded their foes could assuage.

The committee's report was submitted to the Right Honourable the governor-general in council on 1 January 1858 and, within a fortnight of its submission, a decision had been taken to establish a penal settlement in the Andaman islands. In a letter dated 15 January 1858, addressed to Dr F J Mouat and his two colleagues, Dr G R Playfair and Lieutenant J A Heathcote, C Beadon, secretary to the government of India, conveyed "the cordial thanks of the Government of India for the judicious, prompt and effectual manner in which [they had] carried out the instructions" given to them and "the business like and practical shape" in which the results of their investigation had been submitted. The proceedings of the committee from first to last were "entirely approved" and, as recommended by the committee, the old harbour was to be named *Port Blair*.

In another letter, written on the same day, Captain Henry Man, executive engineer and superintendent of convicts at Moulmein, was informed:

> It has been determined by the Right Honourable the Governor General in Council to establish a penal settlement on the Andaman Islands for the reception in the first instance of convicts sentenced to imprisonment, and to transportation, for the crimes of mutiny and rebellion and other offences connected therewith, and eventually for the reception of all convicts under sentence of transporation whom for any reason it may not be thought expedient to send to the Straits or to the Tanasserum Province. His Lordship in Council has determined therefore that a commencement shall be made at the Old Harbour, which will hereafter be distinguished by the name of Port Blair in honour of the officer who discovered and accurately surveyed it upward of 80 years ago, and by whom its advantages were seen and appreciated.

In yet another letter, addressed to Captain Henry Man, he was instructed:

I am directed to request that on your arrival at Port Blair you will hoist the British flag and take formal possession of the group of islands called the Andaman Islands, consisting of the Great and Little Andamans and all the islands adjacent thereto in the name of Her Majesty the Queen and the East India Company.

Captain Man was vested with full judicial and executive authority throughout the Andamans, and also appointed its commissioner. He proceeded to the Andamans on board the *Semiramis* and the British flag was duly hoisted, with all solemnity, on 22 January 1958. On that historic day began a new chapter in the story of the Andaman islands. And this chapter was to last, except during the brief period of the Japanese occupation, till 15 August 1947—another very historic day, when India achieved independence and the sun of the British empire set for all time over the land and territories that were to comprise Free India, including the Andaman and Nicobar islands.

8

The Aborigines: Negritos, Not Negroes

For quite some time it was commonly believed that the aborigines of the Andaman islands were descendents of African slaves once shipwrecked while being carried on board a Portuguese ship. But most anthropologists who have been studying the characteristics of the Andamanese aborigines during the last few centuries have come to the firm conclusion that they are not Negros but Negritos. The theory of the Portuguese shipwreck, therefore, stands totally discounted.

It would appear that at one time the Negritos also existed in other parts of India, because there are traces of Negrito physiognomy in the Kolarian tribes on the Indian mainland. The Negritos seem to have the same ancestors as the

Semangs of the Malacca peninsula, the *Aetas* of the Philippines and other oceanic people, including, perhaps, the now extinct Tasmanians. Some anthropologists have found traces of the customs, which were prevalent among them when they first came into contact with our so-called civilization, even among the people of Torres Strait. There is also a conjecture that the Papuan and Melanesians are Negrito, though they are perhaps crossed with either the Malayans or the Polynesians.

No one has been able to answer the question, with any degree of accuracy, as to how and when they came to the Andamans. The main source that provides any data about the antiquity of the Andamanese are their kitchen-middens, which till recently were found all over the islands. (An excavation of the kitchen-middens reveal fossilized shells at the base.) And then, of course, there are their legends.

As the Andamanese are generally nomads and have had to shift from place to place all through the centuries—consequent upon changes in the monsoon, and because of the scarcity of food in a particular area, most of the food being consumed in a little while—these kitchen-middens, about 50 feet in diameter, were once found scattered all over the place. It seems that as a rule not more than 30 people lived on each site.

That the Andamanese are so ancient that they did not have even any kind of pottery at one stage, was revealed when, in 1952, Lidio Cipriani, an Italian anthropologist, dug up a kitchen-midden in Golpahar in Little Andaman Island. While digging, according to him,

> [they] reached a depth of about four metres from the top of the midden through refuse mixed with only a little earth, very easy to penetrate. Bones, shells and other objects emerged clean, as if only recently rejected. The situation altered suddenly about one metre from the bottom, when the strata became hard and cemented with a mixture of ashes and earth. In these layers the shells were calcified by exposure to fire, and so fragile they could only be recovered in broken pieces. It is clear from this that when they first arrived in the Andamans, the Negrito had no pottery; there are no signs of it at all in the lowest level.

The Andamanese trace back their tradition to a great cataclysm which submerged a greater part of their land which, they say, is responsible for dividing them. According to them, that is why they speak different languages, and the various tribes do not any longer even understand one another's tongue.

The Andamanese, when the British first got to know them, were divided into 12 main tribes; they could be said to belong to three divisions— the North Indian group of tribes, the South Andaman group of tribes and the Ongè group of tribes. The tribes were further subdivided into what is known as septs, with each sept having its own leader or headman. But these divisions and subdivisions notwithstanding, the aborigines of the

Andamans belonged to two main classified categories — *Arioto,* coast dwellers, and *Eremtaga,* jungle dwellers or those living in the hinterland. Both are generally bitter enemies of each other.

The difference between the Arioto and the Eremtaga lies chiefly in the way they collect food. The Arioto's main source of food is the sea. They are, therefore, expert swimmers and divers, also skilful in fishing and shooting with the arrow. They look hardier. The Eremtaga are experts insofar as finding their way through the jungle is concerned, which is natural enough because that is where they dwell. They also know more about the flora and fauna and display great expertise in hunting the pig.

There is a widespread belief that the Andamanese are pygmies, but that is not so. According to M V Portman, who made a thorough and detailed study of the Andamanese, the normal height of the men folk is four feet and ten and a half inches, and that of the women, four feet and six inches. The height does vary because there are some who are a little above five feet. The weight varies between 85 to a little below 100 pounds. (The women are generally steatopygous.)

As already stated, Lieutenant Colebrook found the Andamanese ugly and perhaps "the least civilised in the world". He had described their colour as "of the blackest hue" and their stature "in general small". He thought they were "ill formed and slender, their bellies prominent". As against this, Dr Frederic J Mouat, chairman of the Andaman Committee, has stated:

> They are the most perfectly formed little beings in existence. In proportion to their size, their general framework is well constructed and their limbs present a remarkably good development, and the whole form as elegant as that of any Europeans.

And, in the words of M V Portman:

> In appearance ... the Andamanese men and the young women are not unpleasing, some indeed are distinctly good looking and have fine, well-shaped noses, thin lips, small mouths, even white teeth, bright sparkling eyes, and very well shaped figures.

But he also adds that "the old people often become hideous".

Strangely enough, although they wear no clothes at all, the Andamanese do not like the cold and are afraid of it. Comparatively speaking, they are more tolerant of the sun. They do not like being thirsty or, for that matter, hungry. So the moment they feel thirsty or hungry, they satisfy the need. Similarly, they cannot endure not being able to sleep for more than 24 hours — although, when feasting, they can go on dancing for as many as four days at a time.

The sexual awakening of the Andamanese takes place when they are about 15 years old, but they do not marry till they are about 25. Premarital sexual intercourse among the Andamanese is quite common but once they are married they are strict monogamists and lay great stress on the wife and husband being faithful to each other. Infidelity on the wife's part can result in her being killed and, possibly, her lover too being murdered. Divorce is practically unknown; so is incest. The Andamanese give names to their children while they are still in the womb. After the child is born, another name is added indicating whether a child is male or female. Women are given flower names also; this is done at the time of menstruation, and the young girl is given the name of the flower of whichever tree happens to be in bloom at the time.

The marriage ceremony is simple and has nothing religious about it. As soon as the elders of a tribe get to know that a young couple is interested in each other and would like to get married, the bride-to-be is taken to a newly built hut. And there she sits, while the bridgegroom runs away into the jungle. After some seeming struggle and feigned hesitation, he is persuaded to come back and made to sit in the bride's lap. And that is it. They are now married. The marriage is strictly binding but, after the death of either party, the other can remarry.

The complexion of the Andamanese varies from the near jet black of the South Andamanese group of tribes to the reddish-brown of the Ongès. So does the colour of their hair. It can be black as soot, dark or light brown, red, or even the colour of unburnished gold. Their hair styles vary too. The South Andamanese shave their heads clean; some others in Great Andaman allow their hair to grow long; the Jarawas grow a mop on top of their heads and the Ongès keep it very short. They are never too hairy. In fact, except on the head, they have no hair; only some men have a little beard and moustache and, when they have it, they are very proud of it and never shave it. The skin of the Andamanese is smooth and quite soft, but most Andamanese (though not the Jarawas or the Ongès) are apt to tattoo on their body or scarify it. But the methods differ. According to Portman:

> The tribes of the South Andaman Group cut their bodies with small flakes of quartz or glass in patterns of zig-zag or straight lines running up and down the body or limb. Each cut is about a quarter of inch in length, and is merely superficial. To make a pattern of straight lines, a line of cuts is made, the incisions being end to end and about an eighth of an inch distant, is then cut, and twelve or fourteen of such lines would make the pattern. In the zig-zag pattern only two lines are made, the cut being incised at obtuse angles to each other, and thus forming something like our "dog-tooth" pattern. The making of the pattern depends upon the individual taste of the woman cutting them, but the face and ears, genitals, arm and knee pits are not cut.... Women are tattooed in the same way as men. The North Andaman Group of tribes have a different system of tattooing. The cuts with them are made

by the men with the head of a pig-arrow, and are severe and deep. They are made across the body or limb, and are not placed end to end but parallel to each other. They are about an inch in length and half an inch apart, and as a rule three lines of cuts are made, one in the centre of the back from the nape of the neck to the buttocks, and one on either side of this from each shoulder to half way down the buttocks, these lines are about three inches apart. Occasionally four or five lines of smaller cuts may be seen. Three or four (sometimes five) similar lines of smaller cuts, about two inches apart, are made from the collar bones to the pubes. Other smaller lines of cuts are made down, and sometimes circling round, the arms and legs, the cuts being on a slope like the series of slates of a half-open Venetian blind. The women of this Group are, as a rule, only tattooed when they become elderly.

The Ongès do not tattoo themselves, but use clay mixed with water to smear their entire bodies and draw patterns either with it or with red ochre mixed with turtle or pig's fat.

The Andamanese are very fond of hunting and fishing and their main weapons are the harpoon, which they use for turtle and dugong and large fishes like the porpoise, and bows and arrows with which they hunt everything else, including the pig. They have no idea of agriculture and are a purely hunting and gathering race of men. They are not interested in the chicken and, until the British introduced the dog, they had no use for pet animals. Today, sometimes, there are more dogs than human beings in their settlements. They eat nothing raw; they either broil or bake their food in rough pots over an open fire. An interesting aspect of the dietary habits of the Andamanese is that they do not know the use of salt or sugar in their food. But they love honey.

The pots used differ in shape among the different groups, some rounded at the bottom and others pointed. They are never glazed.

Their burial customs are somewhat quaint. A dead child is buried under the floor of the parents' hut and the grown-ups are generally tied in a bundle and the body placed on a platform atop a tree. The boundary of the tree is marked and festooned with cane leaves, and for about three months no one visits the area. Mourning takes the form of the relatives and friends of the dead covering themselves with grey clay. During the period of mourning, which lasts about three months, there is no dancing or any other festivity. At the end of it the remains of the corpse are taken down from the tree; the bones are washed, broken into sizeable pieces, and used as ornaments. They are supposed to have therapeutic value also, as their mere touch, it is believed, can stop pain and cure disease.

In some cases, however, dead bodies are buried. This is considered to be a great honour to the dead. But, there again, the body is disinterred after the period of mourning is over, the bones washed and broken and kept as ornaments and to cure disease.

The death of a chief is treated differently and has a more elaborate ceremonial. Surgeon F Day was present at the funeral of a chief of one of the northern tribes, who had died on 1 July 1865. He gives a description of the funeral:

> Within two hours his remains were rolled up in leaves by old people and corded with fibre preparatory to their being consigned to the grave. The latter was merely two feet deep, and only a few feet above high water mark. Here the corpse was placed in a half sitting posture with the face turned towards the east. Previous to filling the grave, each took his last farewell of one they had loved so well whilst alive, and one by one in turn gently blew upon his face and forehead. When all was over there did not remain more than six inches of earth above the body, placed there to prevent the ribs from being broken; some stones were now heaped over the grave, subsequently burning faggots, and mourning garlands were placed at the head of the grave on the shore in conspicuous places, to mark a chief's internment. Before retiring, a cup of water was placed at the head of the grave, in case the spirit of the deceased, during the night should feel thirsty. Four months subsequently the nearest of kin went to the grave and brought away the lower jaw which about that time became fleshless; a month afterwards, the shoulder-bone and a rib or clavicle were extracted; and after six months the skull, now freed from impurities. This was slung round the neck of the principal mourner, and subsequently everybody had it in turn to carry about.

A most interesting phenomenon about the Andamanese is that they have never known, even to this day, how to make fire. Therefore, they are very careful and conserve fire by keeping it burning always. They carry fire with them when they go anywhere by sea or travel on shore, taking great care that it does not die. Should the fire do so—which is considered a great mishap—they go to the next village to borrow some.

Apart from hunting, dancing is the main amusement of the Andamanese. They perform at night, generally after a chase. Their dancing is somewhat of a curious and monotonous performance. They use no musical instrument, but drum their feet rhythmically on a special kind of sounding board, which looks something like a Crusader's shield. They sing mostly impromptu while they dance; one of them takes the lead, while the others follow. Then they all sing together. They dance practically every evening, if there are enough of them. The dancing lasts for hours and sometimes all night, particularly if there is a meeting of the tribe. Both men and women take part. A Radcliffe Brown, who saw them dance over 50 years ago, has left this vivid description:

> When all is ready, a man who has volunteered to sing the first song

takes his stand at the sounding board and sings his song through. When he reaches the chorus the women take it up and repeat it after him, and as they do so each woman marks time by clapping her hands on the hollow formed by her thighs, the legs being crossed one over the other at the ankle. The singer continues to sing, thus leading the chorus, and at the same time marks the time of the song by beating on the sounding board with his foot. As soon as the chorus begins the dancers begin to dance. When the singer and the chorus get tired, the singing ceases, but the man at the sounding board continues to sing, thus leading the chorus, and at the same time marks the time of the song by beating on the sounding board with his foot. As soon as the chorus begins the dancers begin to dance. When the singer and the chorus get tired, the singing ceases, but the man at the sounding board continues to mark the time for the dancers. The singer repeats his song several times, and he may sing several songs, each repeated several times. When he gets tired, he is relieved by another man. In a dance that lasts for any time, one singer succeeds another, and the singing and the dancing are kept up continuously.

And it is much the same even today.

Being primarily nomadic, the Andamanese do not build huts of a permanent nature. According to Portman:

A hut is merely a patch of thatch placed on four upright and some cross pieces, about 4 feet 6 inches high in front, and 8 inches high at the back. There is no walling at the sides, and each hut is about 4 feet long and 3 feet wide, which is sufficient for one family.

A typical Andamanese village looks something like this:

```
COOKING            MARRIED                        HEADMAN
┌───┐ ┌─────┐   ┌───┐ ┌─────┐                     ┌───┐
│   │ │     │   │   │ │     │                     │   │
└───┘ └─────┘   └───┘ └─────┘                     └───┘

┌───┐                DANCING GROUND               ┌───┐
│   │                                             │   │
│   │                                             │   │
└───┘ ┌─────┐   ┌─────┐ ┌─────┐   ┌─────┐         └───┘
BACHELORS                                         SPINSTERS
                     MARRIED
```

The religion of the Andamanese is, according to Lieutenant-Colonel Sir Richard Temple, Bart., who was chief commissioner of the islands and conducted the first ever general census in 1901: "Simple animism [consists] of the evil spirit of the wood, the sea, diseases and ancestors, and of avoidance of acts traditionally displeasing to them." They have no rigid ceremonial, nor do they believe in propitiation. But, interestingly enough, they do believe in an anthropomorphic deity called *Puluga* who, according to Sir Richard again, is "the cause of all things, whom it is not, however, necessary to propitiate, though sins, i.e. acts displeasing to him, are to be avoided for fear of damage to the products of the jungle".

But the Andamanese do not believe in either heaven or hell. Contrary to general belief, they are not cannibals. There is no evidence whatsoever of their ever having been so. Human bones are found in proper graves only and, in their kitchen-middens, are never discovered mixed with fossilized bone of pig, shellfish and the like. Besides, as they say, when there is so much natural food available, why should they eat human flesh which, in all probability, will only give them stomach-ache! The charge of cannibalism against them appears obviously a result of observations made by old mariners, because the Andamanese used to kill any stranger they came across. They would burn his body, because they believed in burning the body of any and every enemy. And after that they used to hold weird all-night dances round the fire. This obviously made all those who witnessed this eerie spectacle, believe that the Andamanese were cannibals.

Writing in 1883, on the subject of how the Andamanese navigate from one island to the other, Edward Horace Man, son of Colonel Man, who raised the Union Jack at Port Blair when the second settlement in 1858 was founded, has this to say:

> It is a subject of surprise to all who, during the past fifteen or twenty years, have come in contact with the Andamanese, and have observed the style and capabilities of their canoes, to read the high encomium that have been bestowed on the skill with which they are constructed, and to find that they are credited with such extraordinary speed as to distance easily a cutter, as well as a gig, manned respectively by picked crews of blue-jackets and Chinamen . . . . nowhere on Great Andaman, at all events at the present day, have any aborigines been found capable of propelling a canoe at more than half the speed of one of the ordinary gigs in common use at Port Blair.

It is possible that by the time of Man's arrival there, they had lost their prowess!

According to Man, canoes are made generally in the months of August and September, and it takes about eight men nearly a fortnight to hollow out a canoe and form the prow. (The prow is for spearing fish and turtle.) They generally select a tree-trunk of anything between ten to thirty feet in length. First, they remove the bark and then, with an adze, they shape the exterior of the canoe as also its prow. After that the interior is scooped out, also with an adze. At the bottom level the canoes are about one and a half to three inches thick. They always use an outrigger, which helps maintain the balance. The outrigger is attached to a canoe by three or four pieces of wood which pass through its interior. When alongside the shore, the canoes are propelled by means of the haft of the harpoon spear, which is used for catching fish; when in deep water, paddles are used.

To catch fish, the Andamanese never use a hook and line. The normal method they follow, again according to Edward Horace Man, is:

> At low water the women and children with hand-nets capture such fish and shell-fish as are left by the receding waters in the rocky hollows on the foreshore, and at the turn of the tide the men are usually to be seen standing up to their waists in water, or poling along the shore in their canoes, and shooting with their bows and arrows at the fish as they dart past.

They never catch the turtle (the edible variety which is green) by "turning" it—they spear it when it rises to the surface of the sea to breathe. Their main sport is to chase the pig. But they always kill it with a pointed arrow, as they do the iguana.

Not much is known of the Andamanese language and its grammatical structures. According to Lieutenant R C Temple, then cantonment magistrate at Ambala in the Punjab and later chief commissioner of the islands, in response to a letter Man had written to him enclosing the Andamanese vocabulary and other data that he had collected:

> The Andaman languages are one group; they are like [i.e. connected with] no other group; they have no affinities by which we might infer their connection with any other known group. The word-construction [the etymology of the old grammarians] is two fold, i.e., they have affixes and prefixes to the root of a *grammatical* nature. The general principle of word-construction is agglutination pure and simple . . . . There are of course many peculiarities of grammar in the Andamanese group, and even in each member of the group, but these are only such as are incidental to the grammar of other languages, and do not affect its general tenor. I consider, therefore, that the Andamanese languages belong to the agglutinative stage of development, and are distinguished from other groups by the presence in full development of the principle of prefixed and affixed grammatical additions to the roots of words.

Man's own finding was that they also had "a distinct poetical dialect, and in their songs they subordinate everything to rhythm, the greatest liberties being thereby taken not only with the forms of their words, but even with the grammatical construction of the sentences".

Apart from the Great Andamanese, there are two other tribes in the

Andamans—the Jarawas and the Sentinelese, the latter confined to North Sentinel Island and considered, ethnically, the same as the Jarawas. Very little is known about the Jarawas because they have been hostile to all strangers. There were reasons for this hostility, however. Portman's explanation:

> On our arrival the *Jarawas* were quiet and inoffensive towards us, nor did they ever disturb us, until we took to continuously molesting them by inciting the coastal Andamanese against them. After a few years of this disturbance, the life of the Jarawas became very hard and in retaliation they began to attack us. It was our fault if the Jarawas became hostile.

The Sentinelese, if anything, are even more hostile.

As we shall see later, even petty pilfering from what they considered to be their own legitimate territory, resulted in vicious expeditions being mounted against the Jarawas, resulting in severe punishment. At the same time, their traditional enemies, the Arioto, were given fire-arms. And, as should have been expected, they used them to slaughtering the Jarawas. It is, therefore, no wonder that the Jarawas should have continued to treat the British and us, their then henchmen, as people who were not to be trusted and, whenever possible, destroyed.

9
The Ongés

The Ongés live on Little Andaman Island, which is at the southernmost extremity of the entire Andaman group of islands. Little Andaman has an area of 448 square miles. Although separated by a long stretch of the sea, which extends 31 miles, the identical grammatical structure of the language they speak is an obvious proof of the fact that the Ongés are basically the same as the Negritos of Great Andaman. The vocabularies, however, do differ.

The Ongés too believe in the legend of the cataclysm and that is how, they say, they were separated from their brethren on the other islands in the Great Andaman group. But there is no doubt that they have lived on Little Andaman for thousands of years, because it is proved by their kitchen-middens, which reveal the presence of fossilized shells, the same as those found at the base of kitchen-middens dug up in Great Andaman—a positive proof of the fact that they, like the rest of the Negritos, were once denizens of the Stone Age. And the pottery that appears at the next level (there are no signs of it at the lowest level) shows the careful working of clay, and could perhaps be as old as five thousand years. The upper levels reveal that it degenerated to the extent of becoming as crude as it is today—impure clay carelessly mixed, even with bits of stones, and hardly any firing. The kitchen-middens in Little Andaman also reveal that the pig was introduced into the island about the same time as the pottery. There are no signs of any other animal being present at any time until, of course, the recent introduction of the dog. The Ongés continue to live in the same style, indifferent to the inroads made by so-called civilization elsewhere. Lidio Cipriani describes them as involuted rather than primitive.

The Ongés build for themselves two kinds of shelters—temporary shelters and permanent huts, which are more elaborate than those constructed by the Andamanese. The temporary shelter is quite simple, with no walls and only a sloping roof rising from the ground. The permanent huts they build for themselves are also as uncomplicated. Each hut is circular in shape, and water-proof mats are used as roofing, each mat overlapping well over the other so that the rain does not leak through. The roof, like an enormous umbrella, rests on poles. In the centre of the floor there is always a fire. There is also a fire burning next to each bed—mainly for warmth, for without it the Andamanese would fall ill. Inside the hut there are no partitions or compartments. The beds are arranged like the ribs of an umbrella, but they are so close to the outer edge that everyone sleeps with his or her head towards the centre. The bed itself is no more than several sticks put together, to make it look like a platform; four sturdy sticks dug into the ground at each end act as props. A piece of tree-trunk is used as a headrest. The beds are about 20" above the ground. Most cooking is done in the open, except during the rains when the fire at the centre, which is larger than the fires by the sides, is used. The concept of privacy is unknown; everything is open to every eye.

One reason why the Ongés always keep the fire burning is that they are completely ignorant about the art of making fire. In this sense they are like prelithic people. They are terrified of being without fire. Should it perchance go out, they also show great ingenuity in rekindling it. When lightning strikes one of the trees, they use the smouldering branches of the tree as a source of fire (the tree, naturally enough, continues to smoulder for days together because of excessive humidity).

The Ongés, like the rest of the aborigines in these islands, have no concept of hygiene as we know it. They seldom wash, but are often drenched by the water dripping from every leaf when they are out in the jungle.

The Ongés only gather and hunt. They too are not aware of agriculture. That they are an ancient people is evident, as already indicated, from the presence of calcified shells at the base of their kitchen-middens. The Ongés eat mostly natural food, in which the island abounds. They are very fond of the jackfruit. They generally roast it in hot ashes till both pulp and seed become edible. They also like the Pandanus which, though stringy, tastes something like a pineapple. (Its leaves can sometimes provide roofing for their shelters.) And the yam—some yams are as big as footballs. Then there is food from the sea. They particularly like pilchards. They generally harpoon the fish or shoot it with a bow and arrow. Apart from fish, they catch molluscs, Crustacea, lobsters, crayfish and crabs, even some kinds of hermit-crabs. They also eat the cicada. They collect the pupae as they come out of the ground, and then roast them. Pupae are supposed to be a great treat. Like the rest of the Andamanese, they have no use for salt or sugar.

One of the chief delights of the Ongés is to catch a giant turtle. Once caught, they cut it into pieces while still alive, and throw them into boiling water, or even sometimes roast the entire turtle alive. They are also fond of pork. Nowadays, they make use of the dog to chase a pig and then kill it with an arrow. In fact they find this chase most exciting. They do not eat any lizards, jungle cats, bats, rats or snakes, because, according to them, they harbour spirits of the dead. They are very fond of eating and generally cook and eat at the same time until a state of satiety is reached. The food that is left over they put over a kind of rack and light a fire of green wood underneath, so that it can be preserved for later use. It is at the time of communal feasts that this propensity for eating has to be seen to be believed. It becomes a veritable orgy. Lidio Cipriani, who, during his stay with them in 1952, witnessed several of these orgies, has written:

> During these orgies I have seen a group of about sixty Ongés demolish in a few days ten pigs and a dozen large, wooden vessels full of honey, with basket after basket of fish, caught every night by women.

The crab, the flesh of which the Ongés enjoy eating, also provides them with their roughly made, and also obviously very ancient, smoking pipes. They use the claw, which is cut across the joint with a hole bored at one end, to smoke aromatic leaves.

But what the Ongés love above all is honey. When an Ongé finds a hive of bees, he puts a mark on the tree to establish his ownership. But when the honey is being gathered, everyone helps. An interesting feature is the way the Ongés gather honey. They climb up the trees without providing any protection to their bare bodies. And here nature has come to their rescue. There grow bushes of a plant called *tonjoghe* all over Little Andaman Island. All they have to do is to chew some of the leaves of this bush and smear the pulp all over their body, even in their hair. Some they spit at the bees. This provides total immunity from an attack by the bees. For water in the jungle, they find a substitute in the lianas, from which, when you break the stem and put it into the mouth, you can suck as much as a litre of liquid in a few minutes.

They use the nautilus shell for drinking water. Otherwise, they drink like animals, lying flat on their stomachs, lowering their heads and putting their lips to the water. Another shell they use is that of the Tridacna, a giant clam. They fill it up with water and use it as a mirror when painting themselves.

The Ongés have no clear concept of religion. As in Palaeolithic times, they do have some kind of belief in the survival of the spirit after death, and a fear of its return. But they have no ceremonial of any kind, nor any ritual. They do not have any totems either. They do not believe in sacrifice or, for that matter, in propitiation. They bury their dead under the bed in their hut but exhume the bones, only to reinter them after painting them with ochre. They do not wear bones round their necks.

The Ongés are great believers in the family as a unit—they are monogamous and divorce does not exist. No cases of polyandry, bigamy or incest have ever come to light. Like other Negritos, once they are married, sexual fidelity is the accepted mode. But, of course, before marriage, the young mix freely and no exception is taken to promiscuity. When it comes to the question of marriage, it can only take place with the consent of the family. Before the marriage ceremony the bride and the bridegroom are painted with white clay. One of the elders then addresses them and enjoins them to make a good husband and wife to each other. The actual ceremony is identical with that of the Andamanese (the elders putting the arms of the bride and the bridegroom round each other's necks and then making the bridegroom sit on the lap of the bride).

Interestingly enough, the traditional method of greeting is also to sit on the lap!

Apart from the marriage ceremony which is quite simple, comparatively speaking, they have a somewhat elaborate ceremonial when a girl attains puberty. A Radcliffe Brown, author of *Andaman Islands—A Social Study*, published in 1922, describes it in these words:

> On the occurrence of the first menstrual discharge the girl tells her parents, who weep over her. She must then go and bathe in the sea for an hour or two by herself. After that she goes back to her parents' hut or to a special shelter put up for the occasion. She is not required to go away from the camp. All ornaments are removed from her, only a single belt of *Pandanus* leaf is attached round her waist, with an apron of *cainyo* leaves. Strips of *Pandanus* leaf are attached round her arms near the shoulder and round her wrists, and others are placed as bands crossing her chest from shoulder to the waist on the opposite side, and

crossing her abdomen from the iliac crest on the one side to the trochanter on the other. These are so attached that the long loose ends hang down at the girl's side. Bunches of leaves, either *celmo* or, if these be not available, *poramo* are fastened beneath her belt before and behind. Other leaves of the same kind are placed for her to sit upon. Thus covered with leaves the girl must sit in the hut allotted to her, with her legs doubled up beneath her and her arms folded. A piece of wood or bamboo is placed at her back for her to lean against, as she may not lie down. If she is cramped she may stretch one of her legs or one of her arms, but not both legs or both arms at the same time. To feed herself she may release one of her hands, but she must not take up the food with her fingers; a skewer of *cainyo* wood is given her with which to feed herself. She may not speak or sleep for 24 hours. Her wants are attended to by her parents or her friends, who sit near her to keep her from falling asleep. The girl sits thus for those days. Early every morning she leaves the hut to bathe for an hour in the sea. At the end of those days she resumes her life in the village. For a month following, she must bathe in the sea every morning at dawn.

The Ongés are greatly adept in the art of canoe-making, the making of a canoe being an important event in their lives. The tree selected for the purpose belongs invariably to one of the species of Sterculia. It is first felled and then hollowed out. This is a slow and laborious process because the implement used is a very rudimentary form of the hatchet. They pay a great deal of attention when making the outrigger or the float, because its object is to prevent the canoe from capsizing. Launching the canoe is a ceremonial affair. Therefore, the canoe is decorated with ochre, like they would their own bodies.

They also make their own bows and arrows; the bows are fashioned from the living trunk of a large tree, and the string from long, thin strips of a particular kind of bark which is twisted together. It is from the bamboo that they make their fishing arrow, as also the hunting arrow or the arrow harpoon. It is very cleverly fashioned, the object being not only to shoot the animal with it, but to ensure that it does not escape into the thick jungle, and that it signifies its position by crying through shear agony caused by the piercing arrow.

The favourite pastime of the Ongés, too, is dancing. They have no accompaniment, not even the sounding board. Both men and women participate. Even children. They go round and round holding each other's hands and, while they dance, they sing.

The Ongés, too, have their legends. One of them is the legend of the *Akar-Bale*. According to this, as recounted by Radcliffe Brown:

In the beginning there was no night, no darkness and social life was continuous and was not subject to periods of diminished intensity. Then one of the ancestors [apparently in a fit of temper owing to his lack of success in fishing] crushed a cicada and the cry of the insect brought darkness upon the world.

No wonder, therefore, adds Radcliffe Brown, that:

The Ongés regard darkness as evil. Because, in the darkness, there can be no activity. Consequently, it is a manifestation of a force which is hostile to society.

10

The Birth of the Penal Settlement

Captain Henry Man had, with all due ceremony, raised the Union Jack at Port Blair on 22 January 1858, and thus formally annexed the Andaman islands. Although he had been named the first superintendent of the settlement at Port Blair, the orders for his appointment were soon countermanded, and Dr James Pattison Walker, who had a great deal of previous experience as a jail superintendent, and who was a nominee of Dr Mouat, chairman of the Andaman Committee, was appointed in his place. Accompanied by 200 convicts, an Indian overseer, two Indian doctors and a guard of 50 naval brigadesmen under an officer of the Indian Navy, Dr Walker arrived in Port Blair on board the Company's steam frigate

Semiramis on 10 March 1858.

Walker set up his headquarters on Ross Island. (It continued to remain the seat of local administration, including that of the Japanese, till after the second world war and was abandoned only after the Allies reoccupied the islands in 1945.) It would be interesting to recall here that this was not the first time that Indian convicts were being transported abroad. Actually, it was in as far back as 1787 that Indian convicts were first transported to Bencoolen in Sumatra, which was then under the government of India. They were sent there with a view to developing the place. But when in 1823 Bencoolen was ceded to the Dutch, the Indian convicts were transferred to Penang and Singapore. Interestingly enough, the rules and regulations adopted initially, which were to govern the treatment of the convicts at Port Blair, were identical to the ones outlined by Sir Stamford Raffles in his letter addressed to the Indian government in 1818. He had written: "The object of punishment as far as it affects the parties must be reclaiming them from their bad habits." But he did not think that the systems being followed by them "had been productive of that affect" because, as he put it, "sufficient discrimination and encouragement" had not been shown in favour of "those most inclined to amendment". According to the custom that they had been following, he went on to add:

> It frequently happens that men of notoriously bad conduct are liberated at the expiration of a limited period of transportation, whilst others, whose general conduct is perhaps unexceptional, are doomed to servitude till the end of their lives.

Sir Stamford Raffles, therefore, proposed to divide them into three classes:

> The first class to be allowed to give evidence in court, and permitted to settle on land secured to them and their children; but no one to be admitted to this class until he has been resident in Bencoolen for three years. The second class to be employed in ordinary labour. The third class, or men of abandoned and profligate character, to be kept to harder kinds of labour, and confined at night.

Sir Stamford was also of the opinion that the convicts be encouraged to marry because:

> No sooner [he] marries and forms a settlement then he becomes a kind of colonist, and if allowed to follow his inclination he seldom feels inclined to return to his native country. It rarely happens that any of those transported have any desire to leave the country; they form connections in the place, and find so many inducements to remain, that to be sent away is considered by most a severe punishment.

(Considering the number of ex-convicts who decided to stay on in the Andamans, and now form a major part of the population of the Andaman islands, there was obviously something in what Sir Stamford Raffles said more than a century and a half ago.)

In any case, with certain modifications from time to time, this was roughly to be the approach of the administrators in the Andaman islands as far as the convicts were concerned. Their difficulties only started when, beginning with 1909, the government of India decided to transport political prisoners. (Somehow the "mutineers" and some others also transported for political offences were not considered political prisoners!)

The main problem, which from the very outset compounded the difficulties that the new administrators were to face, was the ambiguity, or shall we say the paradoxicality, of their attitude towards the aborigines, because the orders of the court of directors of the Company and the government of India were that the Andamanese were to be treated well, and not subjected to any injury. Yet at the same time the convicts, who would have to work in clearing the jungles, were to be protected from attacks by the aborigines.

The two objectives were irreconcilable. The Andamanese were the original inhabitants of these islands, which they considered their domain. Anyone else was a usurper. JN Homfray, who was in charge of the Andamanese Home some years later, explained the reasons for their hostility and anger. In 1867, he wrote:

> The Andamanese are the original possessors of the soil, and demand from the usurper some consideration. We have occupied Port Blair and Port Mouat, where they used to live, restricted their liberty, and annexed their fishing grounds. They have had to retreat before us to avoid fights in which they have been killed, and they have suffered much in health by our advent.

On arrival at Port Blair, Dr Walker found that no provision had been made for either accommodating him and his party or feeding them. He had, therefore, to request the commanders of the two ships, the *Semiramis* and the *Mutlah*, which also happened to be there, to come to his assistance. The *Semiramis* was asked to proceed to Moulmein to procure some provisions for the new settlement. She not only brought back provisions but there also arrived on board the brig Captain Henry Man, originally designated as the superintendent, on a short visit.

The work of clearing the jungles was immediately taken in hand, at Chatham and Ross islands, the latter being another small island at the mouth of the harbour. The magnitude of the task can well be imagined, because as Dr Walker described it:

> The jungle is so dense, and the entanglement by gigantic creepers so

complete, as to render it impassable, except along the few pathways used by the aborigines. The jungle, so far as is known, is continuous, no open plains having been observed. Even when cut, often trees cannot be got to fall without great force, nor brushwood when cut removed, owing to intricate binding by creepers of great strength.

The work, however, went apace because, luckily for Walker, it was not yet the rainy season; nor had the aborigines made their appearance. So he was full of hope. But this state of affairs did not last long.

Walker's trouble started not with the aborigines but with the convicts who began to make attempts to escape. (By the end of June, the number of convicts had risen to 773.) The first one to try and escape was Narain, sentenced to transportation for life for having incited sedition in Dinapore, a cantonment now in Bihar. He was chased and caught, sentenced to death, and executed. A number of such attempts followed, some in groups of as many as 21. Most of them were eventually caught and executed. One committed suicide. Another returned in a debilitated state, after having been away for 12 days. He had escaped with some others and, according to his story, had had an encounter with the aborigines when most of his companions were massacred. The punishment meted out to those who had tried to escape was very severe; even some of the British officials thought that Walker had carried it to excess.

The following statement of the state of convicts on 16 June 1858, three months after Walker had established the settlement, speaks for itself:

Total no. of convicts received	773
Died in hospital	61
Escaped and not captured (probably died of starvation, or killed by savages)	140
Suicide	1
Hanged for attempting escape	87

To prevent escapes, the naval guard was doubled. In addition, a Sebundy Corps, consisting of South Indians, was formed. The Sebundies, who were in a way the forerunners of the modern military police, did not prove a success. Three years later, therefore, the Andaman Sebundy Corps was abolished.

The escapes continued, and those who returned were not only shown no mercy but given, in most cases, extreme punishment. For example, during the two months of March and April 1858, as many as 288 escaped, 86 of whom were executed on return. One hundred and forty remained uncaptured. They were presumably killed by the Andamanese.

To add further to his discomfiture, Walker discovered—and this was on All Fools Day, 1 April 1959—that the Punjabi convicts, nearly 200 of them, had been conspiring to capture power. They had planned to murder

Walker, his Indian overseer and all members of the naval guard. Luckily for him, one of the conspirators had ratted and given prior information to Walker about the plot. The attack began in the afternoon as planned, and one of the convicts, Sarwar Shah, aimed his gun at Walker. The gun was snatched by another convict, Muttra Das, who was attacked by Nazzar Mohammad, also a convict. Nazzar Mohammad rushed with the gun towards Walker. Walker fled and was saved by two gangsmen. This led to Walker adopting even more savage measures towards the convicts. (A noteworthy fact about this conspiracy is that it was hatched by ordinary convicts sent to Port Blair under sentence of transportation; no ex-mutineer was involved.)

Dr Walker was so reluctant to have a face-to-face encounter with the Andamanese that, even to obtain thatching leaves (which abound in the creeks of the island), he used to send frigates to get them from Tavoy in Burma on the Tennasserin coast. He was, however, advised to look for them in the Andamans itself. That is how the first conflict between Dr Walker's administration and the aborigines took place. The brig *Mutlah* was out on a search for these leaves but, due to the impudent conduct of a midshipman, one of the officers was killed. In retaliation the men of the *Mutlah* destroyed as many as 40 huts of the Andamanese. Thus began, in right earnest, an undeclared war between the Andamanese and the administration. There was little abatement in the intensity of the conflict between the aborigines and the settlers except that, strangely enough, they were less inclined to attack those who bore signs of being convicts—like those wearing iron rings around their ankles. But they did not spare any of the gangsmen, whose sign of authority was a red turban, a badge and a coloured belt.

Of the many skirmishes that took place with the Andamanese, two were more serious than the others because of the greater loss of life involved. In one figured a naval officer, Lieutenant Templer of the Indian Navy; the other one was what has since come to be known as the Battle of Aberdeen. On 5 August 1858, a signal was made by the schooner *Charlotte*, which was then in harbour, to say that some aborigines were in sight. Under the orders of Walker, Lieutenant Templer, along with Rowe, chief officer of the brig *Sesostris*, one petty officer and eight men, was sent to "reconnoitre and watch their movements". Walker wrote about the incident:

> One man was seen in a canoe close under the mangrove bushes, who was evidently trying to get away. Chase was given, and as the party approached, two more canoes were seen hauled up on the shore. On nearing the first one, the party was received with a shower of arrows.... A native on the shore was shot.... It is to be inferred that the shower of arrows came from the shore, and it was returned with bullets from the boat. Lieutenant Templer then, leaving four men in the boat under Rowe, landed with five men, and after some firing seized the canoe that

was there and then rushed through the village and seized the other two canoes on the other side of the mangroves. The party, after destroying some of the huts which were too green to burn returned with three canoes and the body of the native who was killed, the other natives howling most piteously after them. Not one of the party was touched, but Lieutenant Templer thinks that several of the natives were wounded, as five or six were seen to drop. Lieutenant Templer, in his report, expressed his intention of destroying the village with my permission and this was accorded.

It must, however, be said to the credit of the then government of India that they disapproved of the action, and stated in most unambiguous terms that "on this occasion, as it appears from the papers, our people were the assailants".

The Battle of Aberdeen took place on 14 May 1859, and but for the fact that one of the convicts, Dudhnath Tewari, who had lived with the Andamanese for over a year after having escaped, gave prior information about the intended attack, the casualties would have been much greater, and there would have been much greater loss of life. Dudhnath Tewari was a sepoy of the native infantry regiment and had been convicted for mutiny and desertion and sentenced to transportation for life and labour in irons at Jehlum in the Punjab. He arrived in Port Blair on 6 April 1858. Within 17 days of his arrival he escaped with 90 other convicts (upon rafts made from felled trees bound together with tent ropes), under the command, as it were, of one Aga, who assured them that within ten days he would take them to the capital of Burma. They were joined later by other escaped convicts and eventually totalled 130. They struggled through the jungle and, when they did come across the aborigines, there was an indiscriminate slaughter. Eventually only Dudhnath escaped by feigning death and, when discovered, by supplicating them with gestures to spare his life.

Although badly wounded, his life was spared. He lived with the Andamanese for a year and 24 days. While with them, he went about naked like them, head shaven, and conformed to all their customs. According to his own story, he wandered about with them and thus saw about one quarter of Great Andaman Island. He is also said to have married two Andamanese women. This is obviously not correct, because the Andamanese are strictly monogamous. He, however, did marry an Andamanese woman called Lipaia. Some of the Andamanese later confirmed this. However, since he had served the British well, the governor-general in council was pleased to grant him a free pardon, whereupon he was released and sent to Calcutta.

The battle had been preceded by the Andamanese (in small numbers, never exceeding 20) showing themselves a number of times during April; but no actual conflict had taken place—except when a party landed from the ship *Charlotte*, on 28 April, on a pleasure excursion at North Point in Port Blair. The party had been attacked and one of the European seamen wounded. But, on 11 May, in the words of M V Portman:

> The aborigines attacked Aberdeen and Atlanta Point. Owing to timely warning from two escaped convicts [Dudhnath Tewari and one other], who had been travelling with the aborigines, the attack was provided for and plunder of tools on a large scale prevented. The Naval Guard was landed at Aberdeen; the *Charlotte* anchored between Ross and Atlanta Point; Lieutenant Warden, I.N., landed a party of naval men, and marching to the top of Aberdeen hill put the convicts in his rear for protection; while the *Charlotte's* men stopped the aborigines who were coming along the shore. Lieutenant Warden was attacked from the jungle, and owing to the numbers of savages, retreated into the boats, from whence he protected the convicts who had gathered on the pier, and in water, by firing over their heads. The *Charlotte's* guns too opened fire on the savages, who held possession of the convict station for over half an hour, plundering everything worth carrying off. Lieutenant Hellard, I.N., with a party of Naval Brigademen, Dr Walker's crew, and a number of convicts, rushed up the hill and drove off the aborigines. None of the convicts were wounded, but several of the savages are supposed to have been.

Captain J C Haughton succeeded Dr Walker on 3 October 1859. His arrival was like a breath of fresh air. The first thing he did was to introduce milder measures. Although he too continued to be worried by attacks from the Andamanese, it must be said to his credit that he was the first person who actually laid the foundation of friendly relations with the aborigines. Haughton's overall policy towards the aborigines was:

> I have ... directed that they should never be molested, except when plainly intending to attack our Settlement or parties, I have discountenanced also visits to places which they are known to frequent, and I have even withheld from sending out exploring expeditions likely to bring us in contact with them.

But the skirmishes continued.

However, Haughton was so popular with the convicts that in years to come his regime would be remembered as a golden one. According to Portman: "His policy towards the convicts was reforming rather than repressive, and with him grew up the system which ... made the Penal Settlement of Port Blair ... the first Reforming Penal Settlement in the world...."

Haughton was also fortunate in having been allowed a deputy superintendent, with the result that he found time to travel around the various islands and make contact with the Andamanese in their natural habitat. And although, on taking charge, he had found that a large number of convicts were still continuing to escape, by the time he left the number of escapes had dwindled to a great extent. By then, besides, the aborigines had been made to realize the futility of indiscriminate killing of runaway convicts. Even so, they still continued to deprive them of their brass pots. They would also unfasten the iron rings off their legs and take them away, which the convicts heartily welcomed!

It was during Haughton's regime that the experiment of sending some of the captured aborigines to Moulmein was tried. It did not prove a success. Three of them—who had been named Crusoe, Jumbo and Friday—were among those sent. They developed bad coughs by the time they arrived, and one of them, Jumbo, bore all the symptoms of phthisis. Jumbo died eventually, and the other two were brought back and dropped at a spot on a particular beach they pointed to. They disappeared into the jungle and were never seen or heard of again. The fact of the matter is that whenever any of the aborigines are taken away from their own part of the country, even to another part of the Andamans, they generally sicken and die.

Haughton was also responsible for an innovation. Due to the isolation of the islands, he was faced with serious currency difficulties. In the circumstances, therefore, he had no alternative but to issue redeemable manuscript tokens as currency. A while later, with the permission of the government of India, he issued copper tokens redeemable at the local treasury. It was in these tokens that the self-supporter convict was paid. The system was not a success because both silver money and copper tokens were current at the same time. In 1870 the copper tokens were withdrawn. They have disappeared altogether, and have become so rare that a numismatist would perhaps be delighted to have one at any price!

The settlement experienced its first cyclone during Haughton's days. He described the scene of destruction following the cyclone as "most melancholy and disheartening". According to him:

> The plantain trees, about 12,000 in number, were everywhere laid low; giant trees, between one and two hundred feet in height, were thrown down or snapped in half; the Naval Barracks, the Superintendent's bungalow, and the hospital on Chatham Island were unroofed, the convict building on Viper Island [which had since been built for real hardliner convicts], with the exception of one new barrack, were prostrated; and the convicts' huts in every station were either thrown down or greatly injured.

In May 1862 Captain Haughton handed over charge to Lieutenant-Colonel R C Tytler. In appreciation of his work, the highest mount in Port Blair, which today houses VOR (Very High Frequency Omni Range), was named after Captain Haughton and has since been known as Mount Haughton. Tytler continued to pursue the policy initiated by his predecessor which was, by and large, mild. He concentrated on clearing the land, particularly near what is now known as Mount Harriet (named after his wife). A hundred and forty-nine acres of land were cultivated, out of which 76 acres had been cleared by self-supporters. Tytler also managed to have a pier constructed at Ross Island and started a ten horsepower sawmill at Chatham. During his tenure, the relations with the Andamanese also showed significant improvement. They no longer attacked the settlement or the convicts when they ran into them by chance in the forest.

That peace, however, was broken by an incident which took place on 28 January 1863. As reported at first to Tytler, Petty Officer Smith of the naval brigade, with a large number of naval brigadesmen (including a man named Pratt and two others, John Hamilton and H W Brown), visited an Andamanese camp with a view to establishing friendly relations with them. On landing, they were surrounded by a party of about 30 Andamanese, both male and female, who at first appeared quite friendly. But suddenly the Andamanese seized Pratt and killed him with arrows. The other Europeans in the party retaliated by firing indiscriminately. They then got into their boats and returned to the settlement. This so-called sudden attack was supposed to have been followed by many others on the convicts.

Tytler did not question the story, and made no independent inquiries. What is more, he suggested to the government that he be permitted to conduct a general hunt with a view to catching the guilty Andamanese and transporting them to some other islands. The government of India, not doubting the veracity of the facts as reported, agreed to send further reinforcement in the shape of two companies, one of sappers and the other of native infantry. But they expressed the opinion that, instead of indiscriminate firing, the interests of humanity and civilization would have been better served if two or three "natives" had been seized instantly.

In the meanwhile, Tytler had managed to arrest the two Andamanese who, according to the report submitted to him, were responsible for killing Pratt. They were given the names *Snowball* and *Jumbo*, and Tytler wanted to send them to Calcutta. They never did go there, however, for on further investigation it came to light that the reason why Pratt had been murdered was because he had tried to rape an Andamanese woman. Tytler was severely castigated. In a letter from the government dated 4 August 1863, he was told:

You at once readily adopted the account which Petty Officer Smith palmed off upon you, though there were statements in that account which ought of themselves to have excited suspicion, showing as they did almost certainly that the attack upon Pratt was the result of some sudden anger, and that it was entirely unexpected by the aborigines on the shore, some thirty of whom were close to Smith at the time, and never attempted to touch him.

Loaded with presents, Snowball was sent back to his tribe almost immediately because, apparently, he had been merely present when Pratt was murdered and had taken no part, whilst Jumbo, alleged to have taken part in the killing, was kept for another few months and then returned, on 12 October 1863, on account of "good behaviour".

An indirect result of the detention of Snowball and Jumbo was the decision to establish an Andaman Home, because during the detention many other aborigines had come across to meet them, and they had been allowed to do so. Not only that, they had also been given presents in the shape of coconuts and bananas. Reverend Henry Corbyn, chaplain of Port Blair at the time, was put in charge of the Home. Corbyn, after whom Corbyn's Cove, the most popular beach in Port Blair is now known, had already made friends with a woman called Topsy (known previously as Madam Cooper) and a boy who had come over to see Snowball and Jumbo. A house was built on Ross Island, surrounded by a bamboo fence. This was the nucleus of the Andaman Home. In no time, due to Corbyn's personal friendliness, he had as many as 28 aborigines staying in the Andaman Home.

On 15 February 1864, Tytler was succeeded by Major Barnet Ford.

11

Teething Troubles

It was while Tytler was superintendent that Lord Napier of Magdala (then the Hon'ble Major-General Sir Robert Napier, commander-in-chief, India) came on an inspection of the settlement. He discovered that out of 8,035 convicts that had arrived in Port Blair since the founding of the settlement, 2,908 had died and 612 had deserted; the latter could also be presumed as dead. He found this "deplorable", something that could not be contemplated "without a feeling of grave regret and sorrow". Because, according to him, despite "the depressing effect of banishment and uncongenial climate", much of it could have been prevented if only better housing arrangements had been made.

The term housing is, of course, euphemistic in this context, because they were put up in tents, which provided no protection from heavy rains, the lashing squalls and storms of unimaginable ferocity, which were then and to an extent still are a normal occurrence in the Andamans. Nor did they provide any shelter during the oppressive tropical heat. Even when huts were constructed a little later, they were hardly an improvement because the sides were open and the rain, accompanied invariably by a wind of a high velocity, could easily penetrate inside. According to Napier, the then civil surgeon had reported that during the rainy season not even one-third of the convicts could keep either themselves or their clothes dry. He found that the hospitals were "generally not clean", and the clothes of the prisoners both "scanty and filthy"; very few had *charpoy*s to sleep on. No wonder, then, that once they fell ill they died like flies. He also found among the convicts an "air of depression and despondency".

He also had interesting comments to make on what was described as subsistence allowance paid to prisoners, except to those under punishment. (How those "under punishment" subsisted has not been stated.) The subsistence allowance was supposed to be the amount on which a convict was to feed and clothe himself. It amounted to the magnificent sum of one anna and nine pies. Napier commented: "No able bodied man in such a climate could work on less than a seer of grain which costs an anna; there remains 9 pies, a sum insufficient to admit of indulgence in vegetables or fish in addition to clothing." Napier stated that the causes of the high rate of mortality were:

> The moral depression resulting from exile; the effects of a new and severe climate; malaria from the newly cleared forests; bad and insufficient shelter; insufficient clothing, and want of dry clothes to put on when returning from work in the jungles, where they get wet from frequent heavy showers; want of personal cleanliness and want of conservancy about the dwellings.

He approved of the system of promotion, whereby convicts, who were considered fit for special duties and had shown good behaviour, were appointed orderlies, petty overseers, mechanics, boatmen and the like, and were given an enhanced rate of payment, amounting to four or five rupees a month. By implication, he also seemed to commend the system of those called "self-supporters" because, according to him, they were the ones who, from "capacity and industry [were] capable of pursuing any calling which [was] beneficial to the colony". Further, they could pursue "the occupation they may select—whether fishermen, cultivators or bakers, milk and bottle sellers, sweetmeet-makers, and cobblers, etc.".

Under this system the convicts were released for a period of six months, in the first instance, and received subsistence in the form of poultry, cows, sheep and goats, from the superintendent, to enable them to set themselves up. There was a proviso, though; if at the end of the period of six months it was found that any one of them was not proving "profitable to the settlement", he was liable to be sent back to the working gang.

Napier, however, found very few convicts in irons; they were the ones being punished for attempting to escape. On the whole, he found the general conduct of the convicts "very good". He was all for extending the married section of convicts "to the utmost practicable extent", because he saw that their houses were "good" and their women "well clothed and clean". In fact, in his view, this question of extending the married section appeared "hardly to admit of two opinions". As an *obiter dicta*, he added: "It would be greatly ... regretted if the mild character of the present management were to be exchanged for greater severity". He went on to say that he realized it "necessary to remove these Indians from the scene of their social or political crimes, but in the act of removal their punishment is in a great measure achieved". This was because:

> Transportation beyond sea is, to the Hindoo particularly, and in a less degree to the Hindooised Mahomedans, so terrible a punishment—a separation for ever from every tie and relations, and possession which men held to in life—that it places them in a far different position from the European who is transported to a Penal Settlement.

Most of the recommendations made by Sir Robert Napier were accepted and orders issued to implement them, among which one was "to afford each convict a space of at least 500 cubic feet per man".

Incidentally, it was at Napier's instance that a way was opened to Mount Harriet, a hill—the highest in South Andaman—lying to the north of Port Blair. And it was at the foot of this hill that a few years later Lord Mayo, the viceroy and governor-general of India, was to be assassinated.

When Napier came, as already stated, Tytler was still the superintendent, but most of the recommendations made by him became operative only after Ford succeeded him. So far as the Andamanese were concerned, the love-hate relationship continued. Ford summed up the situation when he wrote: "We shall never be able, I think to do much to *civilise* the adult Andamanese that we now know; if we can arrive at a good and friendly feeling with them, making them understand that their peaceful conduct will win our regard, whilst hostility will be met by withdrawal of all countenance and benefits." However, in addition, he wanted "the educating and civilising of their children". Towards that end he advocated "the establishment of a school under an Army schoolmaster for the Andamanese children on Ross Island, and after educating them there, proposed to send them to Burmah or India".

Meanwhile, differences had arisen between Corbyn and Ford, which led to the former's resignation. J N Homfray took his place as in charge of the Andaman Home. He was to hold that position off and on for nearly ten years. He learnt the Andamanese language and succeeded in establishing such good relations with the Andamanese that he was able to make use of them to capture the runaways and return them to the settlement. Previously, they used to kill them.

In 1867 Ford too, like Haughton, faced the shortage of silver and copper tokens, and had to resort to issuing redeemable card tokens. In the same year Major H Nelson Davies, secretary to the chief commissioner of Burma, visited the settlement for inspection. The administrative control of the Andaman and Nicobar islands had been transferred to the chief commissioner of Burma in 1864. (Till then the government of India had exercized direct authority over the islands.) He wrote a report which was obviously so biased against Ford that not much notice was taken of what he said. Ironically enough, Davies was particularly critical of the self-supporting system which Napier had viewed with such enthusiasm. Some of the recommendations of Davies were accepted, however; among them was the necessity for better food, at least more nutritious food. Another recommendation that found acceptance was that convicts above the age of 45 years were not to be sent to the penal settlement.

Ford was succeeded by Colonel Henry Man in March 1868. It was the same Henry Man (then Captain) who had originally raised the British flag over the settlement in 1858. Though he had originally been named as the first superintendent, his appointment had not materialized.

Colonel Man had been in the Straits Settlements for many a year, and had also acted as governor there; it was while he was acting governor that the decision had been taken to remove the Straits Settlements from the control of the government of India and place them under the colonial office. Man's first act was to introduce formally the discipline of the Straits Settlements in the settlement at Port Blair. It was also during his tenure that once again, in 1869, the settlement at Port Blair was reverted to the administrative control of the government of India. Next year it was decided that for judicial purposes the settlement be placed under the Calcutta high court, an arrangement that has lasted to the present day.

12

The Nicobars and Nicobarese

The Nicobar group of islands were officially annexed by Colonel Henry Man and brought under the British flag on 16 April 1869, after what he described as "an amicable settlement" with the Danish government, who till then had exercised a symbolic kind of suzerainty over them, notwithstanding the fact that they had, in fact, abandoned the islands in 1848.

Before the advent of the British, the main motive of European powers in these islands had been "to convert the natives". They had failed, as Man put it, because "of their lack of sufficient means and often of the bare necessities of life and their ignorance, not only of prophylactics discovered since their day, but also of the most ele-

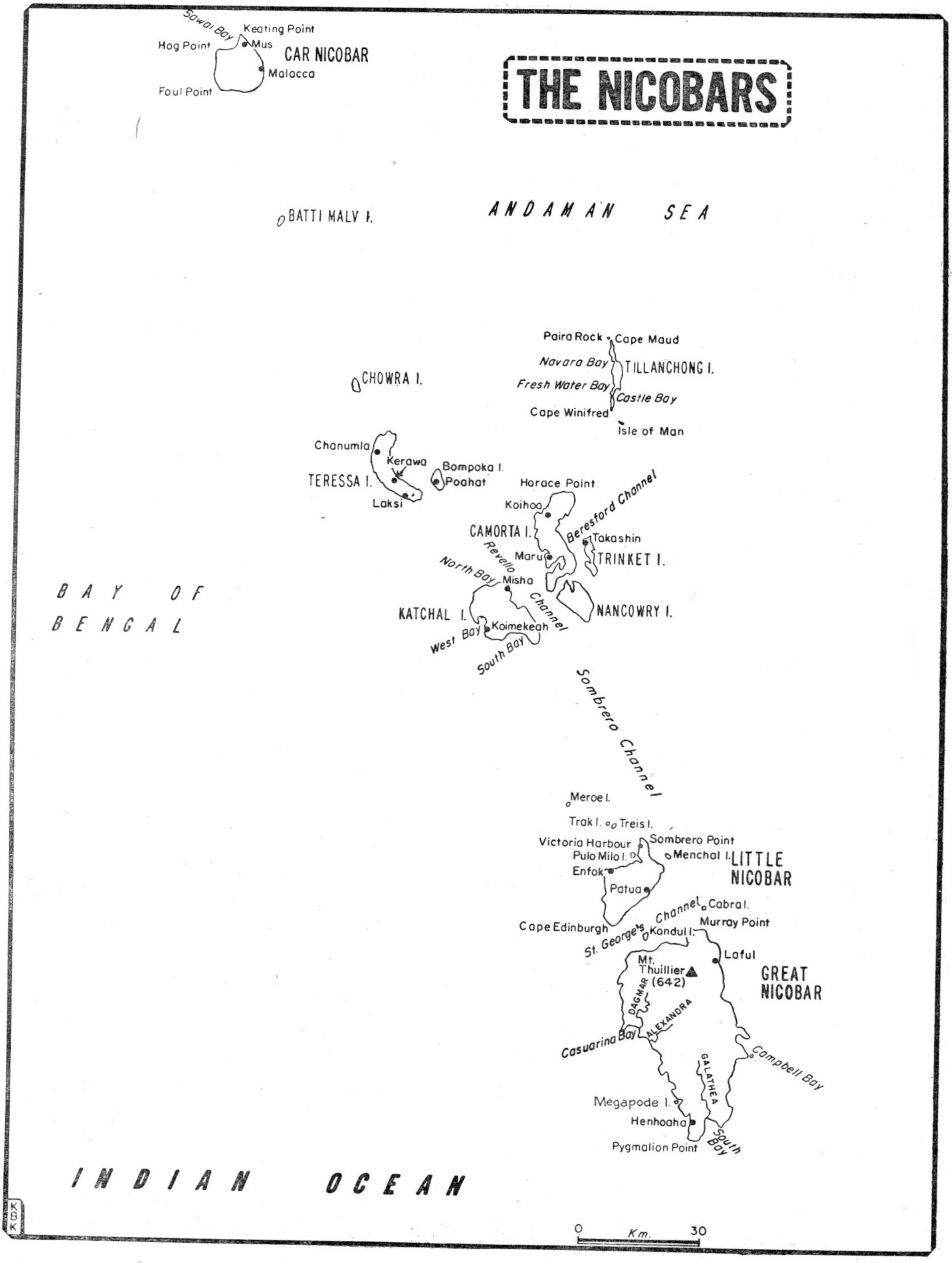
THE NICOBARS
Sawai Bay
Keating Point
Hog Point
Mus
CAR NICOBAR
Malacca
Foul Point
BATTI MALV I.
ANDAMAN SEA
Paira Rock
Cape Maud
Navara Bay
TILLANCHONG I.
Fresh Water Bay
Castle Bay
Cape Winifred
Isle of Man
CHOWRA I.
Chanumla
Kerawa
Bompoka I.
Poahat
TERESSA I.
Laksi
Horace Point
Koihoa
Beresford Channel
CAMORTA I.
Takashin
Revello
Maru
TRINKET I.
North Bay
Misha
Channel
BAY OF BENGAL
KATCHAL I.
NANCOWRY I.
Koimekeah
West Bay
South Bay
Sombrero Channel
Meroe I.
Trak I.
Treis I.
Victoria Harbour
Sombrero Point
Pulo Milo I.
Menchal I.
LITTLE NICOBAR
Enfok
Patua
Cabral.
Channel
Cape Edinburgh
St. George's
Kondul I.
Murray Point
Laful
Mt. Thuillier (642)
GREAT NICOBAR
DAGMAR
ALEXANDRA
Casuarina Bay
Campbell Bay
GALATHEA
Megapode I.
Henhoaha
Pygmalion Point
South Bay
INDIAN OCEAN
KDK
0 Km. 30

mentary rules of hygiene, as evidenced in the case of the Moravians by the wretched site selected by them for occupation".

Ironically enough, it was left to an Indian catechist, Vedappan Solomon from Madras, and his once favourite pupil, Bishop John Richardson, now in his nineties, to spread the faith. (Young Richardson was sent to Rangoon to be educated.) These two have been entirely responsible for converting the Nicobarese to Christianity. Today in a majority of the islands of the Nicobar group, particularly in Car Nicobar, the religion of most of the Nicobarese is Christianity.

After the Danes abandoned the islands in all but name, there were, for the next thirty years (when the Nicobars were left derelict, as it were, in Henry Man's phrase), a number of murders of the crew visiting the islands. As many as 26 vessels were scuttled by the Nicobarese. The culminating point was reached when, in 1866, the brig *Futteh Islam* was attacked at Great Nicobar, and 21 members of the crew murdered.

Car Nicobar, which looks somewhat like Australia, is the most important island in the Nicobar group but, incredibly enough, the Car Nicobarese have no name for the island in their own language. They speak of it as *panam*, which means "the place" or *kuon panam*, "the little place" or "the land". The Nicobarese of the other islands call it *Pu*.

It does not look as though the Nicobarese are the original inhabitants of these islands. They are obviously immigrants, and the accepted belief now is that they must have migrated sometime before the Christian era from what was then a part of India, the land now occupied by the Burmese, Talaings (Mons), Shans and Malays. They are offshoots of some Mongoloid race.

That they have some affinity with the Malays is apparent from *couvade*, one of the customs that they observe. Every Nicobari village has a special lying-in hut where married couples, when expecting a child, are supposed to shift to—a few days before the delivery. And before that, some weeks before the woman's confinement, if the home of the expecting woman and her husband is too far away from the lying-in hut, they must go and live in an *el-panam*, a ceremonial clean house. But the moment the birth pains begin the woman must go to the lying-in hut, else *el-panam* will also become unclean. The husband, when his wife is expecting the child, must not do any hard work. Nor for that matter should the expectant mother. They must also never wear anything tight. They must not even tie a knot, because there is a superstition that by doing so the spirit of the unborn child will get tied up in knots, and delivery will become difficult.

After the birth of the child, the husband must remain with the wife and attend to all her needs. And he should continue not to do any heavy work, nor walk in the sun. He must not even bathe in the sea. All this is to ensure that the child does not get sick, because whatever the father does is supposed to affect the health of the child. In the case of the first child this period is meant to last a month, the period when the father is also treated as an invalid. He is waited upon, like his wife, by friends and relatives who cook for them and also feed them. According to Horace Man, in the case of children born subsequently, this period for the husband's lying-in after the birth of the child is reduced to one or two days only. Bishop Richardson explained that the reason why the man is restrained from doing any work is that the work "affects the health of the baby". But, according to him, "he does not any longer live with the mother in the same place, as the story says, but he is restrained from doing hard work" or going out in the sun. Bishop Richardson said that "he must carry an umbrella to work" and he should not go to the jungle because "the enemy—the devil—will be there and will see him and cause sickness to the young newborn baby". He confirmed that "many things are prohibited—you must not even tie a knot before pregnancy—because the knot will close the womb and the child would not be born. The result will be that the mother will die". With the spread of Christianity, however, most such customs are fast disappearing.

The naming of the child takes place immediately after its birth, and it is the father who gives the name; an additional name is given by one of the friends of the family. The Nicobarese are great ones for feasting. So naturally enough a feast is held. But in addition there is a ceremony to scare away evil spirits. Immediately after the child has been given a name, the women start wailing and gather round a vessel in which they throw a little bit of food, which they would eventually partake of in the feast. This is their way of wishing a long life to the new-born baby. The food collected in the vessel is thrown into the sea. By doing so, they think the evil spirits have been appeased.

By and large, the Nicobarese are monogamous. Some cases of polygamy are, however, known to have occurred, but they are confined, almost exclusively, to the chiefs and those who are more prosperous. Girls have complete freedom to choose their husbands, and no exception is taken to a girl having as many lovers as she likes before she is married. There is no marriage ceremony as such, but the manner in which the wooing and courtship takes place is interesting. According to C Boden Kloss:

> During the night he [the boy] seeks the girl, who will be sleeping among the others. The efforts of the man to embrace and caress her [she] withstands vigorously with blows and scratches, so that his face and chest are often torn and covered with blood. So things continue for several nights perhaps, the man suffering patiently the while, until, if she is willing to take him as her husband, she yields herself. This is their nuptials, and concludes the marriage.

Once married, there is very little infidelity. The marriage can always be dissolved by mutual consent. [How civilized!] But the children go and live with the relatives.

The Nicobarese dwelling is generally circular, with a high thatched roof, and built on stilts quite a few feet above the ground; its genesis is obviously the fury of the monsoon which lashes the island for nearly ten months in a year, and the consequent need for protection from it. The house as such consists of one large boarded floored room with no partitions; it has boarded walls. The entry into the house is by ladder, leading to an opening entrance in the floor of the house. It can be moved away or pulled up and placed in a corner of the house. But, though all members of the family live and sleep in one room, it is amazing how neat and clean everything is inside. There is always a small hut for cooking, separate from the main house. All the worldly possessions of the family are kept in chests either on the main floor or on platforms specially built into the ceiling.

What strikes one most upon entering the house, after climbing up the ladder, is the presence of what they call the *kareau* (spirit-scarers). They are also called devils. Made in various sizes (sometimes as large as human beings), they are often carved human figures bearing spears; today some *kareau* wear European hats, sport pipes and cigarettes; some are representations of mythical animals, though they look like fish or crocodile or various types of bird and pig. Sometimes one can find, just outside the house, the figure of a special spirit-scarer who is "a very bad devil". With the spread of Christianity, there are not many "devils" left in Car Nicobar these days, but there are plenty in village houses in places like Kapanga, on the island of Katchal, or in Nancowry and Teressa and Trinket. The Nicobarese are most reluctant to part with these "devils".

The Nicobarese are very superstitious, and think that every conceivable misfortune is caused either by a witch or a spirit. And to ward it off the evil spirit has to be exorcized. Sometimes this exorcism can be performed privately by getting hold of the doctor-priest or *menluana*, as they call him, to hold a brief ceremony. But in a majority of cases there has to be a general exorcism, for which a family spirit feast has to be held. That is the only way to get rid of evil spirits. And for that, once again, it is essential to seek the help of the *menluana*.

Those present at such a feast are members of the family and a few friends. The men sit and smoke and drink. The women folk go and collect a few eatables, some implements and weapons, and any other old curiosity that they may have. They break up all these things, howling all along, and throw them outside the house. A fattened pig is roasted whole half kept for the ancestors, and the rest for the men and women comprising the party. And now steps in the *menluana* in a state of frenzy, or perhaps escstasy, brought on by drink. Everyone's face is painted red, and they rub their bodies all over with oil. They also start singing a doleful melody and rush around trying to catch *iwi*, the evil spirit that does them harm, while the women howl all the time. Eventually, *iwi* is supposed to be caught. It is put in a miniature decorated boat and taken far out into the sea and left there. They come back, and there is more eating and drinking and singing and dancing. (Such feasts seldom take place now in Car Nicobar, but plenty of them are held in the island of Chowra.)

The religion of the Nicobarese is also pure animism. But, having been exposed to the influence of Christian missionaries for centuries, they have developed a vague idea about there being a Supreme Being. Nonetheless, all their ceremonies are centred around spirits, and these are mostly evil spirits too. According to them, these evil spirits are the cause of all the calamities that human beings have to face. Bishop John Richardson put it this way:

> Nicobarese, they have no religion, but believe only in an evil spirit—the power of this spirit; all sickness, whatever troubles you have got in this world—are caused by evil spirit.... This evil spirit must be continually appeased by offering him pieces of chicken, pieces of pork and so on, every time there is a calamity or sickness about. And people make such offerings to the evil spirit.

The Nicobarese love holding feasts, and their feasts would appear to be precursors of some of our modern-day "Dutch" parties, where everyone contributes something. Sir Richard Temple has described how these feasts are organized:

> A week before the intended feast, a Nicobarese sends friends or dependents decorated with garlands to those who he wishes to invite. When they arrive, they are entertained with betel, cheroots and toddy, and, if possible, a suckling pig. After this the invitation is given, and the intended guest is asked to bring some food with him to help out the feast. If he can, he accepts. If he cannot, he declines. On the night before the feast the guests are reminded by a messenger. At the fixed time, usually at night, the guests arrive with baskets of food which they deliver to the housewife. These consist of pork [roasted or boiled] cut into thick pieces; yams of different kind; plantains and papayes [all boiled]; *ku-wen* or bread fruit pudding—all festooned to strings, in such a manner that each string may be given to one guest; one or two bamboos filled with toddy; a betel-nut neatly folded and fastensed to thin bamboo sticks; and China tobacco [*sonnai am*, or dog's hair as they style it] twisted in dry pandanus leaves and arranged in bamboo holders. The food brought by one guest can be shared with about ten or fifteen other persons. The host slaughters one or two pigs and prepares other things according to his ability. When all the guests have arrived, toddy is served out first in small bamboo vessels or in a clean coconut shell, and then the food is distributed in basket plates made of cane. The chiefs and elders sit in a row in the middle ... and the others here and there scattered about, and while they are eating they smoke cheroots and chew betel-nuts at intervals. After finishing the food the elders commence to sing jovial songs followed by the

younger men. Thus it will be seen that the Nicobarese dinner party costs the host very little; but, on the other hand, he must be prepared to return the obligation to help his friends when his turn comes.

The main wealth—and food—of the Nicobarese is the coconut. They use it for a variety of purposes. From the leaves they make thatch for huts, and torches and sails. From the flowers they make *tari* (toddy). They eat the fruit and drink the coconut milk. (They seldom drink water.) They extract oil from it, and use the shell as a drinking receptacle. Coconut trees are also supposed to be spirit-scarers. Whenever a death takes place, some coconut trees are cut down. The dead body is washed with coconut milk, and some nuts placed alongside the body in the graveyard. The leaves of the trees are placed all round the house. This is all meant to scare the ghosts.

Coconuts are used for lighting purposes too—each half-shell of the ripe coconut placed in close proximity to the other, partly covering the next one, in the shape of a crescent. When one is lighted the next one catches the light from the previous one, and then the next, and so on. This is not only outside the house but inside too. Coconut oil is used for lighting purposes. Coconuts are also fed to the pigs. The coconut was also Nicobari currency, till recently—they used it as barter. Temple has given an instance when the government wanted to acquire eight and a half acres of land for building their agency. Its price—10,000 coconuts.

Next to the coconut, the main food of the Nicobarese is the Pandanus. It is their favourite on the menu. The Pandanus tree belongs to the screwpine variety, and its fruit is sometimes more than a foot long, almost 30 inches in circumference and can weigh as much as 50 pounds. According to Boden Kloss:

> The fruit of pandanus ... consists of a cluster of fibrous drupes, the tops of which are sliced off as soon as gathered .... These divisions are separated from the central core and placed in a pot over a layer of bamboos or gratings below which there is a little water; above them are laid yams, or whatever may be suitably cooked by that process, and the whole is then covered with leaves and steamed for some hours. The pulpy matter that it contains is then scraped out with a shell while the drupe is held on a heavy slab of wood, and then the bristly fibres with which the nutritious portion is intermixed are extracted from the latter by drawing threads of a sort of bass through the pasty mess resulting. Thus is obtained a smooth dough, of a yellowish colour.

This dough is made into balls or rolls, and some of it eaten in that state. The rest is cooked again, perhaps all through the night over a fire, and eaten the next morning. Some of it is covered in leaves and kept for being eaten later. The Pandanus is also used as fodder for the pig.

The Pandanus tree is itself full of thorns, its leaf in particular. There is also a legend about it. Though not of Nicobarese origin. It comes from the Caroline islands in the Pacific, where it also abounds. According to the legend, when the thunder god was descending on earth, he alighted on a Pandanus bush. He found himself in a most painful situation. A woman rescued him. So he bestowed upon her the art of making fire and moulding pots.

The Nicobarese also love fish, but they seldom use nets for fishing. They use a net trap, mostly, which has the bait and is held under water. The moment they see a fish trying to nibble at the bait, they lift the net and catch the fish. They also catch fish by spearing it, sometimes at night in the light of torches made from coconut leaf.

And of course they love pork. But the pig and fowl are reserved for special occasions. They also grow a variety of fruit, most of which was, obviously, imported originally from the mainland. They are very fond of, and can be seen constantly chewing, the betel leaf and betel-nut, and they smoke a great deal. Toddy made from the coconut-palm is their favourite stimulant. In Chowra they eat the dog too.

They are very skilful in the art of canoe-making. Their canoe is very light and is made out of a single log of wood hollowed out. The Nicobari canoe has always an outrigger to balance it, except in the case of the canoe made for racing, which is quite ornamental. Incidentally, the Nicobarese never race a canoe for winning or losing; they do it just for the love of it. This is also true of most of their other sports, among which wrestling is perhaps the most popular.

The Nicobarese follow the partriarchal system and most of them tend to live together in a sort of joint family; their property, which includes their thatch-roof shelters, coconut trees, vegetable gardens and, of course, the pigs, are passed on from father to son. In general, they count property in terms of the coconut trees they own and the number of pigs they rear, the pig being such a favourite that some women are sometimes even seen suckling little piglets.

A very complicated ceremony follows the death of a Nicobarese. The moment someone dies, all friends and relatives are notified. All relatives must be present, and those unavoidably absent must stay away from the village till the first memorial feast is held a few days later. And everyone is expected to bring a present to appease the ghost. In the case of a relative, it is a must.

The eyes of the dead are closed so that the ghost cannot see, and the body is washed in hot water—sometimes as many as five times, depending upon how long it will take before the actual internment takes place. Temple has listed eight obligatory duties: (*i*) removal of all food, as it is tabooed to the mourners till after the ceremony of purifying the hut is over, only hot water and tobacco being allowed before then; (*ii*) destruction of movable property of the deceased, its fragments placed on the grave as a propitiatory sacrifice to the ghost; (*iii*) placing of a little food at the head of the corpse for the ghost (the "remains" of this are thrown on its removal to the dogs and the pigs); (*iv*) construction of a bier made out of a broken-up canoe, belonging to the deceased or a mourner; (*v*) digging of the grave five feet deep and putting two head posts and two foot posts; (*vi*) making fire out of chips from the bier and coconut husks to "bar the ghost on the ground at the hut entrance; (*vii*) completion of the grave by placing the articles sacrificed on the ground or in a destroyed basket belonging to the deceased and (*viii*) throwing pig-tusk trophies, some *kareau* (spirit-scarers) and pictures into the jungle. In order further to appease the ghost, the dead person is buried with all the clothing and other ornaments that he or she may have possessed. The hour at which the burial takes place must be such that the shadow of those attending the funeral must not fall on the grave, because in the shadow lurk the spirits. Therefore, the burial takes place either at sundown, or at midnight or just before dawn.

Temple has also described what happens before and after the burial:

Before removal to the grave, the body is taken to the centre of the hut and placed cross-wise to the entrance, where it is mourned a short while and then carried down the entrance ladder head foremost. Some of the mourners occasionally make a feint of going to the grave with the deceased and the priest [*menluana*] exhorts the ghost to remain in the grave until the memorial feast and not to wander and frighten the living. When in the grave the body is pinned into it by special contrivances to prevent the *mongwanga*, the body-snatching spirit, from abstracting it. The spirits even of those present are finally waved out of the grave by a torch and it is quickly filled in. After the burial the family returns to their hut, in which they are bound to sleep, and about 24 hours after the internment, the hut is purified by mere brushing and washing, and the mourners by bathing, anointing on the head and shoulder by the priest, and the waving of a lighted torch to drive away the spirits. The family then disguise themselves by shaving the head and eyebrows and assuming new names, with the object of deceiving the ghost of the deceased. They then take a meal in silence with all the mourners, consisting of every variety of food procurable, in order that each person present may then and there choose the article that is to be tabued for him till firstly the *entoin* feast, three to seven days after the funeral, and secondly the *laneatla* feast, two to three years later. The balance of the food is placed on the grave.

When the *laneatla* feast takes place, which is two or three years later, the skeleton is exhumed, thoroughly cleaned, and reinterred, sometimes in what is known as communal ossuaries. That, too, has a very elaborate ceremonial. It is a costly festival. The ossuary feast, in fact, is the most important one. It is called *ka-al-awn*, which means, literally, a feast of pig's flesh.

About ten months or a year before the feast, all villagers of a particular village get together to fix the month in which the feast is to be held. They then inform other villages, asking for—and generally getting—their promise of assistance. After sending the invitations, the first duty of the villagers is to make what they call a *no-kopah*, which is food for the burial ground. Fifty or 60 feet high, well-carved poles are prepared and planted either in the ground at *el-panam* (the open communal ground), or in front of the house of the one who wants to commemorate. The poles have cross battens on which are hung a variety of yams, dabs, betel leaves, coconuts, areca-nuts, Pandanus fruit, cheroots, plantains and other eatables. Below the posts are kept boxes containing new clothes and ornaments, bottles of toddy and earthen pots from Chowra. The poles are decorated with flags. When the day of *no-kopah* starts, no killing of pigs is allowed in the village. Huts are repaired, particularly the cooking huts. The grounds are cleared, as also the graveyards. And provisions are collected in large quantities.

A week before the opening day of the ossuary feast, special headstones for the graves are prepared. They are made of well-shaped, round logs of wood—three feet long and nine inches in diameter—with two holes at the end, in which all kinds of objects like soup ladles and cross-shaped iron pikes are fixed. To this are attached toys and dolls and other curiosities to give a festive appearance. The men construct two or three temporary bamboo cages for about a dozen pigs, each pig having a separate enclosure. One cage is kept under the house and the others outside. Even the canoes are decorated. They are filled with eatables and drawn up and kept in front of the house.

The first ceremony, the preliminary ceremony called *vani-patti*, is held a day before the festival, when the houses are decorated, both inside and outside, with coconut-palm leaves, some plants and flags. The bamboo pig-pens are also decorated. A pig is slaughtered as sacrifice and its blood sprinkled all over, and much singing and dancing takes place around the house. On the evening of the actual festival, people come singing with a number of pigs. The pigs that are in the cages, and the ones under the house, are merely for show and kept for a future festival. Those outside the house and the ones newly arrived are to be slaughtered for the festival then taking place. People dance before them.

The second, also the main part of the festival, is known as *kiriam hetpat*, which means dancing in bright light. The men come in new loincloths in various colours, wearing necklaces of silver coins. The women also wear necklaces and, in addition, bangles round their arms and legs and strings of silver coins on their heads. Their garment consists of red and blue cloth stitched together. The special guests bring 10 or 12 pigs as presents for the hosts. Then they dance and sing, men first, women later, with men taking over when the women are tired, and vice versa. This goes on all through the night.

In the morning the dancing continues, but some bring forward strong wooden cages, gaily decorated, and on a platform on top of each a man, a woman and a boy are seated. In the cage is a huge, long-tusked boar. The man, woman and boy sitting on the platform carry some plantains and betel-nuts. All guests are supplied with new red loin-cloths. This is followed by what look like palanquins, but with pigs in the cages below, and they are carried around from house to house in a procession, to the accompaniment of singing and dancing. After the procession is over, the pigs in the cages and most of the other pigs are let off, except those that are to be slaughtered for the guests the same day. The poles of the *no-kopah* are cut and the food strung to the *no-kopah* is scattered in the jungle. The canoes and other things are also broken and thrown away.

Next follows another party; a number of pigs are given away by the hosts to the performers, who kill a few and distribute the flesh among the families of their group. What they cannot eat, after roasting, along with the pigs that have not been killed, they take away to their villages; the live pigs are kept for use on a future festive occasion.

The guests who have come from nearby villages stay on and the merriment continues. It goes on till the climax of the festival is reached, when the digging of the graves is to take place. The women and children and those who are not commemorators, stand at a distance from the graveyard; one or two people from the families of the commemorators open the graves of their deceased relatives, remove the bones and throw them in a nearby bush, which is the ossuary (the burial-place of the bones). Skulls of people who were held in respect, or those of the heads of the families, are replaced after they have been sprinkled with the blood of fowl and young pigs.

After grave-digging and the replacing of skulls is over, new headstones are placed, and the grave-diggers bathe in the sea. They spend the night in a "house of pollution", but not before there has been more feasting and dancing. Two or three days later there is another ceremony when coco-palm leaves are removed from the house and the *el-panam*, but not before there has been another performance of singing and dancing. More ceremonies take place when people from nearby villages are invited to give a performace; they are then feasted and given gifts. When all is over the jawbones of slaughtered pigs are carefully collected, fastened to a long rattan and hung in the public building at *el-panam*—to assess the splendour of the ceremony.

Another custom, a rather barbarous one which, according to Edward Horace Man, was prevalent when he visited Car Nicobar in March 1884, was the one known as "devil-murder". It was based on the superstition that some people have the evil eye and, therefore, can and do exercise a malign influence over others. It only happened when someone died or fell ill for no obvious reason, and someone in the neighbourhood was suspected of being responsible for the misfortune. The punishment that was meted out to him was both dire and cruel. In the words of Horace Man:

> The wretched victim was usually taken unawares and overpowered by two or more young men, who, while forcibly holding him face downwards on the ground, proceeded to bend back each arm in succession until the tendons at the shoulders had either been severed by extreme tension or so stretched as to render those limbs powerless. The legs were then, in like manner, pulled backwards till, it is affirmed, the stout tendons near the groins were so injured as to render the poor wretch powerless to stir, whereon a cord or stout fibre was passed round his [or her] neck, and the ends pulled by the executioners or their friends till death ensued from strangulation. The bodies of such unfortunates, being regarded as unfit for burial, were usually taken out to sea and sunk with stones, in the belief that there was thereby less risk of their spirits haunting the island.

Mercifully, no such custom is known to exist in Car Nicobar any longer.

In the Nicobar group of islands, the other island next to Car Nicobar, which is of great importance to the Nicobarese, is Chowra, but not because of its size or population. Its area is only three square miles and its population, when the British took possession of it, was estimated at a little less than 700. The Portuguese navigators called it Sombrero Island, because it looks like a sombrero — the broad-brimmed Spanish hat. The island of Chowra rises almost to a perpendicular at the southern end, to a height of nearly 350 feet.

According to one legend, the Nicobarese in Car Nicobar were at one time firmly convinced that theirs was the only island in the world; they sometimes even called it *panam*, which means the world. Once in a while, however, some of them would espy one or two large canoes with sails. From a long distance these would look like huge birds with white wings. They thought they were dreaming. How could any other world exist except theirs, they would convince themselves complacently. However, came a day when they decided to make a little canoe, almost the size of a toy, out of the dry spathe of the coconut flower. The leaves of the coconut were fashioned as sails for this toy canoe. They filled it with yams and set it adrift. One day, months later, the little canoe came back. And in the place of yams, it had tiny little pots. They were pretty, but the people of Car Nicobar had never seen a pot. What should they do with it? Someone filled one of the pots with water. The water did not leak. So they put it on fire. The water began to boil. They put some yams into it. When boiled they tasted very good.

So they decided to find out where the pots had come from. Another toy canoe was built and set sailing. But this time they decided to follow it in a big canoe. They sailed all day and all night and eventually saw an island. They sailed towards it and were met by some men who came across to meet them. Theirs was a big canoe. And that is how the people of Car Nicobar first set eyes on Chowra—and on a canoe that could carry as many as 20 men. They also saw big pots, which they brought back home.

Since then, the people of the two islands have not only been friends but, till recently, all pots in Car Nicobar came from Chowra. This is so because all along there has been some kind of belief that, should any food be eaten out of a pot not made in Chowra, it would be an invitation to disaster and possibly death. Besides, a belief was inculcated, perhaps deliberately by the clever Chowra islanders, that if anyone other than one of them attempted to make a clay pot, he was doomed. Therefore, despite the fact that Chowra has no clay of its own (perhaps it was exhausted as soon as they started exporting their pots), they had, till not very long ago, a monopoly of trade in clay pots. It is only women who make the pots; no man ever takes part in their making.

While the people are away in Chowra fetching a new canoe, there are certain taboos that must be observed. The eating of bats is not allowed during that period, because its wings might make one blind. (They do eat bats.) Then, how would a blind man find his way back to Chowra? Also, wood is not to be split, because that might result in the canoe splitting itself.

As in the case of clay pots, so also about the big canoes—the men of Chowra have held a monopoly and, there again, they have no wood in their island out of which they could fashion a big canoe. So the wood is obtained from nearby islands; sometimes they merely act as middlemen or brokers. They buy canoes from other islanders and sell them to Car Nicobarese at higher prices because, basically, Car Nicobarese are very simple people.

Chowra is also known for its wizardry and witchcraft, and it is customary for every Nicobarese boy to be taken to Chowra. It is a kind of initiation into manhood. Before he is taken to Chowra, the blood of a chicken is sprinkled all over the boy's body, and once again when he arrives at Chowra. There are also festivities on his return from Chowra. A canoe race is held, and it is followed by bits of pork being tied or hung over the body of the boy for some hours. Raw eggs are crushed on his head and silver wire tied round his arms and legs; Pandanus seed is also strung around his neck.

Though most customs of this nature have become a thing of the past in Car Nicobar, because of the influence of the missionaries, Chowra still has its witch-doctors, and they continue to practise their witchcraft. A little while ago, Vijay Shankar Sahay, a student of anthropology at the University of Ranchi in Bihar, visited this island. He witnessed one of the witch-doctors performing his ceremony. The witch-doctors at Chowra, he said, "are known as *kamassuns* and they are supposed to have a chief of their own who presumably possesses greater supernatural powers than other witch-doctors and he performs a ceremony called *kumpang* to increase the latter's supernatural powers". The witch-doctors of Chowra, who are considered to be the leaders of society, are concerned with practically every activity of the people there and, according to Sahay, their four main functions are: (*i*) to treat the sick; (*ii*) to prevent the islanders from death and disease; (*iii*) to drive away evil spirits from the island and (*iv*) to forestall and save the people of Chowra from any catastrophe. Sahay, describing a witch-doctor at work, said:

> At the time of the performance of witchcraft, the dress of the witch-doctor is very remarkable. He wears a red cloth, a black hat with a white ribbon round it; beads and coins of the old days are tied around the neck and both the arms, and garlands of tender banana leaves are hung around his neck. He also wears a silver band round his neck and silver anklets and silver chains around his waist. He always applies coconut-oil and turmeric on his face and on the entire body. Sometimes he also has a sword, perhaps of some unknown traveller.
>
> When a witch-doctor is performing his ceremony to cure a sick person, he goes to the sick man's house. He paints his face as black as charcoal and he applies the blood of a pig or a chicken all over his body.... The sick person is advised to lie down under the platform of the house and some blood is collected in a coconut shell which is mixed with dry, powdered leaves. The witch-doctor, after examining the patient, first takes some coconut oil mixed with turmeric and applies it on the chest, on the back and on both the forearms of the patient. And, after uttering some words, he kills a chicken, and the blood is sprinkled over the body of the patient, on his own body and on the persons around them. After this, the blood mixed with leaves is smeared on the body of the one who is sick, and then the witch-doctor puts his hand on the belly of the patient and utters words like *oof ... off ... oof!* Simultaneously, the patient also cries because of the pain caused by the pressure made by the hands of the witch-doctor. This goes on for about three minutes. Then the patient is taken to the seashore to take a bath.
>
> The witch-doctors have different types of performances on different occasions, like, for instance, while treating pregnant women, or at the birth of a child, or at a death ceremony, or when a garden is being laid, or at the time of building a house or when driving away evil spirits. But, in all cases, the dress of the witch-doctor remains the same, and coconut-oil, turmeric and the blood of a chicken or pig and special kinds of leaves are always considered essential.

The burial customs in Chowra also vary somewhat from those of the Car Nicobarese. In Chowra the dead body is tied around with cloth and leaves and placed in one half of a canoe, which acts as a bier, and then laid on top of four posts about six feet above the ground in the cemetery, which is invariably in a thick grove and some distance away from the village. In time the dead body is reduced to a skeleton and, if and when the next communal ossuary feast takes place, the bones are thrown into the ossuary.

Those who were held in great esteem in the old days, particularly in Car Nicobar, used to receive different and more elaborate treatment when they died. An eye-witness has left this description:

> The body was neatly wrapped in cloths under a curtain in the dead room. An open sort of coffin, about seven feet long and four feet wide, was made on the spot, and was fastened by six long, thick, green canes, three on the front side and three on the rear side; each cane was about 60 yards long. When everything was ready the coffin was drawn inside the dead-room on a sloping plank. The corpse was placed in the middle of the coffin and two women lay on either side of the corpse with their hands embracing it, and thus it was dropped below the house; when the coffin had fallen on the ground, two stalwart men fell upon the corpse and lay together in the coffin. The large *el-panam* [public ground] of that village was filled by about a thousand people, both young and old, including those who came from other villages of the island. Of these about a hundred men of the southern villages and about a hundred of the northern villages caught hold of the long cane on either side and dragged the corpse up and down in competition. The canes were broken several times. Thus they occupied themselves till the grave was ready. At last they buried the body at about six o'clock.

Another peculiar custom among the Car Nicobarese is that there is wrestling between two sets of people while the dead body is being carried to the grave, presumably because some are for the burial and others against it. People occassionally get injured in the scuffle and sometimes the corpse falls down. Then they just throw it into the grave along with the livestock of the one who has died.

The largest island in the Nicobar group of islands is Great Nicobar. But the population, till recently, was very small indeed. (Now ex-servicemen are being settled there, but that is another story.) On the coast lived mainly Nicobarese and, in the interior, the Shompens, the aborigines of Great Nicobar. The Shompens live in jungles in the interior, and are today very shy. In the old days, they did resent encroachment upon what they considered as exclusively their island, and the Nicobarese, so far as they are concerned, were strangers. So there used to be the odd incident when "strangers" were attacked.

No one quite knows what their origin is, but it looks as though the Shompens have a Malayan strain which, in all probability, is mixed with the Dravidian; the Dravidians came there either as shipwrecked mariners or when the Chola kings of South India held their sway over most of South-east Asia. Their houses are rather small but, of course, built on piles because of incessant rain. They generally have open sides but thatched roofs. In the old days the men used to go about naked. Now they do wear some kind of a loin-cloth; the women wear bark-cloth petticoats.

The food of the Shompens, like the Nicobarese, consists of coconuts, bananas, various kinds of tubers and the Pandanus. There are also pigs aplenty on the island, and the Shompens love to hunt and eat their flesh.

Besides Car Nicobar, Chowra and Great Nicobar, other important islands in the Nicobar group which have a sizeable population are Katchal, Teressa, Trinket, Camorta and Nancowry. As already stated, it is Camorta, Trinket and Nancowry which form perhaps the most magnificent natural harbour in the world. And until the concluding years of the last century, the best navigational map of this harbour was the one made by Alexander Kyd, surveyor-general of India in 1790 and in charge of the settlement at Port Cornwallis, after Blair.

Penal Settlement in the Nicobars

Because of the large number of murders of the crew of a great number of ships that had been scuttled by the Nicobarese, as indicated already, the British felt that they must have a presence somewhere in the islands of the Nicobars. They thought the best way to do so would be to establish a penal settlement. So they chose the magnificent harbour of Nancowry for the purpose. In June 1869, a beginning was made by bringing to Camorta (in the Nancowry harbour), 262 prisoners. Camorta was infested with a virulent type of malaria, and this would eventually cause the abandonment of the penal settlement there 19 years later.

Camorta began with 262 convicts but their average, while it was a penal settlement, varied between 172 to 308. The police there never exceeded 30 in number. There was also a small detachment of the army, comprising 60 to 65 Madras sepoys. In addition there were some government officials, a few coconut traders and, in later years, children of freed convicts. But the total population was never more than 400.

For the first five years *Blenheim*, an East India-man hulk, was anchored in the harbour; it provided accommodation to some of the officers while buildings for their residence were being built. The official hierarchy consisted of one assistant or extra assistant superintendent, generally belonging to the Port Blair establishment, an officer to command the Madras sepoys and a medical officer. Incidentally, it was here, while in charge of the island, that M de Roepstorff was murdered by a havildar of the detachment of the 2nd regiment of the Madras infantry.

The only interesting event that occurred during the few years when the penal settlement was in existence in Camorta, was in the year 1875, when a number of European astronomers turned up to observe the total eclipse of the sun, supposed to take place on 6 April. Unfortunately, however, they were able to see nothing due to cloudy weather.

It was malaria that proved the killer. The government of India, therefore, decided to close down the settlement. The last batch of settlers left Camorta on 21 December 1888. A few coconut traders were allowed to stay on. And the only representative (of the government of India) to stay behind was a Chinese interpreter; he was to keep a register of the arrival and departure of ships, grant permits to trade and, of course, hoist the British flag every morning! It is a strange coincidence that the British, like the Moravians before them, should have stayed in Camorta also for only 19 years—the Moravians from 1768 to 1787 and the British from 1869 to 1888.

In 1884, an attempt was made to colonize the Nicobars with the help of the Chinese. Fifteen of them arrived from the Straits Settlements. The experiment was not a success, and they soon went back to the Straits. However, it is interesting to recall Horace Man's formulae about the use of the Chinese:

> To colonise the Nicobars, employ Chinese; send them to Great Nicobar: employ agriculturists who are not opium users: maintain quick and frequent communication with the Straits Settlement: assist the colonists in transporting their families: provide them with ready means of procuring food, clothing, medicines, tools and implements.

After the end of the settlement in Camorta, the Nicobars slumbered on. They continued to be under the British but Car Nicobar, the most important island, had only one agent, whose salary was Rs 60 per mensem! He had on his staff one peon, who received Rs 8 per month. Later, about three or four policemen came over. They replaced the peon.

But one of the agents, who was to change significantly the lives of the people of Car Nicobar—as far as their conversion to Christianity is concerned—was Vedappan Solomon from Madras, and his wife. At one stage he was not only an official magistrate but also port officer, meteorological observer, schoolmaster, catechist and amateur doctor. Bishop Richardson was his student. (He was the first representative of the Andaman and Nicobar islands in the first Lok Sabha, and came as a nominated member.)

Many years later, Nancowry was to hit the headlines during the first world war when the government agent there—a woman, popularly known as the *Rani*—was responsible for driving out the German warship *Emden* out of the harbour. She had no soldiers, not even a single rifle. But she was a courageous and resourceful woman. Instead of running away and hiding herself when she sighted the hostile warship, she hoisted the Union Jack. Captain Muller, commander of *Emden*, thought that the hoisting of the flag signified that there were some batteries hidden in the jungle. So he turned tail and departed. The Rani was decorated by the British government for her service to the Crown.

13

A Nicobarese Folk-tale

The Nicobarese have a large number of fascinating folk-tales. Among them is one about Giri and Shoan.

There was formerly a man by the name of Arang, whose wife had borne him three sons and three daughters.

He made himself a nice house and possessed much property.

One day he went out to sea with his eldest son called Shoan.

They wanted to fish with hook and line.

Strong wind got up and heavy sea sprung up.

Then it happened that one of the outriggers of the canoe broke, and both sank into the sea. Arang was drowned, but the boy crawled up on

the back of the canoe and cried:
"What shall I do? My father is dead. What shall I do?"
"Whish! It is the whale arriving."
"Why are you crying, child?"
"Oh, my father is dead. I cannot survive, how shall I get home, what am I to do, my father is dead!"
"Sit down on my back, I know the road," said the whale. "Oh, no, I will not," said the boy. "I am afraid, I do not know the road, as my father is dead!"

But after a while Shoan did sit down on the back of the whale. Whish off they went, quickly, swiftly.

The whale is the chief of the sea. At the sight of him all got afraid. The flying fish flew in all directions, the turtle dived down suddenly; the shark sank down (below) his fin, the sea-snake dug himself into the sand, the *ilu* danced along the sea, the dugong hugged her young one, the dolphin fled, for they were afraid of the whale.

Thus sped the two. By and by they arrived at the country of the whale. It was a big domed stone-house. The walls were of red coral, the steps were made of Tridacna. In the house they saw the daughter of the whale, whose name was Giri.

"Do you like this boy?" said the whale.
"All right, let him stay," said Giri.
"I am willing to stay here."

Then Shoan became servant of Giri. Giri's body was like that of a woman; below she was shaped with a fish-tail, her breasts were the colour of mother-of-pearl, her back like gold; her eyes were stars, her hair like seaweed. Said Giri—"What work do you know?"
"I can collect coconuts in the jungle."
"Never mind, we have no coconuts, but what work do you know?"
"I can make boats."
"We do not want boats, but what other work do you know?"
"I know how to spear fish."
"Don't! You must not do it, for we love the fish; my father is chief among the fish. Never mind; comb my hair."

Shoan remained, he combed her hair; they used to joke together, and they married.

Said Shoan—"How is it, wife, that you do not possess a looking-glass, although your face is so nice."
"I want a looking-glass, look out for one."
"In my private house in the village there is a looking-glass, but I do not know the road."
"Never mind, I know the road; sit on my back and I will bring you near the land."
"I cannot walk in your country, but do, I pray you, return quickly."
"Certainly, wife, you had better stop near the edge of the coral reef on

this big stone; I will return quickly."

Then Shoan returned to his village. He came to his father's house.

"Who is there?" said the mother.

"It is I, Shoan."

"No, you are not; Shoan died with his father on the sea."

"Look at my face; I am Shoan, your son."

He came up into the house. When they heard about it, all the people of the village came. They asked many questions and Shoan answered. He told the story about the whale, and the story about the marriage with Giri. The people laughed and said he was telling lies. Shoan got sorry and angry, and he ran away with the looking-glass. The people went after him and speared him, and thus died Shoan.

Giri stops in the sea near the coral banks, and she sings and calls. In the night when the moon is high, fishermen hear a sound like the singing and the crying of a woman.

They ask other people about it and wonder, for they do not know about Giri. Giri will not return alone, that is why she sings and she calls out: "Come back Shoan, come back Shoan."

Poor, unfortunate Giri!

This tale was rendered into English by de Roepstorff, who was murdered by a sepoy while in service at Camorta.

14

Penal Settlement Grows and a Viceroy is Killed

Colonel Henry Man was by profession an engineer and in 1858 had held the post of executive engineer at Moulmein. He was also in charge of the convicts there as superintendent of the Moulmein jail. As we already know, when the penal settlement was originally founded in Port Blair, Man had been named its first superintendent. Although he performed his duties for a while, it was Dr Walker who in actual fact became the first superintendent. After a lapse of nearly ten years, Colonel Man assumed charge as superintendent of the Port Blair penal settlement in March 1868. (He was a captain in 1858, now a colonel, and was later to attain the rank of field marshal.)

Man was a great believer in Sir Stamford

Raffles' ideal that the "object of the punishment" should be to reclaim the convicts "from their bad habits". He, therefore, introduced the same kind of penal system that had obtained in the Straits Settlements and, accordingly, framed a set of rules and regulations. Though these were amended many a time, basically they remained the same until 1945, when the penal settlement was ultimately abolished.

Colonel Man relinquished charge of his appointment on 16 March 1871. After a brief interregnum, Major-General Donald M Stewart took over as superintendent on 15 July 1872. Stewart had started life as an ensign in the Bengal Army and had served during the Mutiny. He was later to lead an army to Kandahar in the Afghan War, and end his career as commander-in-chief in India, with the rank of field marshal. It was while he was superintendent that the designation of this appointment was changed to that of chief commissioner—though for some inexplicable reason, he was not to be referred to as such in official correspondence.

Lord Mayo, the then viceroy and governor-general of India, had displayed a great deal of personal interest in the affairs of the penal settlement. He therefore decided to visit the Andamans. And it was here that he was assassinated by a Pathan convict named Sher Ali on 8 February 1872.

Lord Mayo's one great desire was to establish a sanatorium for convicts suffering from tuberculosis. He had been told that Mount Harriet would perhaps provide the best site for it. When he arrived at the Hopetown jetty, from where he was to go on board the ship by a motor-boat, it was still not quite dark. So he said: "We still have an hour of daylight. Let us do Mount Harriet."

When he arrived at the top he was most impressed. "How beautiful!" he exclaimed. "It is the loveliest thing I ever saw." Indulging in a flight of fancy, he said he thought there was "plenty of room to settle a million men" at Mount Harriet.

As it was beginning to get dark, Lord Mayo and his party climbed down the hill. He had barely reached the Hopetown jetty, which is at the foot of the hill, when Sher Ali pounced on him. In his book on Lord Mayo in the *Rulers of India* series, Sir W W Hunter has described the scene:

> The ships' bells had just rung seven; the launch, with steam up, was whizzing at the jetty stairs; a group of seamen were chatting on the pierhead. It was now quite dark, and the black line of the jungle seemed to touch the water's edge. The party passed some large loose stones to the left of the head of the pier, and advanced along the jetty, two torchbearers in front...and the Viceroy stopped quickly before the rest to descend the stairs to the launch. The next moment the people in the rear heard a noise as of "the rush of some animal", from behind the loose stones; one or two saw a hand and a knife suddenly descend in

Penal Settlement Grows and a Viceroy is Killed

the torch-light. The private secretary heard a thud, and instantly turning round, found a man "fastened like a tiger" on the back of the Viceroy. In a second, twelve men were on the assassin; an English officer was pulling them off, and with his sword hilt keeping back the native guards, who would have killed the assailant on the spot. The torches had gone out; but the Viceroy, who had staggered over the pier side, was dimly seen rising up in the knee-deep water and clearing the hair off his brow with his hand, as if recovering himself. His private secretary was instantly by his side, and was dimly seen rising up in the surf, helping him up the bank. "Burne", he said quietly, "they have hit me". Then in a louder voice, which was heard on the pier—"I'm all right, I don't think I am much hurt", or words to that effect. In another minute he was sitting under the smoky glare of the re-lit torches, on a rude native cart at the side of the jetty, his legs hanging loosely down. Then they lifted him bodily out of the cart, and saw a great dark patch on the back of his light coat. The blood came streaming out, and the men tried to stanch it with their handkerchiefs. For a moment or two he sat up in the cart, then he fell heavily backwards. "Lift up my head", he said faintly; and said no more.

According to S Yusuf Hussain, author of *Pen Pictures of the Andaman and Nicobar Islands*, the assassin Sher Ali was a highlander who belonged to the North-western Frontier and had been convicted at Peshawar for murdering one of his blood-feud enemies. He was well-built and strong. There was a story going round in the Andamans at one time that, even though he was heavily fettered, he once overturned a lamp with his chained ankle. He was also supposed to have borne down an English sentry by sheer brute strength. He was obviously wily and cunning because, as Yusuf Hussain puts it, he succeeded in establishing "his character as a silent, doggedly well behaved man; and in time [was] set at large as a barber among the ticket of leave convicts".

In order to get him to confess (because he refused to), the British played a ruse on him. They sent an Indian officer in the guise of a man from his native place, who eulogized him as a hero. He told Sher Khan that he had done a "noble deed [which] should be sung in his own country and elsewhere". Before dying, however, Sher Khan said that although he had meant to commit the murder, in actual fact the fatal blow had not been struck by him.

Maulana Mohammad Jafar Thanesvri, who was also in the Andamans at the time as one of the transportees, and later published an autobiography in Urdu, wrote:

For years Sher Khan had been sharpening his dagger. And, when on the 8th of February 1872, Lord Mayo came to the Andamans, he sharpened his dagger again. All through the day he was trying to go to the island [Ross] where he could find Lord Mayo, but he could not. He did not get permission to go anywhere near there. But, when Lord Mayo decided to go to Mount Harriet, it was like fate had brought him to Sher Ali's home. He surreptitiously went up the hill while Lord Mayo was on his way up; he also came down alongside him, but did not get any chance to commit what he had pledged himself to do. So he quickly came down before Lord Mayo could get near the jetty and hid himself behind a rail carriage. And that he said was "my opportunity". He pounced on Lord Mayo the moment he got near the jetty.

When questioned by C Aitchison (foreign secretary), on board the *Glasgow* (where he was taken immediately after the crime), as to why he had committed the murder, Sher Ali replied: *"Khuda ne hukum diya"* (God gave an order). Did he have any accomplice? "No", he replied, *"Mera sharik koi admi nahin, mera sharik Khuda hai"* (No man is my accomplice, God's is my accomplice). But had he done the deed? *"Han, maine kiya"* (Yes, I did it).

Sher Ali was convicted by the chief commissioner sitting as session's judge and sentenced to be hanged by the neck till dead. The high court of Bengal confirmed the sentence.

On the day of his execution at Viper, again according to Maulana Mohammad Jafar Thanesvri: "On going up the scaffold, he [Sher Ali] turned to other convicts and shouted loudly: 'Brothers, I have killed your enemy, and you are my witness that I am a Muslim'. And then he started reciting the *Qalma*, and died while doing so."

By and large, historians have treated this as an ordinary crime. But in actual fact it was a crime committed by one who belonged to the Wahabi Muslim sect and who was driven to murder a viceroy and governor-general as a result of the ideals that underlay the philosophy and way of thinking of the Wahabis. The Wahabis' only obsession was to establish an Islamic state in India and dispose of anyone who stood in their way of achieving that objective. The British being the main stumbling block, it was only fair and just that the big white man be put away.

Lord Mayo had also been keen that special attention be paid to cultivation by the self-supporters, and that they be encouraged to raise cattle.

It was as a result of the special interest taken by Lord Mayo in the penal settlement of Port Blair that J Scarlett Campbell, then home secretary to the government of India, was sent to the Andamans to submit a report on the working of the penal system. He was to work in close collaboration with Major-General Stewart, the chief commissioner. The settlement was also placed under the jurisdiction of the home department, rather than the political department of the government of India, under which it had been hitherto.

Campbell recommended that the convicts be divided into four classes. He began by defining the fourth class or Gaol Gang, which was to be the lowest:

(*i*) Convicts in this class shall be subjected to the strictest gaol discipline and shall be entitled to no indulgences. They shall be employed in gangs by themselves on hard extra-mural labour, or either in workshops attached to the gaol;

(*ii*) All convicts, on first arrival, shall be placed in this class, and shall remain in it for one year, when, if they have conducted themselves well, they shall be eligible to be placed in the 3rd class;

(*iii*) All convicts are liable to be remanded to and kept in this class;

(*iv*) Attached to this class, and forming part of the gaol, shall be a refractory ward, where offenders may be confined and subjected to hard labour and low diet within the enclosure wall of the ward, and there shall be solitary cells for punishment of offenders ordered to be confined in such.

3rd Class:
(*i*) Convicts in this class shall be employed in hard gang-labour by day, and shall be confined in barracks at night. They shall receive rations and gaol clothing, but shall be entitled to no luxury;

(*ii*) After five years' satisfactory conduct in this class, they shall be eligible for transfer to 2nd class.

2nd Class:
(*i*) Convicts in this class shall be worked and confined as in the case of 3rd class. They shall receive rations and gaol clothing, and a monthly allowance of from eight annas to one rupee for the purpose of vegetables and such luxuries as tobacco, etc., as may be sanctioned by the Superintendent;

(*ii*) Convicts of this class shall be eligible for employment in the service of the Government, or of any free resident of the Settlement, subject to such conditions as the Superintendent may lay down;

(*iii*) After five years' satisfactory service in this class, convicts shall be eligible to transfer to 1st class.

1st Class:
Convicts in this class shall remain in barracks or may be located otherwise as the Superintendent may direct. They shall receive dry rations, and from Re 1 to Rs 2 a month, but they shall find their own clothes. In cases in which it may appear desirable, the Superintendent may substitute subsistence money for rations.

Campbell did not want every convict in the 1st class to become a self-supporter. He felt that "only those who bid fair to make such a living as will enable them to support themselves, and any who may be dependent upon them, in sickness and in old age" should be allowed to become self-supporters. Not only that, he suggested that all self-supporters should "pay a considerable tax to the Government". Apparently, that had also been suggested by Colonel Ford, one of the earlier superintendents. Campbell also recommended that only those in the 1st class be allowed to marry.

Woman convicts were to have two classes only. In the 2nd, i.e. the lower class, they were to spend three years. And in the higher, the 1st class, they had to spend two years, and be of good conduct before they would be allowed to marry.

Campbell also mentioned the eventuality of there being European convicts in the settlement, in which case they were to be placed under the same rules "as are laid down for general guidance", except that in their case "good behaviour in gaol previous to arrival at the Andamans may count as time towards eligibility for indulgence". But there is nothing on record to show whether or not any European convicts were actually ever transported to the Andamans.

Campbell would allow a 1st class convict to acquire personal property or to rent land, but denied him "the right of using the Civil Courts to enforce his rights". On the subject of the convicts corresponding with their relatives on the mainland, he was very severe. He suggested that life convicts should have no correspondence with India, and that term convicts could send and receive only one letter every three months.

Campbell also proposed a new concept where life convicts were concerned, perhaps a most unique concept ever propounded before or since. According to him, "when a man is transported for life, he should become *dead to his family* [not his italics] ... I would suggest an Act declaring any such convict to be civilly dead, and property he may have left passing to his next kin." However, he did display considerable foresight when he said: "Such a penal settlement as the Andamans seems hardly the place for political prisoners", because it was to be the beginning of the end of the Andamans as a penal settlement, once the political prisoners began arriving in Port Blair.

Major-General D C Stewart, superintendent and chief commissioner, obviously did not see eye to eye with Campbell because, as he stated somewhat bluntly: "I am no advocate for a system of mere gaol discipline. The circumstances of the case do not require it, and it would, I believe, be a wanton waste of power to enforce it." He did not believe in making a convict "more miserable than the necessity of the case [called] for". He went on to add:

> For my part, I believe that we should follow the example set us in Australia, by granting comparative freedom to the deserving and the industrious convict who had proved himself to be fitted for indulgence by steady conduct for a period of years.... I consider that convicts of ability and good character should be encouraged to raise themselves by their industry to positions of independence, and that they should be permitted to the full enjoyment of the fruits of their labour.

Not all recommendations made by Campbell were accepted, but most were, with some suitable modification and amendment, but the governor-general in council made it quite clear that "the main and primary object for which the Settlement is maintained is to secure that the sentence passed upon convicts is properly carried out under a well regulated system of discipline, and to this object the profitable employment of convicts and the development of the resources of the island must be considered secondary and subordinate". Obviously, a lot of change in political thinking had taken place at the highest level since Sir Robert Napier's visit in 1864, because Napier had categorically expressed the view that "it would be greatly ... regretted if the mild character of the present [the then] management were to be exchanged for greater severity".

The legislative department of the government of India, whilst taking action on Campbell's report, made an interesting discovery. A scribe in the secretariat discovered: "Curiously enough I can find no definition of transportation in the existing law in India. 'Transportation' is made the next punishment to death in the Penal Code; but no statement of what it involves in regard to the treatment of prisoners at the place of transportation is given." Another scribe had this interesting comment to make:

> Numerous letters from convicts to their friends in India have fallen into the hands of the Government and these *all*, and without exception, speak of Port Blair as a most comfortable residence with no drawback but separation from home and its associations; indeed, they often use the most glowing terms to describe it, and no doubt deservedly. Now, it is to be remembered that many Natives voluntarily endure even lifelong separation from their homes and families for objects of ambition or money-making. *Khutrees* of Mooltan, Sindh, Peshawer, and elsewhere, have found their way all over Central Asia and even to Astrabad, Moscow and St. Petersburg.

It does not seem as though the Andamans were going to have much respite from official inspections!

Hardly had the ink dried on the recommendations made in the report submitted by Scarlett Campbell (and their partial acceptance), when in May 1874 there came to the Andamans Major-General Sir Henry Norman (later field marshal and one of the few Englishmen who was to refuse an offer of the viceroyalty of India), for another inspection.

Norman found that on 1 June 1874 the Andaman penal settlement had 7,820 male and 895 female life convicts on its rolls. In addition it had 888 term convicts, 500 married couples, with 578 children, and 1,167 ticket-of-leave convicts, 476 of whom were women.

For some time a controversy had been raging as to whether or not term convicts were to be sent to the Andamans. Term convicts had been sent to begin with, but in 1868 their transportation had been stopped, because it was felt that the "practice of sending limited term men had the effect of lessening the deterrent force of the punishment". General Stewart had dissented with that view because his feeling was that "it is to term convicts we must look in the main for reliable men to fill [the] large and important body of petty officers". Stewart did not think he could rely on life convicts to keep a watch on their fellow prisoners. He was firmly of the opinion that "term convicts... should be sent to Port Blair if security is desired". He also added:

While some may think the whole idea of the Port Blair Settlement a mistake, a view for which there is a good deal to be said, I am convinced it cannot go on with security or without much additional expense unless term convicts are sent there.

The powers-that-be agreed with the views held by Stewart because the governor-general in council decided "to waive the consideration of general policy which restricted transportation to life convicts, and to permit term-convicts to be sent to the Settlement".

As a result of Sir Henry Norman's recommendation, male convicts were to be divided into three classes, as against Campbell's four. These were:

3rd Class:
All convicts on arrival shall be placed in this class. They shall be employed in hard gang labour by day and shall be confined to barracks at night. They shall receive rations and jail clothing, but shall be entitled to no indulgence or luxury. They shall wear double leg-irons for the first six months, and single leg-irons for the second six months, subject to special exemption by the Superintendent. After four years' satisfactory conduct in this class, they shall be eligible for transfer to the second class.

2nd Class:
In this class there will be two grades in each of which a prisoner will pass three years. In the lower grade a prisoner may receive a regular allowance of twelve annas a month, and is to be eligible for posts in barracks or jail or for employment in the artificer corps. In the upper grade the prisoner may receive one rupee per mensem, and shall be eligible in addition for employment in the convict police or in other petty Government employ, as orderlies, or as servants to free residents.

Men in this class will receive dry rations, and be supplied jail clothing or uniform as may be directed by the Superintendent. Any allowance for working in the artificer corps or for serving in any employment may be paid to the men of the second class in addition to their regular monthly allowance.

After three years of approved service in each grade of the second class, convicts shall be eligible for transfer to the first class.

1st Class:
Convicts in this class shall remain in barracks or may be located otherwise as the Superintendent may direct. They shall receive dry rations and an allowance of from one rupee to two rupees per mensem. In cases where it may appear desirable, the Superintendent may substitute subsistence allowance for rations.

They shall do such labour as shall be assigned to them, and shall be eligible for service or to support themselves in such conditions as the Superintendent may impose. In such cases a ticket shall be given to each convict with the conditions entered on it. Convicts of this class who do not live in barracks shall attend muster at such times as the Superintendent shall appoint, but at least once every month. Term convicts shall not be eligible for service, or be permitted to support themselves or live out of barracks. [This would appear to defeat General Stewart's purpose.]

Life convicts in this class may be allowed to send for their wives or children, or to marry.

Sir Henry Norman did not suggest any change in the classification of women prisoners, but he was of the opinion that, subject to certain conditions, it was important for the "well being" and "the moral condition of the Settlement" that "as large a proportion of both men and women as may be practicable should be married". Ticket-of-leave convicts were, as hitherto, allowed to send for their wives or husbands.

Norman also recommended two kind of pardons, with leave to quit the settlement. These were agreed to. They were:

(*i*) The first is to comprise those pardons which are given on extraordinary occasions for conspicuous gallantry or devotion in the service of the Government, regarding which no rules can be laid down.

(*ii*) In the second class the pardon shall be limited: no remission of sentence will be given to any convict who has not been twenty years under sentence at the Penal Settlement. When a convict has served this term of years, the Government may, at their pleasure, take into consideration the nature and degree of his original offence. If it was a kind to make the convict permanently dangerous to society, or to public order, whenever he should be restored to liberty, in that case the life-sentence must run its course. If the offence does not fall within the category above described, the remission of sentence may be recommended by the Superintendent as a reward for approval and sustained good conduct. All pardons to life convicts be granted with the assent of the Government of India.

Norman made some caustic comments about the stone barracks which were "designed on an expensive and ornamental scale". They had cost "a very large sum" and had taken several years to build. He found that as soon as they were completed "one half began to sink, and the foundations were then discovered to be insufficient".

Major-General D M Stewart was succeeded by Major-General A C Barwell on 26 May 1875. During his regime it was discovered that a large number of Andamanese had contracted syphilis, the much dreaded venereal disease, through contact with the convicts. Not only that, in the year 1877 an epidemic of ophthalmia broke out among them. This was soon to be followed by another epidemic of influenza, as also of measles. The result was that the Andamanese, who have a rather delicate constitution, despite the fact that they go about naked, died in great number. M V Portman estimated that in the measle epidemic alone, which had broken out in 1877, "half, if not two thirds, of the whole of the Andamanese in Great Andaman died from its effect".

Not much of significance happened as far as the penal settlement was concerned in the years that followed till Major (later Colonel) A Thomas Cadell took over as chief commissioner on 27 February 1878. With one or two breaks in between, his regime was to last nearly nine years.

Sir Alexander Mackenzie, secretary in the home department of the government of India, came on an inspection tour in 1885. He was quite impressed by the improvements that had taken place in the penal settlement, but he felt that although "it was right to take steps to reduce the excessive death rate", matters had been taken too far and "penal considerations have of late been unduly sacrificed". In his opinion: "There is no reason why we should insist upon reducing the risks to convict life below those of the outside population, if to secure this, we have to wrap the prisoner as it were in cotton wool, and treat him as a precious object whom we are bound to keep alive at all costs, and not to treat with any harshness that might tend to effect his health".

Mackenzie also visited Viper Island, where he found two little Andamanese "the most melancholy objects in the ward". They had been sentenced to five years' imprisonment for killing a convict officer "under grave provocation" because Mackenzie was able to gather that they had been "ill-treated in a way that made it almost natural for them to use their bows and arrows". As he was convinced that they were sure to die if "long in confinement", he hoped that Cadell would "see his way to letting them out after a time". He wrote: "Their pathetic look, like that of a hunted animal, haunted me for days".

It was during Mackenzie's inspection that the question of introducing more Burmese convicts into the settlement cropped up. Cadell was against this. As he put it: "It is notorious how prone Burmese convicts are to escape or attempt to escape from the Andamans." But what he feared even more was that they would take "to committing dacoity on the villages of the self-supporters". However, Cadell did eventually agree to have 600 convicts. The number was later reduced to 500 as Man, who was then in charge of the convicts at Camorta, said that he could accommodate only 50 and not 100, as Cadell had anticipated.

Mackenzie also climbed Mount Harriet and there met "the rascally old *fakir* who lived in a hut under the barracks". This man had been declared a state prisoner after Lord Mayo's murder. But he had set himself up as a holy *fakir* and was being supported "entirely by the offerings of convicts, sepoys, and others who look upon him as a sort of deity". Mackenzie went on to remark that "convicts going to his hut are punished, but all the same they certainly go there".

After Mackenzie came yet another commission, four years later, comprising Charles James Lyall (later knighted), home secretary in the government of India, and Surgeon-Major A S Lethbridge of the Bengal Medical Service (also knighted later in recognition of his work as general superintendent for the suppression of *thagi* and *dakaity* in India). They visited Port Blair in January 1890. Almost at the outset of their report they observed:

> Without a single exception both those who were about to start for the Andamans and those who had been rejected expressed a desire to be transported rather than undergo their sentence in Indian jails. The escaped convict [a Sikh], although he knew that stripes and chain gang awaited him at Port Blair, was most urgent in his request to be sent at once to the Andamans.

Their natural conclusion was, therefore, that "the confinement within the walls of an Indian prison is now a much more severe form of punishment than transportation". In consequence, these two gentlemen wanted the life of a convict in the Andamans to be made more difficult so that the punishment would really act as a deterrent.

The question of term convicts came up for consideration once again. In this instance, the local government and the administration supported the recommendation of the commissioners, with which the government of India concurred, that "the transportation of male convicts who are not under life sentence should be prohibited" and "male term convicts shall not in future be transported to Port Blair". The government also agreed with the recommendation that "the settlement of released convicts at Port Blair should be encouraged". Further, they were of the opinion, on the representation of the superintendent that, "as a general rule habituals should be separated ... and that no one who is not a habitual should be kept with habituals unless it is absolutely necessary". Women convicts were to be segregated completely.

To make the earlier stages of imprisonment more penal, there was to be "a preliminary stage of separate confinement for a period of six months in cells". And that was the genesis of the notorious Cellular Gaol. Recommendations with regard to convicts in the third class were also made. What the superintendent accepted was that "the convicts will be in the third class, including the preliminary stage of two years, for five years, when they will become eligible for promotion to the second class".

The question of remittances made by convicts to their relatives on the mainland, as well as that of bequeathing property left by deceased convicts, was reviewed. So far as remitting money was concerned, it was to be restricted to self-supporters. It was decided that they may "with the sanction of the District Officer ... remit sums not exceeding Rs 100 under special circumstances, such as for the purchase of goods, for passage money for their families, and by self-supporters on obtaining their release". Any sum above that amount would require the sanction of the superintendent. The governor-general in council decided that "the privilege of bequeathing property outside the settlement shall for the future be withdrawn".

Lyall and Lethbridge were categorical that "the provision of more women as wives for self-supporters was one of the chief needs of the Settlement". They therefore recommended—and the governor-general in council, in consequence, directed—that "for the future female term-convicts sentenced to transportation for seven years and upwards shall be transported to the Andamans".

They also suggested that, instead of the pecuniary reward system then prevailing, a new system in which marks were allotted to "convict officers and artificers and other persons employed in different departments" may be devised so that they could become self-supporting convicts in less than ten years, which was the period then in force. Cadell did not quite agree but, after being asked to reconsider, he did introduce a kind of mark system.

While in the Andamans, the two members of the commission also visited Viper Gaol. In their report they gave a description of the Viper prison and its surroundings, including the condemned cells which were "situated outside the jail and adjoining the guard room". About them they wrote: "On the opposite side to the condemned cells are the gallows. The plan adopted is a good one and the platform is on a level with the ground, thus rendering it easy for the prisoner to walk it." In making this comment the two worthies did not obviously realize how risible their remarks were, for what difference would it make to a man condemned to death how he walks to the gallows!

The work of the administration was commended in these words: "The general impression which we received from our brief stay at Port Blair as to the system, order, regularity, and security of the administration was most favourable."

As Colonel N M Horsford only held the post of superintendent and chief commissioner of the Andamans for less than two years, it was left to Lieutenant-Colonel Sir Richard Temple to implement most of the recommendations made by the Lyall and Lethbridge Commission. Temple assumed office on 3 August 1894. The chief commissioner and superintendent was being assisted at the time in the discharge of his duties by a deputy superintendent, some assistant superintendents and overseers—all Englishmen—and several Indian sub-overseers. There was also a military garrison stationed at Port Blair, actually at Ross, which consisted of 140 British and 300 Indian troops, in addition to a few local British volunteers. The police was also organized as a military battalion with a strength of 643.

The penal settlement then comprised an area of 473 square miles, consisting of, as Sir Richard put it, "grazing and arable lands, swamps, dense forests, large harbours and inlets of the sea, hills up to 1,500 feet, and small villages for the tickets-of-leave [self-supporters] convicts, ex-convicts, and free persons, convict stations, workshops and jails". He found that the fundamental principles on which the system was founded were "substantially what they were originally, and had stood the criticism, the repeated examination and the modifications in details...without material alterations". Temple described the system as it obtained during his regime:

> The life convicts are received into the Cellular Jail for six months where discipline is of the severest, but the work is not very hard. They are then transferred to the Associated Jail for 18 months, where the work is hard, but the discipline less irksome. For the next three years the life convict lives in barracks, locked up at night, and goes out to labour under supervision. For his labour he receives no reward, but his capabilities are studied. During the next five years he remains a labouring convict, but is eligible for the petty posts of supervision and the easier forms of labour; he also gets a very small allowance for little luxuries, or to save in the special savings Bank. He has now completed ten years in transportation and can receive a ticket-of-leave. In this condition he earns his own living in a village; he can farm, keep cattle and marry or send for his family. But he is not free, has no civil rights, and cannot leave the Settlement or be idle. With 20 or 25 years spent in the Settlement, with approved conduct, he may be absolutely released.

The women convicts were:

> similarly dealt with, but on altogether easier lines. The general principle with regard to them is to divide them into two main classes—those in and those out of the Female Jail. Every woman must remain in the Female Jail, unless in domestic employ by permission or married and living with her husband. Women are eligible for marriage or domestic employ after five years in the Settlement, and if married

they must leave the Settlement after 15 years with their husbands, all married couples having to wait, each for the other's full term under the rules, which ever comes last, and they must leave together. If unmarried, women have to remain 20 years. In Jail they rise from class to class and can become petty officers on terms similar to those for the men.

Women term convicts were treated more or less on the same lines and the earlier years of their incarceration followed the same pattern as that of male life convicts. But there was one major difference—they could not become self-supporters. Temple described the object of the penal settlement in these words:

> The whole drift of the treatment is that of a long education to useful citizenship, throughout which there runs continuous threads of practice in self-help and self-restraint and of inducement to profit by the practice.... The incorrigible are kept till death, the slow to learn till they mend their ways, and only those that are proved to have good in them are returned to their houses.

The extent to which the system succeeded in its avowed aim of being "a long education to useful citizenship" can be found in Sir Richard's own findings. According to him, although the annual average of those convicts who had committed murders or attempted to do so during the years 1890-99 was a mere 12 per cent per annum, "heredity [seemed] to show itself in both sexes rather in a tendency towards the meaner qualities" but much less in "violence of temperament". He found among young girls "a painful amount of prostitution", a result he thought obviously of a preponderance of males over females and because convict mothers were hardly of a class who could "bring up their girls to a high morality".

He also noted that the locally born population were better educated than their counterparts on the mainland, because education then for the children of all self-supporters was compulsory—for girls till the age of ten and for boys till the age of 14. (This is true even today, because education in the Andaman and Nicobar islands, though not compulsory, is free. One therefore hardly finds an illiterate there, nor is there much unemployment, though people are mostly employed in clerical posts, or as petty traders. This was, and perhaps still is, as Sir Richard said, the result of a tendency "on the part of the whole population to lean on the Government".)

The construction of the Cellular Jail commenced in 1896; it was completed some 14 years later in 1910. It is located at Aberdeen and is built on a promontory lapped by the waters of Sessostris Bay. It faces the island of Ross, which was then the seat of administration. In its original shape, it was a seven-pronged puce-coloured brick building, with the central tower acting as its fulcrum. Each wing was like the rib of an umbrella, and it had three storeys, the tower being the fourth. The tower housed a bell which tolled the hour and, in an emergency, sounded the alarm. On each of the three lower storeys containing the cells, in the central fulcrum, was posted a guard. All he had to do was to walk round like a bullock working the Persian wheel to get a clear, complete and unobstructed view of the verandahs—which faced the cells on each floor of each wing—through the grilled iron doors. In all, the Cellular Jail contained 698 cells. The size of each cell was 13 feet by nine feet with one solitary ventilator, three feet by one and a half feet, built at a height of nearly ten feet from the floor. The prisoner could neither see anything, nor was he able to communicate with any other prisoner. To make communication even more difficult, each wing faced the rear of the other one.

Today the awesome grandeur of the Cellular Jail has departed. Four wings were demolished soon after independence to make room for a hospital. Only three wings remain; one of them is now being used as the local jail. It has 105 cells for prisoners, both male and female. The other two wings, although they still stand, are being used for various other purposes. As though anticipating its ultimate impotent destiny, the tower toppled over during the Great Andaman earthquake in 1941. The new tower is a wooden structure, and no bell tolls.

In 1901 C Boden Kloss visited the islands and, in his book entitled *In the Andaman and Nicobar*, he describes the part of Ross Island which housed the settlement headquarters:

> On the summit stands the pleasant-looking residence of the Chief Commissioner; the church, and the barracks [architecturally modelled on Windsor Castle] for European troops; both the latter built of handsome stone quarried on the mainland. Below these came the mess, containing a fine library and some beautiful examples of wood-carvings executed by Burmese convicts; then the brown-roofed bungalows of the Settlement officers, all bowered in tropic foliage, among which graceful palms and traveller's trees stand prominently forth; and lower still, near the sea, are the treasury, commissariat stores, and other Government buildings. The whole place—in itself of much natural beauty—is kept in most perfect condition by a practically unlimited supply of convict labour.

And, again according to him, the ruling elite did not do too badly even in this remote island, which to an average Indian was *Kale Pani*, the black waters. They had:

> cricket and tennis grounds—the latter both concrete and grass—near which a band of convicts discourses very fair music several times a week. There is a sailing club too, and nearly every Saturday throughout the

year races for a challenge cup are held in the breezy harbour, at which a score of various craft are often found competing; and the Volunteer Rifle Corps has some thirty members, who compete with gun and revolver for a numerous list of prizes and trophies. Good salt-water fishing is to be had with the rod, for fish in great variety are everywhere abundant; and on the mainland, near Aberdeen, golf and hockey are played.

But Boden Kloss did not fail to remark that although "at first sight, it seemed an altogether delightful spot to find in such an isolated corner of the world", he found it rather depressing when he paid a visit to the Viper Jail; so also was the sight of the convicts, who could be seen everywhere "with their fetters, or neck rings, supporting the numbered badges with which the wearers [were] distinguished".

Temple finally left on 9 May 1903 and, after one month, during which F E Tuson held temporary charge, W R H Merk took over as chief commissioner and superintendent. He was the first member of the Indian Civil Service to hold that office.

Merk comments on the prevailing system: "It is an ironical system that gives an easier life to the worse criminal deported to Port Blair than his less hardened fellow prisoner has in an Indian Jail." Apropos the aim of the penal system in the Andamans to reform the convict and give him "a long education to useful citizenship", Merk wrote:

The problem of reform has, it seems to me, to be approached in India from a standpoint differing from that in England. The bulk of the convicts in the Andamans are, from a native point of view, perfectly respectable citizens who respect themselves, whose misfortune, not whose fault it is that they are in transportation, and who on release revert to the places in their family and in their society which they held before conviction, without the loss of their relations' and their neighbours' esteem, and without the loss of subsistence which imprisonment brings them in England.... They are no more outcasts than I am.

Merk's conclusion, and recommendation, therefore, was that the time had come "to stop transportation", because "transportation is a cause of heavy additional expense, that it fails to adequately punish and deter, that it reforms no better [to say the most] than imprisonment, and is therefore a source of weakness to the criminal administration in India".

The government of India did not agree with Merk's recommendation, but it did refer the matter to the provincial governments and sought their opinion. The provincial governments were all for the continuance of transportation—mainly because there was a shortage of space in the jails on the mainland—and felt that if the penal settlement was abolished, they would not know what to do with all the convicts.

The debate continued even after Major (later Lieutenant-Colonel) H A Browning took over from Merk as chief commissioner. And that was on 14 April 1906. But the Andaman penal settlement was not to become a hot issue till the Indian government decided to transport political prisoners in 1910.

15

Taming the Andamanese

The British called it conciliating the aborigines, and the official policy as laid down by the government was "to adhere strictly to a conciliating line of conduct" and "to absolutely prohibit any aggression upon them and not to allow force on any account to be resorted to". But the rub was in the tail of the order which added the proviso, "unless it be absolutely necessary to repeal their attacks". In actual practice, who was to decide when it would become "absolutely necessary" to use force!

For the ostensible purpose of conciliating the aborigines, it was decided to establish special Homes for the Andamanese. In 1863, mainly through the efforts of Reverend H Corbyn, at the time chaplain at Port Blair, 28 Andamanese were persuaded to come and live in some huts on Ross Island. These huts came to be known as the Andaman Home. It was given official recognition and allotted a small monthly grant for its upkeep. A ticket-of-leave convict was appointed as supervisor. (This was to prove a grave error!) The professed aim of Corbyn's policy was to *civilize* the Andamanese. He tried to teach them English and, in addition, "daily employed them in work with native convicts cleaning sites, etc", to use his own words.

Lieutenant-Colonel R C Tytler, the then superintendent, was much more forthright when, in a letter to Corbyn dated 20 June 1963, he laid down the objectives of the Andaman Homes:

Ist—They must see the superior comforts of civilisation compared to their miserable savage condition; and 2nd—Though not immediately apparent we are in reality laying the foundation stone for civilising a people hitherto living in a perfectly barbarous state, replete with treachery, murder, and every other savageness; besides which it is very desirable, even in a political point of view, keeping those people in our custody as hostages, for it undoubtedly secures the better behaviour of these inhospitable people towards our Settlement; whereas their leaving us might injure and abolish all the good that has already been established, and might take years again to regain and recover were we to lose the great advantage we now hold and possess.

In what may be described as a sort of preamble to this letter, Tytler described the aborigines as a "truly savage, treacherous, and ungovernable race of people, devoid of civilisation, in every sense of the word".

Apart from running the Home, Corbyn paid several visits to the hinterland with the object of persuading the Andamanese to come and live in the Andaman Home.

However, notwithstanding the amicable relations on the surface, there was an undercurrent of mutual suspicion all along. What came to be known as the "affair of the dagger" is one evidence of this suspicion. On one of Corbyn's expeditions into the area of Mount Harriet, Corbyn gave his dagger to Joe, one of the Andamanese, to cut a pig into two parts, so that one part could be given to Joe's tribe and the other to another tribe living in one of the camps there. When Corbyn asked Joe for his dagger while the pig was being roasted, he replied: "What dagger?" No amount of threats and persuasion would make him return the dagger. The party returned to Ross carrying the pig and other wherewithals for the feast—with Joe in fetters.

Next morning another inhabitant of the Home, the friendly Topsy, assured Corbyn that the dagger would eventually be returned. And it was. After that, the fetters were struck off Joe in front of a gathering of all the

Andamanese who had been in the party—to teach them all a lesson, as it were. Corbyn recorded: "I held the dagger before Joe to show him that his purloining had been the cause of his imprisonment, and that the restitution of it now was the cause of his release."

Corbyn was, however, far from unsympathetic towards the Andamanese. In his own way he was very fond of them. And while holding charge of the Home he had a wonderful opportunity to study some of their characteristics. One of them is worth recording: Corbyn found that there was not "a single instance of bickering or disputing" between them and "if one asks anything of another it is at once yielded, either as if there was an understood reason for the request, or that it was backed by force of acknowledged and indisputable authority". Another remarkable phenomenon he noticed was that in the Andamanese men and women there was not "the least sign of indelicacy". He also found:

> the women quite modest, but at the same time confiding, free, and familiar; they will place their arms round our necks, sit on our laps, rest their heads in close contact with our faces in a way that the uninitiated would consider most amorous, and take many other sportive and harmless liberties but in the most perfect guilelessness, and without a single conscious thought of doing anything out of course or unbecoming.

However, even at that time Corbyn noticed—and this was some time in July 1863—a "most curious fact":

> They appear to enjoy better health on their own selected swampy grounds, and under their half exposed and feebly protected dwellings, than on this [Ross] island, which is cleared of all jungle, and where they have the comfort of a well-ventilated and thoroughly water-tight house, raised about three feet from the ground, besides the advantage of ample clothing, warm blankets, and simple and wholesome food, with no work to do.

He also found that they suffered most from "coughs, colds, ague, fever, and severe headache". In regard to the charge that the Andamanese had been detained in the Andaman Home against their will, Corbyn wrote: "A simple refutation of this mis-statement may be adduced from the fact that they are now only too anxious to come to the settlement, and that we have much more difficulty in keeping them away from this island than in inducing them to remain here." M V Portman, who was to follow him some years later as head of the Home, did not accept his refutations. "There can be no doubt", he wrote, "that the Andamanese were detained against their will in the Andaman Home, and that considerable and illegal pressure was put on them there".

There was also a difference of opinion between Corbyn and Tytler on whether or not the Andamanese should be utilized for recapturing escaped convicts. Corbyn was opposed to it, for he wrote:

> Colonel Tytler is anxious that I should try to find some means of inducing our Andamanese friends to recapture escaped convicts; and it would perhaps be an act of mercy to do so, if only to hinder Natives from going amongst a people so little under restraint to order, and provoking and instigating them to bloodshed, and all other acts of violence, by the annoyance which they cause them; the result of even one indiscreet or hasty act being committed, may perhaps fatally mar our attempts to conciliate and civilise them; but I fear that, if we invested people of such a turbulent and reckless disposition with a police control over truant Natives, we might let loose their worst passions and encourage their inclinations, which can now hardly be subsided, to attack and ill-use peaceable and unoffending Natives indiscriminately with those who outlaw themselves and forfeit all protection by trying to evade the sentence which has bound them to the Settlement.

Subsequent history vindicates Corbyn.

In October 1863, Corbyn took eight Andamanese on a trip to Calcutta and, according to him, the weather being "propitious" they thoroughly enjoyed themselves. In Calcutta they were accommodated in a small house in the Town Hall compound. The news of their arrival created quite a stir and everybody thronged to have a look at these "anthropophogi". The crowds increased every day, and not all were able to catch a glimpse of them. Therefore, all kinds of rumours began to spread about them. Some said that they had "long tails... that they would, if given a pig, kill it and eat it raw... that the only woman among them [Topsy], who had fallen ill, had said that her life could only be saved if she was allowed to eat the flesh of a white man" and so on. As the crowds swelled, the Andamanese had to be shifted to an encampment on the Ballygunge parade ground.

Corbyn, however, was surprised that the Andamanese "never evinced astonishment or admiration at anything which they beheld". Their favourite spot was the Dharrumtollah market, and there, perhaps even more so, they were harassed by the crowds, and subjected to insults. Jumbo, one of the Andamanese, was spat upon. His reaction was most violent and, wishing to settle scores, he "struck vigorously with his clenched fists right and left". Jacko, when insulted, similarly "vented his wrath on the mob", lashing them with Corbyn's buggywhip.

The Andamanese were shown a lot of other places of interest, but were not impressed. They set sail for Port Blair on 26 November and arrived back on 2 December 1863. Later in the same month Corbyn, this time accompanied by Tytler, took six Andamanese to Rangoon and Moulmein, but nothing of any interest took place, except that the Andamanese proved of great assistance to the crew of the settlement steamer *Diana*, which for some reasons had sailed with insufficient hands.

By February 1864, the number of aborigines on the settlement had risen to 40. They were being employed, along with the convicts, for clearing sites and making thatching and bamboo frameworks, besides other chores. Most of them fell ill, some severely. They also showed dissatisfaction with the prevailing conditions. They hated the presence of convict guards, who did not permit them to move about freely on the island.

In February 1864 Homfray, who was later to succeed Corbyn and was at the time his assistant, was sent by Tytler to visit Port Mouat on the western coast of South Andaman. He was to explore the possibility of establishing a small settlement there for about 500 convicts; they would help in preventing other convicts from escaping to the west coast, and also help in saving the lives of those who might get shipwrecked anywhere near there. Homfray went to Port Mouat by sea, but he trekked back. As a result, shortly thereafter, a 20-feet-wide track was cleared between Port Mouat and Port Blair. Incidentally, while supervising the cutting of the track, Homfray spent a night in one of the deserted Andamanese villages. A little while later Corbyn, accompanied by a party which included Homfray and the much-valued Topsy, went on an expedition in the same direction. While in the jungle, the party was suddenly surrounded by about 200 Andamanese, fully armed with bows and arrows. They formed a semicircle, all ready for an ambush. Corbyn kept his cool. He took Topsy by the hand and started walking towards one who was obviously their chief. Topsy addressed the chief and pleaded with him not to attack. Somehow, she was able to make him relent. The chief handed over his bow and arrow to Corbyn. Others also laid down their arms. Thanks to Topsy, friendship with this group was established. Corbyn took back with him the chief and two of his associates to Ross Island.

On 15 February 1864, Lieutenant-Colonel R C Tytler, who had been acting in an officiating capacity all along, handed over his charge of office as superintendent to Major Barnet Ford. This change was also to effect the fortune of the Andaman Home, because it soon became clear that Corbyn and the new superintendent did not see eye to eye on many points. This was ultimately to result in Corbyn tendering his resignation. Ford writes:

> On my arrival, I found some forty Andamanese on Ross Island at Mr Corbyn's Andaman Home; visiting these people a few days after I found one ... man in irons—the whole party were, as I later learnt, kept under considerable restraint by a large number of convict "parawallahs" about the Home, and a day or two after Colonel Tytler left the Settlement, Mr Corbyn appraised me of the "escape" during the night of several Andamanese prisoners amongst whom were four of the

principal men of the South Tribe—a tribe he was particularly anxious to keep under restraint, who he wished to keep as hostage, and one of whom was "shackled". Mr Corbyn stated the reason for this to be that they had killed many convicts, (though on enquiry I could not obtain any direct evidence against this particular tribe in this respect), "that they pillaged the Settlement plantations and had recently attacked a party of Officer and Brigadesmen at Port Mouat." This escape was effected in spite of the "strict watch" of the "parawallahs" ordered by Mr Corbyn over the Andamanese, who were "on no account to let them leave the premises without my [Mr Corbyn's] permission".

Corbyn's attitude need not surprise anyone because his views on the subject of the Andamanese were unambiguously stated by him, in a letter to none other than Ford himself, that "of one fact I am quite convinced that, unless we forcibly detain hostages of all the tribes, we shall give free license to a reckless and unreasoning people to damage and destroy wherever their impulse leads them, and to continually provoke bloodshed".

On 1 March 1864, only a few days after Ford had taken over, all the Andamanese—except Jumbo and Topsy—escaped. Jumbo and Topsy could not, because they were arrested just before they could do so. Corbyn wanted to put Jumbo in heavy irons; he could not because Ford opposed it. So Corbyn took him in search of the others, but returned a week later only to find that Topsy too had escaped; the dead body of a woman was found near South Point of Port Blair soon after, later indentified as that of Topsy. Why should she have tried to escape while her husband Jumbo was away with Corbyn? Ford explains:

There were many rumours at this time, that of the severity of the "parawallahs" over the Andamanese, towards them, and in my own mind the opinion has always been strong that these people by their harshness or worse drove Topsy and others with her to escape, but that being weak at the time, she took to the water for the nearest [South] point, and had not the strength to reach it alive.

That was the end of "the much-valued" Topsy.
In a report on this incident, ironically enough, Corbyn tried to explain why, in his opinion, the Andamanese would want to escape: "I am not surprised that these people try to escape considering the discomfort which they have to endure and strong yearning which they must feel for their accustomed mode of life". This was in strange contrast to what Corbyn had said when describing the sight of "no less than 28 Andamanese assembled in the Andaman Home", a sight which had elicited "comments expressive of unaffected astonishment and gratification from crowds of Europeans and Natives who witnessed it", because "their submissive and

orderly conduct, good temper, and the pleasure they evinced, were pledges of good understanding which, if discreetly maintained and not interrupted by acts of violence on our part, will, I am convinced, ripen into an intimacy and warm attachment, and be productive of incalculable blessing both to us and this benighted outcast race, with whom our lot has brought us into contact".

Ford wanted Corbyn to either move the Home away from Ross, or do away with "all the buildings he could spare". Corbyn was offended at this suggestion. (The old Andaman Home was no longer in existence and the Andamanese were living in "cattlesheds and styes".) Corbyn would not accept the suggestions made by Ford, who "in order to retain his services", was every time obliged to "give in to him in a humiliating manner". This state of affairs could not last very long. In June 1864, Corbyn resigned and his resignation was accepted. J N Homfray, assistant to the superintendent, took charge. He had volunteered to do so. Some hold the view that perhaps one of the causes of Corbyn's resignation was the description of the Andaman Home as a place where "caged savages were kept as prisoners under guards of Indian felons" by none other than Lieutenant-Colonel A P Phayre, who was at the time chief commissioner of British Burma and agent to the governor-general.

M V Portman assessed Corbyn's conduct as being "certainly most judicious" and, in his opinion, Corbyn was "very kind to the Andamanese" and also "really fond of them". Although his "repressive measures" were "certainly excessive", according to Portman, "his ideas on the subject were correct, and those same measures, however objectionable and illegal they may have been, overawed them, and gave them a sense of our power, making Mr Homfray's subsequent successful dealings with them easier". At the same time, Portman added:

> The principle mistake in our dealing with the Andamanese at [that] period was, that both the Superintendent and Mr Corbyn appear to have been so taken up in guarding against the ill-doings of the Andamanese, that it never occurred to them to take any precautions against the misconduct of the Naval Brigadesman and the convicts who were associated with the savages in the Home.

He went on to say that it was astonishing that none of the powers-that-be should have suspected "the existence of the misdoings of the Europeans and Convicts" and realized that "the Andamanese required to be protected against us, quite as much as we required to be protected against them".

Before Corbyn left, Ford had made two important decisions in the light of the number of escapes that had taken place from the Home at Ross. He felt that "it was impolitic to restrain them on Ross Island; that they must be free to go and come". But, as that might mean having larger numbers on the island, he decided to have two outpost Homes established. As a consequence, two sites were selected, one in the north and the other in the south on the mainland (of South Andaman, i.e. Port Blair). The other decision Major Ford took was that "the Andamanese should be encouraged to recapture the runaway convicts, and bring them in unharmed, and that a reward should be given for every convict so brought in".

Corbyn had strongly objected to these decisions. He was of the opinion that that would give the Andamanese a "police control" over the convicts, as he put it, and he feared that it might arouse "their worst passions". Nevertheless, as decided by Ford, the Andamanese began to perform duties of what eventually became some sort of a "jungle police".

Another incident involving the Andamanese in one of the outpost Homes had taken place when a gangsman named Gilbur Singh had been murdered by an Andamanese by the name of Jacko. According to Ford, Gilbur Singh had disallowed Jacko to enter the upper floor of a hut where food was kept, and that Jacko had tried to steal some. Gilbur Singh had—at least that was the story commonly believed—merely raised his musket to frighten Jacko but, as soon as Gilbur Singh had turned his back, Jacko had shot at him twice. Gilbur Singh succumbed to his wounds. This led to a strain in the relations between the Andamanese and the authorities. Jacko, along with Moriarty, another Andamanese, fled.

Soon after Corbyn left, the allowance for the Andaman Homes was raised from Rs 100 to Rs 200 per mensem. This, perhaps, had something to do with the visit of Major-General Sir Robert Napier, who had come on an inspection in April 1864 and had approved of the policy that was being pursued with regard to the aborigines. Ford's policy vis-à-vis the Andamanese, however, can best be summed up in his own words:

> We shall never be able, I think, to *civilize* the adult Andamanese that we now know; if we can arrive at a good friendly feeling with them, making them understand that their peaceful conduct will win our regard, whilst hostility will be met by withdrawal of all countenance and benefits; ... if from this we can get one step further and by the strict exercise of good faith with them in all our dealings with them they know that we are to be trusted, this is as much as we can expect from them.

But the next step he suggested was "the educating and civilizing of their children". He, therefore, wanted a school under an army schoolmaster so that the children, after their schooling there, could later be sent to India or Burma. The schoolmaster could teach them the English language and, in conformity with the aim of all Victorians, thus pave "the way for the advent of a missionary and eventual Christianity". Well, fortunately or otherwise, the Andamanese, unlike the Nicobarese, escaped this fate.

After assuming charge, Homfray did collect some boys and tried to win their love and affection, and also made an effort to teach them. But he committed the same error as his predecessor—he also employed convicts to act as guards. And so, a few months later, although he found the boys "obedient, affectionate, and well behaved", they had already become very fond of tobacco. As he admitted, their "craving for tobacco" was "the strongest hold" the authorities had over them.

During the next year or so, Homfray did a lot by way of instilling confidence among the aborigines about the good intentions of the British. He was also able to effect reconciliation among some of the hostile tribes. What is more, he was able to persuade Ford to forgive Jacko and Moriarty, who had been involved in the killing of Gilbur Singh, the gangsman, on the plea that they had been "provoked to do what they did". His argument was that, since they had often seen convicts being ill-treated when they did not do what they were told to, they thought it legitimate to take action against Gilbur Singh when denied food. According to Homfray, the Andamanese hated punishment. After his pardon, Jacko lived with Homfray all the time.

By December 1864, the number of Andamanese living in the Home at Ross was 100, perhaps the main reason being that they were taken to the jungle whenever they wished. Nevertheless, odd encounters between the convicts and the aborigines continued, the aborigines, on one occasion, taking away all the articles they wanted. But in certain cases they were also helping the authorities, for instance when they gave Homfray information about some Burmese convicts who had escaped with fire-arms and were on the point of running away from the islands in canoes. They were also beginning to learn the value of money.

Despite the ostensible friendliness between the British and the Andamanese, no real friendship existed. This is evident from an incident, maybe an isolated one, when, after getting the Andamanese to help erect a Home building for themselves, Ford would not allow them to have a fire there. They refused to live there. Ford had to capitulate. (It may be remembered that the Andamanese like to keep the fire burning always.)

About teaching them to read and write, Ford reported that despite Homfray's great patience he had not been able to make them "count beyond four or five". But, to give Ford and Homfray their due, many more tribes had since been befriended, and the Andamanese were now more or less willing to accept, as Ford reported, "all newcomers on their shores [as] their friends and not their enemies" and their general inclination was that "they should succour them". This was in striking contrast to the time when they had "dreaded the appearance of a sail or the landing of a human being upon their shores with a skin less black than their own". Ford, in his report for the year 1865-66, could further claim with some pride that "since June 1864, there has not been one single act of violence on the part of the Andamanese towards any of the inhabitants of the Settlement".

In the course of the year that followed, however, there was one case of violence—not against the residents of the settlement, but against one of the aborigines. In a fit of rage, an aborigine named Jim killed another man of his tribe. In due course Jim was sentenced to imprisonment, but subsequently released. The importance of this event lies not in the murder or the sentence but in the scene that took place when Jim was released and when Homfray presented him to the assembled aborigines who had come to welcome him back. Homfray described the scene:

After explaining to the men the reason for the assemblage and wickedness of Jim with the punishment attached, and on their promising that the like would not occur again, I produced the prisoner before them in irons. At first meeting, they all fell on him with loud crying, which lasted 15 minutes, overwhelming him with embraces, and several of them were almost trembling for a while for excitement and joy. For three nights he gave an account of his bygone days of confinement, accompanying the recital with acting and dancing according to their custom. Having grown very fat and lazy from his idle life, it was with great difficulty he managed this, frequently being obliged to drink water and take rest. The usual crying being over, the women set to plastering him all over with red earth and lard, which is always done to those who may be going to recite, and perform in these night dances, to prevent chill from the exposure they may go through while heated in the dance, as also as a charm and marked decoration on the occasion. His muscles had become so weak that at times he was obliged to be supported, and in the day, so that he might complete the ceremony, they fastened leaves and cord round his body, to strengthen the muscles, and to keep him from pains and cold. When this was all over, I indulged them with some refreshment, and then they took their leave.

Incidentally, it was during Homfray's regime that the dog was introduced to the aborigines. This came about because the pariah dogs on Ross had multiplied so much that they had become a near plague for the islanders. So several of them were caught and handed over to the Andamanese, who straightaway adopted them as pets and began to use them for pig hunting. They found the dogs most useful during the chase.

The debate over the utility or otherwise of the Homes continued. In August 1867 Homfray was once again asked to give his opinion on the subject. He commented:

The Homes were started with the object of charity only, and with no idea of usefulness. The Andamanese are the original possessors of the soil, and demand from the usurpers some consideration. We have taken possession of these islands to prevent other European powers from taking them, which matters nothing to the aborigines, and on that very account some sacrifice in money is justice to the original inhabitants of the Andamans whose territory we are now supposed to be ruling.

The policy of the administration on the subject of whether or not to allow the aborigines to be in close contact with the convicts, and be made use of to catch the runaway convicts, continued to be ambivalent because Colonel Man, who had taken over from Colonel Ford in March 1868, stated: "The Andamanese had been discouraged from visiting our stations in order to prevent any intimacy between them and the convicts, and had been confined to their Jungle Homes, of which six had been constructed for their accommodation in their own haunts." At the same time, Colonel Man considered the Andamanese as useful for recapturing the runaway convicts, for which they now began to get awards in cash. Homfray was in charge of the Homes for a little over ten years.

Colonel Man was the first one to show concern over their dwindling population. He noticed that in one particular year not one of the infants had survived, although there had been an average of at least two births in the Homes every month.

In December 1874, Homfray handed over charge of the Homes and F E Tuson took over. There is no doubt that Homfray had done some good work. He had succeeded in making friends with most of the Andaman tribes, barring of course the Jarawas. He had also been able to establish an orphanage and a nursery. Whether this was a good idea and whether it achieved any success is a different matter. Homfray was even supposed to have supplemented the government grant for the Homes by contributing from his own pocket a sum that amounted to nearly half his monthly salary. It was also during his charge that the Andamanese were obliged to do a variety of chores, such as looking after the gardens (which they rented from the government) or trading cattle, moving pigs and poultry, and selling forest produce. Some were also employed as boatmen. They did not like it at all. The only saving grace was that the profits thus made by the Andamanese were utilized in augmenting the income of the Homes.

Major-General (later Field Marshal and Commander-in-Chief in India) Donald Stewart, who eventually replaced Colonel Man (because in between Major J L Playfair had acted as chief commissioner for a brief period), acknowledged Homfray's contribution: "It must be admitted that his system of management has been attended with the most favourable results." Indirect praise came from the then secretary of state, the Marquess of Salisbury: "Beneficial results appear to follow from the establishment of Homes for the aborigines."

Meanwhile, once again, an experiment was tried by sending two of the aborigine boys to Calcutta. They were christened "Kiddy Boy" and "Topsy". (Topsy, it seems, was a favourite name with the Englishmen then—both for boys and for girls.) They were placed in Burdwan Boys Orphanage and Church Mission Society. Topsy died of inflammation of the lungs, which he had contracted after he and his companion had "yielded to the invitation of a neighbouring gentleman to display their diving powers in the tank", and served with liquor to warm them and then left "lying on the damp ground in their wet clothes". Kiddy Boy recovered but died some months later of "pulmonary consumption".

On taking over in December 1874, Tuson found that the Andamanese on Viper Island were being forced to work as boatmen and cultivators, and that more than 50 convicts were stationed there just to prevent them from running away and also to see that they worked. Tuson stopped this at once and gave the Andamanese freedom to roam about at will. Of course, in no time they had reverted to their life in the jungle.

In February 1875, barely a couple of months after Tuson had assumed charge, four convicts were murdered at a Home on Kyd Island. It later transpired that some Andamanese had been sent by convicts to collect betel leaves, turtles and shells for them. They had not been able to bring any of these things, but they did bring some sugarcane. The petty officer took away from them the sugarcane but refused to give them any fruit. Earlier, whenever they had brought anything, they were given something or the other in return. This infuriated the aborigines concerned. They went away in somewhat of a sullen mood. But they returned later in the evening, when it was dark, and killed the petty officer and his companions. Months afterwards, some other Andamanese captured the ones that had done the killing, and brought them back. One of them, however, escaped almost immediately after being caught. Five of the other Andamanese involved in the murder were sentenced to six months' rigorous imprisonment and placed in the Viper Jail.

Tuson's term at the Andamanese Homes was short-lived. He was succeeded on 19 June 1875 by Edward Horace Man, son of Colonel Henry Man, who had been the chief commissioner a few years earlier. There was now also a new chief commissioner, Major-General C A Barwell, who had taken the place of Major-General Donald Stewart.

Man continued what had by now become an accepted practice of using the Andamanese to work as carpenters, blacksmiths, cultivators and in various other fields. Of course, they were rewarded for their work. But it soon became quite apparent that they were not interested in this kind of work though, strangely enough, women showed greater adaptability. Anyway, in no time at all, they had made it abundantly clear that they wanted to revert to their life in the jungle, which most of them did.

The Andamanese, along with the police, were now being increasingly used, not only for catching runaway convicts but also those Andamanese who had either committed an offence against their own kind or were inimical to the authorities. In one case, when asked what reward he would like in helping to apprehend certain runaway convicts, Maia Biaha, an aborigine, said he would do so only if those aborigines who were then undergoing sentence for killing the convicts on Kyd Island, were released. It thus came about that they were set free; one of them had already died while in prison. (They had, by then, served two-thirds of their sentence.)

Edward Horace Man's overlordship of the Andamanese Homes is notable for the fact that while he held charge it was discovered that a large number of aborigines were suffering from the dreaded venereal disease, syphilis. It was in the Home at Viper Island, in February 1876, that some inmates were seen to be suffering from a certain kind of sores. They were segregated and put into an empty shed. The first official reaction was that perhaps the sores were due to a lack of hygiene and cleanliness. But on further investigation it became clear beyond any doubt that the Andamanese were all victims of syphilis. Further enquiries revealed that the disease had been prevalent for the past three or four years, and that the main culprit, perhaps the sole one, for communicating it to them was Chief Petty Officer Convict Shera, who had been one of the convicts in charge of the Homes for some years. Shera was immediately put back into the labouring ranks, but this could not have been anything but cold comfort to those stricken by the disease! It was syphilis that ultimately proved the primary cause of the decimation of the Andamanese. Major-General Barwell, in a report submitted to the secretary to the home department of the government of India, wrote:

(1) The convicts attached to the "Homes" were all examined by the Medical Officer in charge of Viper, but with the exception of 1st Tindal Shera, all were pronounced free of disease. Shera... was declared to be suffering from tertiary syphilis in its worst form and has since died of it; (2) In addition to his medical proof he was pointed out to by the Andamanese as the worst offender. He was the head Petty Officer in charge of the Homes attached to this duty for several years without any suspicion being apparently raised; and (3) After a careful inquiry it was also ascertained that the disease had been known to the Andamanese during the past 3 or 4 years, and that some of their women had illicit intercourse with convicts from time to time for several years—a child about 3 years old that was shown to me afforded unmistakeable proof of this.

Instead of accepting the responsibility for being remiss, to such an extraordinary extent, for not conducting medical examination of other convicts—particularly those placed in sensitive places of importance, or those living in the homes—the chief commissioner, in a typically sanctimonious manner, tried to shift the blame on to the Andamanese for what he termed as their "immorality". In the fourth paragraph of his report, Barwell drew the conclusion:

It is clear therefore that the opinion hitherto prevalent, that these people were free from any taint of immorality, is entirely unfounded. Nor does it appear that the immorality which has now been disclosed is the result of their residence in the "Homes", for they stated that they did not in this respect differ from the tribes on the other islands.

A typical Victorian reaction! By now he and his colleagues in the official world should have known that the sexual mores of the Andamanese were not the same as those of the Victorians. The aborigines believed in free love, particularly when unmarried. He should also have known that some of the married women were made to yield quite often by the convicts through sheer intimidation.

Man did not quite realize at first the extent to which the disease had spread. But when he did, it must be said in all fairness to him that he did try to prevent its spread; but it was already too late. Besides, the natural habits and propensities of the aborigines came in the way. The Andamanese hate to be segregated. It was, therefore, difficult to isolate those inflicted by the disease. In any case, the disease had already spread so far and wide that there seemed little chance of being able to control it. One cause of its spread was the habit among Andamanese women to suckle each other's babies. The aborigines, by and large, hated being hospitalized. They would rather live in their own homes than come to the Andaman Homes to get cured in a hospital. Apart from that, they like sleeping together, and this resulted in spreading the infection through abrasions on the skin and open sores. In no time, the disease had spread so extensively that there was hardly any aborigine in Great Andaman who had not been affected.

Apparently, Man himself was no less Victorian in his thinking because, after he assumed charge of the Homes, he had given orders that the aborigines living in the Homes should wear clothes. Not because the clothes would provide protection against the elements, but because their nudity was a cause of offence to the European residents on Ross Island! Typical Victorian prudery! He also anticipated the prohibitionist of our day because, in another order, he stopped the ration of rum which was being issued to them. He wanted them to drink tea. Instead they took to opium, which was to become another cause of their extinction. (The fact today is that since then, in all probability as a result of this puritanical order, they are now so addicted to opium that, despite police vigilance and the isolation of the 24 sole remnants of the Andamanese now living on the tiny Strait Island, they still manage to get their daily dose of opium.)

Man was singularly unfortunate during the time he held charge of the Andamanese. He had hardly recovered from the shock of discovering widespread syphilis among the Andamanese when there was an epidemic of ophthalmia. This resulted in many an aborigine becoming either totally blind, or partially so. Man himself contracted the disease, perhaps through nursing others. And to crown it all, a severe epidemic of measles followed in March 1877. It started with some of the local residents; someone had brought it from the Indian mainland. The first to catch it were some boys in the Andamanese orphanage at Ross. It spread like the proverbial wildfire and, since the aborigines had never known this disease and did not possess any natural immunity to it, hundreds of them died. Man attempted to quarantine the sick, but with no success. According to one estimate, half if not two-thirds of the Andamanese population of Great Andaman died from the effects of measles.

An interesting fact noticed by Man was that it was the healthy and the robust among the aborigines who readily succumbed to measles; the lean and the thin showed greater resistance; many of them survived.

Man was kept very busy with the problems of syphilis and the ravages caused by the outbreak of ophthalmia and measles. But notwithstanding that, he did take time off to improve relations between the administration and the Andamanese—particularly with those in the north, with whom there had not been much contact till then. In May 1877, and again in March 1878, he toured around the islands by sea on the ships *Enterprise* and *Rifleman*, and saw for himself the havoc these diseases had caused. At a number of places he was able to land and offer presents to the tribes living there; in some cases they were even persuaded to come and accept presents on board the two ships. To a large extent, Man was the one who cemented friendship between the northern tribes and the British administration. His work received recognition because, in one of his reports, General Barwell wrote: "It is mainly owing to his [Man's] exertions and tact that such satisfactory progress has been made in our relations with the distant tribes", whereupon the government of India, in one of their resolutions, remarked: "The improved relation with the Andamanese appear satisfactory, and Mr Man's services in this matter deserve special notice."

Man's greater achievement was the work he did in the field of research on the customs and languages of the Andamanese. He compiled a dictionary and later published a monograph on *The Andaman Islanders*. It was the first authoritative work which gave a detailed account of the mores and customs of the aborigines of the Andamans.

On 10 July 1879, E H Man handed over charge of the Andaman Homes to M V Portman. Almost about the same time, there was also a change in the chief commissionership, Major T Cadell relieving Lieutenant-General C A Barwell. (Cadell had served in the Mutiny in Delhi and Oudh and had been decorated for his acts of heroism) Portman describes him as "an extremely energetic officer". Portman was able to establish a rapport with Cadell because, in Portman's words, he "gave [him] every facility for visiting the most distant tribes, and for remaining for weeks together in the jungle with the aborigines". Portman's advent, however, was not a very happy one, because a few months after he took over a murderous attack was made upon him—not by an aborigine but by a convict. Cadell reported:

On the 2nd December 1879, at Viper Island, life convict Tokha, No. 21545, who was working in the chain-gang, without any provocation attempted the life of Mr M. V. Portman by striking him on the head with a "patu" while he was passing the gang in a *Jhampan*. Mr Portman was stationed at the Bay at the time, being in charge of the Western Division, and had only come to Viper in order to visit the Andaman Home.

Before Tokha could repeat the blow he was seized by Ahmed, a convict Jemadar of the Andamanese Department. Mr Portman received a severe wound which rendered him insensible.

The convict was tried and sentenced to be hanged. Portman soon recovered. He travelled a great deal, sometimes alone, or accompanied by Cadell. On his visit to Port Campbell, which is on the west coast, he found that nearly every aborigine living on that coast had died of measles. Accompanied by Cadell and Homfray, he also visited the Middle and Homfray Straits—the former divides South and Middle Andaman and the latter Middle and North Andaman. It was the first time that Homfray Strait had been visited by anyone other than Homfray. (It was christened by them as such.)

After seeing what the sea and the jungle could provide in the nature of natural food in the areas they toured, Cadell remarked: "The sea and forests afford sufficient subsistence for the Andamanese, and it is improbable that they will ever take to agriculture." (And they have not so far.) To them what was most noticeable was the obvious diminution of the aborigine population. They also sailed in the creeks running inland from Kyd Island, and many other places, including Colebrook Passage. But everywhere they went it was the same story so far as the aborigine population was concerned. Cadell, quite rightly, attributed this to the aborigines' "contact with civilisation, and to the consequent ravages of syphilis and measles among them". Portman continued his travels, visiting practically everywhere in the north and south of the Great Andamans. He also visited the surrounding islands. He found, to his great satisfaction, that the Andamanese who were with him as boatmen had "behaved excellently and were hard-working and obedient, though on very short commons".

Apart from those Andamanese who accompanied him on his travels by land and sea, Portman also had quite a few living in his own house whom he "had trained . . . to wait at table, row [his] boat, and do other duties which threw them into daily contact . . . and promoted a great deal of intimacy". He said that in the penal settlement "there were many worse companions than the bright and merry Andamanese!"

Partly because of the traumatic experience of being attacked and wounded by a convict in December 1879, and partly because he had contracted a fever during his travels, Portman's health had broken down. He therefore proceeded on leave at the end of the year 1880 and was succeeded by H Godwin Austin, who held charge till October 1883, when Portman once again took over this assignment, though only for a while. Man took over again, but finally relinquished this charge to go to the Nicobars, as Dr Roepstorff, the man there, had been murdered.

The only interesting comment on the subject of the Andamanese during this period was made by Cadell. In one of his annual reports, he wrote that it was "curious that any Officer who is placed in charge of this department soon becomes interested in, and attached to, the poor savages, however little he may have cared for them before hand". Indubitably, this and other factors had combined to make almost the entire Andamanese population of Great Andaman—except the Jarawas—quite amicably disposed towards the British by now, but the picture as to their survival continued to be a bleak one. Cadell summed it up:

> The friendly tribes of Andamanese are, I regret much to report, rapidly dying out. Great ravages were caused among them by an outbreak of measles in 1876, and syphilis has spread from one end of the Islands to the other. Every year shows a decreasing population, the old and middle aged dying, and no children coming up to fill their places. It may safely be predicted that the friendly tribes will be extinct some thirty or fifty years hence. Intoxicating drinks have been successfully kept from them, but it is thought that over indulgence in tobacco has tended to cause sterility among them.

Cadell wrote this some time in the year 1884. Over 200 Andamanese were living in the Homes at the time, but the birth rate was falling and the number of those dying rapidly increased. During the year 1885-86, there were seven births and 23 deaths. And this despite the fact that they had now taken to sending pregnant aborigine women to the jungle when expecting delivery! That the Andamanese men and women had nonetheless got quite used to life in the Homes was testified by Sir Alexander Mackenzie, home secretary to the government of India, who inspected the islands in 1885. In a memorandum dated 29 December 1885, he wrote:

> The Andamanese [men and women] were very merry and amusing, and favoured us with a display of their remarkable skill in archery and also with a dance and chorus. They are in direct charge of a convict petty officer who speaks their language: but are quite free to come and go as they please. They catch fish, gather shells, spear turtle, hunt pigs, and all that they earn is credited to the Home.

This merriment and amusement was ostensibly something on the surface only, because by now it was a foregone conclusion that the Andamanese were doomed. Attempts to keep them alive continued, but it was like keeping someone temporarily alive with the help of oxygen.

By 1891 all those inhabiting Rutland Island and Port Campbell were dead; a few remained in the rest of South Andaman and in the archipelago in general. But to speed them further to their doom, as it were, there was an outbreak of gonorrhoea in the Andaman Home at Haddo. The British, however, have always believed in the adage that the *show must go on*. So from time to time the Andamanese were taken to Calcutta to show them off and—as hithertofore—while there, they were invariably received by the Big White Man, the reigning viceroy of India. The Andamanese had been tamed, no doubt, but by the time the process was near completion, they were already on the verge of extinction.

16
Befriending the Ongés

The Jarawas and the Sentinelese have all along maintained a posture of hostility. The Ongés were also hostile to begin with, but their hostility was eventually converted into friendship. To trace that story, we have to go back to the year 1867. Till then the Ongés, who live on Little Andaman Island, had escaped the attention of the British because the island was virtually unapproachable. There is generally a heavy surfing in the turbulent seas around it and, till recently, there were no landing facilities. Even Dr Frederic John Mouat, chairman of the Andaman Committee, when in 1857 he was looking for a suitable site for locating a penal settlement, had not attempted to land there.

In April 1867 Major Nelson Davies, secretary

to the chief commissioner of British Burma, happened to be on a visit of inspection at Port Blair. (At the time the Andaman islands were under the administrative control of the chief commissioner of Burma.) He had just finished his inspection and was waiting for a ship to take him back to Rangoon. The *S S Arracan* arrived to do so. In the mail that she brought on board was a telegram sent by the shipping agents, Messrs. Bullock Brothers in Akyab, to their office in Rangoon, which read:

Assam Valley arrived under charge of Chief Officer on 21st [in the month of March] at noon. Captain and seven of the crew ashore on the south end of Little Andaman Island to cut a spur, were seen to land and haul up the boat; an hour afterwards a crowd of natives were seen on the beach dancing. No Europeans were seen afterwards. The ship hovered about till Saturday evening, 23rd, and came on here. Report to authorities.

It was assumed that the Europeans had been murdered. Davies handed over the telegram to Ford, who was then chief commissioner, and directed that the station steamer *Kwang Tung* should at once be despatched to the spot because, according to an accompanying second telegram sent by the same shipping agent, the spot was on "the south end of Little Andaman Island, south-east point bearing east half north, south-west point bearing west by north", which was "a sandy beach, quite bold, with a large rock close to the water's edge". Davies outlined the primary object of the expedition: "To endeavour to recover the missing men, or trace what has become of them, and every caution should be taken by the exploring party to guard against a surprise by the natives. No vengeance should be taken on the aborigines unless proof of the murder of some of the Europeans be clearly established."

Unfortunately *Kwang Tung*, as also Homfray—who was supposed to lead the rescue expedition—were away from Port Blair at the time; Homfray was looking for the wreck of another ship, the *Baillie Nicol Jarvie*. But another ship, the *H M S Sylvia*, happened to be in port. It was therefore decided that she should proceed on this rescue expedition. *Sylvia*, under the command of Commander Brooker, set sail on 16 April. She was, however, back in Port Blair two days later. Brooker had found that it was impossible to land on the spot because of the heavy surf. But he reported that he had been able to espy a coil of rope and a sailor's blue cap. He had fired three rockets and had seen a few aborigines emerge from their huts—though after the ship had withdrawn.

By the time the *Sylvia* came back, the *Kwang Tung* was already in Port Blair. She was immediately despatched to Little Andaman. Homfray, who was to direct the expedition, took with him a few Andamanese. Lieutenant Duncan (Royal Naval Reserve) was in command of the ship. The first two attempts at landing—on two successive days, 18 and 19 April—proved abortive. The next day, Lieutenant Duncan decided to go round the southeast end of the island and anchor there. Three large huts could be seen and, there being no surf, a landing was attempted. That too proved unsuccessful. But finally on the 21st, which was a Sunday, three boats were able to land a party, which included Homfray. The boats, however, retreated back into the deep waters of the sea immediately after. The moment the Ongés saw strangers, they appeared on the scene; their objective was obviously to ward off the retreat of the landing party back to the boats. Homfray's party made a quick about-turn. It was followed by a shower of arrows. Two of the settlement brigadesmen were wounded, one in the calf and the other in the finger. The ship fired back. While the party was still wading towards the boats, more arrows were fired at them. Another volley was fired by the men in the boats. The Ongés dispersed.

Davies was very unhappy at the outcome. He wanted to know for certain whether the crew of the *Assam Valley* were dead or alive. He, therefore, directed that another attempt be made and the *I G S Arracan*, which had come to fetch Davies, be sent to Little Andaman on another expedition. The ship was under the command of Captain Barrow and had two other officers, Dunn and Eastwood. Homfray, of course, went again. As previously, he took a few Andamanese with him. The expeditionary party also included a small military force comprising Lieutenant W L Much of the 2nd battalion of the 24th regiment, in command, with ten men from his regiment, seven naval brigadesmen and eight men belonging to the Madras Sappers. Dr C M Douglas was the medical officer in charge, and Lieutenant Glassford, a newcomer to the penal settlement, went along as a volunteer. Before embarkation, Captain W J Dakeyne, who was commanding the troops in Port Blair, gave the following instructions to the party on board the *Assam Valley*:

Supposing the surf admits of a landing being made; the officer must distribute his men in three parties, two for landing and attack, the third remaining in the boats to give support if needed to those on shore. The two parties on shore should keep together, or if extended at short intervals, give support one to the other, no two men being unloaded at the same time.

Should the surf permit of a landing, but the aborigines oppose the party effecting the same, then certain men previously told off should be directed to open fire, wounding only, if possible, but not killing those opposed to them, and a rush then made to capture the wounded and those making off.

In this way, the object in view, viz., that of obtaining information, may probably be attained.

Should decided hostility be shown, then each man of necessity be compelled to make his firing as telling as possible.

Should the aborigines on the other hand come forward in an

apparently friendly way, (every precaution being taken to guard against surprise) then the service of the interpreter and the Andamanese accompanying him will be brought into play.

The officer Commanding will not under any circumstances move inland further than there is any necessity for, certainly not more than a mile or two, the strength of the party under his command nor yet the equipment of force allowing it.

Since this particular expedition is the only one in British military history which resulted in five of the participants being awarded the most coveted British military award—the Victoria Cross—for not exactly fighting "in the face of the enemy", as stipulated in the Royal Warrant governing this award (for the Ongés had not been officially declared belligerants), the report of Lieutenant Much, who was in command of the venture, makes interesting reading. After returning to Port Blair, he wrote:

We anchored in the East Bay [now known as Hut Bay] at 4.15 p.m. on the 6th [after setting sail earlier that day], and went round the following morning to a place about a mile and a half from the spot where the boat's crew of the Assam Valley are supposed to have captured.

At about 8.30 a.m. I left the ship in the second cutter with a petty Officer and six Naval Brigadesmen, and a Jemadar (Mootien) and four privates of the Sappers, and made for the rock which indicated the spot where the massacre is supposed to have occurred.

The second gig containing Mr Homfray, some Andamanese, and a Havildar and two privates of the Sappers followed.

The first cutter containing one sergeant, one corporal, and eight privates of H.M.'s 2-24th Regiment, with orders to act as coverers to the parties when on shore, followed next.

About 150 yards to the west of this rock the surf appeared to admit of a landing being effected, and Mr Dunn, Officer in charge of the boats, ran the boats in stern on, and on a hint from that officer we all jumped out wading to the shore in about from four and a half to five feet of water, rifles in hand and the ammunition slung round our necks, part of which from the swell on was unavoidably wetted. Being thus landed the second cutter moved off outside the surf. The first thing done on landing was to dry the ammunition.

The Havildar and two privates of the Sappers, who according to orders should have landed with us, were unable to do so, Mr Homfray not bringing his boat in close enough to give a chance; nor yet landing himself any part of the day, which undoubtedly was a great drawback to the success of the expedition, as regards obtaining information as might have been done regarding the fate of those we had come in search of from the wounded aborigines. [Portman's comments: "Not at all,

Mr Homfray and his Andamanese could have done nothing, not being able to talk to the Ongés."] The party under my command, the powder then being dry, moved along the shore in an easterly direction towards the rock, the base of which the water at high tide reached. At about 50 yards' distance from this rock, high and dry on the sand, we found the skull of an European (so pronounced by Mr Douglas) and a little further on an ankle boot, such as is worn by sailors; and beyond, nearer still to the rock, the knees and planking of a boat that was painted white, and inside lead colour. Here too, closer into the jungle, the ground had evidently been cleared for the purpose of cooking.

Proceeding on, past the rock, at a point about 100 yards distant, we noticed a party of aborigines who showed themselves from time to time, as they rose apparently to have a peep behind the bushes skirting the jungle, and who discharged their arrows at us as we approached. Noticing that many were retiring, and as I thought probably with the intention of surrounding us, I threw back the left flank of our party and again moved on. On arrival at the point, so to call it, finding that the ammunition was running short, my own in part damaged, and the rest expended, I signalled to the second cutter to come to shore to take us off. I must here mention that the surf since our landing in the morning had increased considerably and was running some fifteen to twenty feet high.

Mr Dunn in reply to my signal backed the cutter in, but in so doing unfortunately the boat was upset—all hands being washed out of her—some gaining *terra firma*, others being dragged out from the surf, Mr Dunn amongst them much exhausted, and one officer, Lieutenant Glassford of the 9th Bengal Native Infantry, a passenger per steamer *Arracan* from Port Blair, drowned. This occurred at about 11 a.m.

Seeing the fate of this boat I marched the party on towards East Bay in the hope of meeting with a spot from whence to re-embark. The first cutter containing 2-24th men coasting along as we advanced, and firing on the natives who were not visible to us.

About 300 yards on we came across the bodies of four men, the heads of whom, mere skulls in appearance, protruded from the ground, the rest of the bodies being partially covered with sand, but to these bodies I could not give more than cursory glance, my whole attention being given to the critical position in which we were placed from the want of ammunition, the apparent little chance of boats ever reaching us, and the knowledge that in our state with the enemy down upon us in any number, our case was hopeless.

Naval Brigadesman Watson picked up a seaman's blue cotton jacket much torn and rotten, which is brought home.

Between 1 and 2 p.m., finding that the boat with 2-24th men on board, as also other boats, did not follow us, but on the contrary were signalling to us to return, we retraced our steps nearly to the place where we had landed in the morning. Here it was that the first cutter sent a raft;

Mr Dunn, one Naval Brigadesman, one lascar and I got on to it. The raft remained fully five minutes exposed to the violence of the surf, from which we were very slowly hauled out. We proceeded, holding on the best way we could, for about 300 yards from the beach, when a surf larger than usual swept Mr Dunn and myself off. We then struck out for the shore, which we all but reached utterly exhausted, and were dragged out luckily by those standing there. About 30 rounds of ammunition, which had been sent from the ship on the raft, reached us all right. This was a great boon, as we were then reduced to two rounds in all. A fresh attempt to send the raft ashore was made, but without success. About an hour later in the day Dr Douglas, 2-24th Regiment, and Privates Thomas Murphy, James Cooper, David Bell, and William Griffith, gallantly manning the second gig with its secunnie made their way through the surf almost to the shore, but finding their boat was half filled with water they retired.

We also, seeing their approach, attempted to meet them part way, but failed to do so, losing in our endeavours the greater number of our arms, and spoiling what little ammunition we had left.

A second attempt made by Dr Douglas and party proved successful— five of us being safely passed through the surf to the boats outside. A third and last trip got the whole of the party left on the shore safe to the boats, when we all proceeded on board the steamer, which we reached about half past 5 p.m., much exhausted and with little clothing, having had to strip to gain the boats.

Saving Lieutenant Glassford drowned, there were no casualties.

We sailed the following morning [the 8th], reaching Port Blair in the afternoon.

From what I saw myself I should say that there were about 30 aborigines killed. The jemadar, who went into the jungle a short distance, says there were fully 100 killed.

I cannot speak too highly of the manner in which all the party who proceeded on shore behaved, both officers and men of both services. To commence with Dr Douglas, who at the risk of his own life gallantly made three trips through the surf to the shore with his soldier crew. This was accomplished by no ordinary exertion. He stood in the bows of the boat and worked her in an intrepid and seamanlike manner, cool to a degree, as if what he was then doing was an ordinary act of everyday life. Privates Murphy, Cooper, Bell, and Griffiths, his four gallant volunteers, behaved equally cool and collectedly, rowing through the roughest surf when the slightest hesitation or want of pluck on the part of any one of them would have been attended with the gravest results, not only to themselves, but also to the party on shore they were attempting to rescue. I can only express for myself and for those who were with me on shore the deep sense of gratitude felt by all for the services rendered on this occasion by Dr Douglas.

I trust that no opportunity will be lost in bringing to the notice of Government the name of one who to save the lives of others, risked his own.

Although the expedition proved infructuous so far as rescuing the crew of the *Assam Valley* was concerned, because obviously they were no longer alive, Lieutenant Much's despatch shows what hazards the expedition led by him had to face.

The Ongés, apparently, had shown up. There were quite a few of them, as soon as the party from the *Arracan* had landed on shore. They had attacked with a shower of arrows, which was returned by a volley of fire, resulting in a considerable loss of Ongé lives. Then again, when Much and Dunn were trying to get off on the raft, the Ongés had directed their shower of arrows on Wilson and his party, still on shore. Wilson's party had fired back, and more Ongés were killed.

Dr Douglas had found a skull near the the rock and thought it to be that of a European, it being "a large skull" from what he could see of its shape, and "from some of the brains remaining in it". Alexander Wilson, petty officer and Naval brigadesman, reported having seen bodies of four Europeans. According to him, they were "buried in a line close together on the shore with their faces upwards and their feet towards the sea". He said he had counted 57 bodies of the dead Ongés.

Whatever the count, there seems no doubt that the casualties among the Ongés were heavy, whereas the British lost only one man – the volunteer Lieutenant Glassford who, as already stated, had died of drowning. Dunn was to die soon afterwards, but not as a consequence of the expedition.

A special additional "Royal Warrant" had to be obtained from the Queen to award the Victoria Cross to five of those who had participated in the venture. They were: Assistant-Surgeon Campbell Millis Douglas, Private Thomas Murphy, Private James Cooper, Private David Bell and Private William Griffiths, all belonging to the 2nd battalion, 24th regiment. The date of the "acts of bravery" was given as 7 May 1867. The citation read:

For the very gallant and daring manner in which, on the 7th May, 1867, they risked their lives in manning a boat, and proceeding through a dangerous surf to the rescue of some of their comrades who formed part of an expedition which had been sent to the island of Little Andaman, by order of the Chief Commissioner of British Burmah, with the view of ascertaining the fate of the commander and seven of the crew of the ship Assam Valley, who had landed there and were supposed to have been murdered by the natives.

The *London Gazette* quoted Lieutenant Much as saying that "seventeen officers and men were . . . . saved from what must otherwise have been a fearful risk, if not certainty, of death". In addition to the award of the Victoria Cross to Dr Douglas and four privates, Toke Secunnie was awarded two months' salary and Private Wilson, a silver watch and chain. Unfortunately, though, Wilson was never able to receive the watch and chain because, by the time they were received in Port Blair, he had already left – not only Port Blair, but even government service. There were reports there of his having been in Bremen. An advertisement was put in the local papers about him, but he was never heard of again. Jemadar Motien of the Madras Sappers and Miners was admitted to the military Order of Merit.

There was some talk of sending another expedition to Little Andaman Island, to know something more about the missing crew of the *Assam Valley*, but it never materialized. Not much is known to have happened during the next five years, so far as the Ongés were concerned. In April 1873, General Stewart decided to pay a brief visit to Little Andaman. He had hardly come back when a report was received that five members of the crew of a junk *Quangoon*, who had landed in Little Andaman in search of water, had been murdered. Stewart decided that it was time an expeditionary party was organized, ostensibly for rescuing the sailors, if alive, but mainly, it was evident, to punish "the guilty Islanders".

An expeditionary force, comprising the usual paraphernalia, set sail on *IMS Undaunted*. They were not able to find any trace of the missing men. But they really went berserk. As reported by Captain Wimberley, the leader of the expeditionary force, they "decided to burn their houses, which consisted of four huts, each distant from the other about half a mile, and in each of which about 40 men could be accommodated, and one enormous about 60 feet in diameter, and which was capable of holding at least some 150 men". While burning one of their huts they were attacked by the Ongés and had "a sharp fight lasting about ten minutes". Naturally enough, the *Enfields* and *Sniders* won. They were able to take one prisoner. (He subsequently died while in the custody of De Roepstorff.) Two of the Indian privates were injured, one of them seriously. This was followed by the burning of "the remaining huts". All attempts to learn the language of the captured Ongé, while in captivity, proved utterly unsuccessful.

Stewart persisted in his belief that the Ongés, like the Great Andamanese, could be brought under the influence of British "rule"; the usual method of paying occasional visits and leaving "presents" for them was tried. Ultimately Stewart, quite rightly, came to the conclusion that "the system of making hurried visits of a few hours at long intervals does little good, and that much time and patience will be needed if [they were] ever to make friends of these savages". And yet nothing more was done for another seven years!

After Colonel Cadell took over as chief commissioner in early 1878, he and Portman (the new officer in charge of the Andamanese), accompanied by other officers and some Andaman islanders, started paying periodical visits. They would go and leave presents for the Ongés. In most cases the presents were collected by them. There was no serious clash. After returning from a visit to Little Andaman in April 1884, Portman recorded: "This trip has been most satisfactory in every way. It is the first time on record that a lengthened visit has been paid to the Little Andaman without our coming into collision with the inhabitants." After another visit in January 1885, there is a distinct note of cheerfulness in Portman's writings. Accompanied by Cadell, he describes how, after he had sent some Andamanese to leave presents for the Ongés,

> about 30 Ongés appeared, some of whom left their bows and arrows and came out in the water towards us. My people swam to meet them and succeeded in persuading one boy, aged about fourteen, to come into my boat. He did not seem frightened, and after keeping him for about ten minutes I sent him ashore with a lot of presents.

They were even able to bring back with them an Ongé named Taleme, "a fine well-built youngman of about 22 years of age".

On another visit, this time to Great Cinque Island, they were able to capture 24 men, women and children, 15 of whom were released soon after. Portman considered this as very important, because those captured were able to converse with the Ongés of Little Andaman. During a trip there the next year, in March 1886, Portman spent the day on shore "dancing, singing and playing about" with them. He attributed this friendliness to their "having captured those Little Andamanese at the Cinque Islands in February 1885, and having kept them for nine months in [his] house, where they were well treated". They had, therefore, become quite friendly.

Presents were now being left at Little Andaman every fortnight. They consisted of "irons of all kind, files, turtles, pigs, red cloth, plantains, coconuts, and yams". Portman believed that the presents should "always be given in large quantities".

So began a period of friendship between the British and the Ongés. (Today they are the friendliest of people.) The credit for this must be given to Portman who, on one occasion, spent as long a period as two months in Little Andaman with the Ongés.

The smooth flow of friendship, however, suffered a slight setback. During a visit in March 1887, Murray, who was chief engineer of the ship *Kwang Tung*, was stabbed while looking at some fish on the beach. There was a sudden thud, and Murray cried out: "I am killed!" The attack appeared unpremeditated. Murray survived, and the Ongé concerned was captured the next day, taken to the ship, "tied up to a gun and given twenty-four stripes". But while being taken to Port Blair on board the ship *Ross*, he got "his hands free from the handcuffs, and once, although his feet were manacled together, slipped overboard and tried to swim to the shore, but was caught by one of [the] Andamanese". In Port Blair, according to Portman, "he was kept under the Chief Commissioner's house, guarded by Andamanese, and seemed fairly well, though he suffered from the wounds caused by the flogging he had received".

Portman and others, in one case Edward Horace Man, continued to visit Little Andaman, and often used to bring some Ongés with them, returning them back after a short stay; some Portman kept for a month or more "in order that they might learn a little Hindustani".

It was in 1896 that a doctor, Assistant-Surgeon Chitts, on one of the ships, the *Elphinstone*, came across a case of condylomata, and came to the conclusion that the Ongés suffered from hereditary syphilis. He was of the opinion that the disease must have been introduced in the remote past. The cynicism, of even a man like Portman, where the "natives" were concerned, can be gauged from his comments on the subject:

> Of course the fact of syphilis being among them has to a certain extent modified our policy towards this tribe. Formerly, our one object, after friendly relations had been established with them, was to prevent them from mixing with the convicts and other Andamanese, and contracting the disease, but now there is no objection to their going about the Great Andaman with other tribes, and there will be no objection to our keeping parties of them up here all the year round.

Incidentally, many years earlier, in 1886, while on a visit to Little Andaman, Portman records having seen "very curious sores on the bodies of the Ongés". But he did nothing about it. In December 1888, during another visit, he saw "one boy with sores at the corners of his mouth". He brought him to Port Blair, and it was diagnosed by the doctors as "sores of constitutional syphilis". He was treated and the malady readily yielded to treatment. But, once again, no steps were taken to save the rest of the Ongés from this scourge!

At the end of January 1895, among those included in a 15-man party of Andamanese being taken to Calcutta, were four Ongés. Calcutta was in the grips of a smallpox epidemic. They therefore saw nothing of the city, except the museum and the zoological garden. Of course, they were received by His Excellency the viceroy, the Earl of Elgin, at Government House in Kharagpur. According to Portman, who took the party, they enjoyed their visit to the viceroy's house, as they were able to get "a good view of the railways, buildings, and bridges, as well as the native fishing craft, etc". He does not say whether their reaction was any different from that of the other Andamanese who had been taken to Calcutta on previous occasions.

After befriending the Ongés and getting to know them rather well, Portman comments: "The Ongés appear to be the least conservative of the

Groups of Tribes, being apparently ready to exchange their own customs for anything which they find to be better." Maybe that is why, comparatively speaking, they have managed to survive so far. But for how long? This is a question for which neither the anthropologists nor anyone else has been able to find an answer.

17

The Untamed Jarawas

The first recorded reference to the Jarawas is contained in the journal kept by Lieutenant Robert Hyde Colebrook (who was to end his career in India as surveyor-general). He made a voyage around the Andamans in 1789-90, in the company of Commodore (later Sir) William Cornwallis, brother of the then governor-general of India, Lord Cornwallis. In an entry dated 26 December 1789, he writes about going up the harbour in Port Cornwallis (now Port Blair). When they "went ashore to look at a hut which appeared to be inhabited", they found it deserted. He wrote:

It was a most wretched little shed, built of sticks and leaves. We found in it some bones, which appeared to be those of a wild hog, suspended to the roof by strings. The ground about the hut was strewed with the shells of oysters, mussels, cockles, and other shell-fish. In returning down the creek, we discovered one of the natives in a tree. The instant he perceived us he ran down with as much agility as a monkey, making a great noise, and calling to two others who were below. One of them we took to be a woman, by her voice, as we could not see her.

In the afternoon, seeing "one of the natives", they stopped "to hold a conference with him". According to Colebrook: "He was a man of the middle size and tolerably well shaped". Colebrook goes on to say: "His wool was rubbed with a kind of red earth, and the rest of his body smeared with mud. He wore round his neck and left arm a kind of ornament which looked like a fringe of dried grass."

In a subsequent monograph, published in the *Journal of the Asiatic Society of Bengal* in 1794, Colebrook again writes about the aborigines he encountered during this particular voyage: "They go quite naked, the women wearing only at times a kind of tassel, or fringe, round the middle; which is intended merely for ornament, as they do not betray any signs of bashfulness when seen without it."

Those who have seen the Jarawas in recent years will find a ring of authenticity in this description. Besides, in the specimen vocabulary of the Andamanese language that Colebrook had compiled and which he published in this monograph, Portman found that nearly half the words he had picked up belonged to the language of the Jarawas!

It is evident, therefore, that the aborigines with whom Lieutenant Blair and others in his administration were on friendly terms included the Jarawas of the South Andamans. Furthermore, in all probability, those taken to Calcutta in 1790 too were Jarawas. And according to Portman, many of the kitchen-middens (near and surrounding the present Port Blair) that he saw were in areas where the Jarawas had lived, because what they contained—as pointed out to him by the rest of the Andamanese—were remains of the sort of things which only the Jarawas eat, things the other Andamanese would not even touch.

Due to some unknown reasons, the Andamanese (as we know them now) had become far stronger by the time of the second occupation, and had occupied almost the entire land around the harbour, having driven the Jarawas into the hinterland. There was constant fighting between the two groups. And Jarawa hostility grew as the British became more friendly with the Andamanese; it soon began to manifest itself against the British in an obvious and concrete manner.

Quite possibly, it was at the time of the first occupation that Blair's men communicated venereal disease to the Jarawas. That may have been one of the causes of the diminution of the Jarawas in numbers, as compared to the rest of the Andamanese at the time.

In July 1863, as is already known, Corbyn led a party to find a passage through the interior from Port Blair to the other side on the western coast. They did not come across any Jarawa as such, but two of the Andamanese, Topsy and Jacko, gave Corbyn to understand that there was a possibility of their encountering "an unfriendly tribe of aborigines of whom they themselves seemed to be in great dread". Ford, in a report written on 3 January 1865, stated that "the aborigines inland on the south side were the most troublesome". It is obvious that he was referring to the Jarawas. A little less than two years later, in March 1867, Homfray was to write:

> I had occasion, in pursuit of runaways, to visit the North Sentinel Island, a distance of about 25 miles to the westward of Port Mouat, with some Andamanese accompanying me. We saw some ten men on the beach, naked, long haired, and with bows and arrows, shooting fish. My friends told me that they were "Jurrahwallahs", who were not friendly to them, having some years past encountered some of the tribe on Rutland Island in which their Chief was wounded.

As it was discovered subsequently, and as is known today, those inhabiting North Sentinel are definitely Jarawas. And they are the most hostile of them all.

Chief Commissioner Stewart mentions the Jarawas when, in a report dated 9 August 1873, he wrote: "They are never found on the coast of the Mainland, and they are not on friendly terms with the tribes we know." All along Stewart had been very anxious to catch one of the Jarawas. He was successful in getting two of them. He describes how:

> The two Jarawas were cleverly caught by Goodur, the convict Jamadar of the Homes. He took out a volunteer party of convicts from Viper, with three days' provisions, proceeded to Jarawa country, and came upon a party of about fifty of these people dancing. Goodur concealed his men in the jungle and told them not to move till he called out, and then walked in among the Jarawas, holding up a pair of looking-glasses. The Jarawas bolted, one man stopping for an instant to examine the glasses and thus being caught. He called to his friends to help him, and after some hesitation these turned and threatened battle, but seeing so many convicts, whom Goodur had now called up, they all bolted without drawing a bow. One unlucky little woman who could not run, being big with child, was also caught. These people were kept for a fortnight, treated with the greatest kindness, and let go where they were caught with a quantity of presents.

Portman, commenting upon this, says that "they were much more well-disposed towards us than now are". He thought "it was a pity that the matters were not pushed on with them, and friendly relations established".

In December 1875, six convicts were captured by the Jarawas. Five of them returned after being kept in captivity for 19 days. Early next year, two expeditions were sent in search of the Jarawas. The Jarawa huts were looted and their weapons and utensils brought back. Of course, as a sort of compensation, some presents were left in the huts but, according to Portman, the presents were unsuitable because they consisted of "matches, pipes, tobacco, and looking-glasses, the uses of which were unknown to these savages".

There were further expeditions in July 1876 and in June 1877, but these proved fruitless. But another one, in April 1878, resulted in the capture of a Jarawa woman and two small children. Within 24 hours of the capture, however, the Brigade Creek Home in which they were housed was attacked by the Jarawas; it resulted in the Andamanese living there getting quite worked up. Man, then in charge, released the woman and children with a quantity of presents.

North Sentinel Island was left alone for nearly 13 years, and it was only after Portman had taken over that he and Chief Commissioner Cadell paid a visit there in January 1880. But they only saw tracks and some villages of the Jarawas. Nothing else. Portman, however, paid another visit on board the *I G S Constance*, and stayed there for a fortnight. One day, he was able to capture a woman and four small children. They were kept on board the *Constance* for a few days, and the woman and two children ultimately released with the inevitable "quantity of presents". A few days later, while in the company of Lieutenant Hooper of the *Constance*, Portman had another encounter, this time with an old man who was with his wife and child. Writes Portman:

Our party were spread out in crescent form, and the Jarawas came to the centre where Lieutenant Hooper and I were. The old man had drawn his bow and was about to fire at Lieutenant Hooper's head when my convict orderly, a Pathan, named Amirullah, who had been stationed at the right point of the crescent, and had got behind the Jarawas, jumped on his back and spoilt his aim. We caught the three unhurt and brought them on board. The next day we took the six Jarawas to Port Blair, where I kept them at my house for some days. They sickened rapidly, and the old man and his wife died, so the four children were sent back to their homes with quantities of presents.

On 20 May, a few months later the same year, Portman once again set out for Constance Bay on a steam barge, taking with him 30 convicts and 120 Andamanese. He camped there for nearly three weeks. The weather being anything but good, he did not meet with much success, except that one day one of the convicts, 1st Tindal Nureddin, who had gone out with a few Andamanese to "look in the hills", returned with one old man, three women and six children. They were taken to Port Blair and Portman kept them with him at Viper. They too sickened and had to be released after a fortnight.

And so it went on—trouble with the Jarawas, followed by expeditions, some captures, and then, inevitably, their release. In his annual report for the year 1882-83, Godwin-Austin (who had temporarily taken over from Portman during the latter's absence on leave) wrote: "The Jarawas have given much more trouble during the past year than hitherto." And perhaps, he surmised, this was due to the fact that "much had been done in the way of opening out tracks through their country".

Many a time in the years that followed, clashes of one kind or the other took place, because it became more and more clear that the Jarawas distrusted everyone, particularly the other Andamanese; they were also in no small measure inimical to the convicts. Attempts to capture them were ultimately unsuccessful because, even when one or two of them were captured and brought and kept in the Andaman Home, they either died after being sick for a little while, or they just sickened and had, therefore, to be released. There was always the odd incident—like when one of the women (out of the two captured by a party of the Andamanese, some convicts and the police on 7 April 1885) fell for one of the Andamanese boys named Mark and tried to persuade him to go back with her. (Mark, however, did not respond to her overtures.) This was a rare case, because normally, there was no love lost between the Jarawas and the Andamanese.

Another Jarawa captured later that year, whose name was Ike, even learnt some Hindustani and appeared to be on quite friendly terms with the Andamanese. When he was being released, he was given "everything he fancied", as Portman put it, in the hope that "he would turn up again and that the kindness he had received had produced an impression on him". But these hopes were belied because a little while later, during a skirmish between the Jarawas and the Andamanese, Ike picked up everything that he could from the Andamanese camp and also indulged in abusing them in the very Hindustani he had learnt during his captivity. Portman writes in his annual report for 1890-91:

> Were I able to get amongst these people [the Jarawas], as I did at the Little Andaman, I have no doubt that in time friendly relations could be established with them, but it is hopeless to try and tame people whom one cannot even see. Few in number, they roam over a large tract of thick jungle, occasionally appearing on the coasts, or visiting the confines of the Settlement and murdering any convicts they may meet. When pursued, the tribe separates into parties of two or three, moving with great rapidity; and on the few occasions we have met with them the meeting has been accidental. The few Jarawas we have caught in the

last ten years, treated well, and returned to their tribes, have not had any effect on our relations with the others.

But Portman had not given up hope. He thought that "by moving parties of Andamanese about in the Jarawa country with strict orders not to show any hostility to the Jarawas", he would "accustom" them to the presence of the rulers, and because: "Eatables, and such articles as they are likely to value, were left in their villages, and none of their property was touched; by such means I am in hopes that friendly relations may be established, as they will learn that we do not molest them, and our advent means to them a supply of the articles they most require." But by 1895 he seems to have given up hope. In the annual report for the year 1894-95, he writes:

> I am of the opinion that the only way to catch the Jarawas will be by sending out armed parties of Police and convicts, as was done on former occasions when they were caught, and using our Andamanese merely as trackers, as they are too afraid of the Jarawas to make any real effort to catch them when alone and unsupported by fire arms.

He explained his return to the big-arm policy by stating:

> There are few Andamanese now alive who are acquainted with the Jarawa country, and those few are old. The jungle, too, has, since the cyclone of 1891, been almost impassable, and in any attempt to capture them, the Jarawas have in every way the advantage of us, nor do I think that, except by some lucky chance, any capture will be made.

He felt that the Jarawas on North Sentinel Island could be tamed, but only "if the Government decide to convert the whole Island into a coconut plantation" and, if they are to be "tamed for scientific or other reasons", then:

> the Officer in charge of the Andamanese should take a steam launch, a lighter with water tanks, a sailing cutter, and some Andamanese canoes over there in the month of February, anchor them in the lagoon on the south side of the Island, and remain there for about two months. Search parties should go through the jungle and catch some of the male Jarawas unhurt, and should keep them in the camp, taking them out turtle catching, and feeding them on turtle, yams, and such food only as they are accustomed to in their own homes. They should be given presents, and half the number caught should, after a few days, be allowed to return to their villages.

Portman suggested a similar policy as far as the Jarawas on Rutland

Island were concerned. But there is nothing on record to show whether or not the policy or the methods suggested by him were ever put into effect. However, the fact remains that the Jarawas of North Sentinel Island happen to be the unfriendliest of them all.

Portman handed over charge of the Andamanese in 1899 and, after a brief interregnum when E H Man was once again in temporary charge, P Vaux, who was then the deputy commissioner in Port Blair, took over in 1901. If anything, the Jarawas became even more unfriendly, perhaps because more jungles were being cleared and there were further encroachments into what they considered to be their domain. There were murders of the convicts employed in the jungles and of those in the service of the forest department. Therefore in 1902, Sir Richard Temple, chief commissioner, decided to send a punitive expedition against the Jarawas. Vaux was in charge of the expedition, and he was accompanied by Rogers, the deputy conservator of forests, and Bonig, assistant harbour master. Vaux was to lose his life in the course of this expedition. Bonig, who kept a daily diary while on the expedition, described the circumstances under which Vaux was fatally wounded and succumbed to his injuries:

24th February (1902)—Left camp at 7.30 a.m. with Messrs Vaux and Rogers, one policeman, three convict servants and sixteen Andamanese. We followed up the Jarawa track and came on the encampment about 9 o'clock. We proceeded on our way and came on another encampment an hour later. As the Jarawas had apparently only just left this, we did not disturb it, for fear of disclosing our whereabouts to the Jarawas, should they be in the neighbourhood. After having rested a little while, we proceeded very slowly till at about 11 a.m., we heard the Jarawas shouting a short distance ahead. Mr Vaux then decided to wait till the evening until the Jarawas had gone to sleep and to attack their encampment as soon as the moon rose. So we waited there the whole day, and when the moon rose we proceeded very slowly to the attack, a few Andamanese going ahead; and Mr Vaux and Mr Roger and myself holding each other's hands so as not to lose ourselves in the dark, slowly crept up to the Jarawas camp. As soon as we got near the camp we waited for a second and when Mr Vaux passed the word, the Andamanese shouted and shot a number of arrows in the Jarawa huts. Mr Vaux then at once with his *dah* in his hand rushed to the nearest hut on the left, while Mr Rogers went to the right and I went straight ahead. When I had advanced a few yards the Andamanese Golat shouted out to me *Sahib, baito, Jarawa tir marta hai, bandook maro* (Sir, please sit down, the Jarawa is shooting an arrow, you should fire): so as I lay down flat on the ground, and not seeing any Jarawa about I fired my revolver in the air. I had not done this before, as Mr Vaux had previously ordered us not to fire till he passed the word. I then saw several children come out of the hut behind which Mr Roger had disappeared. I crept up and secured these with the help of an Andamanese. I then heard Mr Vaux shouting "I am hurt", and turning round I saw him staggering and fall down. I at once went to him, and asked him where he was hurt, Mr Vaux replied "I am done", and the Andamanese showed me that he was wounded by an arrow in the left side. Mr Vaux then said "For God's sake take this arrow out." As I saw that the whole of the arrow head had disappeared in his body, I went for Mr Roger's assistance. I found Mr Roger struggling with a Jarawa woman, and he said he could come in a second, as he did not wish to let the woman go. I then returned to Mr Vaux. The Andamanese were just extracting the arrow and Mr Vaux asked for Mr Roger and myself as if we could do anything for him. As Mr Roger had not turned up then, I became anxious about him, thinking that the Jarawas might have wounded him also. I went to him again and told him that I thought Mr Vaux was dying. We both went back to Mr Vaux, who was only a couple of yards away. We bandaged him up. Mr Vaux asked for light and water, which we gave him. After this Mr Vaux fell back and died. We then awaited in the Jarawa camp till the morning, firing a gun every half an hour to keep the Jarawas away.

It is patently clear that this "punitive" expedition gained nothing. They lost an officer and were not able to capture a single Jarawa. As R F Lowis, who conducted the 1911 census and obviously reflected the official view, put it, this was because "members of the expedition attempted to achieve their end without bloodshed: their object being to capture alive, and bring into the Settlement, as many members of the hostile tribe as they could secure, in order to have an opportunity of impressing them with our power, and also with our friendly intentions towards them." What a paranoia complex about impressing the poor natives with the mighty power of imperial Britain! But according to Lowis: "The expedition into the Jarawa country undertaken in 1902 had for a time an excellent effect on the tribes; but as time passed and the matter was forgotten, they recommenced their malpractices."

So, in 1901, another punitive expedition was organized. It was headed by Fawcett, who was in military command, and comprised a large force. Bonig, who was a member of the previous punitive expedition of 1902, also accompanied this one. It lasted from 14 March to 22 April 1910. But nothing of any importance seems to have been achieved. Not a single Jarawa was captured, although they were able to surround their encampment on 20 March. This is how Fawcett describes the incident in his diary:

Everyone was ready to surround the Jarawas at 3 p.m. but they did not seem to have returned to their huts. At 4.45 p.m. we could still hear no noise, so we sent out 3 Andamanese to see what had happened. These

Corbyn's Cove.

Cellular Jail.

Ruins at Ross.

Great Andamanese on Strait Island ... and their raja.

Timber afloat in a creek.

An Ongé Grand Dame smoking a pipe made out of crab's claw.

Harpooning the fish.

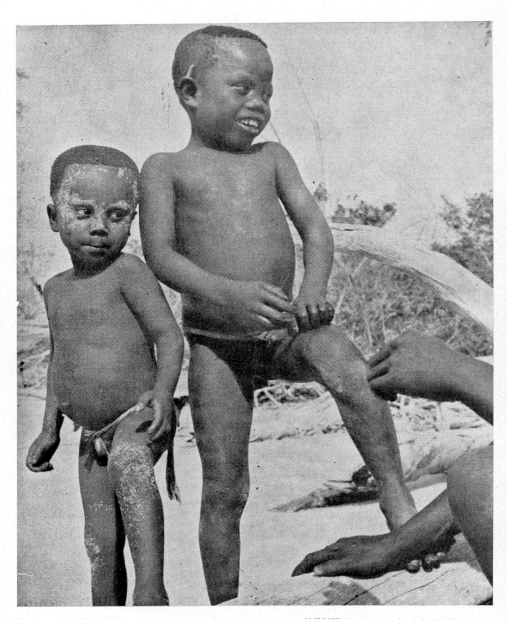

The young ones.

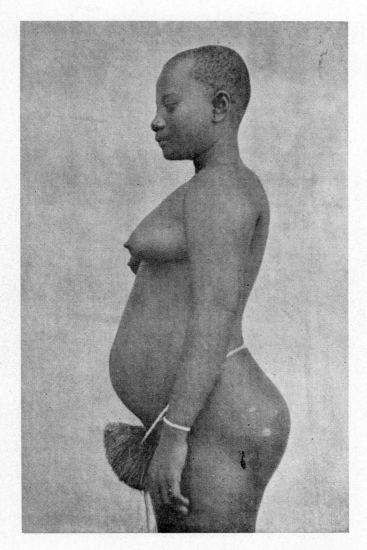

Statue in ebony.

An Ongé hut.

The family within.

Another happy family.

A Jarawa comes aboard.

A trio.

Outside his habitat.

A couple decorating themselves.

The Ongés are amused.

A Jarawa foursome.

A Nicobari canoe for racing. In the foreground is an ordinary canoe, with its outrigger.

The pig is their wealth.

A Nicobari hut.

Nicobari devils.

Bishop Richardson.

A Nicobari damsel.

The nutritious Pandanus.

The Shompens of Great Nicobar.

Three brothers.

A proud mother.

Saudagar : he lived to tell the tale.

Mercy ship ; the I N S Narbudda.

Seas and skies.

Port Blair.

returned at 5.15 p.m. saying that no Jarawas had yet arrived, but they could hear them returning. We gave them another 15 minutes and then commenced to surround them. It was about 5.40 when two parties went right and left. It took some time moving off as every man was told to go 10 yards apart and as quietly as possible. The Andamanese were in the majority in front and the tails of the lines were entirely sepoys, also Burmans helped to surround. As soon as we had commenced to send off our two parties we heard the Jarawas breaking wood and shouting. When the two lines had divided right and left we got the two tails together and marched straight on the Jarawas; we were directed by their dancing which grew louder as we advanced. We seemed to be making a terrible noise crashing through the jungle. At last Mr Bonig and I had arrived within about 15 yards of the nearest hut. Not until this minute did they hear us, in spite of the noise. Mr Bonig wanted me to give the signal for the firing at once, only I waited about 3 minutes as I was not sure whether the flanks would round; as it happened this wait was unfortunate as it enabled the Jarawas to collect their bows and arrows]. I fired my gun in the air which commenced the firing which was carried on round both flanks. The noise was deafening. It was unfortunately now quite dark and very difficult to distinguish people. A general advance was made on the huts and the firing continued. It was at this moment that the Jarawas escaped.

Fawcett explained the failure thus: "This was a difficult position to surround and it was almost impossible in this country to keep the distance of the men of the surrounding parties equal. The darkness was solely responsible for the failure. If we had been 15 minutes earlier I believe we would have caught every man."

The British still hoped that the Jarawas had learnt a lesson!

The only effect it had was that for a while their activities were largely restricted to their own territories, but the odd raid continued to take place. However, once again, in 1917, their raids became so daring that in one case a train on a tram line was held up. So yet another punitive expedition was organized.

D L Morgan was the leader of this one, and his party consisted of 12 Andamanese, 16 policemen and 35 coolies. He has left a description of his encounter with the Jarawas, which took place on 26 February 1918:

At 7.30 a.m. we came across a pool of running water, and almost immediately afterwards heard the Jarawas ahead of us. The Andamanese fell back, and with 5 sepoys I crept along the nullah. Before we came within killing distance, the Jarawas heard us and raised the alarm. One of these voices was peculiarly like an Indian. We rushed towards the village. Abandoning everything the Jarawas fled headlong into the jungle. I saw an unclothed woman with her child—a Jarawa youth with red cloth round him and a full-grown Jarawa. I put two barrels of buck shot into the last at about 15 yards distance. He dropped his bow and arrows, but slipped into the jungle. Sepoy Kirpa wounded a Jarawa with buck shot at close range. The men behind were armed with rifles— I do not think they hit anybody. There was a great deal of blood in the nullah, and the Andamanese followed this for a while. They (the Andamanese) then came to a running stream and some thick jungles and the track was lost.

Morgan does not say whose blood this was, but it must have been that of the wounded Jarawa.

Morgan also described the Jarawa village: "The village consisted of 10 huts, inhabited by 20 to 30 Jarawas. Each hut was about 3 feet high and 6 feet square. The diameter of the village was about 20 yards. There was thick jungle on all sides, a small nullah running down one side." He said he had been able to destroy two communal huts, but does not specify whether there were any Jarawas inside the huts at the time of destruction. Morgan went on to report:

I came across over 20 old Jarawa villages. Each village had between 7-15 huts. The jungle is full of well beaten tracks. Each of the two communal huts which we destroyed was capable of holding 100 persons. There were several women and children in the village which we raided on the 28th of February. Wherever we found grown-up Jarawa footprints we also found footprints of their children. We recovered a large number of nets and small bows. The nets are made by the Jarawa women, and the small bows are used by the children.

In Morgan's opinion, the number of Jarawas was considerably larger than what had been estimated earlier. He felt certain that "30 Burmans armed with guns and daos, with some Andamanese to track them, would wipe out every Jarawa in the place in 2 or 3 years". It is evident that the administration did not share his view, because no attempt to wipe them out with the help of Burmans "armed with guns and daos" was made.

The Jarawas continued with what had become their normal activity of attacking the convicts. In one such raid they attacked a camp of convicts working on the collection of cane, killing five and wounding three. And this camp was supposed to be in an area considered by the British as outside the territorial limits of the Jarawas. So one more punitive expedition. The officer who commanded this one was C G Fields. He was accompanied by Baines, another officer, a party of 15 policemen, six Andamanese and 40 convicts. Fields wrote in his diary about the happenings on 8 March 1921:

Set off at 7 a.m. with eight Police, 20 convicts and 5 Andamanese. At

9.30 a.m. we suddenly came on a big camp half way down a hill and at the head of a fresh water nullah. The camp was empty, but according to the Andamanese it had been occupied about three or four days previously. We spent half an hour three collecting any material we could find. There were twenty huts, small leaf affairs, each occupied by two people. Among the things found was an old strip of cloth with blue convict stripe on it. This was only an evidence procurable to show these particular Jarawas had been engaged in any of the recent raids on the settlement. No traces were found to indicate that there were any runaways living with them. From this camp, two well defined paths—one northwards towards the creek, and the other southwards .... As this party of Jarawas had gone northwards we followed after them. At 2.30 p.m. we came down to the creek after very hard marching through the densest jungle. I decided it was time to look for fresh water, and a suitable place to camp. We followed the creek for about a mile until we came to a place where a small nullah branched off. My three leading Burmans and one Andamanese went up this nullah to see if there was any fresh water there, while the rest of the party halted, Mr Baines, the Sub-Assistant Surgeon and myself were seated within five yards of each other, the convict porters altogether slightly behind us, and the Police as usual when a halt was made, all round. The Burmans had hardly gone five minutes, when we heard a cry of *"Bandooq lao"*. [Bring the gun.] Mr Baines and I jumped up with the intention of taking the Police forward as fast as we could, when the Sub-Assistant Surgeon lost his head and fired his shot gun in the air. Immediately after the Police Havildar hearing one shot fired from near where Mr Baines and I had been seated, and realising that the Jarawas were somewhere about thought that I had given orders to fire. By the time I had found out the real reasons for these two shots being fired, and had prevented further firing; the Burmans had rejoined our party in considerable state of excitement. It appears that they had run into a party of 8 or 9 Jarawas about 200 yards up the nullah. The Jarawas had jumped up and pursued them; and were close behind them rapidly approaching our main party when the two shots were fired; at once they turned and fled. By the time we reached the spot where the Burmans had first seen them there were no traces of them; nor could our Andamanese pick up any definite tracks; as the jungle they had taken was hard and leaf strewn. After casting round for about three quarters of an hour or so, we decided that nothing more could be done, as it was then about 4 p.m. and our porters were about tired out. In fact it was felt to be useless trying to run down this particular party now that they knew we were armed with firearms. The whole expedition had been vain.

This "expedition had been vain", Field admitted, but so had been the previous ones, and one would have thought that the government would have realized that to lead punitive expeditions against the Jarawas was no way of solving the Jarawa problem. That way they had neither been able to tame, nor terrify, nor befriend them. To terrorize them into submission, they thought, was the only answer. As time would show, this was not going to succeed.

The years following 1921 witnessed an increase in the activities of the Jarawas. They began to come more frequently into the settlement area, waylaying people: in the course of the next three years as many as 21 convict settlers were killed by them. So in 1925 one more punitive expedition was mounted. The services of a special military officer, Captain West, were placed at the disposal of the administration to lead this expedition. He was also provided with a platoon of 30 Kachin military police. This is what happened:

> Captain West divided his party into a number of patrols which started operating simultaneously at Alipur, Jatang, Middle Strait, Ike Bay, and the Northern extremity of South Andaman. These patrols came into contact with the Jarawas on eight occasions during the four months they were out. The principal attack by Jarawas on one of the patrols was at Ike Bay. Some 40 Jarawas participated in the attack and the shouts of a man among them in Burmese proved the presence of a runaway. During the course of the operations thirty-seven Jarawas were claimed to have been shot and were seen to have dropped, but only six were actually found dead.

As with previous expeditions, this one did not put a stop to Jarawa raids either. To contain the Jarawas in their own territory—at least what the rulers had decided was Jarawa territory—the British had also organized a Bush Police in the year 1905. It comprised a few selected, friendly Andamanese with a Burmese as their head. The Bush Police was to expand a great deal in later years and, eventually, it was to be a Bush Police officer who would break the ice and establish some rapport with the Jarawas.

18

Penal Settlement—to be or not to be

The Andaman penal settlement was often described as being *sui generis* which, in English, means that it had developed on its own volition. The first person to describe it as such was Lieutenant-Colonel Sir Richard Temple, who was in effect the chief commissioner and superintendent at the turn of the century—from 3 August 1893 to 9 May 1903. As a matter of fact, the term *sui generis*, strictly speaking, is not quite correct. The penal system in the Andamans was inspired by the concept of a penal system as propounded by Sir Stamford Raffles who, as governor of Sumatra, had enunciated certain principles which he had followed whilst managing the convicts in Bencoolen. The broad features that obtained in the Andamans over the years continued to be more or less the same, notwithstanding the numerous inquiries into the system and the frequent visits paid by various luminaries from the citadel of power as embodied in the government of India. It was obvious, therefore, that the Andaman penal system was just muddling through, and everyone was conscious of the fact that, to quote Shakespeare: "There was something rotten in the state of Denmark."

The attitude of the government to the proposals made by W R H Merk of the Indian Civil Service, who was chief commissioner from 9 April 1904 to 14 April 1906, was somewhat ambivalent. It was once again suggested, by the home secretary, government of India, to the chief secretary of the government of Burma, that the Burmese government should take over the administration of the Andaman and Nicobar islands, mainly, it would appear, with a view "to abolish the Andaman Commission, transferring its junior officers to the Burma Police, where some of them might, with the concurrence of the Lieutenant Governor of Burma, fill existing vacancies in the cadre, and retaining the senior members (for whom it is unlikely that suitable employment can be found in Burma) in the Andaman until they retire".

A half-baked solution indeed! And as one would have expected, nothing came of it, the main question of transportation, the abolition of which was the principal recommendation made by Merk, being "allowed to stand over for the moment".

But in no time, Merk himself had changed his mind! In a letter to Sir H H Risley, home secretary to the government of India, which Merk wrote when he was commissioner of the Delhi division, he said: "I have changed my mind about a total abolition of transportation. I think the Government of India scheme is excellent, provided the convicts transported to the Andamans are put through at least ten years of severe intra-mural existence there, and after local release from intra-mural jails, are never allowed to return to India." And as an excuse for his change of mind he quoted from a report published in the *Pioneer* of Allahabad, which stated, *inter alia*, that:

Maiku Pasi of Shahjehanabad District was convicted of making a murderous assault on Durga Singh, a convict warder, while in Central Jail, Bareilly. During appeal being heard by Justices Knox and Richard, the judgement—"In the present case he had received no provocation, and his assault was that of a desperate man, disappointed in his attempted escape, and as he himself adds in his not being sent to the Andamans."

The report in the *Pioneer* was dated 18 March 1907, and Merk's letter is also of the same date.

There was no let up as far as the formation of the committees was concerned. Another committee, consisting of H W W Reynolds as president, our friend W R H Merk and W W Drew (all belonging to the Indian Civil Service) as members, was appointed vide a letter dated 7 February 1908 from H H Risley. This inquiry resulted in a note on the subject being written by Reynold and Drew, with a separate note by Merk. The government ruled, in brief: "After an exhaustive inquiry into the subject, the Government of India have decided that the existing system should continue, subject to the introduction of such improvements as may from time to time be found practicable."

All along, meanwhile, the question whether term convicts should continue to be sent to the Andamans was still engaging the minds of the powers-that-be. Government continued to prevaricate. At one time the proportion of term convicts, as against those sentenced for transportation, was fixed at 33 per cent. But by 1906 that limit had been exceeded. So the transportation of term convicts was suspended temporarily. But, due to the usual lack of coordination between the authorities back home and those on the spot at Port Blair, it was suddenly discovered at the end of the year 1909-10 that the proportion had come down to 19.03 per cent; this, naturally enough, created problems in the Andamans. For instance, due to a lack of sufficient labour force, revenue from the forests had come down to Rs 23,198 in 1908-09, as against more than Rs 300,000 in 1906-07. So the question was taken up again. In a note dated 24 August 1910, J L Jenkins, home secretary to the government of India, said that as there was "not the slightest prospect of transportation to the Andamans being abolished", he was of the opinion that they may "agree to the transportation of term convicts under the former conditions". Jenkins himself paid a visit to Port Blair, and on his return stated:

> As a penal system it is certainly superior to that which is in force in Indian jails. There is a great variety of useful labour on which the convicts are employed according to their aptitudes. There is no reason to suppose that the punishment involved in transportation is not sufficiently deterrent, and I do not for a moment suppose that any man has ever been induced to commit a crime, which he would not otherwise have committed, by the consideration that he might be sent to the Andamans instead of being imprisoned. The system has a very decided reformative effect. The convicts, of whom we saw many employed in occupations of all kinds, are cheerful, willing and law abiding. The hang-dog sullen look which marks the long-term convicts in Indian jails is entirely wanting. In my opinion the system now in force in the Andamans, though capable of improvement in matters of details, is essentially a sound system, which, while being sufficiently punitive, is humane and gives a convict some chance of preserving self-respect.

Jenkins' note is dated 27 April 1911. The game of snakes and ladders continued. Jenkins, in an *obiter dicta*, had also stated: "It is not uncommon for a life convict to return to India with some hundreds of rupees, and cases are quoted of men who have accumulated much larger sums than this. One man died leaving Rs 7,000, but he had taken to money-lending in his self-supporter days".

At the time of Jenkins' visit, the number of male working convicts was 10,844, and those of female convicts in the female jail 255.

The next visit by an important official to the Andamans was in November 1913; it was that of the home member of the governor-general's executive council—the Honourable Sir Reginald Craddock. The report written by Sir Reginald is different from other such reports, particularly on one count. He gives a graphic picture of what Port Blair and its environs were like at the time of his visit. He first describes what he calls the islet of Ross:

> Owing to its comparative freedom from danger in the event of a rising among the convicts, Ross has been selected as the headquarters of the Administration. Its total area is only about 70 acres, and it is now so site-crowded that there is no room for further building upon it. On Ross are Government House, the barracks of the detachments of British and Native Infantry, the houses of their officers, the combined Mess and the Station Club; the Club for the subordinates of the Settlement, the Officers' tennis courts, the church, the European Hospital, the Treasury, the Post and Telegraph offices, the Store godown for the Commissariat supplies of the whole Settlement with its flour mills, bakery, ice and mineral water factories. There is also a bazaar; and an anchorage for the ferry launch plying between Ross and Aberdeen, and for boats allotted to the officers residing on Ross. Besides these there are barracks and hospitals for the convicts serving on Ross; these men are specially selected and the barracks in which they live are walled off from the rest of the Island and carefully guarded. Although Ross is overcrowded and there is some inconvenience in having the main European settlements on this detached Island, yet there are also great advantages, not the least one being that with the concentration of the food supply on the Island, if the convicts were to mutiny in large numbers, they would before long be staged into submission.

Ross has since been abandoned. Now one can only see derelict ruins of the glory that once embodied the representatives of the British Raj on the islands of Andaman and Nicobar.

Craddock also described the island of Chatham, which is three miles further up the harbour and where Blair had built his first headquarters: "It contains a yard and sheds for the minor repairs of boats that belong to the Department; steam saw mills which have been at work for many years and are about to be replaced by more up-to-date machinery. This Island also contains the houses of the various officials whose work necessitates their residence on the spot, their offices and such barracks as they require for resident convicts." Chatham had, by then, become the headquarters of the forest department, which it still is.

Craddock described Viper as being "another three miles south-west in a sheltered nook" and he said that it was "quite out of date as a jail, the building being old and of an unsuitable pattern". Viper then was the headquarters of the western district and contained the offices (along with the residences) of the district officer and his subdivisional officer. Viper too has since been abandoned and is now only used as a picnic spot.

Craddock described Cellular Jail as "a large starshaped three storeyed brick structure, with an encircling wall", which contained "cells to accommodate 703 convicts and work sheds between the radiating arms. He thought that it was "the most up-to-date institution in the Settlement" and was "one establishment where penal discipline [could] be properly enforced". The women's jail, he thought, had been "rendered somewhat unhealthy by its proximity to a brackish water swamp that [bred] the *nyssomyzomya ludowi* [the principal local carrier of malarial poison]". But, he added, this swamp was "being rapidly filled in" and it would soon "cease to be a cause of sickness".

Craddock also gave in his report the breakdown of the convicts in the Andamans at the time:

Life Convicts	8,626
Term Convicts	2,218
Total	10,844
Female Convicts	265

He gave an outline of the penal system then in force and wrote: "The system on paper purports to be a very perfect one. There are manifold forms of labour, hard and light; there appears to be every incentive for good behaviour; the bad are punished and the good are to be rewarded, but *the whole success depends upon the manner the system is worked.*" (The italics are not his.) On the subject of the reformative aspect, Craddock's remarks were telling and incisive:

The Settlement Officers stoutly maintain that the system reforms, and they point to certain respectable domestic servants in European employ, and to the few cases in which men appear to have risen to better things. Now no one could be so rash as to deny that some men may be reformed after a life in the Andamans. But in the first place the point is not whether some individuals have been reformed or not, but whether the tendency of the place is towards reform; a large percentage of reformed characters is requisite before success can be claimed. In the second place it is by no means certain that the respectable men who leave the Andamans have become respectable in spite of them. Men who have been guilty of offences such as dacoities, etc., in which theft has been an element are never permitted to enter domestic service, and respectable men may be found among the murderers who have in a moment of passion committed a murder, who have shot an enemy in a frontier feud or taken part in a religious riot. But if we turn to the system, not a theoretical system of Codes and Manuals, but the system in actual working, it is easy to perceive that *the incentives before the convicts are not incentives which tend to reform but incentives which tend to debase them.* [The italics are not his.]

Where the punitive aspect of the penal system was concerned, Craddock's comments are also far from devoid of interest. Talking about the theory that "transportation was in itself a deterrent and to be complete and real it should be permanent expatriation", he wrote:

When life convicts return after 17 to 20 years and term convicts at the expiration of their sentences, any idea of permanent expatriation has vanished. In these days when ships carry a number of Indian emigrants to distant colonies like Fiji and British Columbia and when crowded steamers carry labourers from Madras to Burma, from India to Ceylon and the Straits, the mere terror of crossing the *Kalapani* is an exploded bogey. The journey to the Andamans is nothing to a Burman and little to the native of India, but it would be going too far to say that the convict regards the Andamans as a delectable residence. He certainly does not.... It is plain that the really important factor in the system is the introduction of wives into the self-supporting and refugee colonies. The well meant endeavours of the Andaman Code to comply with these conditions by means of self-supporters and convict marriages have not succeeded because, first, such a small percentage of self-supporters of convicts are self-supporting, secondly, because such a small percentage of self-supporters marry, and thirdly, because a marriage of this kind is not regarded as a really binding tie.

He concluded by saying that "the taste for sodomy may and does, once created, get such a hold over men as to ruin married life". From this remark one would naturally conclude that homosexuality among the convicts was widely prevalent. Could they be blamed when there was such a shortage of women in the settlement?

Craddock said that the government had three alternatives before them: (*i*) to end the settlement altogether; (*ii*) to patch the system so as to mitigate as far as possible its worst defects; and (*iii*) to reform completely the entire system of the Andamans, which could not be done without very radical amendments of the penal system as a whole, of which the Andamans formed a very small part. In the circumstances, however, Sir Reginald Craddock felt that there was no alternative but that "the subject must be investigated and examined in detail by a carefully chosen Commission which would go into the whole system of Indian jail life and not merely confine itself to the Andaman".

After Sir Reginald Craddock's return from the Andamans and, apparently, after the submission of his report, the Honourable Rama Rayaningar moved a resolution in the council of the governor-general of India, which met on 24 February 1914 in the council chamber of the imperial secretariat in Delhi; His Excellency Baron Hardinge of Penshurst, viceroy and governor-general, presided. The resolution read:

> My Lord, I beg to move—That this Council recommends to the Governor General in Council that a joint commission of officials and non-officials be appointed to investigate the whole subject of jail administration and to suggest improvements in the light of the experiences of the West.

In accepting the resolution on behalf of the government, Sir Reginald Craddock said:

> I have recently returned from a visit of inspection of the Andamans where I have studied as closely as time would permit the system in force in the Penal Settlement at Port Blair, and nothing struck me so forcibly as the fact that our penal system is still far too rigid and makes no sufficient attempts to differentiate between crimes committed in the heat of passion and cold, calculated crimes implying a vicious and degenerate nature. The compartments into which criminals are divided are still far too few; the diagnosis is too rough and ready; and the treatment too uniform.

Sir Reginald finished his brief speech with a rhetorical flourish: "Our wishes and those of the Honourable Member [the mover of the resolution] may be expressed in the words of a poet who is very frequently quoted in this country:
>>That men may rise on stepping stones
>>Of their dead selves to higher things."

This was in early 1914. Soon after, however, the first world war broke out in Europe. As a natural consequence, therefore, everything about the penal settlement in the Andamans or the appointment of a jails committee was forgotten. Therefore, the position of the convicts and the penal settlement, as such, remained much the same in the Andamans. But after the war had been fought and won, an Indian Jails Committee was appointed. Its members were Sir Alexander Cardew of the Indian Civil Service, member of the executive council, Madras (chairman); Sir James H DuBoulay, secretary to the government (home department); Colonel James Jackson, late inspector-general of prisons (Bombay); Lieutenant-Colonel Sir Walter J Buchanan of the Indian Medical Service (retired); Khan

Bahadur Khalifa Syed Hamid Husain (Delhi); D M Dorai Rajan of Pudukottah; Norman G Mitchell Innes, Esquire, inspector of prisons (Home Office, London); Donald Johnstone, Esquire, Indian Civil Service (secretary); and John W Steadman, Esquire of India Office, London (assistant secretary). As was to be expected, among the directives issued to the Jails Committee there was one on the subject of the Andamans, which stated that since "recent inquiries . . . have led the Government of India to doubt whether the administration of the Andamans as a penal settlement is not susceptible, with advantage, of material change, or whether in fact the continuance of the settlement in its present shape is in itself expedient", therefore, "an enquiry into this direction may be expected to yield results of special value".

The committee, apparently, had a gala time visiting various countries all over the globe and inspecting jails there. The countries they visited, besides Great Britain, were the United States of America, Japan, the Philippines and Hongkong. Of course they toured all over India and Burma as well. This took them nearly two years, and the report they submitted after a mountain of labour could be said to have produced only the proverbial mouse.

But their comments on the penal settlement were by no means lacking in interest. They harped back on the subject of the insufficiency of women. They were critical of the administration because they felt that "in order that there should be a reasonable chance of the convict population becoming the nucleus of a decent community", after a prisoner was released, the administration "should [have] at any cost provided [him] with the necessities of domestic existence". This was not done. Instead, they said, "marriages, known as local marriages, were allowed to be contracted between self-supporting male convicts and female convicts. These women were frequently too old for child-bearing". Besides, they said, as "they were often of bad character...union between such women and released criminals were hardly likely to produce a respectable community". Another result of that, according to them, had been "wholesale immorality on the part of the women". They also mentioned "unnatural practices" being prevalent to a very large extent.

One of the recommendations—that women prisoners be brought back to India—was actually put into effect more or less straightaway. Some exceptions, however, were made. There were only 242 in number when the committee visited the Andamans.

The Jails Committee considered the various alternatives that had been suggested about the future of the penal settlement: one of them, which had been put forward by a previous chief commissioner, Lieutenant-Colonel M W Douglas, was that the penal system should "be developed and continued as a reformatory system for the more decent class of prisoners". This they rejected out of hand. Another suggestion that had been made was that a new settlement be opened in Middle Andaman. This they also rejected because, as they put it: "After the most careful consideration we have come to the conclusion that it is not advisable for the Government to incur the responsibilities and the expenditure that would be involved in the creation of a fresh penal colony."

Other alternatives considered by them, according to their report, were: "(*i*) The continuance of the present system at Port Blair with such improvements as experience has proved to be necessary; (*ii*) the entire abandonment of the Andamans as a penal settlement...; and (*iii*) an intermediate course by which, while the Andamans are not entirely abandoned, the character of the system there would be radically changed." They gave reasons for rejecting the first two alternatives, and recommended the following for adoption:

> We have come to the conclusion... [that] the solution of this important and difficult question which we advocate is the retention of the Andamans as a place of deportation, not for the great mass of the prisoners who now go there but for a small class of selected prisoners whose removal from British India is considered by the Governments concerned to be in the public interest. Our recommendation accordingly is that deportation to the Andamans should cease except in regard to such prisoners as the Governor General in Council may, by special or general order, direct. Eventually the population will be reduced to this small body of specially dangerous criminals who will then be confined only in the healthier localities where the Cellular and Associated Jails are placed. We consider that no female should in future be sent to the Andamans and therefore the female prison there will be available for the special class of convict whose future deportation we contemplate.

The committee also recommended the abandonment of the then existing self-supporter system. That was logical, perhaps, in the circumstances, because if there were to be no female convicts "the convicts hereafter released on the self-supporter system would have to live a life of celibacy", as they put it. The remedy suggested by the Indian Jails Committee would appear to have been worse than the disease.

One of the members, D M Dorai Rajan of Pudukottah, disagreed with the majority in the committee and recommended that "the prisoners in the Andamans should be transferred to the local jails". Why, he asked, could temporary jails not be constructed if accommodation in Indian jails was insufficient?

In his minute of dissent, Dorai Rajan also joined issue with his other colleagues on the committee on the definition of "habituals". They had defined a "habitual" as being "specially dangerous to the interest of the community". His very cogent argument was that this definition was very vague and, he asked: "Who is specially dangerous?" He found this special classification "objectionable" and saw no need for it, saying: "Every criminal who commits a crime although for the first time, which involves moral turpitude, is a possible danger to society. Habituals are certainly a menace to the public, in so far as they have formed habits of crime". But this class, he feared, might even include a "casual" because, as he put it, "the line to be drawn between dangerous and specially dangerous is ... very thin indeed."

At a meeting of the Central Legislative Assembly, held on 11 March 1921, the Honourable Sir William Vincent, now home secretary to the government of India, announced that "subject of course to any advice from [that] Assembly", the government had decided to "abandon the penal Settlement altogether". In the course of his speech, he mentioned the visit to Port Blair and the report submitted by his predecessor, Sir Reginald Craddock, which had resulted in the formation of the Jails Committee, the appointment of which had been delayed because of the first world war. But, he said, as a result of Sir Reginald's visit, certain reforms had been introduced as an interim measure. They included "the abolition of chain gang sentences" and "the systematic reclamation of salt swamps". In addition, he went on to say that "additional allowances for food [had] been sanctioned for convicts engaged in labour at a distance from their station" and "the system of local marriages [had] been regularised" as also "allowances paid to married self-supporters had been increased, and marriages between convicts and freeman [were] no longer permitted". He announced the government's final decision:

> The time has now come to end this penal settlement altogether. Of course, there must necessarily elapse a considerable time before this proposal can be carried out completely, because we have to deal with 12,000 to 15,000 prisoners, and they have to be accommodated somewhere as obviously they cannot be released forthwith. But we are taking certain steps in this direction immediately, and we are also impressing upon local Governments the necessity of adding to their jail accommodation without delay.

On 5 September later in the same year, in reply to a question by the Honourable Rai Bahadur Lala Ram Saran Das in the Council of States, the upper chamber of the then legislature, the Honourable H D (later Sir Henry) Craik stated:

> Government have decided to abandon the Andamans as a penal settlement and not to retain it in the modified form suggested by the Jails Committee. Deportation accordingly ceased in March last, and Government will shortly introduce legislation with a view to the abolition of transportation as a form of punishment. Orders have been issued for the return of political prisoners, and of those who are diseased or unfit to remain in the Settlement. We are also issuing orders for the repatria-

tion of females (except those who wish to marry and remain in the Settlement) and adolescents. The repatriation of the general body of convicts, however, presents many difficulties and cannot be carried out at one stroke.

A new element that had been introduced in the settlement, sometime in the early years of the present century, was the deportation of political prisoners to the Andamans, but that will be discussed in a subsequent chapter.

In actual fact, as stated previously, the only recommendation of the Jails Committee—and the decision of the government of India thereon—which was put into effect was the abolition of the deportation of female convicts and the closure of the women's jail in Port Blair. Because, in reply to a question by Rai Bahadur Pandit J L Bhargava in the Central Legislative Assembly on 6 February 1922, the Honourable Sir William Vincent stated:

> Owing to the stoppage of deportation to the Andamans and the inability of Local Governments to find funds at the present moment for the construction of new jails, overcrowding in existing jails in certain provinces has unfortunately become most serious. This is particularly the case in the Punjab, North-West Frontier and in Madras, in all of which the existing accommodation is taxed to a point which gives rise to serious apprehension. In the circumstances, the Government of India have very reluctantly come to the conclusion that there is no alternative except to reopen temporarily the deportation to the Andamans of prisoners sentenced to transportation from certain provinces.

So back to square one. Three years later, in October 1925, the Honourable Sir Alexander Muddiman, member of the executive council of the governor-general, who was also at the time president of the council of states, paid a visit to the Andamans. After his visit, a government of India resolution outlined the position then obtaining in the Andamans, and also went into the question as to why it had not been found feasible to abolish the settlement: "In the first place there was the considerable number of self supporters in the settlement who were enjoying a life of semi-independence. To have transferred these persons forthwith to Indian jails to serve the remaining of their sentences in close confinement would have been a serious hardship". For once, this reasoning carried conviction. Not only would it have meant hardship to the self-supporters, it would have been inhuman.

Another reason advanced also carried conviction. It was the question of the locally born population, people who were born and brought up there and were, in most cases, of mixed parentage. (The communities to which they belonged and the provinces from where they orginally came were different.) In the words of the resolution: "It would [have been] a very serious hardship to them if Government abandoned the settlement altogether."

Then, quite rightly, the resolution stated: "Another consideration was that the islands occupy an important strategic position in the Bay of Bengal, have a fine harbour, and are a very distinct asset to India from the naval point of view." It also spoke of the "inherent wealth of the Islands, agricultural and forest", stating further that during the previous 18 months as many as 276 men and 31 women convicts had gone to the Andamans as volunteers from jails in India.

The government had also made an effort to settle married convicts in the Andamans. Except in the case of the Moplahs, the scheme had not proved very fruitful. But the resolution described the scheme, as far as Moppilahs (*sic*) were concerned, to have proved "an unqualified success". Of the 1,133 Moplahs transported to the Andamans, 258 had been given agricultural tickets and they had brought to the islands their wives, children and in some cases also their relatives; they then numbered 468. But, for some unspecified reason, the transfer of more wives and families of the Moplahs had been stopped.

"MOPILLAHS" OR MOPLAHS

Since ancient times, Malabar was known as the traditional centre for trade in pepper, and Arab traders and sailors had been frequenting its coastal ports for many a century. Some time in the 9th century, however, a number of Arab Muslims came and actually settled in Malabar. They married the local Dravidian women, who were obviously Hindu, and began to sire a new community which came to be known as Moplah. But they were Sunnis and continued to remain fanatically Muslim. Though they paid taxes and rent to their Hindu overlords in Malabar, their spiritual leader was still the Caliph of Turkey.

When the Indian National Congress took up the cause of the deposed Sultan of Turkey and started what came to be known as the *Khilafat* movement, the Moplahs came to the firm conclusion that the British were against Islam. So they declared a sort of "independence" in the areas in Malabar where they were in preponderance. Some Moplah gangs donned a kind of uniform and, with the aid of an assortment of weapons, mostly countrymade, they began to picket police posts. Economically they were the underdogs, as the landlords to whom they paid their rents were mostly Brahmin Hindus. The movement therefore took a communal turn. What followed can only be described as a holocaust. The effort of the British to arrest their leaders proved infructuous. Mobs numbering anything from 5000 to 10,000 attacked post-offices, railway stations, official residences, liquor shops and plantations. There was arson, loot and murder. They went to the extent of setting up a *Khilafat* kingdom under one Mohammed

Haji as the *Khilafat* king. And, since they had not forgotten that the Hindus were *kaffirs* (infidels), the movement turned primarily anti-Hindu. According to one official account, "almost every Hindu house where loot could be obtained was attacked and plundered". Besides, there were a number of forcible conversions and, as it happens in all such times of chaos, many women were raped, and some forcibly taken as wives.

On 25 July 1921, in a clash with the police in which as many as 5,000 Moplahs were involved, a British Army officer and a police officer were murdered. A railway station was set on fire and burnt, and the railway line torn up. In one clash with the Moplahs, the army lost two officers and several men. It was not until reinforcements arrived in the shape of army contingents of Burmese, Gurkhas, Garwahlis and Kachins of the Burma Rifles that the authorities were able to control the situation. It is difficult to gauge the enormity of the Moplah rebellion. In the words of Lieutenant-General Sir George MacMunn, writing in his *Turmoil and Tragedy in India in 1914 and After:*

> To show, how formidable the galvanised Moplahs could be, the instance of the attack on Pandikkah post during one of the drives may be cited. Here the post was attacked at dawn on two fronts. They lost 67 killed inside and 150 outside, but of the small garrison one British officer and eight other Ranks were killed and two Gurkha officers and 27 other Ranks were wounded.

But once the British had their reinforcements, they too did not in any way lag behind. Mohammed Haji, the *Khilafat* king, along with 21 of his followers, was captured, court-martialed, and shot. So were six of his followers. Moplah casualties totalled 2,266 killed in action, and 1,615 wounded; those captured numbered 5,688. As many as 38,256 Moplahs surrendered. Many prisoners were also court-martialed and shot. One particular act of British reprisal was reminiscent of the Black Hole tragedy of Calcutta. Ram Gopal, in his *Indian Muslims—A Political History*, has written: "A ghastly chapter of reprisals was enacted in a goods train. About 70 (one version says 100) Moplahs were packed into a goods wagon going from Calicut to Madras. South India's summer sun was scorching the iron wagon, and when the wagon was opened at the Podanoor railway station, it was found that 66 Moplahs had died of suffocation, and others were in a precarious condition."

It was these Moplahs—who had either been captured or had surrendered, and were after trial sentenced to transportation—that formed the nucleus of the Moplah community in the Andamans.

However, to go back—the government of India's resolution following Sir Alexander Muddiman's visit also mentioned the possibility of the settlement, in the islands, of domiciled Europeans and Anglo-Indians. As a matter of fact, this scheme was the brainchild of the Anglo-Indian leader,

Lieutenant-Colonel Sir Henry Gidney. The government of India did not seem very enthusiastic about it, because in the words of the resolution:

> The Government of India are prepared to receive applications for land from these as well as from persons of other classes, but they consider it necessary to give expression to a word of warning by making it clear that the climate of the Islands is definitely tropical and that any form of agriculture involving hard physical labour in such a climate is unlikely to be congenial to persons not accustomed to manual work in moist heat.

Muddiman's noting on this resolution is rather interesting. His comments are pithy and incisive and show that not only did he know his own mind, he was also not the type to indulge in the usual officialese—vague and full of prevarication—which bureaucrats are normally prone to. He wrote:

> (1) The Islands cannot be abandoned. I do not think we could contemplate this. In my mind it is a promising possession which may develop into a really valuable asset to the Crown; (2) The convict system cannot be done away with at once and we must endeavour to obtain voluntary convict labour to carry us over the transitional period ... ; (3) I would at the same time encourage free colonisation .. ; and (4) As regards the Forest Department ... my impression at present is that it will be a very good thing to try and interest some big firm in England to undertake forest development.

The last suggestion never materialized. It just remained a pious hope!

Despite repeated assertions by the government that conditions in the Andamans had improved, the penal settlement continued to be described by the press in India, as well as by the politicians, as *Kala Pani* or "Hell on Earth". This cut to the quick Lieutenant-Colonel M L Ferrar, who had had three spells as chief commissioner between 23 April 1923 and 12 April 1931. (Today, Ferrarganj, a township, is named after him.) Ferrar wrote:

> The general ideal prevalent among their [the politicians'] class ... is one of disbelief in the Andaman ever becoming fit morally or materially for colonisation and development. They are the slaves of phrases and have determined that this place was, is and always must remain a "Hell on Earth". ... There is in actual fact a marked change in the general moral atmosphere. The quota of work done is not less and almost certainly more than before, there is better behaviour, more happiness, more stamina, better health and less, enormously, malingering. Bad hats are shipped away and better men take their place and so we progress if slowly.

Ferrar repeated the refrain which had been voiced again and again during the previous several decades: "Women remain the great want." And yet the women's jail was abolished and the transportation of women stopped!

The Andaman penal settlement formed the subject of another debate in the Council of States, when the Honourable Vinayak Vithal Kalikar moved a resolution on 11 September 1933 with regard to terrorist prisoners incarcerated there. Sir Harry Haig, the then home member, describing the state of the settlement, recapitulated that "the penal settlement had not been closed and the cellular jail had never been closed", and he gave various reasons for not having been able to do so. The reasons are already known. He found it strange, he went on to add in somewhat of a caustic vein, that "a sufficient number for a good many years past [had] been found to volunteer from the ordinary jails to go to a place which I have noticed ... described as a 'Hell on Earth' ". The number of prisoners then, according to Sir Harry Haig, was 6,536.

By 25 March 1935, the number had come down to 5,604. For that is what the Honourable Sir Henry Craik, the new home member, told Mohan Lal Saksena, when the latter put a question on the subject in the Central Legislative Assembly.

Sir Henry Craik was to visit the Andamans on a tour of inspection in 1936, when he would virtually raise a hornet's nest by describing the Andaman islands as a prisoners' "paradise". For many years the Andamans would be referred to sarcastically, as "Craik's paradise". (Today, most of those who have lived there realize how apt that description was!)

The scheme for the colonization and development of the Andamans, which in a way replaced the policy of the abandonment of the penal settlement (or shall we say the immediate abandonment of the penal settlement), was introduced during the regime of Chief Commissioner Ferrar (who, incidentally, was a contemporary of the Right Honourable Sir Winston Churchill at Sandhurst, and died only recently). The idea was to have a larger population at Port Blair, it being no longer mandatory that all prisoners sentenced to transportation must come to the Andamans. Convicts were now allowed the option of volunteering to spend their period of penal servitude in the Andamans. And the emphasis was to allow only those who were comparatively young and who had no history of habitual crime. They were also permitted to bring their families if they so desired. There was no longer the compulsory period of being ten years on probation as labouring convicts. The new system meant only a few months in jail, after which the convicts were given a wage. Besides, it was no longer essential, for those transported, to wear convicts' clothes. Naturally enough, in consequence, there was a change in the outlook of the convicts; in fact what could be described as their moral standard, also improved to a certain extent.

As stated already, a large number of Moplahs who had taken part in the notorious Moplah rebellion were transported to the Andamans. They were allowed to send for their families, and a new experiment, of allowing them to live in separate villages, was tried. They named some of the villages after those left behind, like Calicut for instance. (Later on, this practice of living in separate villages became less rigid, and now most of the villages have a mixed population.) Similarly, Burmese convicts were also given the choice of living in separate villages and sending for their families. As a result of this policy, many families of the Indian and Burmese convicts came in. Among them were also many Sikhs.

Another consequence of the closure of the penal settlement in its old form was that the forest department was faced with the problem of insufficient labour that could be employed in the jungles. Because, notwithstanding the changed situation, *Kala Pani* was still a dreaded name, and those who went there felt that they would always carry this stigma of having been sent there. So the administration sent out a call to a number of Christian missions in India to help persuade some young Christians to volunteer for service with the forest department in the Andamans. There was no response from the Indian mainland. But from the American Baptist mission in Burma the response was positive. The Karens, who were known for being a sturdy people, were prepared to come. So there arrived in the Andamans, in March 1925, 45 Karen families under the leadership of Reverend Lu Gyi. They were settled in a village called Webi near Mayabunder in Middle Andaman. (They are there even now, despite the fact that the Burmese government offered to repatriate them to Burma in 1967, when they repatriated all those Burmans who had not taken up Indian citizenship after India became free. They are a content and happy lot and, according to my talks with their leaders, there is no question of their ever going back to Burma. Webi is their home and that is where they propose to stay for all time.)

The settlement of Anglo-Indians and domiciled Europeans which, as already mentioned, was the brainchild of Sir Henry Gidney, had something of a still-birth. Some of them did go but were not happy, and could not get used to conditions there, which were of a primitive nature. They needed a real pioneer; George Docherty was one. He came and married a Karen women. Happily, he is still alive and lives in Webi. He did quite well in the forests and jails departments and was a prisoner of war of the Japanese in the last war. He recalls: "In the scheme... most of the colonists came from the Calcutta zone [who] were accustomed to the social facilities existing in towns. They returned almost immediately after landing." According to Docherty, this scheme was formulated because "Sir Henry Gidney, president of the Anglo-Indian community of India, felt that the Anglo-Indians should have a homeland apart from India", and it "was a failure from the very beginning as the government would not by any means help the Anglo-Indians". He feels that if Sir Henry Gidney had only known "the moral and physical and financial requirements of would-be colonists he would have never launched this scheme".

What is more, he said, "no appraiser came to these islands to find out the state of affairs". By and large, most of the Anglo-Indians came and saw and went back after a little while. A few, like Docherty, stayed back. And the elders among them are happy and contented and would rather live there than anywhere else. For Docherty: "It is the peace and the quietness and the freedom to live the sort of life that we want, which is the main attraction."

This, however, is not true of the younger generation. They find living there a bore and their future prospects dim, so they leave and look for flesh-pots in the big cities of this country; some have migrated abroad. For the few who are there, the future is rather dim. When the present generation of older people is dead and gone, there will be none left, in all probability, to till their land and tend their vegetable gardens and fruit orchards.

Another tribe of people, who were brought to the Andamans during this period of colonization, were the Bhantus. The Bhantus are classified as a "criminal tribe" and belong to Uttar Pradesh. They found the new surroundings rather congenial. They have stayed and prospered, and some of them are today holding responsible positions. No one ever talks of their origin; now they form an integral part of the community.

19
The Early "Politicos"

It is something of an irony that, although the penal settlement at Port Blair in the Andamans was founded primarily to get out of the way those who had taken part in the 1875 Mutiny, not many other "political prisoners" were sent there for the next few years. In any case, the term "political prisoners" was then unknown. The purpose underlying transportation was that the sentence should be regarded "with peculiar fear"; those who had drafted the Indian Penal Code had explained the necessity for the sentence of transportation. According to them:

The consideration which has chiefly determined us to retain that mode of punishment is our persuasion that it is regarded ... with peculiar fear. The pain which is caused by punishment is an unmixed evil. It is by the terror which it inspires that it produces good, and perhaps no punishment inspires so much terror in proportion to the actual pain which it causes as the punishment of transportation in this country. Prolonged imprisonment can be more painful in actual endurance, but it is not so much dreaded before hand, nor does a sentence of imprisonment strike either the offender or the bystanders with so much horror as the sentence of exile beyond what they call *Black Water*. This feeling, we believe arises chiefly from the mystery that overhangs the fate of the transported convict. The separation resembles that which takes place at the moment of death. The criminal is taken for ever from the society of all who are acquainted with him, and conveyed by means, of which the natives have but an indistinct notion, over an element which they regard with extreme awe, to a distant country, of which they know nothing from which he is never to return. It is natural that this fate should impress them with a deep feeling of terror. It is on this feeling that the efficiency of the punishment depends and this feeling would be greatly weakened if transported prisoners should frequently return, after an exile of seven or fourteen years to the scenes of their offences, and to the society of their former friends.

The penal settlement in the Andamans was by no means the first experiment in transportation that the British had tried. Earlier, some Indian convicts had been transported to Bencoolen (in Sumatra), to Penang, to Malacca, to Singapore and to Moulmein (in Burma). But transportation on a scale as large as the one which followed the outbreak of the Mutiny had never taken place. Some mutineers were being tried and sentenced till as late as in 1876, as one of the daily newspapers reported:

> On the 20th of March last, a native General Court Martial was assembled at Poona for the trial of trooper Ram Pursad, of the 1st Regiment of Light Cavalry, who was tried on the following charge: for having, on or about the 28th day of May 1857, at the Mutiny of the Bengal troops at Nusseerabad shamefully abandoned the garrison of that station which it was his duty to defend.

The newspaper report does not indicate what the sentence was but, presumably, the trooper was to be transported for life! After the 1957 mutineers, the next batch of political prisoners to be transported were the Wahabis.

The Wahabi movement originated in the Arabian peninsula, where it was started by one Mohammad Abdul Wahab with the object of ending what he thought was tyranny against the Muslims in the name of religion. In due course, this movement infiltrated into India. Sayed Ahmed, born in 1786 in Rae Bareli (Uttar Pradesh), took upon himself to initiate in India what subsequently came to be described as the "great" Wahabi movement, a counterpart of the original one in the Arabian peninsula.

Sayed Ahmed was a Muslim fanatic. He called himself a Messiah who had come to spread the holy word. He recruited Muslims from Uttar Pradesh, Bihar and Bengal and, having done that, proclaimed himself *Khalif*. He even struck coins in his name, which bore the inscription: *Ahmed, the Just, Defender of the Faith, the glitter of whose scimitar scatters destruction among the infidels.*

Collecting his followers from Uttar Pradesh, Bihar and Bengal, Ahmed shifted his scene of activity to the North-west Frontier, with the object of putting an end to Sikh rule. His followers and the Sikh armies were involved in many a minor clash; sometimes the Wahabis did achieve a certain amount of success. Both sides were ruthless. Eventually, however, in the year 1831, Sayed Ahmed was killed in a battle against the Sikh army under Prince Sher Singh.

Sayed Ahmed's followers described themselves as *Mujahideen*s (crusaders). For some years they lay low. Came the Great Mutiny of 1857. They joined hands with the mutineers, the seizure of the North-west Frontier as their objective. Once again, they failed. However, their sole aim was still to drive out the British from India. At the end of 1863, due to the highhandedness of the British, a *jang-i-azim* (great war) was started by them against "Yaghistan" (Tadzhikistan) on the frontier. General Chamberlain was the British commander-in-chief. The *mujahid*s joined the fight in full force, along with the neighbouring Afghans, and fought with great valour. The war went on for three months. Chamberlain was grievously injured. Nearly seven thousand of his soldiers were killed, and the British had to send for reinforcements from all the cantonments of the Punjab.

It was while he was involved in helping (with men and money) the cause of the *mujahids* in Tadzhikistan that Maulana Mohammad Jafar Thanesvri—one of the most notorious Wahabis who was eventually to land up in Port Blair—was apprehended and finally sentenced to transportation for life in the Andamans. It would be interesting to quote here the judgement of Sir Herbert Edwards. While convicting Jafar, Sir Herbert remarked: "It is impossible to exceed the bitter hostility, treasonable activity and mischievous ability of the prisoner. He is an educated man, and a Headman in his village. [He was what in those days used to be described as a scrivener by profession.] There is no doubt of his guilt and no palliative of it."

Jafar was caught red-handed, as it were, when his house was searched in Thanesvar, a village near Panipat, in the Karnal district of Haryana. Incriminating evidence was found in some of the documents captured, which revealed that he had been responsible not only for recruiting men for the "cause" but had also been collecting gold *ashrafi*s (sovereigns) for the Wahabis. This was in December 1863.

On his return from the Andamans, he published a book in Urdu entitled *Kala Pani*. In it he says that it was due to an Afghan informer that his house was searched; this had led to his prosecution and eventual sentence of transportation to the Andamans for 20 years. He and his accomplices had been sentenced to death, but the chief court in Lahore reduced the sentence to one of transportation for life.

An interesting part of his story is that it took him and his companions 11 months to get to Port Blair from Ambala, the journey from Ambala having started on 22 February 1865. They were first taken to Lahore and lodged in the Central Jail there. From Lahore, they were taken to Multan; from Multan they went on a long voyage down the Indus river in a steamer to Sukkur, because then the Indus river had not been bridged. From Sukkur to Karachi, from Karachi to Bombay on board the *S S Bagla*, and then confinement in the jail at Thana. The last part of the voyage, which lasted 34 days (from Bombay to Port Blair), was on board the *S S Jamuna*. Jafar says that except for one convict, Motilal, no one spoke English and the crew was all British.

All through the journey, whether by train or steamer or ship, or while they were lodged in various jails, Jafar and his companions had to wear the regular jail dress, besides being shackled. But once, in Port Blair, his fortunes took a turn for the better. One gathers from his story that in fact, things could not have been better. On arrival, he was immediately lodged in the house of Ghulam Nabi, a peon in the marine department. He was given new clothes to wear and his shackles were removed; the food, he writes, was excellent.

Luckily for Jafar, he also escaped being branded, as all convicts till then had been, because shortly before he arrived orders to do so had been rescinded. Within a few months of his arrival, he was able to inveigle himself into the good books of the chief commissioner, because he first became his *moharrar* (court clerk) and then *mir munshi* (superintendent). There were no longer any restrictions on his movements. He had a paid servant to administer to his needs, and a house to live in.

Jafar writes that, during all the 18 years that he spent in Port Blair, every day for him was a day of feasting—either at his own house or at the homes of others living there. And no sooner had he settled down, he found himself a Kashmiri woman to wed. She did not live very long. But he soon remarried, this time a Brahmin girl from Almora; but the girl needed some persuading, as she was not a Muslim. He, however, did succeed, not only in wooing her but also in converting her to Islam. She was to be his companion throughout his stay in the Andamans and, according to what he was written, gave birth to ten children. They went back home with eight. What happened to the other two, he does not specify. (And all this while he had a wife and three children back home!) But there is no doubt that Jafar, even according to his own written memoir, was a very smooth character. He managed to curry favour with every chief commissioner who happened to be there during Jafar's 18 years' sojourn in the Andamans. What is more, he even admits that, when there were complaints against him and he was in fact guilty, the chief commissioner took his side and exonerated him. He had not shed his Muslim fanaticism either; he was responsible for creating a lot of communal tension when he insisted on sacrificing a bull on the holy day of Id. He also did a certain amount of proselytizing. And the chief commissioners —mainly Colonel M Prothroe—always backed him, he writes.

It was while he was there that the Earl of Mayo, viceroy and governor-general of India, was assassinated by an Afridi Pathan named Sher Khan. (That story has already been told.) There was an obvious suspicion that the Wahabis as such, and maybe in a covert way Jafar himself, had something to do with the murder but, in the words of Jafar, it was thanks to the then chief commissioner, General D M Stewart, that the Wahabis were "saved from being implicated."

Jafar was also lucky, in a way, because, though after his arrival rules did begin to get more and more strict, they were not to apply to those who had already been there. Obviously a man of a certain amount of talent, he utilized his time in learning to speak English. He also started teaching Persian, Urdu and *Nagari*!

The government of India eventually issued orders for his release. They were received in Port Blair on 22 January 1882 but, since his wife was not due for release just then as she had not finished her 14-year term, he stayed on. Then he found that she was again pregnant; so he stayed on still further, and finally said goodbye to the islands on 9 November 1883. He took back with him a wife, eight children and 8,000 rupees. And this time the voyage on the *S S Maharaja* took four days and four nights from Port Blair to Calcutta. So, as far as Maulana Mohammad Jafar Thanesvri was concerned, the Andamans proved to be a veritable paradise.

Then, there were also those who were sent to the Andamans for their part in what came to be known as the Manipur revolt. It was Senapati Tikendrajit who in September 1890 first raised the banner of this revolt. All went well for a while but, in March the following year, the British forces arrived and demanded Tikendrajit's surrender. He was indignant and refused to do so. Not only that, he somehow cajoled three generals of the British Army to meet him; they were assassinated. The British reacted by attacking the Manipur fort, but the attack was repulsed. The fort was attacked again, this time at midnight; once again the attack was beaten off. Senapati Tikendrajit was hailed as the saviour of Manipur.

But the Senapati's was a Pyrrhic victory, though it did provide him with a temporary respite. To begin with, even reinforcements from Burma did not help. The fort was stormed with heavy guns, and that caused heavy damage. Senapati Tikendrajit, however, managed to escape. But some of his other generals fell into the hands of the British and within a fortnight the Senapati too was captured, albeit after he had put up a brave, though desperate fight. A kind of mock trial was held and the Senapati, his younger brother and another general were sentenced to death and hanged. Some of the others were ordered to be transported, among them being members of the royal family and their attendants. And it is thus that they arrived in the Andamans.

For once, the British did show a greater sense of fairness, and did not treat them as common criminals. They were housed in a bungalow on Mount Harriet with some land to cultivate a garden, and also given facilities to carry on some kind of business to maintain themselves.

But for those who really were political prisoners, even though the government refused to accept that nomenclature for many years, the Andamans were to prove a hell on earth. Many years later, however, when some of the well-known political prisoners were to demand similar treatment, the government of India was to comment that there was a difference between the Manipuri prisoners and those who were described by the government as seditionists, because "the former [the Manipuris] had no trial and [were] confined under Regulation II1 of 1818, whereas the latter [the political prisoners] have been convicted of definite offences under the Indian Penal Code".

20
Come the Political Prisoners

The idea of sending political prisoners to the Andamans was first mooted by Sir J P Hewett, governor of the United Provinces, when he wrote to the secretary, government of India, seeking the central government's permission to transport Hoti Lal and Babu Ram Hari (both editors of *Swarajya*, a newspaper published in Allahabad), who had been sentenced to various terms of imprisonment. As transportation of term prisoners was not allowed at the time, the governor was seeking permission because he felt that it was "desirable to get these people out of the country". The government of India first agreed but apparently, on second thoughts, conveyed the Indian government's decision, telegraphically, to the effect that they thought it "inexpedient to relax rules in case of two convicts in question and desire that they should be dealt with in the usual way". They did eventually arrive in the Andamans and in Port Blair's Cellular Jail, but that was much later.

Swarajya will find perhaps a unique place in the history of Indian journalism, because it has been the only newspaper in history, not only of India but perhaps of the entire world, whose eight successive editors were convicted for sedition. The Sedition Committee summed up the case of the *Swarajya* in these words:

> The first determined and persistent impulse towards a revolutionary movement in these now peaceful provinces came from the establishment of *Swarajya* (Self-Government) newspaper in Allahabad in November 1907, by a certain Shanti Narain, a native of U.P., who had formerly been sub-editor of a Punjab newspaper.... Eight successive editors ... were prosecuted and sentenced to long terms of imprisonment for objectionable publication. Seven of these editors came from the Punjab.

On what frivolous and minor excuses the British government was willing, those days, to impose savage punishment where so-called sedition was concerned is apparent from the fact that one of the two editors—Babu Ram Hari of Qadian (Gurdaspur)—was sentenced to an aggregate term of 21 years for writing and publishing the following poem:

> Oh! My dear Motherland why
>   are you crying?
> The rule of the foreigners is
>   about to end.
> They are packing up!
> The national shame and misfortune
>   will not last long!
> The wind of freedom has
>   begun to blow,
> Old and young are yearning for freedom!
> When India becomes free,
> "Hari" will also enjoy his freedom.

The sentence of transportation for ten years was pronounced on another editor, Ladha Ram Kapur from Gujrat in the Punjab, because he had commented on a case in which an Englishman had raped an Indian woman. He had written:

> Normally speaking, she was a sister to all of us. This Englishman, in a most cowardly manner, destroyed the chastity of a respectable woman!

While sentencing him to transportation, the judge pontificated:

> I do not see what stronger language could be used by the writer for bringing into hatred or contempt or for exciting disaffection towards the Government established by law in British India.

In the year 1910, a dozen young men were tried in what came to be known as the Khulna conspiracy case. The charge against them was that they were members of a group which had conspired "to wage war against the King". Eleven of them were convicted. The officiating chief secretary to the government of Bengal wrote to the home secretary, government of India, that "in the Khulna Conspiracy Case, which was tried in the High Court, Calcutta, by a special tribunal... eleven persons were convicted and sentenced to transportation varying from 7 to 2 years". He went on to say that:

> In passing the sentence, the Hon'ble Judges [had] observed... that these prisoners were the most deeply implicated and the most prominent members of the conspiracy, and that they must be removed from the scene of their criminal activities for a considerable period.... It [was] very desirable that all the eleven prisoners should be prevented from mixing with the prisoners in other jails in India and inflaming the mind of ordinary criminals with revolutionary doctrine.

In the circumstances, he went on state, the lieutenant-governor of Bengal considered it essential that "the Government of India may be moved to consider their deportation to Port Blair". The government of India agreed. This became a precedent for other provinces; it was to be followed by a regular stream of political prisoners pouring into the Cellular Jail at Port Blair, and creating a situation for which the authorities were neither prepared nor equipped.

The next to arrive were those convicted in the Alipore conspiracy case, and included Barindra Kumar Ghosh (whose brother had achieved fame as Sri Aurobindo. Also involved in anti-British activities, Sri Aurobindo left British Indian territory, and moved over to Pondicherry in French India. There he founded an *ashram*, and was more or less worshipped as a living god by his devotees all over the world, specially by those who chose to live in his *ashram* at Pondicherry.) What came to be known as the Alipore conspiracy case was the culmination of a long watch kept by the Bengal police on several premises in Calcutta. In simultaneous searches conducted on 2 May 1908, the police had discovered a mass of seditious literature, loads of explosives, arms and ammunition, along with detailed written instructions on the techniques of manufacturing high explosives. The searches were followed by arrests of as many as 41 persons, out of whom 38 were tried.

By far the most well-known prisoner transported to the Andamans was Vinayak Damodar Savarkar. Several decades later he was to gain notoriety for his alleged complicity in the murder of Mahatma Gandhi, soon after India achieved independence; he was acquitted of that charge for lack of evidence. He had also the unique distinction, if one may describe it as such, of having an elder brother, Ganesh Vinayak Savarkar, in the Andamans under the sentence of transportation for life during the time he himself was there.

The Savarkar brothers were both convicted in what is known as the Nasik conspiracy case. There were two conspiracies—the first Nasik conspiracy and the second Nasik conspiracy, the former preceded by what was described as the Gwalior conspiracy. All three were interlinked. The charges against those accused, according to the *Roll of Honour* written by K C Ghosh, were that at Nasik

> and at other places in British India, Vinayak Damodar Savarkar in London (*i*) attempted to wage war, (*ii*) conspired among themselves to wage war, (*iii*) conspired among themselves to commit offences punishable under Section 121 of the Indian Penal Code, (*iv*) conspired to deprive the King Emperor of the sovereignty of British India, (*v*) conspired among themselves to overawe either by criminal force or show of criminal force the Government or the Government of Bombay, (*vi*) collected arms and ammunitions, with the object of waging war, and (*vii*) concealed by an illegal omission the existence of a design to war.

In addition, the accused in these conspiracies had also been implicated in one way or another in two incidents—in the bombing of the car carrying Lord Minto, the viceroy, in November 1909, and the murder in December of the same year of the British district magistrate at Nasik. Among the documents produced during the trial, there was one which contained the exhortation:

> Terrorise the officials, English and Indian, and the collapse of the whole machinery of oppression is not very far ... the campaign of separate assassination is the best conceivable method of paralysing the bureaucracy and of arousing the people. The initial stage of the revolution is marked by the policy of separate assassination.

(Incidentally, section 121 of the Indian Penal Code, under which they were "punishable", reads: "Whoever wages war against the Queen, or attempts to wage such a war, or abets the waging of such war, shall be punished with death, or transportation for life, and shall also be liable to fine.")

In the judgement pronounced in the first Nasik conspiracy case, on 24 December 1910, Vinayak Damodar Savarkar was sentenced to transportation for life—and once again, to another term of transportation, also for life, for his complicity in the second Nasik conspiracy case, the judgement of which was delivered on 30 January 1911. Strangely enough, unlike what happens normally (the sentences run concurrently), in his case it was specifically stated that the sentences were to run consecutively, which meant transportation to a term of fifty years!

Savarkar, who had been living in England while he was being tried in India, had temporarily fled to Paris. But he obviously hated being a fugitive. So he returned to England and was, of course, immediately placed under arrest and sent on board a ship to India. At Marseilles, he jumped ship and tried to swim his way to freedom. The British police gave chase, of course with the help of the French police, and succeeded in capturing him. As this had happened in French waters, Savarkar contended that the action was illegal, and he challenged it in the International Court of Justice at The Hague. His plea was turned down. About the same time, the government of India also gave their final decision on his plea in regard to the legality of the two sentences running consecutively. Savarkar was informed, according to *The Story of Transportation for Life*, the book he wrote after his return from the Andamans: "You are sentenced to fifty years' transportation. The International Tribunal at the Hague has given judgement that England cannot be constrained to hand you over to France."

"The word fifty kept ringing in my ears," he was written. He felt, however, that he could at least console himself that "for this purpose it [the government] has subscribed to the Hindu doctrine of re-birth, and had disowned the Christian doctrine of resurrection", because the government decision, as conveyed to him, was tantamount to saying: "You [are] to run your first life-sentence first, and your second life-sentence after it, that is, you have to take a second life to run it."

In a way, the vicissitudes in the fortunes of Vinayak Damodar Savarkar affected and reflected the fortunes of other political prisoners during his sojourn in the Andamans—in the Cellular Jail at Port Blair, to be precise.

Savarkar described conditions on the ship which carried him to the Andamans:

The party of 50, who were my immediate neighbours on the ship, came from the dirtiest class of Indian population. Hindus, Muslims, thieves, dacoits—they were all inured to filth, cruelty and crime. Some of them were stricken with foul diseases, some knew not what it was to brush their teeth, and all had piled their beddings one upon the other, and lay by each other without an inch of space within them.... My feet touched their heads, and their feet came near my mouth.... Right in front of me, I saw a big cask almost half cut and open... and I discovered they used it all during the night as a chamber pot and commode.

Notwithstanding all that, his first glimpse of the islands did not fail to enchant him: "The Island ornamented the sea like a palace built in the land of the fairies.... It was so picturesque and compact that it could not fail to ravish the mind of even a prisoner in chains like me."

For some time, the political prisoners were treated like the others; they were all even allowed to live under one roof, under the supervision of one Pathan warder. They were given the task of what was known as "picking oakum". It consisted of picking threads from the hard surface of a coconut shell, which was first broken into pieces. Apart from the fact that the work was very tedious, it was also very hard on the hands. But worse was to follow. A high official on a visit from Calcutta, on seeing the political prisoners working together, decided that they should not be allowed either to live together or work together. So they were divided and put up not only in different "*chawl*s" but also in separate cells. And the moment they were seen talking to one another and, if the wardens thought that what they were talking was of a suspicious nature, they were handcuffed and, according to Savarkar, subjected to all kinds of punishment. He writes:

> The sentence of picking oakum was substituted by work round the grinding oil mill.... We were to be yoked like animals to the handle that turned the wheel.... Twenty turns of the wheel were enough to drain away the strength of the strongest cooly and the worst brawny *badmash* [bad character]. No dacoit past twenty was put on that work. But the poor political prisoner was fit to do it at any age.

What he and his other fellow political prisoners found most galling was that "there was no water for washing hands". Drinking water was even more scarce, and water for a bath practically unobtainable. And as regards sanitary arrangements, the less said the better; they were non-existent. The prisoners were allowed out for the purpose only three times a day – morning, noon and evening—and at no other time, not under any circumstances. Another form of punishment was to harness convicts, instead of horses or bullocks, to the carriages carrying government officials.

The first time people on the mainland got an inkling of conditions obtaining in the Andamans was when the *Bengalee* of Calcutta published an article on the plight of the political prisoners there. This, according to Savarkar, was based on a letter which Hoti Lal, one of the political prisoners, had managed to smuggle out of jail. He had not only managed to send it out, but had somehow seen to it that it reached Surendranath Banerji, then proprietor of the *Bengalee*, a weekly, who was later to be elected, twice over, as president of the Indian National Congress. Hoti Lal, as readers would recall, was one of the editors of *Swarajya*, whom the government were at first reluctant to send to the Andamans.

The *Tribune* of Lahore, in its issue dated 3 May 1912, mentioned what the *Bengalee* had stated about hardships which political prisoners had to undergo. Confirming what Savarkar states in his book, it stated: "Four men are tied to the mill [i.e. the oil-mill] and they have to go round a centre-post just as bullocks do. They have to press out 30 pounds of oil during the day." In addition, it gave details of other kinds of hard labour:

> Chopping coconut bark [the outer husk] is another species of work. One gets a huge log of wood about half a maund [about 40 lbs] in weight and a wooden mallet about 4 pounds in weight. The prisoner has to place strips of coconut upon the wood-block and go on striking them with the mallet. In this way a sort of fine dust is pressed out of the coconut strips and only a fibrous substance remains. . . . There is [also] a kind of broad-based thorny plant called *ramkhan*. The prisoner is given 80 or 90 of these leaves and out of these he has to beat up 4 lbs of white flax. If even a drop of its juice touches the body it begins to itch and ultimately produce a kind of sore. Among the work outside the jail may be mentioned felling of trees and piling them up in a large heap; running about with heavy lumps of clay and reaching them to the workmen, laying of 1,230 bricks in the day or hoeing a plot of tea-land 40 by 4 yards in area; and all this one has to do in all sorts of weather — in heavy rain as well as in the fierce heat of the sun.

Giving details of the punishment for not being able to complete the tasks allotted, the article in the *Tribune* went on to state:

> The regulation about punishment for short work is that if the prisoners are unable to go through the full quantity of work or fail to turn out the required amount of work they will be handcuffed for a week. This is the punishment for the first offence. For the second offence a week's handcuff and four day's starvation diet. For the next offence the punishment is fetters for a month or two, then cross-bars for ten days— a punishment which compels the victim to keep his legs apart—and for further repetition of the offence, fetters for six months or so and solitary confinement.

The fat was really in the fire. The home department was now worried because, as one of the scribes there noted on a file: "It is very likely to attract attention in the House of Commons." Therefore, it was felt that they "had better have a report". The home member, however, was of the opinion that "conspirators can hardly expect to escape hard labour in the Andamans subject to their medical fitness for the same". He further declaimed: "Anarchists whose objects are murder can scarcely be said to be suffering for their opinions, any more than any other criminals." Nonetheless, a letter on the subject was addressed to the chief commissioner,

Lieutenant-Colonel H A Browning (of the Indian Army) who was up in arms straightaway. Couched in somewhat acerbic terms, his reply was:

> The Government of India laid down that these prisoners should not be styled "political" prisoners, a nomenclature which no doubt tends to give them spurious importance. ... These prisoners are not locally styled "political" prisoners and that orders have been issued that these convicts were "ordinary transportees" convicted under the Indian Penal Code and were to be styled and treated as such: that they had not been "employed as writers or clerks nor had there been any intention of so employing them".

(Only privileged prisoners were given work as writers and clerks.) Browning was very positive in his assertion that "they will continue to be employed on *ordinary labour*". M S D Butler, deputy secretary (home), who had written the letter to Browning, and to whom Browning had sent the above-quoted reply, commented somewhat wryly: "Colonel Browning has obviously taken offence at being called upon to report. It is probably very hot at Port Blair just now."

In an article dated 4 September 1912, the *Bengalee* again returned to the charge of harsh and inhuman treatment being meted out to political prisoners in the Andamans. It stated that "all of them without exception come from respectable families" and that "most of them know English ... [some] having a thorough education in English, Sanskrit, Mathematics, Science, Philosophy, History and their vernaculars" and were men brought up "amidst ease and plenty, susceptible to all the best sentiments that culture can evoke". Yet how were they being treated? "Up till last January they were left in the Cellular Jail [and were] made to dress exactly as other prisoners, i.e., a pair of jangias [shorts] up to a little above the knee, white coat with sleeves up to the elbow and the neck-ring with a large wooden ticket hanging to it." Later, the *Bengalee* went on to state: "The order was ... given to scatter them all over the jail. Deprived of the only congenial company of their fellow sufferers and put on hardest labour that Cellular Jail could produce, their condition was really pitiable." The article concluded:

> Whenever they claim special treatment and privileges as political prisoners they are given to understand that they are ordinary criminals and must not expect anything more than they can get in the usual course of things. Again, as ordinary criminals they get nothing what their fellows get. Murder cases are given plain tickets and are eligible for all sorts of easy jobs.

That, indeed, was the paradox; they were getting the worst of both worlds!

Meanwhile, one of the political prisoners, Indu Bhushan Roy, committed suicide by hanging himself in his cell. Indu Bhushan Roy had been involved in what came to be described as the Manicktala conspiracy case, for the simple reason that some of those accused were arrested at 32 Muraripukar Road, Manicktala. But, in actual fact, this was a part of the Alipore conspiracy. Savarkar has recounted the circumstances under which Indu Bhushan Roy was forced to put an end to his life:

> Indu Bhushan Roy ... was one of those who were sent out to work. But he found the work outside more fatiguing and humiliating than the labour inside.... If a prisoner outside happened to fall ill he was sent to a hospital relatively better than the hospital in jail. But if a political prisoner became sick, he was punished all the more for his sickness.... Indu Bhushan was fed up with it and returned to the jail of his own accord. Chains were put on his arms and hands, and he was marched on to his old residence, but he refused to go back to work in the settlement. He was punished for this recalcitrance.... He was disgusted with his own life.... Every evening I saw Indu Bhushan returning from the "Kolu", dead tired, with drops of perspiration on his face, the chaff of coconut clinging like saw-dust to his body from top to toe, a weight of about 30 lbs on his head, and a sack of chaff on his shoulders.... One fine morning as our doors were unlocked for the day and we were all coming out, a warder approached us and, requesting not to disclose his name, broke the news that Indu had hanged himself last night.... He was found dangling from the top of the window, hanged by a noose made of his torn clothes.

Of course the official story was that he had committed suicide in a fit of insanity, and because he had had a personal quarrel with someone!

The case of another political prisoner also created quite a stir. Ulaskar Dutt lost his sanity as a result of cruel treatment meted out to him. Having refused to work, he had been handcuffed and kept standing for seven days. And it was during this period that he said that he had been tortured. Again, according to Savarkar, Ulaskar Dutt said:

> Even in semi-conscious state of mind and under severe pain of the body, I could clearly feel that the Medical Superintendent had played his electric battery upon me, the shock of which it was impossible for me to stand, the electric current went through me like the force of lightning. Every nerve, every fibre and muscle in it seemed to be torn by it. The demon seemed to possess it. I uttered words such as had never passed my lips before. I roared as I had never done before, and suddenly I relapsed into unconsciousness for three continuous days and nights.

As a result he was declared insane, and was in a lunatic asylum for nearly 12 years. He was removed to Madras, from where he was eventually discharged after having completed his period of sentence. Ulaskar Dutt was also one of those convicted for his part in the Manicktala (Alipore) conspiracy case.

Then took place what can truly be described as the first recorded hunger strike—not only in the Andamans, but perhaps on the entire Indian subcontinent. In a letter, the chief commissioner, Major H A Browning, informed W H Wheeler, home secretary to the government of India:

> Two of the "Seditinists" prisoners, Ladha Ram and Noni Gopal Mukherji, having persistently declined to take any food are now being forcibly fed twice a day in the Cellular Jail by an oesophageal tube passed either through their nose or through the mouth. Both these prisoners are under punishment of separate confinement with all work and indulgence removed for absolutely refusing to do any work.

Ladha Ram was one of the editors of *Swarajya*. Noni Gopal Mukherji had been sentenced for having thrown a bomb on the car of a high police dignitary. He was only 16 years old. Prison regulations did not allow anyone of so tender an age to be put on hard labour. But he was, and that too on an oil mill. The fiery youngster refused. And all hell was let loose. Once again, according to Savarkar:

> He was kept standing with manacles on.... He was given clothes made of gunny bags. He stopped wearing clothes altogether.... He was put in chains. Hands and feet were both tied up.... He was sent to solitary confinement. He would not turn out even for bath. Then he was bodily lifted, stark naked, to be washed on the reservoir. He was stretched flat upon it, and the *Bhangis* [sweepers] washed his body. They rubbed his body with a piece of dry coconut shreds. And they rubbed it so hard that the skin was almost blood-red with rubbing.

Noni Gopal Mukherji's hunger strike lasted 72 days. Meanwhile, sympathetic strikes had also followed till nearly every political prisoner had struck work.

Overtures were made by Browning, chief commissioner and superintendent. He promised to look into their grievances and also forward them to the government of India for their final decision. But his overtures were of no avail. Eventually, the government deputed Sir Percy Lukas, director of medical services in India, to make an on-the-spot study and resolve the impasse; this he did. L P Mathur, in his *History of the Andaman and Nicobar Islands*, writes that: "After the visit of Lukas a policy of conciliation was instituted." He, however, adds that, according to the official version, that happened because the convicts had undertaken "to give no further trouble to the authorities, provided they were allowed to leave the Cellular Jail and were given light and congenial forms of labour". Following this understanding term political prisoners, like other convicts, were given light work and the freedom to do it outside the jail. This relaxation, however, did not apply to those transported for life, like Savarkar or his brother.

The comparatively relaxed atmosphere was not to last very long. On 9 August 1913, 19 of those who had gone on hunger strike—and that was the total number—were brought back to their cells. It was alleged that they were discovered hatching a plot, and that they had actually made a bomb and exploded it in a *nullah* near Bamboo Flat (one of the suburbs of Port Blair). The plot, as usual, came to light because one of their locally enlisted accomplices squealed.

Captain R Anderson, commandant of the military police in Port Blair, stated in a report dated 29 August 1913:

The seditionists for some time back have been meeting one another regularly, chiefly on Sunday; this they have been able to do as the petty officers in charge of them and others, though they have no intention of joining them, are ready to help them and have been doing so.

On the 13th of July 1913 ... Lal Mohan [a convict] ... reported that several seditionists and other Bengalis were corresponding with one another and with India, and were procuring medicines and chemicals with a view to making bombs. They were holding their meetings on Sunday.

In June 1913 [sixteen of them] attended a meeting.... At this meeting it was asked, "Who of us knows how best to make bombs?" Upendra Nath Banerji said he knew how to do so if he could get the things.

After consultation they said, "We must kill all the *sahibs* with bombs at the same time, then it will be very good for us because a convict will then be able to go to his own country when he likes."

The short term convicts then said, "It will not be so good to kill all the *sahibs* because it will be very bad for us, but we must kill the Chief Commissioner and his bungalow must be blown up."

This was unanimously agreed to and then it was decided that Evan *Sahib* [one of the jailors] must be taken because he punishes the convicts a lot.

After this they dispersed, one by one, by different routes.

The discovery of this plot shook the administration. Although a sympathetic character, comparatively speaking, the new chief commissioner and superintendent, Lieutenant-Colonel M W Douglas suggested that all political prisoners be confined in future to the Cellular Jail. And since there was a lack of accommodation in that jail he proposed that the total number of political prisoners, at no time, exceed 14 life convicts, confined, two each, in the seven different wings of the jail.

Perhaps as a result of this, or because of mounting criticism in India and abroad about the state of affairs in the Andamans, the Honourable Sir Reginald Craddock, home member of the governor-general's executive council (who was later to become governor of Burma), decided to pay a visit to the Andamans in the winter of 1913. While there, he went into everything in detail and also granted interviews to leaders like V D Savarkar, Barindra Kumar Ghosh (brother of Sri Aurobindo), and three others who had submitted petitions to him. Besides these five, he wrote: "I saw all these [meaning Hoti Lal Varma, Nand Gopal and others] as I went through the jail, and heard all who had any complaints to make." He also accepted written petitions, and said:

> The majority of them dislike the idea of being shut up in the Cellular Jail, and profess to prefer the rigours of an Indian Jail with such alleviations as the Indian jail system affords. If they are to remain transported, they urge that they should enjoy the benefits and privileges of the transportation system, e.g., the right to earn remission by marks and the opportunity of being employed as convict overseers and convict warders.

Sir Reginald admitted that the position was "a very difficult one", because "if they are locked up in the Cellular Jail, they are being treated with less indulgence than the ordinary well-behaved criminals". And yet he saw the dilemma: "On the other hand, if they are allowed the same freedom of movement, they are certain to plot escape and other misdeeds."

Among the petitions submitted to Sir Reginald, V D Savarkar's began by requesting him to "put an end to this anomalous situation in which I have been placed, by either sending me to Indian Jails or by treating me as a transportee just like any other prisoner". Interestingly enough, however, he concluded his petition, saying:

> The latest development of the Indian politics [he could only have been referring to the Minto-Morley reforms] and the conciliating policy of the Government have thrown open the constitutional line once more. Now no man having the good of India and Humanity at heart will blindly step on the thorny paths which in excited and hopeless situation of India in 1906-07 beguiled us from the path of peace and progress. Therefore if the Government in their manifold beneficence and mercy release me, I for one cannot but be the staunchest advocate of constitutional progress and loyalty to the English Government.... As long as we are in jails there cannot be real happiness and joy in hundreds and thousands of His Majesty's loyal subjects in India, for blood is thicker than water; but if we be released the people will instinctively raise a shout of joy and gratitude to the Government, who knows how

to forgive and correct, more than how to chastise and avenge. Moreover my conversion to the constitutional line would bring back all those misled young men in India and abroad who were once looking up to me as their guide. I am ready to serve the Government in any capacity they like, for as my conversion is conscientious so I hope my future conduct would be. By keeping me in jail nothing can be got in comparison to what would be otherwise. The Mighty alone can afford to be merciful and therefore where else can the prodigal son return but to the parental doors of the Government

It seems incredible that a man of Savarkar's calibre, known for his revolutionary activities and for his hatred of the British Raj in India, should have written in such cringing terms! But there is no doubt that he did. Craddock reacted by saying:

Savarkar's petition is one for mercy. He cannot be said to express any regret or repentance, but he affects to have changed his view.... It is quite impossible to give him any liberty here, and I think he would escape from any Indian jail. So important a leader is he that the European section of the Indian anarchists would plot for his escape which would before long be organised. If he were allowed outside the Cellular Jail in the Andamans, his escape would be certain. His friends could easily charter a steamer to lie off on the Island and a little money distributed locally would do the rest.... There seems to be no alternative but to keep them (the life convicts of Savarkar's class) in the Cellular Jail; when they have served a sufficient time of hard labour in the jail, and if their behaviour is good, they may be given the indulgence of simple imprisonment.

Barindra K Ghosh's plea was mainly on grounds of health. He had submitted:

Hoping that you will be graciously pleased to lay this humble petition before His Excellency Lord Hardinge's Government for kind consideration. With due respect and humble submission I beg to state that this sentence of 20 year's transportation for me amounts to a death sentence. My physique is extremely poor owing to malarial fever and I had been a lifelong invalid due to this reason, my weight at present being only 92 lbs. Port Blair is a hot-bed of malaria and the natural hardships of life in incarceration added to that will in the long run undermine my health to such an extent as to bring on an untimely death.

Craddock found the case of Barindra Kumar Ghosh "in some way most interesting of the whole lot" because "he professed repentance, but denied any knowledge of the local plot which led to the incarceration of all the anarchists". Sir Reginald Craddock added that "his denial was obviously untrue [because], as he went on, he let slip a statement that he could sincerely assure us that nothing could go on of that kind among the seditionist prisoners without his [Ghosh's] knowledge". Therefore Craddock's surmise was that "Barendra's unwillingness to give any information [was] due to the knowledge that he would be murdered if he were to speak; and that but for [that], he would not be unwilling".

Staying on for a while, Craddock met a whole lot of political prisoners and carried out his inspection of the penal settlement in the Andamans. His most important recommendation vis-à-vis the political prisoners was that: "(a) Savarkar and others like him carrying the sentence of transportation cannot be allowed out, much less sent to any jail on the mainland, and (b) political prisoners carrying what was known as term sentences may be sent back." On the basis of his second recommendation, the government of India addressed letters to provincial governments. Madras, Punjab, Bombay and the Central Provinces governments agreed to take this class of prisoners back; others declined because of overcrowding in their jails.

By a strange irony, while Sir Reginald Craddock was writing his report (which he did on board the *S S Maharaja* on 23 November 1913), an article on the subject of the treatment of political prisoners appeared two days later in *India*, the London journal. It reiterated the story of the hunger strike which had led to Sir Percy Lukas' visit and his report, which had not seen the light of day but had resulted, presumably, "in a point blank refusal to regard them as political prisoners or first class misdemeanants". The writer of the article went on to emphasize that "they are not ordinary criminals, and we do not believe that their countrymen regard them in that light". And he wrote:

> Whatever may have been their crimes, it is perfectly well known by the Government of India that they were committed at a time of great general excitement. Methods of coercion have been abandoned in India itself. Why should it be continued in Port Blair in the case of men who are already suffering the loss of every hope and comfort in life?

Savarkar writes that they kept on waiting for some reply from India in answer to his and his co-prisoners' petitions, but none came. So they "decided that something had to be done, [they] could not take it lying down". The result was, as reported by J Hope-Simpson, officiating chief commissioner and superintendent of Port Blair, to the home secretary on 9 May 1914: "I regret to have to report that of the prisoners confined for sedition, in connection with political murders and allied offences, sixteen have struck work.... It will be noticed that action has been concerted from which it is reasonable to conclude that, notwithstanding our attempts at separation, these convicts are in fact in easy touch with each other."

He also mentioned in his report that the conversations which the prisoners, according to them, had had with Colonel Douglas (chief commissioner) and Captain Flowerdew (medical superintendent) earlier, had, as far as he could judge, "a most unfortunate and unexpected effect", because:

> Apart from creating in the minds of the convicts a false impression of their own importance as prisoners and tending to obscure the essential villainy of their crime, these conversations have led the term convicts to believe that Col. Douglas had recommended to the Government of India the grant of remission in their cases on the same scale as those granted to prisoners confined in Indian jails and that the prisoners (both term and life-convicts) allege as the reason for their refusal to work, the failure of the Government of India to issue orders giving effect to the supposed proposal of Col. Douglas.

Hope-Simpson, however, added that "a search of the records in my office, both public and confidential, has not resulted in the discovery of any letter on the object, despatched by Colonel Douglas".

The main demand of the striking political prisoners was that they were not being given remission in their sentences, as was being granted to prisoners on the mainland. Savarkar states that they had prepared a manifesto containing three specific demands: "(1) As political prisoners, we should have all the privileges of the first class; (2) we should, otherwise, be put in the category of ordinary prisoners, given all the facilities accorded to them and the periodical visit to this jail be permitted by members of our families; and (3) we should be sent back to serve our term in the jails of India, so that we may get all the facilities of that jail life, including reduction in the period of the sentence on certificate of good behaviour." While the strike was on, the government began to repatriate term political prisoners to the mainland. Savarkar states that there was a special notification issued in terms of which:

> (1) all prisoners who were sentenced to definite period of time, short of life sentence, shall be sent back to their respective prisons in India, where the remission of their sentence will be duly considered and followed; (2) prisoners on life-sentence shall be detained in this [Cellular] prison for a continuous period of fourteen years, whereafter they will be set free for some labour of light character. This shall operate only in the case of those prisoners who give proof of their good behaviour duing their period of incarceration; (3) during the period of fourteen years, the prisoners shall be given decent food to eat, and decent clothes to wear. After five years, he shall be allowed to cook his own food and given from twelve annas to a rupee per month as his pocket allowance.

And so it went on.

Even a man like Hope-Simpson was beginning to feel uneasy. On 13 June the same year, that is a little over a month after he had reported the strike, he wrote to the home secretary:

> I am perfectly alive to the fact that their crimes were heinous and deserved condign punishment, and I refuse and have consistently refused to admit that because they were dubbed "political" they were in any sense venial. At the same time I am of the opinion that the treatment meted out is entirely unsuited to the temperament of these prisoners, that no reformatory effect can be expected from that treatment, and that elimination of the hope of better times to come [a hope which supports the usual criminal] partakes of the nature of cruelty in treatment.

Hope-Simpson seemed quite emphatic in his opinion that "the Cellular Jail is not suited to the requirements of the case". He said that "it was created for criminals of a very different stamp, and for them it possesses certain elements of value". He was therefore of the opinion that: "Educated men who have been convicted of offences against the state such as these should not be transported, but should be distributed in Indian Jails." The note was subjected to the usual bureaucratic noting. The home secretary commented on Savarkar's case, saying:

> The Hon'ble Member [Sir Reginald Craddock] ... came to the definite conclusion that Savarkar above all others could not be given any liberty in the Andamans or transferred to a jail in India. But the Hon'ble Member considered that a certain number of years of hard labour would satisfy the punitive requirements of his case, and that the remainder of his term would be of the nature of mere incarceration, because he would be dangerous to the community outside. ... Hon'ble Member also advocated the same treatment being meted out to other lifers who are being retained in the Andamans and confined in the Cellular Jail.

For some unknown reason, the file does not seem to have reached the table of Sir Reginald Craddock until 4 September, a little short of three months after Hope-Simpson had submitted his note. In Savarkar's case, Craddock's views would appear to have remained the same because, while talking of the lifers in the Andamans, he writes: "The position is that they are all shut up in the Cellular Jail because they might be very mischievous and in Savarkar's case, at all events, because there is extreme probability that he would make his escape." However, he hastened to add: "But men of education and intelligence who have also in most cases a poor physique cannot be kept on hopelessly and indefinitely in physical labour of the kind suitable for a day labourer. The punishment tells much more on them mentally than on the ordinary prisoner, and it embitters them and contains in it no element of reform." He even went on to say:

> Last, but not the least, I think that they must be given a glimmer of hope. If they continue unreformed, and if their former associates are still actively conspiring, it would be sheer folly to let them out altogether, but the hope might be that after a period of 14 years from the date of their conviction, the conditions of their incarceration will be further considered. It is quite possible by that time their views may have entirely changed, their potential influence outside waned, and that some paid employment be found for them in the Settlement. I think that some action of this kind must be taken if their only hope is not to be, as Barendra Nath pathetically put it, in "either a lunatic asylum or a friendly grave."

In addition, Craddock also indicated that he would like that "the superintendent should be asked to make recommendations . . . to find these prisoners, on conditions of their good behaviour, work which will keep their minds occupied. . . . Good behaviour should be allowed to earn them certain alleviations, while misconduct would entail reversion to manual tasks. Among the alleviations to be earned by good behaviour might be certain occasional holidays, access to books, which should be carefully selected". The net result was that the atmosphere did ease to some extent. They began to get occasional holidays and also some books. But they were to continue their incarceration in the Cellular Jail until they had completed their term of 14 years.

21

During the Great War and After

While scribes in the government of India's citadel of power were debating the fate of political prisoners in the Andamans, world-shaking events were taking place in Europe. On 28 June 1914, Archduke Franz Ferdinand, heir to the Austrian throne, was shot dead by Gravilo Princip, a fanatic, at Sarajevo. Events moved quickly, because the German Kaiser reacted with great indignation, the Archduke being one of his personal friends. Within less than a month, Europe was at war. Neither France nor Russia or England nor, for that matter, Serbia, whose officials had been accused of being behind the murder of the Archduke, wanted war. But Austria did, aided and abetted by the sinister General Staff in Berlin.

Although this war, which was to turn into a great Armageddon, was being fought thousands of miles away, it was to affect in some way our tiny islands in the Bay of Bengal.

As a natural corollary India, being part of the British empire, declared war on the side of the Allies, and our soldiers, in hundreds and thousands, were sent to fight on the battlefields of Europe. They covered themselves with glory. But it is unbelieveable that Savarkar, a declared freedom fighter and inveterate enemy of the British, should have been so carried away as to write to his brother, in his once-yearly letter dated 9 March 1915:

> It was thrill of delight in my heart to hear that Indian troops were allowed to go to Europe, in their thousands, to fight against the best military power in the world and that they had acquitted themselves with such splendour and were covered with military glory. ... You may be knowing [sic] by this time that some of us have already volunteered to go to the front of the war, and I am glad to inform you that Government have made a special note of it, though no answer could come yet.

There is no official confirmation of Savarkar's offer, but the very fact that the letter was allowed to be sent, obviously after being censored officially, proves the veracity of this offer!

Some of his other countrymen, who also belonged to the revolutionary party, were obviously less enthusiastic about the war—which was nothing but a struggle for hegemony among the big powers in the west—or the part Indian soldiers were playing as mercenaries of the British, for there soon arrived in the Cellular Jail the first batch of some of those who had been sentenced in the Lahore conspiracy case.

In this so-called conspiracy, which was followed by trials in two other conspiracy cases—known as the first supplementary case and the second supplementary case—as many as 212 men were tried (between April 1915 and January 1917), of whom 36 were sentenced to death and as many as 77 sentenced to transportation; some of the death sentences were changed to those of transportation for life by the viceroy. Those accused in the cases were charged with conspiring to wage war against the king.

The genesis of the conspiracy lay in the United States, and practically all those implicated in the three cases were members of the *Ghadar* party. The aim of this party was to start an uprising in India and, to formulate their *modus operandi*, the first meetings had taken place in the United States and in Singapore. On arrival in India, members of the Ghadar party were to spread into the villages (particularly in the Punjab, since most of them were Sikhs), and collect recruits with the idea of committing decoities to begin with, presumably to fill up their coffers for the work in hand. They were also to encourage the disaffected troops to mutiny and, if successful, with their help seize magazines, attack arsenals, even make an attack on the artillery, and then indulge in the massacre of Europeans in general. These were some of their aims and objectives.

The story of the Ghadar party is a long one and somewhat complicated. Yet, it is a fascinating story. *Ghadar*, as most readers would know, means rebellion.

The first Indian immigrants arrived in Canada and in the United States some time in the early years of this century. No one really knows what urged them to leave the Punjab, their beloved land of the five rivers. One story has it that some of the Sikh troops passing through Vancouver in British Columbia (on their way back after celebrating Queen Victoria's diamond jubilee) told stories, when back home, about this continent of wide, empty spaces which flowed with milk and honey. So some Punjabis took off for Canada, and some for the United States. There is an interesting, though rather sad, description of the first group that arrived in Canada. Wrote an observer:

> They were a forlorn looking lot, sad-eyed and silent. ... They wore only cotton clothing, the rain dripping from their soaked turbans and falling on the pathetic bundles besides them which contained all they possessed. ... I am sure that most people who saw them were quite convinced that they would sicken and die very quickly in a climate so different from the heat of the Punjab.

They neither sickened, nor did they die. They were much too hardy. But they faced a bleak future. How could they be honoured in a foreign country when they had no honour at home?

It was in America that the Ghadar party took birth. A few Indians got together and formed what was called the Indian Association of Pacific Coast. Their main grievance was that Indians were refused entry into certain countries and often refused jobs. In 1908, the association changed its name to Indian Independence League. Some Indians carried on an agitation in Oregon; others organized themselves into a party called the Hindi Association. This association later transformed itself into the Ghadar party, with its headquarters in San Francisco. On 1 November 1913, it brought out the first issue of its journal, known as *Ghadar*. (A Punjabi edition came out in 1914, and also one in Urdu. The *Ghadar* openly claimed to be "the enemy of the British Raj". It was edited by Har Dyal, a well-known revolutionary who had fled India in 1911, and had become, within a year of his arrival, the professor of Indian Philosophy and Sanskrit at Leland Standfort University in Palo Alto, California.

The first conference of Indian revolutionaries abroad met at Stockton (California) in February 1914, and the party soon had its branches in Canada, Panama and China.

The Sikhs in Canada were becoming increasingly discontented at the discriminatory restrictions being imposed on them. (By 1908 there were

8,000 of them, and more were coming.) The Canadian government wanted to put an end to Indian immigration. So in 1911 they passed a law which required every intending immigrant to have 200 dollars with him or her. Besides, they were to travel by ship, which would bring them directly (without changing ships) from India to Canada, knowing full well that no such shipping service was in existence.

To fox the Canadian authorities, Gurdit Singh, an enterprising Sikh, a wealthy contractor in Singapore and Malaya, went to Hongkong and chartered a Japanese ship, *Koma Gata Maru*. After picking up Indian passengers from Shanghai, Moji and Yokohama, he sailed into the Vancouver harbour on 23 May 1914. Barring 22 passengers who were returning to Canada, the others were not allowed to land. Then followed a kind of state of seige, which lasted over two months, during the course of which food and water on the ship were exhausted. Ultimately, force was used. It included the use of *Rainbow*, a British warship, to force *Koma Gata Maru* to return. On the way back, the *Koma Gata Maru* went through many an unpleasant experience whenever the ship touched shore—Yokohoma, Kobe, Hongkong, Singapore. On arrival at Calcutta, the reception was even worse. Some of the passengers who had landed, and were on their way back home to the Punjab, were kicked around and pushed and beaten up. They were even charged with bayonets and fired upon. According to official sources, 14 (and according to unofficial sources, 40) lay dead. A hundred and twenty were arrested.

In September 1914, an organization was formed at Zurich, which called itself the International Pro-Indian Committee. Its president would later go to Berlin to work in the German Foreign Office. The Indian National Party was formed in Berlin and, in due course, it expanded its activities into West Asia; some Indian revolutionaries arrived in Turkey, others went off to Baghdad (via Persia) and Damascus (via the Suez). Besides, some even surfaced in places as far off as China, Japan, Burma, and of course the North-western Frontier Province in India.

There is no doubt that the Ghadar party was supported by the Germans with both arms and money, and one of the German plans, according to James Campbell Ker—about which he has written in his book *Political Troubles in India, 1907-1917* was to take over the Andamans. He writes:

> First of all an agent was to go to the Andamans, in the guise of a merchant, and to land arms supplied from German sources: he was then to get in touch with the released prisoners who were working on their own ground, and arrange with them to destroy the wireless station on the appointed night. One or two of some twelve German ships laid up in Sabang [in Sumatra], after getting together the fittest of the crew of all the vessels and taking as many Germans from Deli [also in Sumatra] as possible, were to leave for the Nicobars; here they would pick up quickfirers, guns and ammunitions, which would be previously deposited

by pre-concerted arrangements. The ships would then proceed to the Andamans so as to arrive there on the night fixed for the destruction of the wireless station, landings being effected at the same time both on the East and the West side of the Island. After this had been done, and the place had been captured, as many of the convicts as were fit and willing, were to be shipped, under German leadership, to a place near Rangoon.

The take-over of the Andamans was to be a prelude to engineering a revolt in Burma and India. Sir Reginald Craddock, in *The Dilemma of India*, a book he published after he ceased to be a member of the viceroy's executive council, has also made a reference to this proposed venture of the members of the Ghadar party. He has written:

The anarchists and seditionaries in America had another string to their bow, viz. to obtain arms by Government [presumably German government] help and land them on the coast. The idea was to set free all the convicts on the Andaman Islands and land them in Burma and then trust to a rising of the population.

But to go back to the prisoners sentenced for their involvement in the Lahore conspiracy cases; the first batch arrived sometime in 1915. It consisted mostly of Sikhs who had, in one way or another, been associated with the Ghadar party. They included Bhai Parmanand, who had earned for himself the reputation of being a great revolutionary. In subsequent years, unfortunately, he was to associate himself rather actively with Hindu communal politics and become a pillar of the Hindu Mahasabha, a purely communal organization, which stood for the supremacy of the Hindu *dharma rajya*, in which the minorities had no place except as second class citizens.

Bhai Parmanand, who had obtained his master's degree from the Punjab university, was for some years a sort of travelling lecturer, whose main aim was to preach the doctrine of the Arya Samaj, a Hindu reformist organization which believed in converting Muslims back to Hinduism. (According to strict Hindu doctrine, you have to be born a Hindu; there can be no Hindu converts.) Later, Bhai Parmanand was a professor at the Dayanand Anglo-Vedic College at Lahore for a while. His activities, however, attracted the government's attention; he was, consequently, bound down; he retired to his village near Jehlum in the Punjab.

But in October 1910 he sailed for Europe on the pretext that he was going to study medicine. After a brief sojourn in Paris, he went off to Georgetown in British Guiana, where he started his Arya Samaj activities, ostensibly with a view to saving the locals from turning to Christianity, and of course to provide himself with bread and butter. Within six months, however, he had arrived in California. While there, he did take up a course in medicine, but the moment Har Dyal was back in Berkeley (California) from Palo Alto—and that in 1912—the two joined together and became close associates. And that was the beginning of Bhai Parmanand's career in the Ghadar party. He left the United States in 1913 and, after visiting most of the centres of Indian revolutionary activity in Europe, returned to India in December 1913, to start the Ghadar movement in the Punjab. Convicting him in the Lahore conspiracy case trial, the tribunal said about Bhai Parmanand: "Finally, we can only say that we have examined and considered all the available evidence with the utmost care; and the only conclusion to which we can come is that this accused [Bhai Parmanand] was not only one of the persons concerned in the present conspiracy, but was one of the most important revolutionaries."

Of the three judges, two agreed that he be sentenced to death. The third did not. Though sentenced to death, the viceroy reduced the punishment to one of transportation for life. And that is how Bhai Parmanand, along with some of the others transported for life, found himself in the Cellular Jail.

Perhaps one of the worst jailors that the Cellular Jail was to see in its long and tortuous career was a man named Barry, an Irishman, obviously a frustrated man and something of a sadist. He had been there for many years, had had several brushes with Savarkar and others, and was responsible for inflicting corporal punishment on many a political prisoner. Part of the reason why Savarkar had it so rough was because of Barry's firm belief that all unrest in the Cellular Jail had stemmed from Savarkar.

Barry soon had a brush with Bhai Parmanand. As the former Ghadar party leaders had come to the Andamans with the reputation of being incorrigible, Barry decided, at the very outset, to be tough with them. They were to be kept under strict control. Bhai Parmanand and Ashutosh Lahiri, a revolutionary from Bengal who was also to end up as a leader of the Hindu Mahasabha (the Hindu communal organization), were singled out for special treatment. They were subjected to all kinds of abuse. Being unable to put up with that kind of treatment, the two of them, one day, just picked Barry up physically and flung him on to the floor. Luckily for him, no bones were broken. But this was something unprecedented and caused quite a stir. Something therefore had to be done to preserve the white man's prestige and authority. The punishment had to be exemplary. The two men were sentenced to be flogged, twenty stripes with the cane in each case. According to Savarkar: "Parmanand was tied to the framework and given twenty stripes with the cane. Every stroke made a deep cut in the body and blood spouted from the wounds. . . . The caning was done and Parmanand bore it unperturbed."

However, it was obvious that there would soon be another show-down. The situation reached boiling point when one of the political prisoners, Bhan Singh, found himself locked up in his cell for having had a mild skirmish with his *tyndal*. (The word *tyndal* has its origin in the Malayalam word *tandal*, which was applied originally to a petty officer of the lascars.) Barry did not leave it at that. He went to the cell and showered Bhan Singh with abuse, and of course the hot-headed Sikh returned it in full measure. Five warders were immediately sent for, and the poor prisoner was beaten up black and blue.

Now the prisoners decided that something had to be done. On a prearranged day, therefore, 100 prisoners in different wings of the jail struck work. It was the largest number of prisoners in the history of the jail who had simultaneously taken such action. Two of their leaders—the Sikh, Sohan Singh, in his sixties, and Prithvi Singh, a Rajput from the Punjab—wanted to present a statement of their demands. The authorities would not hear of it. So they both resorted to hunger strike. After a period of 12 days, the government yielded. The strike was called off.

Another incident that created quite a stir, and was ultimately to result in the death of one of the political prisoners, was the refusal by the jail authorities to allow Rama Rakha to wear the sacred thread. (Every devout Hindu is supposed to wear a sacred thread round his body all the time.) Rama Rakha, a Punjabi Brahmin, had been convicted for spreading sedition in the army with a view to bringing about an armed revolution in Burma and Siam (now Thailand). No sooner had he arrived in the Andamans and set his foot in the Cellular Jail, he was asked to take off his sacred thread; apparently, that was the rule in the jail. Rama Rakha refused to oblige; so the thread was forcibly removed. He went on hunger strike and even refused water to drink. As usual he was fed forcibly, which resulted in his falling seriously ill. It was given out that Rama Rakha had developed tuberculosis. Savarkar takes the credit for having been able to persuade him to start eating. Nonetheless, within two months, he was dead.

The number of political prisoners continued to increase. In Europe the war eventually ended with an armistice. The hopes of political prisoners soared high, because they thought that, as a part of the victory celebrations, there would be an amnesty; but they were to be disappointed.

In the meantime, the long-awaited Jails Committee had been formed; it visited the Andamans. At about the same time, there was a general demand all over India for the release of the long-suffering political prisoners in the Andamans. The National Union of Bombay organized a petition demanding their release, which was signed by as many as 70,000 of its members. The government of India did react this time. Whether it was due to the agitation, or just because they felt unable to cope with so many political prisoners who had necessarily to be kept incarcerated in the Cellular Jail, is arguable. But the fact is that there was a general amnesty for most of the political prisoners, including Bhai Parmanand—but excluding Savarkar and some others who fell in the same category. (These numbered 300.)

An article written by Colonel Wedgwood, a member of the British parliament, which appeared around then in the *Daily Telegraph* of London, also attracted a great deal of attention. It was entitled *Hell on Earth: Life in the Andamans*. Colonel Wedgwood had, quite coincidentally, travelled in a railway compartment with a man, "one of those white-dressed men with a soft voice and saintlike face", who had lived for five years in the Andamans, and had once been a professor of history at the Lahore university. The "saintlike man" had given a very graphic picture of the tyranny and moral corruption in the Andamans; he told him how, in the midst of it all, many a political prisoner (he had mentioned the name of Ganesh, the elder Savarkar), "after ten years of this hell...now permanently in hospital, awaited his end—a release from this world to one where there are no tyrants and prisons."

The working committee of the Indian National Congress had also passed a resolution "demanding the release of Savarkar brothers". At long last Savarkar, and some others like him, were allowed out of the Cellular Jail and permitted to live as ticket-of-leave prisoners in Port Blair.

Like Maulana Mohammad Jafar Thanesvari, Savarkar, once outside, took to proselytizing and launched a *shuddhi* movement in the Andamans. However, when orders came for Savarkar to leave the Andamans, he petitioned to the government: "If I was not to be set free on my stepping into India, I prefer to be kept back in the Andamans to serve my whole term of imprisonment." He suggested that for the rest of his time he "should be allowed to settle in the Andamans as a free person with [his] family, or alone on a ticket granted of that purpose". His plea, of course, was turned down. (He was subsequently released while in Yerwada Jail at Poona, after a meeting with the governor of Bombay, Sir George Lloyd, when, according to him, he was made to sign "a pledge of enforced abstinence from current politics".

The decision to repatriate political prisoners to the mainland synchronized, more or less, with the decision of the government of India to abolish the penal settlement in the Andamans altogether. Sir William Vincent, home secretary to the government of India, admitted in the Central Legislative Assembly 11 on March 1921: "For some years we have had misgivings about the Settlement." And in reply to a question by the Honourable Rai Bahadur Ram Saran Das in the council of states a few months later, the Honourable H D Craik stated categorically: "Government have decided to abandon the Andaman as a penal settlement.... Deportation accordingly ceased in March last." Within less than a year, however, government had had second thoughts. Home Secretary Sir William Vincent told the Central Legislative Assembly on 6 February 1922:

> Owing to the stoppage of deportation to the Andamans and the inability of Local Governments to find funds at the present moment for the construction of jails, overcrowding in existing jails in certain provinces

has unfortunately become most serious. . . . In the circumstances, the Government of India have very reluctantly come to the conclusion that there is no alternative except to open temporarily the deportation to the Andamans of prisoners sentenced to transportation.

The position continued to be much the same for the next few years, because government reaffirmed, in a resolution on jails dated 27 February 1926, after Sir Alexander Muddiman, home member of the governor-general's executive council, had visited the Andamans that "the task of closing the penal settlement has not been found an easy one".

While the government was prevaricating about the fate of the Andamans as a penal settlement and had, finally, come to the conclusion that it had to continue, the freedom struggle on the mainland went on, if anything, with greater vigour, particularly by those revolutionaries who had no use for Mahatma Gandhi's non-violent methods, or for *satyagraha*. There were many cases in which terrorists—as the British described them—were involved, cases like the Chittagong armoury raid, the Kakori conspiracy and the Lahore conspiracy cases. Some of those convicted in these cases found themselves transported to the Andamans.

The three conspiracy cases mentioned above could well be described as some of the most daring in the history of the terrorist movement in India.

The Chittagong armoury raid was conducted on 18 April 1930; April 18 was chosen because that was the day when the Easter rising had taken place in Ireland. The leader of this exploit, if one may call it so, was Surya Sen. Manmathnath Gupta, in his *History of the Indian Revolutionary Movement*, describes what happened and how the raid was organized:

> Nirmal Sen, Lokenath Bal, Anand Singh, Ganesh Ghosh, Ambika Chakrabarti and Upendra Bhattacharya were to lead the attack on the various key points of the district [of Chittagong]. Anand Singh and Ganesh Ghosh were to spearhead the attack on the police line and armoury and Ambika Chakrabarti was to lead an attack on the telegraph and telephone exchange. Most of the youths were below 20, some even in the age group 16-17. The vehicle carrying Singh and Ghosh was followed by the vehicle carrying Surya Sen. The revolutionaries were able to surprise and capture the armouries and a huge amount of arms and ammunition came into their hands. A few guards and an English officer were killed. All the tasks were carried out according to schedule and Surya Sen was given a guard of honour. When the Europeans heard of the shooting and bomb blasts, they left their houses and fled.

This initial exploit was followed by many others all over the neighbouring hills, where the revolutionaries had escaped, and there were many encounters between them and the police. There were heavy casualties on both sides; according to one source as many as 160 soldiers were killed. That may be a slight exaggeration. But 32 revolutionaries were put on trial in this case. Some were hanged, some sentenced to various terms of imprisonment and, of course, quite a few sentenced to transportation for life. The leader, Surya Sen, escaped capture for quite a while; he even spent some time in Chandernagore, which was French territory. He was caught finally, tried and sentenced to death, but one of his companions, Kalpana Dutt, who was also tried along with him, was sentenced to transportation for life.

The Kakori case had its birth at a meeting in Shahjehanpur (in the then United Provinces), at the house of Ramprasad, who had achieved fame under the name of *Bismil*; this was in as far back as early 1924. All those present assumed names like *Nawab*, *Quicksilver* and the like; Ashfaqulla, a Muslim among them, decided to wear the garb of a Hindu and called himself *Kunwarji*.

On 9 August 1925, they stopped a passenger train by pulling the alarm chain near a railway station known as Kakori. The moment the train came to a halt, 16 of them entered the brake van of the train and removed the chests which carried money. While this operation went on, some of them kept watch on the passengers—a Gurkha in the act of picking up his rifle was shot dead; a passenger who leaned out of the window was wounded by a revolver shot fired by a raider; a European carrying a rifle, when trying to alight from the train, was fired at and wounded in the leg.

Following the raid, extensive searches were carried out in the entire province of Uttar Pradesh, and most of those involved were arrested. A trial ensued and, as was to be expected, some were executed, and others sent to the Andamans on transportation for life.

The case which really caught the imagination of the people in India, and became something of a *cause célèbre*, was the Lahore conspiracy case. It was in this case that Bhagat Singh was involved. Bhagat Singh's is the greatest name among the revolutionaries who fought for India's freedom. He had become a legend in his lifetime and today he has become an integral part of Indian folklore. Despite Bhagat Singh's belief in violence as a legitimate weapon in the fight for freedom, Gandhi, the apostle of non-violence, pleaded mercy him with Lord Irwin, the then viceroy of India.

It all began with the appointment by the British government of a commission to recommend constitutional changes that could be introduced in the political structure of the governance of India. The commission was headed by a Liberal member of the British parliament, Sir John (later Lord) Simon. One of the members, incidentally, was Major Clement Attlee (later the British socialist prime minister of England, known subsequently as Earl Attlee). But what incensed the public in India, and particularly the Indian National Congress, was that no Indian had been included in the commission. The Congress, therefore, decided that the commission be boycotted and, wherever it went, it met with processions demonstrating against it and the shouting of the slogan: "Simon, go back!"

The commission arrived in Lahore (now in Pakistan) on 30 October 1928. As elsewhere in India, a procession had been organized and it was being led by Lala Lajpat Rai, one of the foremost leaders of the Congress, who had spent many years in exile abroad. As the procession was marching towards the Lahore railway station, it found itself faced by a barbed-wire fencing. It stopped; at the head near the fencing stood Lajpat Rai and some other local leaders. Although the procession had so far been absolutely peaceful, suddenly, for no ostensible reason, the police started raining blows on the processionists. Lajpat Rai received many blows and, although it appeared at the time that the injuries were of no serious nature, they ultimately proved fatal; a few days later, Lala Lajpat Rai had a severe heart attack. He died on 17 November 1928. The man who had beaten Lajpat Rai with a *lathi* was J A Scott, the senior superintendent of police.

Some time earlier, Bhagat Singh and some of his associates had formed themselves into a revolutionary party under the name of the Hindustan Socialist Republican party. The council of the party met in Lahore on 10 December and decided to kill Scott, because he was the man who, they said, was ultimately responsible for the death of Lala Lajpat Rai. A week later, on 17 December, Bhagat Singh and three of his other colleagues, including Rajguru, gathered near the *kutchery* (which housed the offices of the Lahore police) to await Scott's arrival. Fortunately for him, it was not Scott who came out first, but one of his junior superintendents of police, J P Saunders. Rajguru rushed forward and fired with his revolver. The shot hit Saunders in the head. He fell to the ground. Bhagat Singh fired another half a dozen shots, thus applying the *coup de grace*. The assailants decamped. (Incidentally, I was living in a room in the new hostel of Government College, Lahore, which was less than 100 yards away. I heard the shots and rushed out. Saunder's body was lying in a pool of blood. The police were running helter-skelter, in a state of utter confusion!)

The police started a massive man hunt and, during the course of the next two or three months, several arrests were made. But it was not until several months later when another event involving high drama took place in the Central Legislative Assembly, resulting in the arrest of Bhagat Singh, that they were able to unravel the various skeins of what came to be known later as the Lahore conspiracy case.

It was 8 April of the year 1929. Vithalbhai J Paiel was the president of the legislative assembly. As he was about to give his ruling on the introduction of the Public Safety Bill, which the leader of the Congress party, Pandit Motilal Nehru, had described as being "aimed at Indian nationalism and at the Congress", two bombs exploded on the floor of the House, followed by two revolver shots. The two young men responsible for this sensational act were 24-year-old Bhagat Singh, and Batukeshwar Dutt, 22 years of age. (Dutt was to spend many years in the Andamans.) Bhagat Singh and Dutt offered themselves for arrest without any show of resistence.

Bhagat Singh was wanted in many other cases and was one of the principal accused in the Lahore conspiracy case. A total of 24 persons were accused—six at the time were absconding and seven had turned approvers. Those accused were charged with "a conspiracy and war against the King-Emperor by murder, dacoity, and other methods, including the manufacture and use of bombs". The trial started on 10 July 1930 and the judgment was pronounced on 7 October 1930. Bhagat Singh and two others—including Rajguru, who had fired the first shot at Saunders—were sentenced to death. Seven others were sentenced to transportation for life.

These seven were among those who arrived in the Andamans in the year 1932.

L P Mathur, in his *History of the Andaman and Nicobar Islands*, writes:

The first batch of terrorist prisoners arrived in the cold weather in 1932. Fresh batches continued to reach the Andamans upto the beginning of 1933. ... The huge Cellular Jail in which they were confined was dilapidated, with crevices in the walls everywhere. ... Many of them ... were [made] to lie on wooden boards on the cold floor. ... There were no proper medical arrangements. ... The meals were of the worst quality and sometimes contained dead worms. ... They were given hard tasks. ... They were not allowed to purchase books nor were they provided with books by the Government. There were no facilities for recreation or games. ... The attitude of the authorities was vindictive, callous and discourteous.

The only way to protest against such inhuman treatment was to resort to the only weapon the political prisoners had—hunger strike. Bejoy Kumar Sinha, author of *In Andamans, the Indian Bastille*, who was at the time a prisoner in the Andamans himself, confined to the Cellular Jail, recalls that after a discussion among themselves a few of them went on hunger strike in early January 1933. They, however, agreed to give it up after an assurance by the then chief commissioner that their grievance would be looked into. Apparently, nothing much happened and there was no substantial improvement in their living conditions. So, once again, they decided to go on hunger strike. A communique, dated 28 May 1933, and issued by the home department at Simla, was read out on the floor of the house of the legislative assembly by the Honourable Sir Harry Haig, home member:

The Government of India have received information from the Chief Commissioner of the Andamans that on the 12th of May twenty-nine prisoners convicted of crimes connected with the terrorist movement went on hunger strike in the Cellular Jail as a protest against certain alleged grievances not being redressed. They have since been joined by several others.

The communique went on to state that one of the Lahore conspiracy case prisoners, Mahavir Singh, had died on 17 May. The official reason given for his death was that "the patient's resistance [to forcible feeding] in his weakened state [had] caused a severe shock to his system and led to his collapse and death". But Benoy Kumar Sinha's version is that, while being fed forcibly, the milk went into his lungs, and although Mahavir Singh knew what had happened he had kept quiet, thus inviting death.

The government communique also announced the death of another political prisoner, Mankrishna Nam Das, who had been administered food on 17 May "through his mouth without resistance". But on the 19th he had been admitted to hospital with lobar pneumonia. "Throughout his illness he took whatever was prescribed for him and gave no trouble whatever", it stated, and his death "was due to natural causes and was in no way accelerated by his abstinence from food for one day". Mohan Kishore, another prisoner, also died as a result of forced feeding, it was presumed.

As one would normally expect, there was a great deal of concern all over India about the fate of the prisoners who had gone on hunger strike. A delegation of members of the legislative assembly met Sir Harry who, apart from expressing "appreciation of their feelings", did precious little—except to despatch a special emissary, Lieutenant-Colonel Barker, who was inspector-general of police in the Punjab at the time. Whether it was due to the terms offered by Barker or due to a more conciliatory mood of the local authorities (because the hunger strike had gone on for an unprecedented prolonged period of 46 days), most of the prisoners' demands were accepted. Simla was therefore able to announce, in a communique dated 27 June 1933: "The Government of India have received news from the Chief Commissioner, Andaman and Nicobar Islands, that the hunger strike was abandoned by all prisoners on June 26." And Sir Harry Haig was in a position to state:

> Since the termination of the strike the Government of India have been in communication with the Chief Commissioner, Andaman and Nicobar Islands, with a view to considering whether there were any matters in regard to which it might be reasonable to amend the rules. As a result the Chief Commissioner, with the approval of the Government of India, has now introduced certain changes in the treatment of prisoners.

In the words of L P Mathur, who writes that what he has stated in this connection is based on Bejoy Kumar Sinha's book, the government agreed that:

The political prisoners were to be supplied with bed-sheets, mosquito nets, pillows, towels and bed-steads. The quality of rice, food and vegetables was to be improved. Fish was to be supplied to Bengali prisoners on alternate days. The kitchen was to be left under the supervision of the political prisoners. ... Facilities for indoor and outdoor games were to be given to them. The Government of India recognised the right of the prisoners to subscribe [to] prescribed newspapers and magazines.

Though unofficially this class had existed for a long time, now the term "permanently incarcerated prisoners" was given an official status.

Burma being administratively a province of India then, all those who were sentenced to transportation for life there were also being sent to the Andamans. However, it was not until the Tharwardy Rebellion (as the British called it) was crushed that the largest ever batch of Burmese transportees, who could also be described as political prisoners, arrived in the Andamans. They numbered 535. According to a statement made by the then home member of the Burmese government, on 24 February 1935, as many as 274 Tharwardy "rebels" had been sentenced to death and 535 transported.

The Tharwardy Rebellion

The general council of Burmese Association was the only political party in Burma. It was under the control of a few Burmese landlords and intellectuals at the time, whose political objective was to achieve Home Rule for Burma under the British empire.

However, at its annual conference held in Mandalay in 1928, Dr Saya Sen, who was the leader of the extremist faction of the general council, moved a resolution that their goal, from then on, would be to achieve complete independence, and that they believed in a mass movement to achieve that objective. The moderates, of course, quit the conference. According to Jiten Ghosh, one of the Indian revolutionaries who was also a transportee in the Andamans: "Dr Saya Sen was elected General Secretary [and set up] a big volunteer corps. ... He considered raising a rebellious army with the agricultural population of Burma."

Dr Sen started a workshop for manufacturing locally-made guns and other ammunition at his secret headquarters in the thick forests of Tharwardy. Youths from all over Burma rallied to his cause; they were given training in the use of arms. Having thus organized a volunteer army, Dr Saya Sen raised his flag of rebellion one night in December 1930. Writes Jiten Ghosh:

He issued a proclamation revoking all agricultural loans. ... Buddhism was declared the State religion. ... Railway lines and bridges, telephones and telegram lines were destroyed at Tharwardy, arms and ammunitions of the police were snatched, prison gates were broken, freeing prisoners. Headmen of villages and towns were disarmed.

For seven days, until the British Army arrived on the scene, Dr Sen's volunteer army held sway over Tharwardy; even the British magistrate was made to surrender and declare that British rule had ended. It took the British Army three days to quell the rebellion, and they had to even resort to shelling. (Dr Saya Sen escaped.)

Tharwardy once again came under British sway, but the rebellion had spread to all parts of Burma. Dr Sen's men captured police lines and jails in most towns. The British retaliated with all the force at their command. Reprisals were both heavy and brutal. Again, in the words of Jiten Ghosh: "Village after village was blown up by gun fire and shelling. ... Government officials indulged in plunder, loot and rape. Heavy punitive taxes [were] imposed on villages."

Four years were to elapse before the British could put a complete end to the rebellion. And it took another four years to capture Dr Saya Sen, "while sick of fever in the forest of Mandal through the treachery of a friend".

There were trials all over Burma and, as already stated, 274 "rebels" were hanged. Five hundred and thirty-five others arrived in the Andamans to join their counterparts from the rest of India.

For three years following the settlement of the issues that had led to the hunger strike in May-June 1933, the life of political prisoners in the Andamans ran at a fairly even pace. Of course, they suffered from a sense of frustration, but that was not due to harsh treatment meted out by the jail authorities, but primarily because the life of a permanently incarcerated prisoner, no matter how free from petty irritations, was far from pleasant. Even though more letters, to and from relatives, were now being allowed, difficulties of communication being what they were, the concession made no substantial difference. The same applied to the laxity in the rule with regard to interviews with relatives. Very few of them could travel all the way to *Kala Pani*. Besides, there were the usual minor clashes; in one case, again according to Mathur (quoting Bejoy Kumar Sinha), there was a work strike in 1934, because of the rough handling of a prisoner by a jail warder. The situation was resolved after threats and counter-threats (the authorities threatening to stop all facilities). Both sides realized the futility of the exercise, and the authorities agreed to revert to *status quo. ante*. Sinha says that the new chief commissioner, who had taken over in 1936, was of a "haughty nature". (If he means W A Cosgrave, he had taken charge on 6 February 1935, and not in 1936. No new chief commissioner took office in 1936.)

Captain B Chaudhuri of the Indian Medical Service, who later retired as lieutenant-general, was posted as senior medical officer in the Andamans from April 1935 to September 1939. As he was chief of medical services there, Cellular Jail was under him, and he was official visitor of the jail. In an interview with me in New Delhi, he said that far from being a man of "haughty nature", Cosgrave was a very sympathetic person, who fully agreed with Chaudhuri's postulate that, since most of the prisoners were educated people, they should be treated accordingly.

Unlike his predecessor J W Smyth, who used to inspect the jail standing in the central tower, Cosgrave would go to each cell and talk to all the prisoners individually, although that would take hours. (Perhaps Bejoy Kumar Sinha was referring to Smyth and not Cosgrave when he spoke about the chief commissioner being "haughty". (Smyth was in office from 7 December 1931 to 6 February 1935, when Cosgrave took over.)

Chaudhuri had made it a regular practice to pay a weekly visit to the jail and meet practically all the prisoners; some of their leaders like Ganesh Ghosh, Dr Niranjan Roy and Sardar Gurmukh Singh became his personal friends. According to him, each one of them had a cell to himself and, although food was rationed, they ran their own mess. He thought that the food used to be "fairly decent" and better than what was given to prisoners in Indian jails. They were given both fish and meat, though there was some argument about the quality and (interestingly enough) about the sex of the goat whose meat was to be eaten! When anyone was sick in hospital, Chaudhuri's orders were that there should be no limit to the food served to prisoner-patients.

With regard to library facilities, Chaudhuri conceded that there were some difficulties about the kind of books which were to be allowed. Most prisoners—at least a majority of them—were from Bengal, and they wanted to read mainly Marxist literature, which did not meet with the approval of the authorities in Bengal, whose prior permission was necessary. In consequence, therefore, prisoners from other provinces also suffered. According to Chaudhuri, it was decided at his suggestion that as far as books required by prisoners from other provinces were concerned, the approval of the authorities in those particular provinces may be obtained. This the government agreed to. And, since prisoners from other provinces were not interested in Marxist literature only, they had no difficulty in getting the books they wanted. "So 99 per cent of the books they wanted, they got them", said Chaudhuri. Exercise and recreation, of course, were confined to the jail compound only. "But they were even allowed a rifle drill", added Chaudhuri, "and they had a workshop where they made rifles". This facility had to be withdrawn because of "trouble among themselves". They were allowed to play football in the compound, but in batches. The story told by Bejoy Kumar Sinha, as quoted by Mathur, is quite different, however:

> The quality of food gradually deteriorated. Worthless books were purchased by the Government. ... Many political prisoners were flogged for slight violation of the rules of the prison. The continuous stay of

terrorist prisoners in the dingy cells in the harmful climate of the tropical island, shattered the health of nearly all of them.

Be that as it may, there is no denying the fact that the prisoners were in a state of mental turmoil and were most restive. Political parties on the mainland, particularly the Congress, were also displaying a great deal of interest on the fate of prisoners in the Andamans. (In reply to a question by Mohan Lal Saxena in the legislative assembly on 25 March 1935, Sir Henry Craik gave the number of terrorist prisoners as 219.) The total number of questions asked in one year alone, i.e. in 1936, was 61.

In the midst of it all, Sir Henry Craik, who was home member of the governor-general's executive council, decided to pay a visit to the Andamans to see things for himself. This was sometime in the middle of the year. On arrival back in Simla he scandalized everyone, particularly the press, by stating that the Andamans were a "paradise". For a while the Andamans were freely described, rather facetiously, as "Craik's Paradise". Craik, however, replying to a question asked by Bhai Parmanand in the legislative assembly, said that "the phrase which is so often quoted as 'Paradise' was not the phrase I used". He explained that he had said that "it was a "Paradise for prisoners". And he categorically added: "In comparison with any other jail or convict settlement in British India, it is a paradise." During the course of his reply to the same question by Bhai Parmanand, Craik further said: "I found no serious defects in the administration of the Cellular Jail, Port Blair, which required to be remedied; and . . . according to the Public Health Commissioner's report for 1934, the death rate was 11 per cent per thousand of the total convict population".

Apart from that, Sir Henry submitted no detailed report because, as he said, he was not the kind who believed in writing reports. But he did say that all they (the prisoners) wanted was their release; otherwise, they had no major grievances.

Craik's statements led to all kinds of protest from the leaders of various political parties in India, particularly the Indian National Congress and members of the legislative assembly. Obviously, to appease the latter, and to quieten them down for a while, Craik agreed to send two members of the legislative assembly—Raizada Hans Raj of the Congress and Sir Mohammed Yamin Khan of the Muslim League—to visit the Andamans and see things for themselves.

Sir Mohammed Yamin Khan and Raizada Hans Raj, accompanied by his wife and son, set sail from Calcutta on 9 October 1936. Like everyone else who visits the Andamans, they too were fascinated by the natural beauty of the islands, for Sir Mohammed Yamin Khan wrote, in a report which he submitted on 30 November 1936, after his return:

> From the sea we could see the Andaman Islands, and the Port Blair Settlement looked just like a well-kept park. The portion of the hill

near Aberdeen Town looks like the Malabar Hill of Bombay, and Raizada Hans Raj on seeing the jail thought that it was the Chief Commissioner's Castle. The Ross Island is a beauty and looks beautiful from the sea .... [We] were much impressed by the beauty of the Islands.

Sir Mohammed Yamin Khan wrote that, on the very first day of their arrival, the first thing they did was to spend "two hours in the hospital which is exclusively for political prisoners". They spoke to every patient, and found that "some indoor patients were suffering from the disease with which they have been suffering even in India". They found the number of patients—25—comparatively small. Most looked "as if they had recovered from their ailments and were kept in the Hospital till the doctor was fully satisfied that they were perfectly cured". Yamin Khan, incidentally, was put up as a houseguest of Captain Chaudhuri, the senior medical officer, because the official guest-house had apparently only enough room to accommodate Raizada Hans Raj, his wife and son.

The next day, according to Yamin Khan, he and Hans Raj met the political prisoners in the jail and, as desired by the prisoners themselves, without the presence of officials. What surprised Yamin Khan "was to learn that the political prisoners had great cliques amongst themselves and one party had no confidence in the other parties". So they had to meet them in three separate batches, and a few individually. They talked to them for several hours, and listened to their complaints, which were:

Health: About health they laid stress on the question of there being 25 patients in the hospital, 73 being convalescents on the day of our first visit. On this I had a long talk with the Medical Officer and Superintendent of the jail, who has given us a full and detailed account of the causes which were responsible for so many political prisoners being in the hospital.

(This illness, presumably, was "on account of the influenza which they had contracted on account of exposure after exercise which generally people do in the Andamans after the Monsoons". People do so even today, if they are not careful.)

Water Supply: I learned that water supply was not insufficient, but on certain occasions only through the mistakes of someone or the other it was not available during certain hours of the day. The Chief Commissioner and the Senior Medical Officer took action on this. It was also brought to their notice, that sometimes the political prisoners wanted a second bath in the evening after games, which was generally responsible for the shortage of water, as each can be allowed one bath either in the morning or in the evening.

Climate: The chief complaint about the climate was that the variation was very small, 89-66. (Yamin Khan's comment: "Calcutta was hotter when we left than Port Blair when we arrived there. Humidity is really very great.")

Food: The chief grievance of the political prisoners on this score was that a large variety of vegetables do not grow on the Island. Some kinds of vegetables are imported from Calcutta and Rangoon which remain fresh for a few days, after which they have to depend on local produce. About fish and mutton they said they always got fresh supply, except during the height of the Monsoon.

(More than forty years since this report was written, the position in the islands vis-à-vis food and other eatables, even consumer goods, is still the same.)

Sir Mohammed Yamin Khan goes on to say that Raizada Hans Raj went into the kitchen, where food for ordinary C-class prisoners was being cooked. He tasted *dal* and *chappati*, and he thought that the food was better than that "cooked and prepared in the Punjab jails".

The political prisoners also complained about the lack of sufficient newspapers. The visitors found that the following newspapers were being supplied to them: (*i*) *Statesman Weekly* (overseas edition); (*ii*) *Illustrated Times of India*; (*iii*) *Sanjavani*; (*iv*) *Bangabashi*; and (*v*) *Chief Commissioner's Bulletin*.

They also looked into complaints with regard to library facilities—that the prisoners had to purchase a lot of books themselves and that the government grant of Rs 200 was inadequate; recreation and sport facilities, too, were not enough.

But both Sir Mohammed Yamin Khan and Raizada Hans Raj felt that everything boiled down to one simple fact, which was the gravamen of their grievances—*they wanted to be repatriated*. When faced with the categorical question as to what they would prefer—to be kept in the Andamans together, or repatriated to India and kept in separate jails, their answer was: "We have nothing to choose between the two. Each is equally bad. We want to be repatriated immediately and kept together."

Sir Mohammed Yamin Khan was of the opinion that "this great stress on repatriation . . . in spite of the fact that they enjoyed greater facilities in the Cellular Jail" was "chiefly on account of their not meeting outside people so often as in India". Pending their repatriation, however, they wanted certain facilities:

(1) To play outside the jail walls, preferably on the Gymkhana Ground;
(2) Sea-bathing;
(3) Some sort of entertainment like cinema or any other show to break the monotony; and
(4) Cells to remain unlocked during the night and only the doors of

the verandahs kept locked in order to allow one prisoner to visit another.

In this context, Sir Mohammed has also given a description of the cells in the Cellular Jail. He writes:

The cells are of the size which ordinarily a middle class man or a clerk at Simla or in Calcutta does not have for his bed room. ... Each cell has got a cot with a blanket, a bed sheet, one pillow and a sheet. ... Each prisoner is allowed to purchase articles which are sanctioned by the jail authorities as each B class prisoner can get Rs 20 a month and C class prisoner Rs 10 a month from their relations or friends.

But Sir Mohammed Yamin Khan was definitely of the view that "some of the prisoners ought not to have been sent at all to the Andamans". And in that category, he included "(1) Those whose health was not good enough at the time they were sent to the Andamans; and (2) Those who are very young and are sentenced to short terms of imprisonment."

As far as the youth of some of the prisoners was concerned, it is an interesting coincidence that, while the two worthies were still in the Andamans, Sir Henry Craik should inform D K Lahiri Chaudhuri, in reply to a question put in the legislative assembly, that of those sentenced to transportation in connection with the Chittagong armoury raid case "one of the convicts at time of his conviction in March 1932 was 15; the ages of the rest ranged from 17 to 26".

Sir Mohammed Yamin Khan's report contrasts strangely with the observations made by Bejoy Kumar Sinha, as quoted by Mathur: "Many political prisoners are flogged for slight violation of the rules of the prison. The continuous stay of terrorist prisoners in the dingy cells in the harmful climate of the tropical Islands, shattered the health of nearly all of them."

Nowhere in his report does Sir Mohammed Yamin Khan mention any complaint made by the prisoners that they had been flogged; nor does his description of the cells makes them out to be "dingy". The author, who has seen them, agrees that they are depressing no doubt, but so are cells in any jail all over the world—even in the contemporary world when there is so much talk of "hate the crime but not the criminal". In his report, Sir Mohammed Yamin Khan also wrote: "I did not see mosquitoes in the Andaman Islands even 5 per cent of what I found in Calcutta." Obviously, he failed to notice the irony of his remarks!

Anyway, the visit of the two legislators raised the hopes of the political prisoners. They all thought that something was bound to happen. They waited in vain. Government, on the whole, was of the opinion that conditions obtaining in the Cellular Jail were by and large satisfactory. What spurred the prisoners' hopes still further was when Congress ministries in seven Indian provinces were installed, as a result of the introduction of provincial autonomy under the Government of India Act of 1935. And yet nothing happened. The political prisoners were at the end of their tether. On 9 July 1937, in the words of an official communique:

> A large number of terrorist convicts in the Andamans... sent a petition to the Government of India requesting that throughout the whole of British India [not Andamans alone]:
> (1) All detenues, State prisoners and convicted "political" prisoners be released;
> (2) All repressive laws be repealed and all orders of internment withdrawn;
> (3) All "political" prisoners at present in the Andamans be returned to India and no more sent to the Andamans;
> (4) All "political" convicts be treated as class B prisoners.

The communique stated that the petition in question had not been received by the government of India till 20 July but, two days earlier, "terrorist convicts" had already informed the chief commissioner that unless "the Government of India's reply was received by the 24th July they would go on hunger-strike". On 23 July, "the orders of the Government of India rejecting the petition were conveyed to the prisoners". And, according to J A Thorne, home secretary to the government of India: "The mass hunger-strike commenced on the 24th of July (1937). The number of strikers was 177."

Gradually, the strike gathered momentum. By 19 August, again according to Thorne, the number had swelled to 225.

A wave of indignation spread all over the country; the people were, naturally enough, anxious about the state of health of the striking prisoners. S Satyamurthi of the Congress party in the Central Legislative Assembly moved a motion of adjournment of the House. During the course of discussions on the adjournment motion, Bhulabhai Desai, leader of the Congress party, summed up the situation when he said:

> From one end of this land to the other appeal has gone forth that these prisoners should be repatriated; You [Home Secretary Thorne] were good enough to thank the President of the Congress for an appeal to the hunger-strikers to give up hunger-strike and if those thanks had any grain of sincerity in them, I want to aid you in a cause, not merely of mercy, but of good to yourself, the maintenance of the Government. If you wish to make more terrorists, by all means carry on with your fetish of discipline; by all means carry on with all those shrouds and fuel facing those men, [There was horror at the report that the local administration had been arranging for shrouds and fuel, on a large scale, for those who might die as a result of the hunger-strike.] and if you do so, you will find that the Government will dig its own grave

with the ashes of these men.

Even M A Jinnah joined in making a plea on behalf of the prisoners:

We are not urging upon you now that you should repatriate them because they are on hunger-strike. But they should be repatriated on grounds, on reasons that we feel that, whatever may have been the reason five years ago in 1932, these reasons do not exist now and the question should be reviewed.

The motion was carried by 62 votes to 55, and the government was defeated. To say that there was a great deal of sympathy for the hunger-strikers all over the country would be a gross understatement: not only did most of the chief political bodies and leaders join in voicing their sympathy and indignation, a large number of political prisoners in India also staged sympathetic hunger strikes in their respective jails.

Meanwhile, authorities at home had to resort to forced feeding. The prisoners had to be kept alive, come what may. But apart from the fact that they had learnt from past experience how to go about it without the use of undue force, both the chief commissioner, W A Cosgrave, and the senior medical officer, Captain B Chaudhuri, were fortunately sympathetic and humane, and they had also been able to establish cordial relations with some of the prison leaders in the Cellular Jail. This fact did make Captain Chaudhuri's task of "force feeding" them comparatively less arduous. And Cosgrave had backed him all along.

The striking prisoners did respond to this approach of the chief commissioner because, according to Chaudhuri, they sent a note to him (Chaudhuri) to tell the chief commissioner that their protest was not directed towards the local administration, but was one of principle—against the British government for holding them in the Andamans. This was an insult, they felt. They also made a specific mention of the fact that, if they did not greet Cosgrave or Chaudhuri when either went on his rounds, it was not to be taken amiss, because it was not meant as a personal affront to them.

Chaudhuri says that he had instructed all medical officers to consider the hunger-strikers as patients and not as prisoners, and that no notice was to be taken of any insult they might be subjected to.

To keep the prisoners alive, he said that forced feeding had to be resorted to. But he proudly pointed out that, though the hunger strike had lasted 56 days, not one was allowed to die. The veterans among the strikers were very serious about their willingness to die for the cause, and stuck all along to their resolve about not eating voluntarily. But the younger people, added Chaudhuri with a chuckle, were different. He had given instructions that outside the cell of each of the youngsters some cheese and other small eats were to be left lying overnight. And next morning, if these had disappeared, he said with a merry twinkle in his eye, of course it was said that they had been eaten by rats! He chose one of his junior officers, Dr Todd—for the part he had played in trying to make the striking prisoners understand that dying would not help—to tell them that all their complaints were being duly forwarded.

Chaudhuri also recalled how he and Cosgrave insisted on going on their rounds to see the prisoners, despite the fact that there was a possibility that some prisoners might abuse them, throw shoes at the chief commissioner, or even spit at him. But Cosgrave went, undaunted, and unaccompanied by a policeman. Perhaps that, in its own small way, put the political prisoners in a more receptive frame of mind at least as far as abandoning the hunger strike was concerned.

Strangely enough, they were so sore at the visit of Yamin Khan and Hans Raj having produced no tangible results, that they did not want any politician or minister to come and see them while they were on hunger strike. The only exception they made was that of a visit by Mahatma Gandhi. They had full faith in him, they said, and would welcome his visit. Curiously enough, the only other person they said they would be willing to meet was one B P Singh Roy, because, they said, being a sportsman, he would do something once he had promised to.

Mahatma Gandhi was unable to come. He, however, sent a telegram on behalf of the poet, Rabindranath Tagore, Nehru, the Congress Working Committee and himself, appealing to them to abandon the hunger strike. (The Central Legislative Assembly had already passed a motion to the effect that the government repatriate political prisoners from the Andamans.)

So the hunger strike was at last abandoned. It had had the largest ever number of prisoners participating—a historic event in the Andaman penal settlement. It had lasted 56 days, though fortunately not one prisoner had died. And, to give the devils their due, the parts played by Cosgrave and Chaudhuri were commendable. J A Thorne, home secretary to the government of India, duly acknowledged this when, during the course of his speech in the Central Legislative Assembly on the motion for adjournment, he said:

We are fortunate in that we have as Chief Commissioner, Mr Cosgrave, a gentleman well-known to the older members of this house, and an officer of proved merit and earnest goodwill. The Senior Medical Officer, Captain Chowdhry—and Raizada Hansraj and Sir Mohammed Yamin Khan will, I am sure, bear me out in this—is a doctor admired by all for his skill and his devotion. The heaviest burden falls on the doctors and we are fortunate in having Captain Chowdhry there in this crisis in charge of the medical staff.

Thus ended a very sordid chapter in the history of the penal settlement in the Andamans.

On 9 September 1937, Thorne announced that "the question of repatriation of terrorist prisoners who have given up hunger strike is under consideration". For some unspecified reason 8 prisoners had continued their hunger strike. Three weeks later, on 30 September, Horne was able to tell members of the Central Legislative Assembly that 72 political prisoners had already been repatriated. The rest were to follow.

The point is, was the Andaman penal settlement a paradise or a hell on earth? If you were Maulana Mohammad Jafar Thanesvri, and in the Andamans during the 1860s, and could wangle to ingratiate yourself with the right people, the Andamans were a paradise. But if you were a Savarkar and were sent to the Andamans on transportation and treated as a common criminal, even without the facilities allowed to a common criminal (like being given a ticket of leave after a few months' incarceration in the Cellular Jail) and had to suffer the indignities and hardships that were the fate of common felons, murderers and cut-throats, then the Andamans were, undoubtedly, a hell on earth.

Niether the Andaman penal settlement, nor those who administered it at the locall evel, nor for that matter the government of India, were equipped to handle the new breed of educated and intellectually far above-the-average prisoner. The system, therefore, as originally conceived and instituted, was doomed to come a cropper when faced with this complex and unexpected situation. And it did.

22

The Mikado's Shadow

While political prisoners in the Cellular Jail were fighting for their rights, war clouds were hovering over Europe. To those with any political insight, it was obvious that peace could any day be shattered in Europe; and the entire continent, followed inevitably by practically the rest of the world, would then be engulfed in flames. The peace treaty at Versailles, which had been signed after the end of the great (first world) war, had sown the seeds of a further conflict. The Weimar Republic in Germany had neither the will, nor for that matter the muscle, to tackle the colossal problems which faced that country.

To retrieve the situation, a "redeemer" emerged in the shape of a tiny tooth-brush moustached ex-corporal: an Austrian named Adolph Hitler, house painter by profession, who had served in the great war. Adolph Hitler had, in fact, lain blinded with gas in a German hospital while still in service.

Hitler had great admiration for the "Duce"—Benito Mussolini of Italy, who was the son of a blacksmith. The "Duce" had formed what he described as a party of action, and given it the name *Fascisti*. The Fascisti wore black shirts and were the first storm-troopers to be seen in western Europe. They were not averse to killing their opponents in cold blood. On 30 October 1922, Mussolini had marched into Rome and taken over the state; the king had been allowed to remain as nominal head.

Hitler set out to devote all his energies in the formation of a party based on the Italian model. Someone described him as "a tough, resentful, visionary figure, half crazy with anti-Semitism, as an orator violent, abounding, and hysterical, but disinterested, patriotic, and charged with Teutonic pride". It is difficult to better that description.

Hitler formed the notorious Nazi party, which he euphemistically described as the Nationalist Socialist party, whose avowed aim was "to clear Germany of the Jews, to stamp out communism, and to revive the Military renown of the German people". On 30 January 1933, Adolph Hitler became Chancellor of Germany and when, in August the next year, President Von Hindenburg died, Hitler had himself "elected" as "the leader". And that indeed was the beginning of the end.

Hitler began furiously arming the Germans; and he tore every clause of the Versailles peace treaty. On 25 July 1934, he made an unsuccessful attempt to stage a pre-Nazi revolt in Austria, in the course of which Chancellor Engelbert Dollfuss was assassinated. (Hitler was to annex Austria in March 1938.)

Not to be outdone Mussolini, Hitler's mentor, who was soon to start playing second fiddle, invaded Ethiopia on 3 October 1935, and within a few months had captured Addis Ababa. But the actual rehearsal of the second world war started when civil war broke out in Spain in the month of July 1936. Both Germany and Italy sided openly with the rebel forces who, under the leadership of Generalissimo Franco, even imported the Spanish Moors to fight the Loyalists. On the side of the Loyalists came the Russians. An international brigade was formed. But the French and British refused to intervene on the side of the government established by law, which had been elected legally. The ultimate result, in the circumstances, was a foregone conclusion.

The Spanish Civil War started on the night of 17 July 1936. On 25 October later the same year, Germany and Italy announced the formation of the Rome-Berlin Axis. Exactly after one month, on 25 November, Germany and Japan announced the signing of the Anti-Comintern Pact. With that the triangle was complete.

In Asia, Japan had tasted blood when she scored a victory over Russia in 1903, and, according to one historian, the result of this was that "the whole Orient trembled with delight and the Occident began to talk of the Yellow Peril and to wonder whether the day of the Yellow Man might not be near at hand".

However, Japan in the thirties was a strong power—with a modern army, navy and air force, and not without dreams of imperial domination over China and the rest of South-east Asia. So, on 18 September 1931, Japan embarked on its infamous career of conquest by invading Manchuria.

Events in Europe had moved at a rather quick pace, and it was becoming increasingly clear that Hitler, combined with Mussolini, represented not only something of a sinister combination but also a formidable one, determined to imperil peace in Europe as well as in the entire world, with Japan playing its own infamous role in the Far East.

Hitler had annexed Austria on 13 March 1938, and then gone on to acquire Sudetenland. The Allies felt that something had to be done now. So Neville Chamberlain, prime minister of England, flew to Munich along with his French counterpart. The meeting between the three heads of state lasted two days—29 and 30 September—and the outcome was a piece of paper which Chamberlain displayed with a flourish when he arrived back in London. It proclaimed "peace in our times" but amounted, in fact, to a total surrender to Hitler's demands, because it had given an overt approval to Hitler's occupation of Sudetenland.

Hitler did not let the grass grow under his feet. On 15 August 1939, he occupied Czechoslovakia. On 17 April, a few months earlier, Mussolini, whose appetite had been whetted by his conquest of Ethiopia, had invaded Albania. On the Spanish front, the gallant Loyalists had lost their battle, the insurgent forces having completed their conquest of Spain by the end of August. It was clear that nothing could now stop Hitler's dream of conquering the whole of Europe.

He signed a non-aggression pact with Soviet Russia, which confounded not only Britain and France but even the United States of America. The pact was signed on 23 August; there was nothing now to hold back Hitler and his Nazi hordes. On 1 September he invaded Poland, leaving Britain and France no alternative but to declare war on Germany. Both France and Britain gave a final warning to Hitler, saying that unless German troops were withdrawn from Poland at once, they would, without hesitation, fulfil their obligations towards Poland. On Sunday, 3 September 1939, Prime Minister Neville Chamberlain of England informed the House of Commons:

We decided to send our Ambassador to Berlin instructions, which he was to hand at 9 o'clock to the German Foreign Secretary and which read as follows: "I have ... the honour to inform you that unless, not later than 11 A.M., British Summer Time, today September 3, satisfactory assurances to the above effect have been given by the German Government and have reached His Majesty's Government in London, a state of war will exist between the two countries as from that hour.

Later, broadcasting to the nation, Chamberlain said: "I have to tell you that no such undertaking has been received, and that consequently this country is at war with Germany."

At 5 P M the same day, after the expiry of the time-limit given in their ultimatum, the French government made an official announcement to the effect that a state of war would exist thenceforth between France and the German Reich.

The USSR were not to lag behind, so the Soviet forces invaded Poland from their side of the border. The battle was truly joined.

All along President Roosevelt had tried, through diplomatic channels, to prevent war; but his efforts had been of no avail. And once the war had broken out openly, there was no doubt on which side his sympathies lay, although officially the USA was neutral.

Between the outbreak of hostilities in Europe and by the time Hitler made the fatal mistake of invading the USSR, thus creating a second front for himself and his armies, Europe lay ravaged. The entire continent lay at the feet of Hitler, and Mussolini, now his puny disciple. Soviet Russia, not to be left behind, had also embarked upon a career of aggression by invading Finland, their tiny neighbour.

But before the war started between Germany and Russia, the pace of the Axis aggression had quickened, particularly with the advent of spring in 1940. On 9 April 1940, the Germans had begun the invasion of Norway, and had seized Denmark, and then, barely a month after, launched an attack on the Netherlands, Belgium and Luxembourg. In less than 20 days, these countries had surrendered. Next would be France. The British, realizing the hopelessness of the situation, started evacuating their troops from France, and by 4 June their evacuation from Dunkerque was complete, thus making the task of Hitler's army easier. On 14 June, German troops entered Paris, and on the eighth day of their arrival the French, led by Marshal Petain, signed an armistice. Two days later the French-Italian armistice was also signed. Fighting ceased on 25 June.

On 10 July began the Battle of Britain.

Mussolini was waiting for fine weather in Africa; on 5 September he invaded British Somaliland, and on the 13th, Egypt. But that did not satisfy his appetite for aggression. On 28 October began his invasion of Greece. But Hitler was not going to allow him to receive all the kudos. Besides, Mussolini's fascist troops were hardly covering themselves with glory. So in February 1941, Hitler despatched to Tripoli (in Libya) one of his ablest generals, Erwin Rommel, to take charge of the North African campaign on behalf of the Axis. And to make a show of his so-called invincibility, he sent the Axis forces to invade Yugoslavia and Greece. That was in the month of April.

Meanwhile, in Japan, General Tojo and his forces, armed to the teeth as it were, were straining at the leash, and waiting impatiently for an opportune moment to join in the kill. The Allies, since the Nazi attack on Soviet Russia, had been involved in a fight-to-death struggle on the eastern front; their fortunes appeared to be flagging, and that, decided Tojo, was his hour.

On 26 November 1941, in one of the most well-guarded secret moves the world has ever witnessed in the history of warfare, the Pearl Harbour striking force sailed from the Kurile Islands and on 7 December carried simultaneous aircraft attacks on the United States naval bases at Pearl Harbour, Hawaii, and nearby army air-bases. At the same time, Japanese destroyers bombed Midway Islands. The next day saw Japanese planes raid American air-bases in the Philippines, and Japanese forces invaded Thailand and Malay. They also seized the Shanghai international settlement, attacked the mainland territories of Hongkong and bombarded Wake and Guam. On 10 December they sank two British warships—the *Repulse* and the *Prince of Wales*.

And on 11 December began the Japanese invasion of Burma.

On 20 May 1942 they would complete the conquest of Burma. The British, however, had evacuated Rangoon earlier, on 7 March. According to S Woodburn Kirby, author of *History of the Second World War*: "Early on the 8th of March, the *Heinrich Jensen* [a requisitioned ship]...weighed anchor and steamed down the Rangoon river." Kirby recalled with a certain amount of nostalgia that: "Two ships of the Royal Navy had formed the spearhead of the attack when the British captured Rangoon in 1824. One hundred and eighteen years later the Navy was the last to leave the post." He further added: "One of the repercussions of the loss of Rangoon was the evacuation of the Andaman Islands. These islands had considerable strategic importance for they flanked the approaches to Rangoon."

The British were obviously fully conscious of the military importance of these islands because at one stage, according to an administrative reconnaissance report submitted to the Far East general headquarters (Singapore), the admiralty had decided "to instal certain defences at Nankauri with a view to rendering the harbour fit for use as a naval fuelling base in case of need". The Japanese also, it would appear, appreciated the importance of the Andamans, because, again according to Woodburn Kirby:

As early as the 7th of February (1942) Imperial General Headquarters [Japan] had issued orders for their capture. The opportunity to do so occurred when reinforcements were being sent to Burma by sea after the occupation of Rangoon. A battalion of 18th Div, which was en-route to Rangoon from Malay, together with a naval component consisting of detachments from *9th and 12th Special Base Forces*, sailed from Penang on the 20th March and three days later Port Blair was occupied and an air base quickly established.

The entire strength of the army stationed at Port Blair had consisted of one British company. In January 1942 it had been replaced by a battalion of the Gurkhas. But when it was realized that it was not possible to hold Rangoon, on 12 March 1942 the Gurkhas were also withdrawn under General Wavell's orders, thus abandoning the poor unfortunate people of the Andaman and Nicobar islands to their fate. And that fate was going to be far from kind.

The military authorities were more than apprehensive about the loss of the Andaman islands, and not purely from the strategic point of view. They feared that, if and when Japan occupied the Andamans, it would obtain control of military convicts there, which numbered 180 at the time, as also of the large number of revolutionaries who were still in Port Blair, despite the fact that the transportation of political prisoners, as a compulsory measure, had come to an end. This question was discussed as far back as on 31 January 1942, at a meeting of the Chiefs of Staff Committee. According to the minutes of this meeting, the committee felt that there were "many uses to which these convicts might be put". They felt that:

(a) Both revolutionaries and convicts could be used for propaganda purposes;
(b) Both could be used as leaders for fifth column activities;
(c) Military convicts could be used (i) to suborn prisoners of war (ii) as the basis for a unit formed from prisoners of war (iii) as spies (iv) as Military fifth columnists.

It was therefore recommended that "they should be evacuated to India in order of priority: (a) Military convicts; and (b) political convicts". Of course, no notice was taken of these recommendations.

Interestingly enough, the latest batch of military personnel to arrive in Port Blair under sentence of transportation were men of the Central India Horse. Philip Mason, in his book, *A Matter of Honour*, gives an account of how that happened:

When the Central India Horse was ordered overseas, the men entrained without any unusual signs, but at Bombay there was an unexpected delay; they were shunted into a siding and kept there for a day and night, during which the four Sikhs who had really been infected by *Kirti Lehar* propaganda had their chance. Two-thirds of the Sikh squadron refused to go overseas. Their officers reasoned with them but nothing would shake them; the regiment sailed without them and a squadron of Dogras was sent later to take their place. The mutinous Sikhs went before a court martial and the leaders were transported to the Andamans where they fell into Japanese hands.

(*Kirti Lehar* was a communist-oriented movement.) Philip Mason gives an interesting explanation as to why the Sikhs at the time were more prone to radicalism than others in the Indian Army. According to him:

> Of all the people of India, the Sikhs were at this moment perhaps the most inflammable. They were prosperous by Indian standards; their lands were fertile, and they did not subdivide them indefinitely but sent their younger brothers to the army or to the police in Hong Kong or Singapore, to drive taxis in Calcutta, to work as electricians or carpenters in Kenya. They were better educated than most peasant communities; like the Scottish peasantry they were a people of their book. Such people cannot be isolated; it is among the thriving, the go-ahead, the intelligents, not among the destitute, the lacklustre and the hopeless, that radical doctrines take hold.

Back in Port Blair: in a telegram dated 16 February 1942, Burma Army headquarters were informed that on that day "Port Blair had been raided by three bombers"; the raid had lasted 65 minutes and ground defences and aerodrome had been the target. It added: "No casualties. Slight damage to property." A note appended to the telegram stated that this had been "the second time within three days that Port Blair had been raided".

During the next few weeks a number of Japanese planes flew over the islands, ostensibly for the purpose of reconnaissance. The Bay of Bengal also saw naval activity. The Indian Navy lost *HMIS Sophie Marie*, after she had struck a mine. According to the official history of the Indian Armed Forces during the second world war, edited by Bisheshwar Prasad:

> When the Japanese submarines were detected Indian ships went into action to protect the convoys under their charge, and when Japanese aircraft appeared over the coast of Eastern India they met with an effective opposition from naval guns. On 28 January 1942, the paddle steamer *Idar* was shelled by a submarine off the north coast of Ceylon . !. . At least four ships [mostly merchant vessels] were sunk off the east coast during the month. On 5 February 1942 HMIS *Ramdas* was attacked.

After the fall of Rangoon and Singapore, and the sporadic Japanese air-raids on the Andamans, it was obvious that it was only a question of a few days before the Japanese would mount their invasion of the Andaman and Nicobar islands. So the first step the authorities took was to shift all offices, officers and their families from Ross Island to Aberdeen.

Ross Island would appear to have already fallen into a state of decay.

It is a strange coincidence that one of the last important persons to have spent a night in Ross Island, while fleeing from Singapore to England, should have recorded her impressions of this place. It was no other than Lady Diana Duff Cooper, the famous beauty and socialite, wife of the then British commissioner-general of South-South-east Asia based in Singapore. She has written:

> We arrived at the penal settlement of Port Blair, Andaman Island, at about three [on 16th January 1942]. I took a hasty dislike to it .... Ross is the select patch where the Chief Commissioner has a residency. There is a barracks, a post office, a club, a church and parsonage, a village institute, and that is about all, except for an old Circuit Home lately turned into a rest house for air-travellers .... The House indescribable, very large and wandery and shapeless, with strange devil carvings mixed with suburban taste. A huge haunted bedroom....

After shifting from Ross to Aberdeen, the next step was to evacuate from the Andamans the officers, their families and other civilians who wanted to flee the proverbial sinking ship. The last ship set sail from Chatham jetty at Port Blair on 13 March. Chief Commissioner C E Waterfall decided to stay on, whereas at the last moment the British deputy commissioner fled. One of those who stayed behind despite being given the choice to leave, was Dr Diwan Singh Kalepani, an official doctor who was to play a very significant role during the Japanese occupation, and would ultimately die of Japanese torture.

In any case, the idea was that the ship would act as a ferry and come back to collect more of those who wished to be evacuated. The ship's destination was Calcutta but, with enemy activity in the Bay of Bengal, she was diverted to Madras. Unfortunately however, on her return voyage, she was sunk by a Japanese U-boat. So that was the end; no one was to leave the islands for years, except either as Japanese prisoners or under Japanese tutelage.

23

Japanese "Sphere of Co-prosperity"

On the night of 23 March 1942, ships belonging to the Imperial Japanese Navy swooped on the islands of Ross and Chatham. At 4 o'clock in the morning they fired their first shot from one of the guns aboard a naval ship. There was no firing in return. But shortly after was heard the sound of a loud explosion; the wireless station and the telegraph office at Port Blair were blown up. The Japanese fired a second shot. This was followed by complete silence, a kind of deathly silence as though everyone in Port Blair had stopped breathing. At 6 o'clock the Japanese started landing. The crowds that had collected at the jetty the previous evening, anticipating the arrival of the Japanese, had been told by the police to go back home.

Immediately after they landed, the Japanese began the business of installing themselves and settling down. One Colonel Bucho was appointed civil governor, and his first act was to arrest Chief Commissioner Waterfall and release all convicts incarcerated in the Cellular Jail. This act, of course, caused a great deal of satisfaction among those who benefited from the clemency. (One of the convicts, a "gentleman" criminal who pretended he was an erstwhile freedom fighter, was later appointed chief commissioner for a short while. His name was Pushkar Bagchi.)

On the third day of their arrival, the Japanese called a general meeting of the public, where Colonel Bucho spoke first. He then asked some others to address the gathering. Dr Diwan Singh, who was the main spokesman of the people, said in the course of his speech:

The Japanese, like us, are Asians. The British were *ferungees* [foreigners]. We fought many a battle of freedom against the British, but we never succeeded, because they believed in dividing us. The Japanese now assure us that they will help us attain freedom from the British. They give us that pledge and, therefore, they want us to co-operate with them in every way. In the light of what they say, they deserve our co-operation. But I want to warn you that freedom is not something which anyone can give us on a platter. To achieve freedom we have to fight. Therefore, my dear brothers and sisters, I appeal to you to stand on your own legs and come forward to fight for freedom. To depend on the help of anyone else is meaningless. You have to build up your own strength. You must stand united and have faith in yourself and in India's ultimate destiny. You must have courage. You must be ready to sacrifice your all for the freedom of your country.

The Japanese obviously could not have appreciated this, and maybe by making such a speech Diwan Singh was laying the seeds of future suspicion, and his ultimate destruction. But the Japanese were aware that Diwan Singh was a man of substance and commanded the respect of the citizens of Port Blair; so he was promoted to the rank of chief medical officer, and also assigned a number of other tasks, like being in charge of ambulance and Red Cross, public welfare, publicity and the Grow More Food campaign. He was also appointed chairman of the Peace Committee, which had ten other members.

Diwan Singh, who had suffixed the *nom de plume* "Kalepani" to his name (because he wanted to be totally associated with the Andamans), was a remarkable man. Although he was a government doctor belonging to the Indian medical department of the Indian Army, he had got into trouble with the British government many years earlier. He had been so carried away at a meeting held in Dagshai in the Simla hills (where he had been posted) that he had actually made a speech in support of Gandhi's non-violent movement, which had just then been launched.

Of course he was arrested and put on trial, but the prosecution case had failed because not a single independent witness was willing to testify against him. While in the Andamans, he had not only gained for himself the reputation of a healer but of being a very religious man who took interest in every aspect of people's welfare. Besides that, he was a Punjabi poet and something of an innovator, because he was among the very first Punjabi poets who wrote in what came to be known in the west as *vers libre*. One would think that he was also something of a seer. Much before the war actually broke out, and the Japanese invasion took place, he wrote a poem entitled *Haneri* (The Storm). In translation, the opening lines read:

The storm is coming, the storm!
Pitch dark, blinding, and with such speed!
It will be night; there'll be darkness all round,
The sun, the moon, the stars—will be eclipsed,
The source of light will be extinguished.

The storm is coming, the storm!
Maybe in the past there has been such a storm—
But we've not seen it; we don't remember it!
The storm is coming, the storm
Of revolution, of destruction, of change,
All will be topsy-turvy, no one will be able to see anything,
None will recognize one another—
All values will change.

Diwan Singh Kalepani became a legend in his lifetime; he is a legendary figure even today.

According to a Japanese report written on the history of the Japanese administration, which fell into the hands of the British naval intelligence:

Two weeks after landing of the Japanese on South Andaman Island... the Peace Committee was established, and it was organised by a Chairman and ten members for the purpose to settle land problems, supply goods, arbitrate disputes, and also, judge all civil affairs. This committee lasted for nearly eight months, until the time of the completion of *Gunseisho* (Military Administration Office) on December 2nd of 1942.

For a little while, during which the Japanese were busy occupying places of strategic importance and consolidating fortifications left behind by the British, the Japanese were by and large quite friendly towards the general public. So, by changing masters, the people thought they had not lost much. But soon the Japanese started showing their fangs. That became obvious when, according to several eye-witnesses with whom this author has spoken, an incident took place near the Muslim mosque in Aberdeen. A few Japanese soldiers, obviously in a state of inebriation, started stamping on the ground with their heavily shod feet, thus raising a lot of dust and frightening a number of chickens which scampered into the houses nearby. The Japanese soldiers followed them inside the houses and started taking liberties with the women folk, to which the latter objected. A youngster named Mohammed Nasim, incensed at this insult, took out an air-gun and fired at them. The Japanese fled, but returned soon after and shot Mohammed Nasim dead. It created a stir in the city. This incident was followed by several other acts of misdemeanour on the part of the Japanese soldiers. Although Diwan Singh, as a doctor, was fully occupied in tending to the sick and needy, he could not possibly shut his eyes to what was happening; he was also chairman of the Citizen's Peace Council. So he protested.

But there were elements working against Diwan Singh. Among those who were trying to poison the mind of the Japanese against him was his own junior colleague, Dr Rama Nand, who aspired to be chief medical officer. Another ambitious person was Bagchi who, to curry favour with the rulers, even went to the extent of supplying the Japanese with what came to be known as "comfort girls". With the help of the police, he would forcibly abduct young women for the purpose. This angered the people. Diwan Singh continued to protest, and with some effect because, fortunately, till then his equation with the Japanese was still quite high.

Then another incident took place.

Chief Commissioner Waterfall had been removed from the islands, but his assistant, Major A J Bird, was still under house-arrest. During the days of the British, Bird had been invested with some judicial powers also, and he had, on one occasion, convicted Bagchi to six months' imprisonment for accepting a bribe. For Bagchi now, here was an opportunity to settle old scores with Bird. So with the help of a lifer he managed to plant some life belts and broken-down spare parts of a transmitter near where Bird was living under house-arrest. Both Bird and the lifer were arrested and handcuffed, and the lifer made to "confess".

There was an announcement with the beat of a drum in the streets of Port Blair that Bird was to be publicly punished. A large crowd gathered and Bird was brought to the open *maidan* in Aberdeen in handcuffs. A posse of Japanese soldiers was present with loaded rifles at the ready. According to an eye-witness, Bagchi read out the charges against Bird:

(i) You have taken undue advantage of the facilities provided to you by the Japanese while under house arrest;

(ii) You have through the lifer [Sarup Ram] been instrumental in spreading the rumour that the British forces are expected back in the Andamans in the near future;

(iii) You have been sending messages to the British through wireless;

(*iv*) You have tried to flee, while under house arrest, by boarding a British submarine; and
(*v*) You have been secretly corresponding with the British.
Though you have not confessed to having committed any of these crimes, there is sufficient circumstantial evidence to prove these charges. Therefore, you are guilty of having committed all the above-mentioned crimes. Your punishment is *death*.

There was pin-drop silence. The firing squad was ready. But no orders came to shoot. What followed was something which exceeded the worst act of bestiality. First, one of the Japanese stepped forward to where Bird stood handcuffed, and twisted his ankle until it broke. Then he started beating him in the stomach with his fists. Bird crumbled and fell down. While he lay in what appeared to be unendurable agony, he was kicked again and again, and then made to stand. His arms were twisted and his shoulders broken. Finally, another Japanese officer rushed at him with his naked sword and severed his head with one stroke. He wiped his blood-smeared sword with the body of the dying Bird and said: "An enemy must be killed by the sword."

It must be said to the courage and forbearance of Bird that at no time did he cry out, or in any other way demean himself by asking for mercy. He showed exemplary courage and submitted to the inhuman torture without uttering a sound. He died like a man. Those who had known Bird testify to the fact that he was a good, humane and kind officer.

To crown it all, Bagchi announced to a stunned crowd that Bird's so-called accomplice, Sarup Ram, was being given a pardon because he had confessed his crime, because he was an Indian and, since the Japanese had pledged to free India, they did not want to maltreat an Indian!

Bagchi and others of his ilk notwithstanding, the Japanese, with each day that passed, were establishing their hold ever more firmly over the islands. At the same time, they were paying lip service to the work of the Peace Committee.

The Japanese, in their history of their administration, do acknowledge the work of the Peace Committee. It states that: "Peace and order of this [Andaman] island was maintained, mostly by the activity of the Peace Committee, *until the establishment of Gunseisho on May 1942* [author's italics]." After the military establishment was put into operation, "as the Chief of this office, the Commandant of the Naval Forces in this island was appointed". And then the report goes on to state: "Under this organisation, the Assistant Commissioner's office, Police Station, Jail, Supply Office, School and Hospitals were placed, and this organization executed the administration until the arrival of *Miniseibu*'s civil officers." They were not to arrive until February 1943.

The Allies were fully aware of the importance of capturing Port Blair. As early as on 19 August 1942, an India Command Joint Planning Staff memorandum speaks of capturing "Mount Harriet, High ground west of Matta Bay [500 feet] and Mount Haughton" which would do much to "make Port Blair untenable". At the same time, the memorandum adds: "No information [is] available regarding enemy strength or disposition". This, evidently, shows that the Allies' intelligence activities had not yet started.

However, Bagchi, aided and abetted by many other opportunists and time-servers, continued his nefarious activities. And what was a source of great anguish to Dr Diwan Singh and his other colleagues were Bagchi's unceasing attempts at forcibly kidnapping many young girls, some of them not so young, for the Japanese. The Japanese administration was making itself unpopular with such unsavoury activity.

But, on the other hand, they still wanted to impress the Indians overseas in South-east Asia by posing as champions in the cause of Indian freedom. So they started establishing the Indian Independence League in various countries in South-east Asia, all of which were, by now, under Japanese occupation.

To help establish one in the Andamans, they brought to Port Blair Baba Hari Usman, one of those who had been on board the *Kama Gata Maru*, had escaped British bullets at Calcutta, and fled. He had somehow arrived in Sumatra and lived all these years in a village there under the name of Usman Ali. He had earlier been involved in throwing a bomb on Lord Hardinge, the viceroy. Baba Hari Singh Usman set up a branch of the Indian Independence League at Port Blair, with Diwan Singh as chairman. But while in Port Blair, he also became aware of the havoc Bagchi was playing with the lives of the local people. When Hari Singh tried to persuade Bagchi to put an end to it, not only did the latter refuse to listen to him but, in the course of a heated argument, struck Hari Singh with a staff with such force that one of Hari Singh's arms was fractured. That was the end of Bagchi. When the matter came to the notice of the admiral, Bagchi was stripped of all power and sentenced to six months' imprisonment.

Things nonetheless continued to be much the same. There was some kind of peace on the surface but underneath, there was turmoil. And there was no end to local rivalries, or to the ambitions of those who wanted to advance themselves by kowtowing to the Japanese. But since the Japanese thought they could still make use of Diwan Singh, they are supposed to have succeeded in persuading him to attend a conference at Bangkok, where representatives of Indians from most South-east Asian countries were present—including General Mohan Singh, founder of the first Indian National Army. (There is some controversy about whether Diwan Singh attended the Bangkok conference. According to some, he did. But most people living in Port Blair, at the time, say that he did not even once leave the shores of the Andamans. Most probably, the latter are right.

The Indian National Army was born when a few Indian army officers (who had been taken prisoners in the war), along with a few local Indian leaders, met in Kotabaru (Sumatra) on 11 December 1941; the meeting was followed by a discussion between some Japanese generals and Mohan Singh (then captain) of the 1/14 Punjab regiment. The result was that all Indian prisoners of war were placed under Mohan Singh's control. He was given the rank of general and asked to form an Indian National Army which would cooperate with the Japanese to help drive away the British from India. Simultaneously, the Indian Independence League had taken official birth, and Rash Bihari Bose, who had been living in Japan as an exile from India, became its *de jure* president, although he had been the *de facto* president since its formation after the outbreak of the Sino-Japanese war in 1937.

There were 100 delegates at the Bangkok conference, and its sessions lasted nine days, from 15 June to 23 June 1942. A Council of Action, with Rash Bihari Bose (as chairman) and four others, was formed. The conference resolved that "the formation, command, control and organisation of the Indian National Army be in the hands of Indians themselves" and that the Japanese government may formally declare that "immediately on the severance of India from the British Empire, the Imperial Government [of Japan] shall respect the territorial integrity and recognize the full sovereignty of India free from any foreign influence, control or interference of a political, military or economic nature". Furthermore, the Japanese government was requested "to hand over the properties owned by the Indians . . . and left by them owing to the exigencies of war to the Council of Action".

In yet another resolution, which was to have perhaps the greatest effect on the destinies of Indians in South-east Asia, and indirectly on Diwan Singh's ultimate fate, the conference requested Japan to make necessary arrangements to bring Subhas Chandra Bose, who was requested to be "kind enough to come to East Asia".

The Japanese government failed to give an official assurance of the status of the Indian National Army (INA) vis-à-vis the Japanese forces. This resulted in the resignation by the entire Council of Action, barring Rash Bihari Bose. And that was the end of General Mohan Singh's career, who was to spend the rest of his days under house-arrest in Sumatra.

Shortly before the Bangkok conference, according to the Japanese history of their administration in the Andamans (quoted already):

The Andaman *Miniseibu* was established in February 1943, due to the request made by the Naval Headquarters to the Japanese Government, and the administration organisation was the same as that of *Gunseisho* [Military Administration Office]. The staff of *Miniseibu* being so few, and fulfilment was attempted many times, but all attempts were overturned when the ships were sunk on its way with the *Miniseibu's* staff. The objective of *Miniseibu* was, supposedly, "to protect the local population and also to promote their public welfare". The paper goes on to add:

> Consequently, *Miniseibu* ... made every efforts to the maintenance of public peace and order, development of industries, repairing of roads and prevention of epidemics in the islands, but its main work was to increase the production of food stuff by establishing a self-sufficiency system. On the other hand, recognizing their religious freedom, much attention was given to education and also attempts were made to make the local people happy, by encouraging wholesale amusements.

This report reads like something out of *Alice in Wonderland*. Of course, the Japanese did improve the condition of roads, and built some new ones. They also lengthened the airstrip. But it was all done in the interest of defence, and by no means for the welfare of the people.

Hardly anything was done by way of "development of industries"; perhaps it was not practicable at the time. As far as religious freedom was concerned, orders were given at one stage that every Sikh must shave off his beard and cut his hair, something which is considered the ultimate defilement in terms of the basic tenets of Sikh faith. But they were forced to do so. (This author met a police-officer in Port Blair who, he said, had been subjected to this.)

As regards the prices of food and clothing, there came a stage when *ghee* was sold at Rs 200 per seer and each egg cost Rs 3. Rice was practically unobtainable. Diwan Singh encouraged people to grow whatever food they could, and also introduced a kind of rationing system.

The fact of the matter was that the Allied blockade was becoming so stringent that the Japanese were finding it almost impossible to bring any consumer goods into the islands. The shortage of cloth, and even of medicines, was becoming very acute because neither of them could be manufactured in the islands.

Diwan Singh and members of his Punjabi Study Circle, which he had founded before Japanese occupation, along with members of the Peace Committee, did whatever they could to ameliorate the conditions of the citizens. He was very active and paid frequent visits to practically every nook and corner of South Andaman Island. Meanwhile, Diwan Singh's detractors, and those seeking to replace him, were just as active in plotting against him and carrying cooked-up tales to the gullible Japanese officers. What made the situation worse was the fact that the Allied bombing of the islands by air and sea was becoming quite frequent; they were attacking defence installations on the islands, and with success. The Japanese suspected espionage. They were right, but neither Diwan Singh nor any of his comrades in Port Blair were responsible for it. How information was being gathered and supplied to the Allies, which resulted in Japanese defence installations being bombed, is another story, and will be dealt with later.

The plot was thickening and the heat was on as far as Diwan Singh was concerned. The purpose of his visits to the suburbs was deliberately misconstrued, and the Japanese were told that he was plotting against them. So an order was issued restricting his movements. He objected because, apart from anything else, he was chairman of the Peace Committee. Things came to such a pass that, in one instance, a Japanese officer is said to have slapped him!

The Japanese started indiscriminate arrests on charges of spying; those arrested were accused of switching on torchlights and lighting flares at night to help British intelligence agents. Once again Diwan Singh protested, trying to assure the Japanese that none among those suspected was an enemy agent.

All kinds of plots were hatched to implicate him, but they proved abortive. As an additional provocation, he was asked to vacate the Gurudwara building so that a batch of Korean women, who were being imported as "comfort girls" for the Japanese, could be housed. He again protested. But his strongest and most vigorous protests were on behalf of those who were being arrested every day and lodged in the Cellular Jail on the false charge of espionage, and subjected to third degree methods to extort "confessions".

Diwan Singh was also asked to hand over all stocks of medicine, so that they could be reserved for the exclusive use of the Japanese. He refused. All the other doctors followed suit. (Diwan Singh was also president of the local Doctors' Association.)

Eventually, some Japanese stooges tried to implicate him in a plot which, they hoped, would "prove" Diwan Singh to be a spy. That too failed. But these men assured the Japanese that if they wanted to arrest Diwan Singh it would not be difficult to find proof of his "guilt". The Japanese had already started feeling insecure because they saw the tide of war turning against the Axis. (In Europe, in the middle of May 1942, the Royal Air Force had begun a major air offensive against Germany, the like of which the world had never seen before.) On 3 September 1943, a few weeks before Diwan Singh was to be arrested, the British Eighth Army had crossed over from Sicily and had landed on the Italian coast: five days later, the Italian armistice had been announced.

Now the poor, tortured and unhappy people of the Andamans were in for a period of unprecedented repression. It was also the end of the so-called period of Asian "co-prosperity", for that had been the professed aim of the Japanese.

24

Japanese Reign of Terror, Netaji's Visit and their Ultimate Doom

On 23 October 1943 Diwan Singh, along with all active members of the Indian Independence League, the Peace Committee and the Punjabi Literary Society, was arrested. They were confined in the Cellular Jail. Diwan Singh was subjected to torture which can only be described as unmatched in savagery. It was inhuman. He was suspended by his hair from the ceiling of his cell and beaten mercilessly. Hung upside down, his hands and feet were tied and the various parts of his body burnt. Pins and needles were thrust into his nails and toes. Electric shocks were administered to his body. His eyeballs were gouged. He was tied at the stake, beaten, put into a stock and pressure applied until his bones crunched.

The torture and beating was so severe that by the time they had finished with him there was not one unbroken bone or joint or rib left in his body. But they were not able to break his spirit—nor make him confess, for he had nothing to confess.

After having failed to make him "confess", they adopted the stratagem of pressurizing a young girl, Kesar Kaur, to say that Diwan Singh used to visit her and had told her that he was a British spy. She refused, so she was tortured. Her husband, too, was tortured. In short, every conceivable method was adopted to force her to say what they wanted. But they met with little success.

Ironically enough, on 29 October—within a weak of Diwan Singh's arrest—the Provisional Indian Government had been installed at Singapore, with all due ceremony, under the leadership of Netaji Subhas Chandra Bose. Just when Diwan Singh and his colleagues were undergoing tortures of a satanic nature, General Tojo was making an official announcement that the Andaman and Nicobar islands would be handed over to the Provisional Indian Government. This announcement was made in the Japanese *diet* (parliament). Subhas Bose was jubilant, as is apparent from a statement he made in Tokyo, at the house of his host, Baron Shibusawa. It has been quoted by the Japanese author, Tatsuo Hayshida, in his book on Bose:

> Premier Tojo's announcement of the transfer of the Andaman and Nicobar Islands to the Provisional Government of Free India is in consonance with Japan's oft-repeated statement that it will support the Indian Independence Movement. The sincerity of Japan in honouring commitment will surely impress the world. The return to the Provisional Government of Free India of the Andaman and Nicobar Islands, which are the first part of India to be liberated by the Japanese Army from British rule, has infused a new hope and great confidence into our fight for freedom. The liberation of these islands has a symbolic significance because the Andaman Islands were used by the British as a prison for political prisoners sentenced to penal servitude for conspiracies to overthrow the British Government—and there have been hundreds of them—were locked up in this Island. Like the Bastille in Paris, which was the first to be stormed in the French Revolution, setting free political prisoners, the Andamans, where our patriots suffered, are the first to be liberated, but it is always the first piece of territory that has the most significance.

Maybe it is hindsight, but Bose's belief in the sincerity of the Nippon government does appear somewhat naive, for surely he must, by then, have heard of the fate of General Mohan Singh and his first Indian National Army!

The disappearance of Subhas Chandra Bose from Calcutta, his journey to Europe and his eventual appearance in Japan reads like a James Bond story. Subhas Bose had been in a British prison in Calcutta, but had been released and put under house-arrest because he had undertaken a fast while in prison. Despite a constant vigil by as many as 62 men of the Criminal Investigation Department posted all round his house, he managed to escape disguised as a Pathan and travelled to Kabul in Afghanistan, from where he managed to get to Germany. While in Germany, he tried to rally around him all those working for India's independence. And then, after the outbreak of hostilities in the Far East and the consequent collapse of the British there, he travelled in a German submarine to Madagascar, from where he was picked up by a Japanese submarine; he arrived in Japan on 30 July 1943. His Provisional Indian Government was immediately recognized by the Japanese satellite governments, like Thailand, Manchuria and Nanking—and of course by Japan's Axis partner, Germany, and one or two of her European satellites.

At the installation ceremony of the Provisional Indian Government, and the resurrected Indian National Army at Singapore, Bose said, while pointing out the significance of the historic event, that he had "not the slightest doubt that the entry of the Azad Hind Fauj (Indian National Army) into the Indian borders will unleash a revolution in India and British rule will crumble into dust". It was to prove a hope forlorn.

After the formation of his government, Bose sent his ambassadors to all those places where Indians were concentrated—Hongkong, Shanghai, Canton—but no one was sent to the Andamans.

Bose himself decided to visit the Andaman islands. Before he came, there was some talk of an Indian National Army battalion being sent to the Andamans as a symbolic gesture. It would have given much heart to the oppressed people of the Andamans, but the Nippon government vetoed it. In the circumstances, Bose arrived alone to pay his first, which was also to prove his last, visit to what, in theory at any rate, was his "territory" and should have been the seat of his government. He landed at the Port Blair airport on 29 December 1943 and was accorded a ceremonial welcome. He was received by Admiral Ishikava, the overlord of the islands, and the commander-in-chief of the Japanese army. He also inspected a guard of honour. But as one would expect, there was a complete lack of enthusiasm among the local people, because none of them could foretell what was going to be his fate on the morrow! How, then, could they be interested in something as far-fetched as the Japanese pledge to Bose to help him fight for India's freedom?

Bose was escorted by the admiral and taken to stay with him on Ross Island, in what was previously the chief commissioner's residence.

One of the objectives of Netaji Subhas Chandra Bose's visit to the Andamans was to settle with the local admiral, who was head of the administration there, the question of the appointment of a chief commissioner of the Andaman and Nicobar islands, to function on behalf of the Provisional Indian Government led by Bose. Hugh Toye, in *The Springing Tiger*, his book on Subhas Chandra Bose, writes: "The Admiral in agreeing to the appointment of an Indian Chief Commissioner told Bose that for cogent strategic reasons there would be no complete handover during the war, but that if the Commissioner was prepared to co-operate, some departments of civil administration could be transferred." There is nothing on record to show that Bose either raised any objections to the proposed arrangement with the admiral, or took up the matter with Prime Minister Tojo at any stage.

Along with some chosen Japanese officers, five local youngsters, who knew both English and Japanese, were allotted the task of being in constant attendance on Netaji. Among the Indians was Mushtaq Ali, who is now working in the chief commissioner's secretariat at Port Blair. Mushtaq Ali says that on Bose's arrival, none of them was able to get a word with him all day, because they were terrified of the Japanese officers who stuck to him like leeches. In the course of the evening, however, he found that the Japanese officers had become quite high. Mushtaq Ali thought that a god-sent opportunity to whisper into Netaji's ear about what was happening in the Andamans. He specially told him that, on his scheduled visit to the Cellular Jail the next day, he should ask to be shown the sixth wing of the jail, and visit every cell in that wing. He singled out the case of Diwan Singh and told Bose about the tortures he was being subjected to. Suba Singh, a subaltern in the Indian National Army who later came to Port Blair as one of the five representatives of Netaji Subhas Chandra Bose, with the avowed objective of taking over the administration of the Andaman and Nicobar islands on behalf of the Provisional Indian Government, and who has written a book, in Punjabi, on Diwan Singh, writes: "If that be so, I don't understand why, when he visited the jail the next day, he never asked to be taken to that particular cell or even that particular wing." But, since Suba Singh is obviously an apologist for Bose, he later goes on to cast doubts on the authenticity of the statement made by Mushtaq Ali. And yet Suba Singh also writes that it was surprising that a man of Subhas's acumen and intelligence should not have been able to perceive or sense that the local people looked so sullen—those tortured and unfortunate people—and wonder why!

On the second and last day of Netaji's visit, there was a public meeting in his honour which he addressed. Hugh Toye says it was at this meeting that Bose received the freedom of the city of Port Blair. Subhas talked about the formation of the Provisional Indian Government, and dwelt on his aim to seek the help of the Japanese government in the fight for India's freedom. Therefore, he said it was incumbent upon the Indians to cooperate with the Japanese; he and his government would only gain respect in the eyes of the Japanese government if, by working hard, the Indians could prove to the Japanese government that "we deserve freedom". He even chided his audience for being lazy and lethargic. Not one word about the tortures Diwan Singh and many other innocent people were being subjected to, nor about the miserable plight of the people. One wonders why he never asked what had become of the president of the local Indian Independence League, who was none other than Diwan Singh!

That he was aware of what was happening in the unhappy city of Port Blair is evident from the fact that he decided to send a five-man commission to the Andamans under the leadership of Lieutenant-Colonel E G Loganathan, who was to take over as chief commissioner. While briefing the commission, again according to Suba Singh, who was one of its members, Subhas Bose told them to look into the alleged case of espionage, as a result of which Diwan Singh and many others were being persecuted. He asked them to submit a report to him on the subject. But that was in the future!

In the meanwhile, the tortures continued and there was no let-up in their intensity. If anything, the relentless brutality increased because the Japanese began to realize that they would never succeed in making Diwan Singh confess—and confess to what? He had done nothing, nor had any of the others, who were accused of being spies. The Japanese torturers did not rest even after reducing Diwan Singh's body to pulp. They went still further. They subjected him to the ultimate indignity that can be inflicted on a devout Sikh. His hair and his beard were forcibly shorn. Even then his spirit was not broken.

But there is a limit to what the flesh can bear. Within a few days, he was dead. He passed away in the dead of night on 14 January 1944.

By the time Lieutenant-Colonel Loganathan, accompanied by four other officers of the Indian National Army—Major Mansoor Ali Alvi and Lieutenants Mohammed Iqbal, Srinivasan and Suba Singh—arrived in Port Blair, which was on 22 February 1944, Diwan Singh and many others, who had been incarcerated and tortured in the Cellular Jail, were already dead.

Loganathan was supposed to take over as chief commissioner. But, although he was received with all due ceremony and accorded full honour, it was obvious that the Japanese had no intention of allowing him any effective power. He and his companions were accommodated in an ordinary bungalow near the Gurudwara. There is nothing on record to show that any official oath-taking ceremony (of Loganathan's appointment as chief commissioner) took place in Port Blair, or that he ever took over formally as chief commissioner. Anyway, they were told that they could assist in administering the departments dealing with education, civil supplies and agriculture. But they would have no say in important departments like jail or the police. After a great deal of haggling, when the matter was taken to the admiral, who gave them a lecture on the activities of "spies" like Diwan Singh and others, some compromise was arrived at; they were told that they would also be allowed to have some say in matters pertaining to jails and the police. But it seems patently clear that the Japanese had no intention of handing over any effective power. Suba Singh admits that, to begin with, the colonel and his men were considered by local people as Japanese stooges. But later on, after they had been able to intercede with some success on behalf of one or two who were to be executed for their supposed implication in crimes connected mostly with espionage, the attitude of the local people underwent a slight change.

The living conditions in Port Blair, however, were pretty bad. There was no cloth, no rice, no fish, no sugar. Japanese currency had lost all value, and the price of a coarse, handspun shirt, if and when available, was Rs 150!

What position Loganathan and his mission occupied is clear from Suba Singh's book, in which he says that right opposite their residence, in the windows of the barracks, binoculars and telescopes were installed so that the names of all those who came to see them could be taken down. Even the names of the Japanese who came to visit them were noted.

Loganathan had an occasion to go to Singapore and report to Netaji about conditions obtaining in the Andaman islands, and what had happened to Diwan Singh and others (about 90 of those arrested, according to some survivors, were shot dead by a firing squad one morning in November, somewhere near Humphreyganj), and also how the Japanese rulers were behaving. In addition to this personal report, Loganathan and his colleagues were regularly sending reports to Netaji. Therefore, there is no reason to doubt that Bose was not aware of how the Nippon government officials were treating the Provisional Indian Government and its representatives in the territories occupied by Japan, of which by far the most important was the territory of the Andaman and Nicobar islands, because it was supposed to have been handed over officially to Bose and his government!

And yet, on 6 July 1944, Netaji Subhas Chandra Bose, in an address to Mahatma Gandhi broadcast over Rangoon Radio, said:

> There was a time when people used to say Japan had selfish intentions regarding India. If she had them, why should she have decided to hand over the Andaman and Nicobar Islands to the Provisional Government of Free India? Why should there now be an Indian Chief Commissioner of the Andaman and Nicobar Islands stationed at Port Blair?

What chief commissioner! What an incredible act of self-deception! The solitary reference to the Provisional Government of Free India headed by Subhas Bose in the "official" history of the Japanese occupation of the Andamans reads: "Rieutenant-Colonel Roganadan [sic] with four officers of the Free India Provisional came to this island on February 1944, and established their office. But on July 1945, orders were received to evacuate, and consequently, all the members of the staff left this island in the beginning of August 1945."

Not a word about Loganathan being appointed, or acting as chief commissioner of the islands, nor about what their functions were, or their accomplishment, if any. And yet Subhas Bose, in his broadcast addressed to Mahatma Gandhi, spoke about "an Indian Chief Commissioner of the Andaman and Nicobar Islands [being] stationed at Port Blair". No wonder then that this myth of the Japanese government handing over the Andaman and Nicobar islands to the Provisional Government of Free India, or an Indian chief commissioner being appointed there, was the subject of many a raised eyebrow. The extent to which Subhas Bose himself believed in this make-believe fantasy is anyone's guess!

Perhaps it would be of some interest, in this context, to quote the assessment of Subhas Chandra Bose made by Philip Mason, who was for many years in India and belonged to the Indian Civil Service. At the time of the partition of the subcontinent, he was defence secretary to the government of India. Author of many well-known publications, Philip Mason has written in *A Matter of Honour*, which is an account of the Indian Army, its officers and men:

> Subhas Bose ... was a man of burning enthusiasm .... What he wanted to believe, he believed, and here he was naive, not to say gullible. But he was utterly sincere, and he proclaimed his doctrine with tireless energy and devotion. He was arrogant, cock-sure, ruthless, quite without humour; he saw everything in stark terms of right or wrong, good or bad; there was no hesitation or indecision. All this made him a most effective orator.

To turn now to the question of espionage, which was the root cause of the horrific tortures inflicted upon the poor citizens of Port Blair, the chief victim of which was Diwan Singh. The leader of this operation, which was assigned the task of going to the Andamans to gather intelligence, was Denis McCarthy, an officer of the Indian Police who had served in the Andamans before the Japanese invasion. He seems to have had the amazing foresight to have made some kind of an arrangement with the headman of a village named Ferrarganj, which is a suburb of Port Blair, before he was evacuated from the Andamans just before the Japanese took over. In October 1942, he was posted in Rae Bareli in the United Provinces (now Uttar Pradesh) when, according to him, he received a telegram from Bob Scott, who was at one time assistant commissioner at Car Nicobar. Scott wanted to see him because he wanted to ask McCarthy whether he would "consider going back to the Andaman Islands to make an appreciation of conditions there under the Japanese Occupation". McCarthy readily agreed. He was commissioned into the Sikh regiment, and he selected a party of five to accompany him. They were: a British other rank wireless/telegraph operator, Sergant Dickens; two ex-military policemen, who had served in the Andamans and were now in the army; Jemadar Habib Shah; Havildar Gyan Singh and two Ranchi coolies who had also previously worked in the Andamans—Havildar Joseph Bakla and his cousin, Peter.

After weeks of intensive training, McCarthy and his party set out on this very hazardous, but nonetheless very exciting, expedition. Colonel Christopher Hudson, commander of force 136 (group B), who was responsible for all operations in the Andamans, made the necessary arrangements for their being taken there. Hudson, who now lives in Chicana in Cadiz (Spain), told this author in a letter:

> My part in these Andamans operations were arming and equipping the parties, persuading the Dutch Naval authorities, with whom I was on friendly terms, to nominate one of their submarines for the first sortie, drawing up the operation orders in conjunction with the leader of parties, Major Denis McCarthy, and finally to authorise his plan of action within the Island on arrival.

The party travelled from Colombo on board a Dutch submarine, with Commander de Vries in command, and landed on 18 January 1943 on the west coast of Middle Andaman, four miles off Flat Island (which is 70 miles from Port Blair). In a hitherto unpublished report McCarthy has written:

> The submarine journey was quiet and uneventful. From the third day we stayed submerged in daylight. The fourth evening we made our landfall and soon picked up our beach. After dark we made our landing, everything going smoothly ... and within half an hour all our equipment was ashore. By midnight the camp had been set up well back in the jungle, near, but not on a stream.

They were carrying folboats for use as transport and were armed with sten guns.

After a week's preparation, McCarthy, accompanied by Habib Shah and Joseph, set out for Port Blair, travelling by night in two folboats— Habib Shah and McCarthy in the first, towing Joseph, who was in the second with a fishing line.

After more than a week of travel by folboats in the creaks, followed by trekking through jungle and across steep ridges, treading on thorny trees and jungle growth and plagued by leeches, they eventually arrived at a main road, which McCarthy was able to recognize as being within half a mile of Ferrarganj. They pitched their camp in the jungle and, leaving Joseph to cook a meal, walked across to the headman's house. And in McCarthy's words: "The Headman was most surprised. He said he had forgotten all about the arrangements I had made before leaving, but was delighted to see us. He took us to the *bhoosa* (straw) store in between the walls of the house, so that his wife and son, who were asleep, would not get to know we were there." The headman told McCarthy of the conditions prevailing in the Andamans, the brutality of the Japanese and how the inhabitants of the islands had been terrorized. The headman also told him that:

> They [the Japanese] had publicly executed poor Bird, the Chief Commissioner's Secretary, early on, just to impress the inhabitants, and had continued with a string of summary executions, brutal assaults, and rape. Sir Francis Waterfall [the British Chief Commissioner] and the remainder of the officials had been taken away by ship, which put paid to any attempt to evacuate them.

While McCarthy and Habib Shah were with the headman, they heard someone call. It was a Japanese and a local intermediary, who wanted the headman to give them a census of all the people in the village. This he did, while McCarthy and Habib Shah were in the safety of the *bhoosa*.

McCarthy goes on to tell the story: "When the Jap and his companion moved off the Headman came back to us. Habib Shah's own cousin Wilayat Shah was in the post at Ferrarganj, and the Headman was to arrange a rendezvous with him next day back in the jungle." As they moved out of the headman's house, they narrowly escaped being captured by the Japanese. This is how McCarthy describes it:

> We moved out and were just stepping back into the main road when we saw two Japanese soldiers in the moonlight, standing on the road less than ten yards away. We turned sharp right down the road, and strolled back as fast as we could in the opposite direction. I remember thinking "we must not keep in step." Nothing happened, perhaps the Jap took us for census takers, or just could not be bothered, but we were glad to slip back into the jungle.

It is difficult to believe even for a moment that the Japanese would have let them off if they had seen them, particularly since one of them happened to be a white man. In all probability, the Japanese did not notice them, since they were all dressed in very dark jungle-green clothes, and if they did, perhaps they were so drunk that they could not be bothered.

On the day following, McCarthy and his companions "were a bit chary about the rendezvous". They were afraid that they had aroused suspicion, "but the Headman came all right .... He gave us further information, and messages from Wilayat Shah for his cousin. We arranged a post-box, and moved back into the jungle. We intended to return within a fortnight, but thought it better not to tell this to the Headman". They did not speak to Wilayat Khan either, as he was working in a room occupied by a Japanese. All communication was through the headman, and the post-box was in a hole in the ground under a particular tree.

It was then that tragedy overtook them. They had started back on a different route, which meant crossing some creeks. As Habib Shah was unable to swim, they had to make a raft for him. When climbing a bank, McCarthy tells us: "Habib Shah slipped and banged the butt of his sten gun on the ground, and the gun went off. The bullet passed right through him, killing him almost instantly. We buried him there, using a mess tin as a spade, and piling large stones over the grave to shelter it from disturbance."

On arrival at the camp, writes McCarthy: "We sent a Wireless/Telegraph signal back to Headquarters, and were much cheered to see three Flying Fortresses come one day and bomb what we assumed were targets indicated by us, and then return intact without any fighters in pursuit."

Their mission accomplished, McCarthy and his party set out to get back to the submarine. The arrangement was that at the end of the operation two canvas squares would be put up on the beach by way of a signal and, as soon as the crew of the submarine would espy them, they would elevate the periscope high, as an acknowledgement that the party had been identified. The periscope came up, but along with it also a part of the conning tower. That was not because the crew of the submarine had seen the signal but because the submarine had grazed a coral reef, torn off the Asdic in the process, and surfaced. The party was taken on board, but one wonders what would have been the fate of McCarthy and his companions had the submarine not had this accident!

On board the submarine, there was some talk of McCarthy staying on in the islands, but it was ruled out because he was not considered fit enough. Obviously, his wandering in the Andamans, in order to collect intelligence for the Allies, in conditions which were most trying and difficult, had taken a heavy toll on the health of Denis McCarthy. According to Colonel Hudson: "He looked so ill when he reached Colombo after spending some time in the Andamans on what was to be his last attempt that I had him brought ashore on a stretcher and doubted whether he would survive for long."

But he survived. Denis McCarthy now lives in Bristol.

The submarine brought the party back to Colombo on 29 March. Most people in the Andamans are under the impression that Major Denis McCarthy and Subedar Bakhshish Singh, also an ex-policeman, were in the same operation which, incidentally, was code-named Baldhead I. Bakhshish Singh was not with him, but in Operation Baldhead IV and possibly, thinks McCarthy, also in Baldhead III as well.

While on Baldhead I, McCarthy had arranged a post-box near Ferrarganj as the point where the information was to be gathered. McCarthy is not sure, but it is possible that Bakhshish Singh also used the same box. McCarthy says he had also heard that "Bakhshish Singh ran into a party of the defecting India Liberation Army near Wimberleganj [another suburb of Port Blair], and got away pretending to be one of them, who had got lost!" Beyond that, not much is known of what Subedar Bakhshish Singh accomplished and how. (All attempts by this author to contact him have proved unsuccessful.)

According to the records available in the India Office Library and Records of the Foreign and Commonwealth Office in London, Bakhshish Singh was one of the 12 men aboard the *HMS Taurus* when this particular submarine, commanded by Lieutenant-Commander M R G Wingfield, left Colombo on 14 December 1943 and arrived off Port Campbell on the western coast of South Andaman on 19 December. Her task was to land a party of two officers and 12 men (one of whom was Subedar Bakhshish Singh) with 8,000 pounds of stores, for the purpose of reconnaissance. The two British officers were Major Grieg and Captain Falconer. This was Operation Baldhead III. (No information is available about Baldhead II.)

The *HMS Taurus* sailed again on 19 January 1944 with two more British officers (names not known), two British sergeants, eight Indian other ranks and 9,000 pounds of stores. The party left behind by the previous operation was successfully contacted and the stores landed safely on 24 January. The party, comprising Baldhead III, was found to be in excellent health. This was Operation Baldhead IV.

There was yet another operation—Baldhead V. Its objective was to pick up the entire party left behind by Baldhead III and IV. They wanted to do so before the onset of the monsoon. The mission was eminently successful and the entire party, along with leftover stores, embarked once again on *HMS Taurus* and returned to Trincomalee in Ceylon on 27 March 1944.

It does not speak much for the Japanese intelligence or the efficiency of the Japanese administration in the islands that they were not able to capture anyone involved in these operations. What is more, they obviously did not have even a clue of what was happening.

So far as Bakhshish Singh is concerned, there is nothing on record to show whether he remained behind on the islands after Baldhead III till such time as Baldhead V collected the party still on the islands. But it was obviously due to the clandestine and apparently highly successful activities of these four operations that the Allies were able to gather intelligence about Japanese defence installations in Port Blair, and consequently able to bomb, severely damage, and in most cases destroy them. Hence the persecution of the people in Port Blair.

Suba Singh is of the opinion that the Japanese had some inkling of how intelligence was being leaked to the Allies. This writer thinks they had not the foggiest idea. It should be clear to the dispassionate observer that it was because they were completely at sea that the Japanese resorted to such extreme measures. Otherwise, obviously, it would have been in their interest to keep the people happy and contented in order to gain their cooperation. No one can deny that the Japanese were no fools; admittedly they were drunk with power, and had become gullible to the extent of being influenced by local "jackals".

The tug-of-war between the Japanese and the representatives of Subhas Chandra Bose went on. Loganathan and his colleagues did succeed, as already stated, in interceding on behalf of some; they were even able to prevent one or two executions. But these were stray cases. However, they did manage to allay, to a certain extent, the suspicions of the local people, who began to think that maybe Subhas's men were not merely Japanese stooges. They began to talk openly with Loganathan and his men; they told them their tales of woe. The unfortunate result of this, as readers know, was that the Japanese started keeping a strict watch on those who came. This frightened them, and they stopped calling on them.

While the struggle for recognition by the Japanese of the status of the Provisional Indian Government representatives was going on, Allied raids on Port Blair and the neighbouring areas were gaining momentum. Port Blair suffered very severe bombardment one night at the hands of Anglo-American bombers. A number of petrol dumps caught fire and the entire city of Port Blair was enveloped in thick black smoke. This, according to Suba Singh (an eye-witness), was followed by attacks by Allied fighter planes which machine-gunned Japanese defence installations. On another night, in the light of the full moon, a British submarine made its appearance in the waters lapping the island of Ross, and began to shell a number of sites in Port Blair.

The next morning a large number of people, between 60 to 70, which included some local leaders and acknowledged stooges of the Japanese, were rounded up, lodged in the hated Cellular Jail and kept in solitary confinement. Even the wives of some were not spared. And once again the merciless beating began, with recourse to all the third degree methods the Japanese had perfected.

Suba Singh admits, although somewhat obliquely, of his and his colleagues' helplessness, saying quite pathetically, "But what could we do?" And yet, almost in the same breath as it were, he says that it was due to their reports to Netaji, as a result of which Bose had taken up the matter with higher authorities in Tokyo, that the admiral was transferred and a new one had taken his place. But was it not after the new one had arrived that this fresh wave of oppression commenced? Well, he says rather complacently, the Japanese then sent two judges!

It was presumably after the arrival of the new judges that the most atrocious deed, to crown the innumerable foul deeds already done by the Japanese, was committed. Suba Singh is silent on the subject. Mohammad Saudagar is still alive to tell the tale.

Saudagar was in his teens when he arrived in Port Blair on 15 August 1935, under sentence of transportation for life. In an interview with this author, he swore that he had not committed the murder for which he was convicted, but had taken on the blame to save his elder brother, who had a wife and family. Be that as it may, he had already completed his statutory term in the Cellular Jail and was living a "free life" on a ticket of leave when the Japanese arrived. When they, on arrival, ordered a general clemency, he became entitled to employment.

Apparently, since he had known Bagchi earlier, Saudagar became his orderly when he assumed power as the short-lived chief commissioner of the Andamans, under the tutelage of the Japanese. He continued to serve the administration in some post or the other even after Bagchi's fall from grace. But he continued to be in touch with Bagchi. One day, according to him, Bagchi told him that the days of the Japanese were numbered because the British were expected to come back soon. Bagchi said he had received a letter and that the Allies were expected around mid-August. Who had written to him, and from where the letter came, Bagchi did not tell him. Saudagar says that he was at the time very friendly with one Sher Singh, and they were staying together under the same roof. Since Saudagar had implicit trust in Sher Singh, he confided in him about what he had learnt from Bagchi.

Saudagar did not know at the time that Sher Singh had turned informer, and that he belonged to the Japanese equivalent of our Criminal Investigation Department. Sher Singh duly reported to his Japanese masters what Saudagar had told him. After two days Saudagar was arrested. And then followed torture—merciless beating, being put in a stock, and starvation. I asked him why he had not told the entire story when interrogated. That would have implicated too many people, he said. He underwent all that suffering to save the others just as he had taken upon himself the onus of the crime committed by his brother. That brother has long since been dead, but Saudagar is alive and kicking, married, rearing a family, and settled in Port Blair. He went back to Badaun, his village in Uttar Pradesh, but the enchanting Andamans called him back. So he came back and has no intention of ever leaving his adopted home.

One evening, Saudagar continued, in the month of July, the monsoon was at its furious worst: there was rain and thunder and gale. The weather gods seemed to have gone berserk. It was pitch dark. (Being close to the equator, the sun in any case sets very early on the islands.) At about 6 o'clock in the evening, about 600 inmates of the Cellular Jail were herded into trucks: they were told that they were being taken to help lay a garden somewhere in the suburbs. The prisoners rejoiced. But not for long. About 300 of them were asked to board the steamship *Akbar*; the rest were loaded into two small boats, 200 in each. The boats set sail in the darkness, which was impenetrable at about 7 P M. They were like animals squeezed in a stifling pen. No food of any kind was served. Hungry and soaking wet, those who could find a little space anywhere dozed off. Saudagar says that he had just fallen off into an uneasy slumber when he was rudely awakened—in fact, so were all the others—and ordered to disembark. It was about 1 o'clock in the morning. He could see no signs of any jetty, nor even a ladder. So, naturally enough, he tried to push himself backwards. At this he was beaten. So he jumped into the sea, and started swimming. He swam and he swam. In the morning he found himself on three feet of marshy shore, and he recognized that the island lying in front of him was Havelock Island. There were corpses floating all round; his estimate is that about 300 men had died that night. Four hundred survived, but there was hardly anything to eat and very little water to drink.

Suddenly, ten strange Burmans appeared from nowhere. But they were no angels of mercy come to help. On the contrary, they were out for what they could get. And they stationed themselves near where fresh water was available. Some of those who had managed to swim ashore had earlier, while in jail, been able to smuggle some jewellery. They had it now with them. The Burmans dispossessed them of all that and killed those who resisted. According to Saudagar, they killed nearly 100, and then disappeared. The survival rate among those left was very low, because all they could find to eat was some kind of grass and tubers. Only eight survived eventually, and one day, when a Burman from among them died, they cooked his dead body and ate it. Saudagar says he did not share in the first cannibal feast because he was asleep. But after that, according to Saudagar, if anyone died, they ate up the carrion. Most of those who had eaten human flesh began to suffer from stomach-aches and beri-beri. But somehow, he says, it did not have an adverse effect on him. He had found the flesh too salty.

Ultimately, there remained only two survivors—he and another person named Goverdhan. They stayed on that island for a month and 29 days.

During that time, unknown to them, the Japanese had accepted defeat and surrendered. There was, therefore, a lot of aerial activity. They found a number of planes flying overhead. In order to attract attention they hoisted a white piece of cloth on a bamboo pole. One day, soon after, they sighted a ship. A tall white man came in a canoe and took them on board the ship. They were taken to Rangoon, then Penang, and finally to Singapore. In Singapore, says Saudagar, he gave evidence in a trial against the Japanese.

I have checked Saudagar's story with many of those who were in Port Blair during the Japanese occupation. Most of his facts, according to them, are substantially correct; only, perhaps, he has embellished some and embroidered others.

Another deed, just as foul, was committed by the Japanese two days before their surrender—on 13 August 1945. A few days before that, the Japanese had rounded up about 300 people from the villages and taken them to a village known as Guracharana. This operation was called the *Round Up*. All the people—men, women and children—were kept in a hut under strict watch. No amenities were provided, least of all any food. On the third day, 13 August, all of them were herded into trucks and taken overland, besides the coast, to Tytler Ghat, which is at a distance of 13 miles. From Tytler Ghat they were taken in small boats to a tiny island known as Tarmugli. And there, they were all lined up and machine-gunned. Not a single person survived.

After the Allies reoccupied the islands, they sent a search party. All they could find were heaps of bones. Rama Krishna, editor of the local news-sheet, the *Andaman Shimbun* (sponsored by the Japanese who at first was a great favourite of the Japanese but had subsequently fallen from grace, testified to the veracity of this incident.

While the inhabitants of these unhappy islands were going through the agonies of hell, in Europe, on 6 June 1944, Operation Overlord had begun, and the Allies had landed on the coast of Normandy. On the other side, Russian troops had broken into eastern Czechoslovakia. On 7 May 1945 the German High Command surrendered all forces unconditionally at Rheims and the Russians finally captured Breslau. The war in Europe came to an end. Officially, all hostilities ceased on 9 May 1945, at 12.01 A M.

The year 1944 had been a bad one as far as India was concerned. On 31 March the Japanese had surrounded Imphal, and on 8 April they had reached the outskirts of Kohima. But their advance had been halted there.

It was not until the war in Europe had ended, and the Allies had dropped their first atomic bomb on Hiroshima, that the war was to end in the Far East. The atom bomb on Hiroshima was dropped on 6 August. (The representatives of the Provisional Indian Government in the Andamans had left Port Blair nine days before.)

That the Allies remained conscious of the strategic importance and value of the Andaman and Nicobar islands is apparent from the fact that in as far back as August 1943, the India Command's Joint Planning Staff were talking about the "capture and retention" of the Port Blair settlement in South Andaman Island, because "it would virtually secure [them] (the use of the Andamans as an advance base". In another paper, dated 20 October of the same year, the Joint Planning Staff indicated that the capture of Port Blair would secure for the Allies the following advantages:

(a) It increases the scope of our [Allies] intelligence activities, especially as regards the Japanese army aspect of intelligence, for which at present we lack satisfactory bases;
(b) It affords us an advance base for attacks on enemy shipping;
(c) It provides a number of sheltered anchorages; and
(d) It denies to the enemy an advance base for naval and air forces.

Talking about the moral value of the operation, the paper went on to add: "We are perturbed at the apparent disinclination of the general public at home really to interest themselves in the Eastern Theatre." They, therefore, thought that "the successful completion of this [Andaman] operation would have a more beneficial effect on creating an interest in this theatre than would the capture of Akyab, which would inevitably be regarded as yet another minor operation in Burma, in which country they appear to evince little interest". Besides, they felt, "the Japanese army and people would be more sensitive to the loss of the Andaman Islands, with consequent threat towards the centre of their strategic position in South East Asia, than to a withdrawal from Akyab". What is more, in an annex to this paper, they added: "Reliable evidence... indicates that the Japanese expect us to attack the Andaman Islands in the near future."

The only time the recapture of the Andaman islands was seriously considered was at a conference of the British chiefs of staff on the eve of the Cairo conference, code-named *Sextent*, and held on 22 November 1943. The operation to capture the islands was to be known as *Buccaneer*. In his book *The War in the Far East*, Basil Collier has written:

> *Buccaneer* was an expedition to the Andaman and Nicobar.... The British Chiefs of Staff considered this the most promising operation they could undertake in the Bay of Bengal with the means they thought likely to be available. But in the context of the Cairo Conference, with the forthcoming assault on Hitler's Fortress Europe in the forefront of their minds, they were not satisfied that *Buccaneer*... would make the best use of resources which might, they thought, be more profitably employed in Europe.

Apart from that, Chiang Kai-shek was proving difficult. Basil Collier continues: "Chiang Kai-shek's attitude was such that they doubted whether any inducement the Allies could offer would extract from him a firm and unequivocal promise to contribute to an offensive on land." To illustrate how irascible and cussed he could be, Collier tells us that "at one stage he insisted... that the air lift to China must in no circumstances be curtailed, although it was obvious that no offensive on lines discussed with him could be launched unless some aircraft were deviated from the air lift to the support of the Allies".

This attitude of Chiang Kai-shek is of special interest to us in India, because he was posing as our great friend at the time!

Earlier in August that year, one of the decisions taken at the Quebec conference, code-named *Quadrant*, was to appoint Rear-Admiral Lord Louis Mountbatten as the Supreme Allied Commander in South-east Asia. So one of the plans that he brought to the *Sextant* (Cairo conference) was Buccaneer. But according to S W Roskill, in his book *The War at Sea*:

> The British and American Chiefs of Staff were by no means yet agreed over the correct strategy; and the Chinese were demanding that any offensive by them should receive diversionary support from a strong seaborne expedition across the Bay of Bengal. As President Roosevelt

had already promised the Chinese that this would be done, the British Chiefs of Staff found themselves committed to carry out *Buccaneer* in March 1944.

However, Roskill goes on to say that both the British and American chiefs of staff were agreed that "in no circumstances should the operations in Europe be prejudiced". There was, therefore, a basic difference of opinion between the two because, again according to Roskill, "whereas the Americans were insistent that the Burma operation and *Buccaneer* should take place as planned, the British were equally insistent that any seaborne expedition in the Indian ocean would undoubtedly lead to a diversion of strength from Europe."

One of the two parties had to give way. In this case, it was President Roosevelt who did. Prime Minister Winston Churchill received a terse cable from the American president, which read: *Buccaneer is off*. Thus ended the solitary seriously-proposed attempt to recapture the Andaman and Nicobar islands.

There is no point in speculating its effect on the lives of the people of the island. That will always remain one of the ifs of history. There is no gainsaying the fact, however, that had the Allies mounted Buccaneer, they would have had no difficulty in recapturing the islands, because by then the strength of the Japanese forces had been much depleted, and most of their lines of supply had been seriously affected due to Allied action in the air and at sea.

Buccaneer was scheduled for March 1944. By that time, of course, Diwan Singh had succumbed to the tortures inflicted upon him in jail; but many of his companions were still alive. Perhaps they, and many others who were also undergoing terrible suffering and hardship, would have been spared. And perhaps also Saudagar and the hundreds thrown into the sea and those massacred at Tarmugli. But one thing is clear: to those deliberating in Cairo or in Quebec or at Mountbatten's headquarters of the South-east Asia Command, the Andaman and Nicobar islands were a mere chain of islands in the Bay of Bengal in the Indian Ocean, and their importance or otherwise was judged solely from the military point of view, and how their capture was to affect the course of the war; no one at any stage thought of the miserable people inhabiting the islands. Human beings obviously do not matter when a war is being fought.

Buccaneer was off, but that did not mean the Allies were sitting idle while it was being planned, or even after its abandonment. The systematic bombing and destruction of Japanese targets continued. In one of the reports pertaining to the period between 24 June 1944 and 25 May 1945, the extent of the damage caused by Allied action was summarized as follows:

The main item of interest consists of severe damage to the previously slightly damaged Saw Mill on Chatham Island which has now been rendered completely unserviceable. There is also some damage to the main wharf of the island. The coal sheds at *Hope Town Station* have been completely damaged at the Marine Yard at Phoenix Bay. Throughout the various districts a number of barrack-type huts and identified barrack buildings have been damaged, destroyed or removed. The total number of such buildings affected throughout the area is 17. On Ross Island a considerable number of unidentified hut-type buildings, some of which may be barrack huts, have been destroyed, in addition to even probable godowns in the vicinity of the jetty. Throughout the whole area covering about 40 dwellings, mostly of a medium or small size, have been damaged or destroyed. At the Cellular Jail at Atlanta Point a considerable amount of demolition and removal has taken place and still seems in progress.

Pointing out an instance of Allied air attacks, the report adds that "on the 6th December (1943) 12 Liberators (B-24) raided Port Blair area. No shipping was seen and the attack was therefore directed at Chatham Island .... Thirty-five hits on the target are claimed".

The very fact that the Allies were able to effect so much damage on the islands, with more or less impunity (though in one case five or six Japanese fighters had attacked Allied formations), shows that had Buccaneer been put into operation, the Andaman and Nicobar islands could have been liberated from the pernicious grip of Japanese rule much before they actually were.

Although the end of the war was nowhere in sight, the headquarters of the Supreme Allied Commander of South-east Asia had already planned on the kind of administration the islands would have once they were recaptured from the Japanese. In a communication dated 11 November 1944, addressed to the government of India, it was stated: "Upon reoccupation of the Andaman and Nicobar Islands it will be necessary to establish military administration in them and as these islands fall within this theatre this will be the responsibility of South East Asia Command." But, it added:

> In view, however, of the fact that the islands constitute part of India and that after a period of military administration, which may be short, responsibility for administering them will revert to the Government of India. There would be obvious advantages if the Government of India could see its way to provide the Civil Affairs Staff which will be required for the military period so that when civil government is restored continuity of staff will be ensured.

In a Joint Planning Staff paper, dated 15 August 1945, it was recommended that "C-in-C India be invited to accept responsibility for the re-occupation of the Andaman and Nicobar Islands after a Japanese recapitulation".

But before this decision was taken, sometime at the end of the month of February earlier in the year, there was something of a spurt in Japanese shipping activity in the Andaman Sea. As stated by S Woodburn Kirby in the fourth volume of his book, *The War Against Japan*: "With Mountbatten's approval, [Vice-Admiral, Sir Arthur] Power carried out a series of anti-shipping sweeps by destroyers in these waters: targets in the Andaman Islands were bombarded on the 24th and 25th February and again on the 13th and 19th March 1945." Then, in April 1945, writes Kirby:

> Vice-Admiral Walker sailed from Trincomalee with two battleships, the *Queen Elizabeth* and *Richelieu*, four cruisers, the *Cumberland*, *Suffolk*, *Ceylon* and *Tromp*, two escort carriers, the *Empress* and *Shah*, and five destroyers, the fleet being accompanied by two oilers escorted by a sixth destroyer. This force bombarded airfields and other targets on the Nicobar Islands on the morning of the 30th [April] and then set course for Port Blair in the Andamans where, in the evening, airfields, batteries and shipping were attacked by air strikes and by gunfire. The force remained in the area till the 7th May, during which time it attacked Margui, Victoria Point and Port Blair and the Nicobars for the second time.

After the Allies dropped their first atom bomb on Hiroshima on 6 August 1945, events in the Far East moved quickly. Two days later, on the 8th, the USSR declared war on Japan. The next day, on the 9th, the Allies dropped another atom bomb, this time on Nagasaki. On the same day the Russians invaded Manchuria; by the 12th, they had also entered North Korea.

On 14 August 1945, the mighty Japanese surrendered unconditionally.

On 6 October it was decided, writes S Woodburn Kirby, that "Japanese forces in Malaya, the Andaman and Nicobar Islands and Sumatra were to be collected on Rempang Island in the Rhio Archipelago at the Eastern end of the Strait of Malacca as soon as its 400 or so mainly Dutch inhabitants had been brought to the mainland".

According to *The War at Sea*, a compilation made by the historical section of the naval staff admiralty, the operation to occupy the Andamans and Nicobars was code-named *Popcorn*. The expedition, which was to bring the 116th India Infantry Brigade from Calcutta to Port Blair, was for some reasons delayed. Therefore, *Bandra*, a "mercy ship" carrying supplies for prisoners of war and those living in Port Blair, escorted by the Indian Navy sloop *Nerbudda*, left Calcutta on 22 September and arrived in Port Blair four days later, on 26 September, and remained there as a kind of guard-ship.

Operation Popcorn, comprising the convoy for Andaman and Nicobar islands, states *The War at Sea*, "left Calcutta on October 3, and landing at Port Blair took place on the 7th" and, because of the mines in the harbour, the disembarkation of stores was greatly delayed, because it was not possible to use the Chatham jetty or the dockyard.

However, the 116th brigade, which had been detailed by the South-east Asian Allied land force under the command of Brigadier A J Salomon, to reoccupy the islands, landed on 7 October.

On 7 October 1945, Brigadier A J Salomon took the formal surrender of the Japanese.

Thus ended one of the most tragic and perhaps the unhappiest chapter in the history of the Andaman islands.

25

The Nicobars During the Occupation

Except for Car Nicobar, the Japanese left the rest of the islands in the Nicobar group very much to themselves, except where their presence was essential from the military point of view. But in Car Nicobar, it was a different story. Fortunately, Bishop John Richardson, who had assumed the duties of the assistant commissioner when the British left, is still there to tell the tale.

One Sunday, at the end of July 1942, Bishop Richardson tells us, he was coming back home after attending a Sunday morning service when he and his congregation spotted a warship. When the warship come closer, they recognized the ship's flag, which carried the emblem of the rising sun; it was a Japanese warship.

Bishop Richardson hurried home, which was in the village Mus, from where he could see two boats trying to land. "The surf was very bad", he says, "and one of the boats capsized, but the other landed safely". The Japanese went round the island, rounded up most of the village headmen and inquired about their nationality. The headmen replied that they were Indians. Were there any troops on the island—any Sikh, Gurkha or Scottish soldiers, was the next question. There were none.

They put up a post on which they wrote that Car Nicobar had been occupied by the Japanese. After sitting around for a couple of hours, by which time it was beginning to get dark, they left.

The next day, recalls Bishop Richardson, he went to the assistant commissioner's office and burnt all the secret and other important papers. "If the Japanese had found me doing so, I would have been killed there and then," he says. But luckily for him they were not around.

The Japanese came back on 2 August 1942, and it was then that the total occupation of Car Nicobar took place.

To begin with, they did not treat the Nicobarese very harshly. A few days later, however, they demanded and took away 1000 Nicobarese to work as labourers. Then they took away some more, and then some more, thus denuding Car Nicobar of all her able-bodied men. Bishop Richardson says the Japanese had given him a solemn promise that they would treat the Nicobarese they were taking away very well. "But when they were there, the Japanese did not treat them well. They were cruelly beaten, and given only a ball of rice to eat with water, and nothing else. And many died."

But worse was still to come. "One day three [Allied] planes flew over a ship that was at anchor in the waters off Car Nicobar. The planes pounded it with bombs and sank it." And that, said Bishop Richardson, was the signal for a long reign of terror in Car Nicobar. All the headmen and other important men in Car Nicobar were arrested and accused of giving information to the enemy. Bishop Richardson continues:

We all denied that we had given any information to the enemy. Of course, they didn't believe us. So we were all put in a concentration camp in the jungle in the centre of the island. We could not escape, because the camp was surrounded by Japanese guards. We were in that concentration camp till the end of the war. Every few days, the Japanese would come and take away some Nicobarese, telling us that they wanted them for work. None of them ever came back. They were all killed. My son was murdered; so was my son-in-law, my brother-in-law and my nephew. Anyone who was educated was taken away and killed. I was to be their last victim. One day I was taken to the Japanese headquarters. I was handcuffed and questioned all evening and all night. I was asked where I had hidden three hundred rockets. I said I had no knowledge. I didn't even know what a rocket was.

They said I was a liar. They threatened to kill me. I said I was not afraid to die. But they must shoot me, so that I was spared pain.

The next morning, however, when Bishop Richardson was taken to the Japanese army headquarters, expecting to be beheaded, the major-general commanding the occupation forces in Car Nicobar stepped up to him and said: "You are the luckiest man in the world, because our Emperor has decided to stop the war. He doesn't want to shed any more blood. So you are now free." Bishop Richardson was given a yard-long piece of red cloth and some rice. He rushed home to his wife and his young child and told her: "I have escaped with my life. The war has ended."

Thus came to an end the nightmare in Car Nicobar. The only good the Japanese occupation did to the people of Car Nicobar was that when war came to the island, all traders who were outsiders, and who had been exploiting them for many a decade, fled. After the war the land which the Nicobarese had mortgaged to the traders reverted to them. They have managed their own affairs since, having set up their own cooperative. "We are now enjoying prosperity and can look the world in the face," Bishop Richardson concluded.

26

Liberation... and Horrors Recalled

Arfat Ahmed Khan first went to the Andamans in 1926 and was evacuated in 1942. He worked in the food department of the government of India all through the war and was among those who came back to Port Blair on board the *S S Dilwara*, the troop-carrier which brought back the first party of soldiers and civilians. He recalls:

Before the actual re-occupation we were based in Calcutta for about six months for making arrangements for provisions and the like. Ultimately, we sailed from Calcutta in a fleet of 4 ships, *Dilwara* being the mother ship. I was one of those civilians who were eventually to take over and run the civilian Government,

N K Patterson was the chief commissioner designate and the troops were commanded by Brigadier A J Salomon. When we reached the Andaman waters, we anchored off the Ross Island and one of our boats was sent in advance to contact the commandant of the Japanese forces. They still numbered nearly 20,000. After having established contact, the advance party returned. And then Brigadier Salomon and his troops landed in commando formation. [No civilian was allowed to land that day.] After Brigadier Salomon's men had taken position on shore near the jail, the Aberdeen jetty and other strategic places, the civilians on board the 4 ships were allowed to land. But that was not till the next day.

Khan said that before they had set sail from Calcutta, they were given strict instructions that after landing they were *not* to drink any water or eat any food in Port Blair, lest it be polluted or poisoned. And of course they were not to mix with the Japanese. When Khan landed at Aberdeen jetty, he found about 50 or 60 old friends waiting there to welcome him and others who had arrived.

It was a pitiable sight. I found that one of my old friends, once a very wealthy man, Akbar Ali, was wearing a vest and a pair of shorts made out of a gunny bag.... I was so moved that tears came into my eyes. He was in tears, too, because he said that his son had been killed by the Japanese. When I asked some of my other friends about their families, most of them were not even able to speak, because they were in such agony.

About living conditions, Khan said:

The sanitary conditions were appaling. It is indescribable. There were no lavatory arrangements anywhere. Flies were in abundance. You couldn't even eat. Garbage, even human excreta, had not been removed for God knows how long. Everyone looked anaemic. The conditions were so bad that we were asked not to go and mix with the local population. So we couldn't even go and meet our friends.

On 9 October 1945, the formal ceremony to mark the surrender of the Japanese took place. Brigadier H J L Addison was in overall charge as far as the administration was concerned, but Brigadier Salomon took the surrender. Khan had asked Brigadier Addison's permission to watch the surrender ceremony. Permission granted, he went across to the Gymkhana grounds where it was going to be held. From what he could recollect:

One table was laid just facing the Andaman Club. All officers were gathered there; the military was in charge. A car drove up. It carried the Commanding Officer of the Japanese naval forces. He was in full uniform and was carrying his sword. He was accompanied by two Aides. Brigadier Salomon was seated on the other side of the table. The Japanese Admiral saluted. Brigadier Salomon stood up and shook hands with him. Then the Japanese Admiral took his sword out of the scabbard, surrendered it to Brigadier Salomon, unbuckled his belt and stripped himself of all other decorations and badges of honour. A prepared document was read out.

Brigadier Salomon signed the document on behalf of the British Government and the Japanese Admiral on behalf of the Japanese. Despite instructions to the contrary, the crowd that had gathered burst into cheers. The whole ceremony did not take more than two or three minutes. The ceremony over, the Japanese Admiral walked quietly with his bowed head to the car; his two Aides were walking behind him. They got in and drove away.

The Japanese Command was given instructions that all Japanese troops should move out of the city and be at least four miles outside its limits. They were also divested of arms, and given wooden staffs instead. After a few days, Khan visited Guracharana, a neighbouring village, where a large number of Japanese troops had been housed in barracks. He found them in very poor shape—no proper clothing, nothing to eat. They had planted sweet potatoes, and that is what they were living on.

He also heard stories of Japanese atrocities. He had read a great deal about the atrocities committed in various other countries—Germany, Russia, China and others, but they were nothing compared to the barbarous acts committed by the Japanese occupation forces. He heard about Diwan Singh and others, who had been victims of Japanese terror.

Khan narrated an incident about a close friend of his, Khan Sahib Dr Nawab Ali. According to him, Nawab Ali was a very respected citizen, and used to mix freely with Englishmen even in those days. Perhaps that is why he had been arrested and tortured; eventually, he had died in jail. But before he died, he was made to sign a document to "confess" that he was a spy of the British. He did. In Khan's words:

Two of his daughters, both very beautiful, Saira and Sofia, were brought before the father stark naked, and their legs were forcibly stretched. Then the Japanese lighted newspapers and placed them under their open thighs. The father covered his eyes. The girls shrieked. They cried, "*Abba Jan, bol do han! Abba Jan, bol do han*" (Please, dear father, say yes). So, he said, "Yes, I am a spy", and signed the paper.

There were hundreds of other such cases.

India and the world outside heard, for the first time, what had happened in the Andamans when a correspondent of the *Hindustan Times*, the Delhi newspaper, paid a visit to Port Blair a week after the British had taken over. In a despatch datelined 16 October 1945, he wrote:

> Scepticism breaks down under the weight of authentic evidence piling up of Jap atrocities during three and a half years of occupation.... The Andaman people still remember him [Dr Diwan Singh] with deep love.... His fall began when in one of the monthly Independence Day meetings held on the 21st of each month to commemorate the so-called liberation of the islands by the Japs, he spoke with brutal frankness and said that what they had hailed as liberation had become worse than slavery. After that he came under Jap suspicion and they took the first opportunity to kill him.

On the subject of Colonel Loganathan, he wrote: "He was told by the Jap authorities to learn the work during the first year and study local conditions before he was given full powers of his office. During the year of apprenticeship he could not helplessly watch the police terror and is, therefore, reported to have feigned illness and went back to Singapore where he seems to have protested against the state of affairs in the island." That protest, as we already know, was received by none other than Netaji Subhas Chandra Bose! The correspondent added:

> The most hated men in the Andamans are the 300 or so men of police whom the British left behind when they evacuated. They supplied the new rulers with details about each and every family or individual in the Andamans and that explains why the dossiers kept by the Japanese police, which have now come in the hands of the British, are so rich in detail about each individual. These policemen, the population alleged, took prominent part in torturing people during the espionage trials. It is said that the property of those who were executed or torturted to death in these cases was shared between the Jap "Thokumuhan" and the Indian Police. This police force has now been disbanded and its men have been put in jail.

The correspondent wondered why people had collaborated! He could only explain it thus: "The fact... is that the morale of the people became so low during the Japanese rule that even children, a large number of whom have learnt the Japanese language, became informers." He quoted the example of one of the young men he had met "whose brother-in-law was shot in an espionage case and whose father-in-law was tortured and a sister roughly handled. After that to save his skin and keep above suspicion he contributed an article to the *Andaman Shimbun* praising the co-prosperity sphere. After all there was no other alternative".

In another despatch by the same correspondent, which is datelined 18 October 1945, he wrote of 151 people found in the prison camp in the Andamans, who had since "left for India on board the troopship Dilawar". He went on to say:

> Most of them are Punjabis and VCOs [Viceroy's Commissioned Officers] or belonging to other Indian ranks. While there is no officer among them, most of them were brought there on March 23, 1942, and have been completely cut off from the rest of the world. Now they are returning home as Rip Van Winkles looking very thin and worn out, which explains the allegation they made about their none too nutritious rations which did not include either meat or vegetables and very hard work from 5 a.m. to 5 p.m.

According to the correspondent, the government of India also toyed at that time with the idea of attaching the islands "to some Indian province so that its people may share the advantage of electoral representation and constitutional reform with the people of other Indian provinces". But, obviously, nothing came of it. Just as well. The islands might have gained some ephemeral advantages, but they would have lost their identity!

Stormy weather, and difficulties encountered in clearing mines, had meanwhile held up the despatch of troops to Car Nicobar. The troopship finally sailed from Port Blair on 17 October. Car Nicobar was reoccupied by the British on 18 October 1976.

By the end of October, disarmament throughout the islands had been completed. The total number of Japanese troops awaiting evacuation was 18,846. A hundred and eighty-six Japanese were being held in custody as war criminals. This number was later reduced to 112.

The population of the islands, by the time the British reoccupied them, had been reduced to a mere 18,000, whereas before the Japanese occupation it had been 34,000. The figures speak for themselves.

One of the first decisions that the government of India took after the re-occupation was to abolish the penal settlement. In the words of N K Patterson, the chief commissioner designate:

> After very careful consideration the Government of India decided with the approval of the Secretary of State to abolish the Penal Settlement. This decision led in turn to the question of the future of convicts numbering nearly 6,000 who had to remain on the Island at the time of the Japanese occupation in 1942. The Provincial Governments eventually all agreed to the proposal made by the Government of India that all convicts who had still some balance of sentence to serve should be given remission of that balance, and should be allowed to return to their homes if they so desired.

This was in October 1945. Four thousand and two hundred convicts availed of this offer. They were repatriated to their homes, thus further reducing the population of the islands.

Patterson, as already indicated, was among the officers who had come on the troopship *Dilawar* along with Brigadier Salomon and his troops. He has also written of the condition of the population of Port Blair, who had extended the British forces "a tremendous welcome":

> The population was obviously in extremely bad shape as regards nutrition, clothing and health, and the general deterioration and destruction was found to be very heavy in regard to such matters as roads, drains, buildings, marine dockyard, saw-mills etc.... The population was suffering from starvation and malnutrition. The incidence of disease was very high. Clothing in most cases consisted of gunny sacking or old rags. There were literally no consumer goods of any kind available in the whole of Port Blair. The roads were in shocking condition. The sanitary conditions were indescribable with drains blocked and destroyed.... Buildings were in dilapidated condition and in many cases partitions, ceilings and fittings had been removed, or destroyed.

But it was the prevalence of disease that needed urgent attention. According to Patterson: "The incidence of malaria was extremely high but the main diseases which had to be dealt with arose from sheer starvation, and beri-beri in particular was very prevalent. There was a severe epidemic of scabies throughout the whole of the Port Blair area."

Fortunately, things were not so bad in Car Nicobar. As Patterson put it: "Owing to their somewhat peculiar methods of living, the Nicobarese had not suffered as severely as the population of the Andamans, and their rehabilitation proved to [be] very much simpler and very much more rapid than in Port Blair."

Patterson says that right from 8 October 1945, the day of their arrival: "The whole energies of the civilian staff were directed to the immediate task of relief." He found that "the close and easy cooperation of the Civil Staff with the military administration" was an outstanding factor which proved to be an "important asset during the four months of the Military Administration".

One of the first steps that the authorities took was that: "All Government servants who were still in the Islands were reemployed immediately and all Departments reemployed as many of their old employees as were available." Another factor that proved a great asset was the presence of nearly 10,000 Japanese troops who, in the words of Patterson, "provided an adequate labour force".

On 28 November 1945, the islands were honoured by a visit from Rear-Admiral Lord Louis Mountbatten, the Supreme Allied Commander of the South-east Asia Command. (He is now the Earl Mountbatten of Burma.) Lord Mountbatten kept a private diary while in South-east Asia. The entry for that day begins characteristically with a reference to his wife,

Edwina, because 28 November also happened to be her birthday. He wrote: "Edwina's birthday, I only hope she gets home in time to be with Pamela [their daughter] for it." About Port Blair, the entry reads:

At 14.30, we landed at Port Blair, the capital of the Andaman Islands. Here I was met by M Patterson, High Commissioner [sic], Brigadier Salomon, Commanding 116 Indian Infantry Brigade, Group Captain Pope and Captain Blair, R. N. R., the great nephew of the original Captain Blair who founded the Port. After inspecting the Naval Guard of Honour, I visited and addressed practically the whole of 116 Brigade in groups, and later went round the magnificent harbour with Blair and went on board H. M. I. S. "Kistna". The population consists of some 12,000 natives and 6,000 convicts who have been released and pardoned. Wherever we drove, every single native, without exception, stood up and saluted as we passed, a relic from the Japanese who beat them if they did not salute. However, I think they were pleased to see us as they were being starved to death by the Japanese.

Lord Mountbatten spent only one night in Port Blair. Another very important visitor, who followed soon after, was the viceroy and governor-general of India, Lord Wavell. He was accompanied by Lady Wavell, the vicerene.

The military administration was supposed to last for six months, but in actual fact the administration was handed over to civilian authorities on 7 February 1946. And, by that time, according to Patterson, "practically the whole of the Japanese forces had been repatriated, the evidence necessary for the trial of Japanese war criminals had been obtained and communicated to the appropriate authorities, and steps for the repatriation of displaced persons had been taken".

N K Patterson handed over charge as chief commissioner in February 1947, and Inam-ul-Majid, of the Indian Civil Service, was the first Indian ever to be appointed to that post.

Less than a couple of weeks after Majid had taken over, there arrived in Port Blair the distinguished writer, Compton Mackenzie, who was subsequently knighted. He was at the time engaged in writing a book on the contribution of the Indian Armed Forces in the second world war. Coincidentally perhaps, Sir Compton arrived in Port Blair on board the *R I N S Narbudda*, which had originally come there along with *Bandra*, a "mercy ship", before the Japanese had actually surrendered. Sir Compton landed on 23 February 1947, and his main purpose was to find the truth or otherwise of the atrocities committed by the Japanese on the islanders.

Mackenzie's host was the deputy commissioner, Michael Sullivan, who had been at Cambridge and was an Olympic runner. Sullivan was married to an Assamese girl, Sherin, who, it was said, was his one-time gardener's daughter, and had by now learnt to speak English like a "native". Sullivan took him around and told him about the Japanese horrors.

Mackenzie was charmed by the Andamanese jungles. He wrote: "The Andamanese jungle seemed to be even richer than the Burma jungle in variety of trees, for it had some of the characteristics of the Malay jungle added. Besides, there were many coconut groves and wide valleys of paddy."

About the horrors: "My mind was too full of the horrors of the Jap occupation ... to settle down to diary writing when we got back to the ship. Of 20,000 people they managed to exterminate in one way or another over 7,000." On the subject of Major A J Bird:

When the British and Indian authorities escaped in March 1942, the Indian Government asked for volunteers to look after the local population. Among those volunteers was Major A J Bird [as was his chief, Waterfall]. A Bengali convict called Bagchi, who when manager of a cinema [I think in Calcutta] murdered a man and received a life sentence, had been employed by Bird and sacked for malingering, to revenge himself, after the Japs appointed him Chief Naval Intelligence Officer, he forged a letter from Bird which purported to give instruction about the establishment of an espionage service.

The version of the story given to him varies slightly, but it corroborates the fact that Bird was "tortured to make him confess". According to Mackenzie, just before his execution, "Bird moaned for water, whereupon the executioner, a Jap naval officer, called for water which he poured on his own sword before cutting off Bird's head by the edge of a trench dug to receive his body".

When Mackenzie visited the Cellular Jail, he had a glimpse of Bagchi. He wrote: "Then I saw a small young man with the face of a weasel and the eyes of a viper." When Bagchi saw Mackenzie, "a greasy propitiatory smile began to trickle over his face". Mackenzie stared at him without response, whereupon he turned his face away. Mackenzie was told that "appeals were being cabled from Bengal to the Chief Commissioner on behalf of Bagchi". Mackenzie, quite rightly, felt that Bagchi "deserved to be stamped out like a cockroach". But he was not. He managed to get away with all his atrocious deeds, and live in Calcutta. Of course he was forbidden to visit the Andamans, although he was very keen to do so. It was said that he had stolen a lot of gold and jewellery from some of his victims, and he had buried it somewhere. He wanted to come back to recover it. But A K Ghosh, the then chief commissioner, firmly refused to allow him to do so. That was the end of the story of this despicable man.

Mackenzie was able to confirm all the horror stories—the drowning of hundreds of people on Havelock Island, the Tarmugli massacre, the tortures of men, the women being forced into prostitution and much else. He said: "The kindest explanation for the Japanese atrocities is to attribute them to panic. They were in a panic throughout occupation." He was told how, when the wireless station had been blown up resulting in a loud explosion, "the Japs all fell down on their faces and did not move for twenty minutes". Mackenzie's conclusion was:

> The atrocities committed in the Andaman Islands upon the unhappy people there cannot be dismissed as propaganda. They are all too foully true ... and the Indian Nationalists who with patriotic intent allied themselves with the Japanese will stand at the bar of history as the tools of a sub-human nation. It is intelligible that for the freedom of his country a patriot might accept the help of apes, but he should not try to pretend afterwards that apes were civilised human beings, and whitewash their essential bestiality.

Sir Compton Mackenzie was most impressed by the atmosphere in Port Blair. Before leaving for Car Nicobar, he wrote: "The atmosphere of the place was extraordinarily genial. Everybody liked the other fellow; I did not hear a word of criticism by one official against the other. Co-operation was the rule."

At Car Nicobar, Mackenzie learnt: "At first the invaders behaved fairly well, but when we [the Allies] started bombing the airstrips they indulged in the same spy scare as on the Andamans. In all seventy-five Nicobarese were tortured to death."

The most moving story he heard was that of a captain of Arong, a village in a very remote part of Car Nicobar, where everyone then was completely animist. He was told: "The captains of all the villages were ordered to surrender the Union Jacks which they had, and this was done by all except the captain of Arong. He buried his and would not reveal the place under torture. The flag was finally discovered by the Japs two years later, and after being tortured again the captain of Arong was put to death."

In Car Nicobar, the Japanese had applied the same kind of tortures as in the Andamans, except that they would make a man (they wanted to torture) climb a coconut tree, and force him to stay there all day, balanced on a precarious branch.

Mackenzie also visited the solitary local store which he found "well run and well stocked". But he was amused to find an inscription on a board just inside the entrance. It read:

Always tell the truth.
Give up your bad habits.
Might is right.
God Almighty.
Don't spit here.

Mackenzie called on Bishop Richardson. (Everyone who goes to Car Nicobar meets him.) He visited the chapel, and there, to his surprise, he found lying a dry pomelo (a grape-fruit, larger and more sour). He wanted to know what the pomelo was doing there, and heard an interesting story. A sailor from the *H M I S Krishna*, when she was there at the time of the Japanese surrender, apparently cheated a Nicobarese by buying two pomelos for the price of one. Back on board the ship, he found himself stricken with paralysis. Apparently, he was so conscience-stricken that he sent one of the pomelos back, and requested that prayers be offered for his recovery. And the story has it that he recovered immediately!

Mackenzie was anxious to visit Great Nicobar, but the assistant commissioner of Car Nicobar, Major J d'Issa-Boomgardt, was very keen to visit the island of Chowra. Although the island fell under his jurisdiction, he had never been able to visit it, because in those days the administration had no ships at their disposal. So he wanted to take advantage of the *Narbudda*, which was carrying Mackenzie. Mackenzie seems to have regretted going there, because he found the people there ugly and the villages dirty. He wrote:

> The ground round the villages was littered with coconut shells and refuse, and flies were thick everywhere .... The most depressing thing about the island was that practically the whole population was infected with venereal disease, not to mention elephantiasis, tuberculosis and malaria .... The people had no medicine of any kind.

27

Independence—and After

When independence came to India, as also to the Andaman and Nicobar islands, Inam-ul-Majid was still chief commissioner. In the annual administrative report for the year 1947-48, he wrote:

The most memorable event of the year was the achievement of Independence. The flag of the Indian Dominion was hoisted in the Gymkhana Ground on the 15th of August 1947 with great reverence and solemnity. The population, though meagre, gathered in their thousands and the orderly way in which they took part in the ceremony was most impressive.

It was during this period that the Bhantus, the

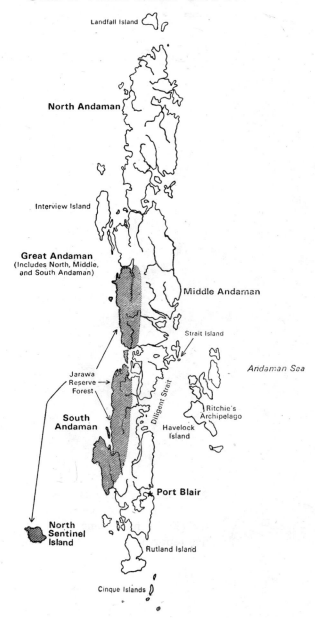

GREAT ANDAMAN GROUP

criminal tribe which had been specially imported some years earlier, were given the choice of going back. So 500 of them left, leaving only a few behind. And in the words of the report: "Soon after their arrival in their province of origin a great number of them petitioned to return". And many did.

It was also for the first time, during this period, that the cosmopolitan character of the population of the Andaman islands was officially taken note of because, in a note written obviously by the then chief commissioner, it is stated:

The most noticeable feature of this population is its cosmopolitan composition. The local inhabitants are descendents from people belonging to all castes and creeds and from various provinces from India. In spite of all derogatory remarks that one hears about these islands, familiarly known as *Kala Pani*, yet the people are setting an example as to how people of different origins can compose their differences and live in amity. In fact the evolution that is peacefully proceeding might be termed as a laboratory carrying out an experiment on an all-India basis showing how a secular State which the Indian leaders are laboriously trying to establish for the Dominion is being successfully founded. Due encouragement and guidance is required to ensure progress along right lines.

Mercifully, this cosmopolitan character of the population, despite attempts by Muslim and Hindu evangelists to convert members of one religious community to the other, still persists. The success of Christian evangelists like Solomon and Bishop Richardson, in converting most of the Nicobarese to Christianity, lies in the fact that—as Compton Mackenzie noticed when he was there—they "did not make the mistake of interfering too much with the old customs". The result is that even today the Nicobarese continue to observe certain old animistic customs, like *couvade* and the ossuary feasts! Besides that, however, it is a fact of history that, when animists do take to any religion, it is either Islam or Christianity.

Another remarkable observation made in this particular report relates to the question of the *lingua franca* of the Andaman islands. It proudly speaks of having solved this question "which has been agitating the minds of the educationists in India by having *Hindustani* as the *lingua franca*". Since then many attempts have been made, and are still being made, to impose from above a more Sanskritized form of Hindi on the people. But they have been far from successful, because the people there, without exception, still speak simple Hindustani or Hindi. As a matter of fact, it is a legacy left behind by the British, unintentionally of course, because it was their practice to ensure that no convicts belonging to one state or to one linguistic group be allowed to live together. They were afraid that, while incarcerated in jail, or living together in barracks as ticket-of-leave prisoners, they would find it easy to hatch conspiracies against the rulers, were they to speak the same language. So they were mixed together and, in order to communicate with one another, they took recourse to developing a new *lingua franca*, and the *lingua franca* thus evolved was simple Hindustani.

And it continues as such even today. No matter what your origin, whether you are from the south, north, west or east of India, you speak Hindustani. In fact no one gets employment in any of the local offices of the administration, unless he or she can speak simple Hindi.

Majid, apparently, was a very popular man and considered a "man of the people". He used to go about everywhere in a weapon-carrier, because he had no car, and would stop and give lifts to poor men, women and children. (There was no public transport at the time.) He is also considered the father of the cooperative movement in the islands. According to one who knew him well and served under him: "In the Andamans he [Majid] got *Panay Hanay* cooperative stores formed in the Nicobar islands. They are managed by the tribal people. Today these *Hanay*s are a great force and the tribals are proud of them."

Apart from that, he advised the local people to buy land and housing sites, because he could foresee that the development of the islands would take place at such a fast pace in the future that "not an inch of land" would be available. He was right. Today it is difficult for anyone to acquire land anywhere in the neighbourhood of Port Blair. According to the same gentleman who served under him: "Today, you go to any village and the name of Inam-ul-Majid is on the lips of every *kisaan*."

But Majid soon fell from grace, and was transferred, telegraphically, at very short notice. It is said that there were two allegations against him; he was accused of having agreed to the settlement of about 500 or 600 Muslims from East Bengal and, therefore, suspected of trying to create an imbalance between the Hindu and the Muslim population, and also of trying to ensure that the Muslims became a majority. (The Hindus, at the time, were in a very small majority, of perhaps 500 or 600.) Secondly, it was suspected that he had, perhaps indirectly, encouraged some of the Nicobarese to petition to the British parliament, saying that since geographically and ethnically the Nicobarese had nothing in common with Indians, the Nicobars be declared a separate British Crown colony.

It is not possible to verify the veracity of these allegations. But it is a commonly held belief in the islands that these were supposedly the two reasons for his summary transfer. (Understandably, when contacted, Majid did not want to talk about it. His successor merely said that he, too, had heard something to that effect.)

In July 1949 came A K Ghosh, also of the Indian Civil Service, to take over as chief commissioner. But before his arrival the first batch of settlers, consisting of 128 refugee families from East Bengal, had already arrived. This was in accordance with the scheme formulated by the government of India to increase the population of the islands. Most of them were in poor health. A majority of them were settled in and around Port Blair as agriculturists, and some as artisans.

In an interview with the author, Ghosh said that the first thing he noticed after taking over was that although the Nicobar islands formed a very large part of the territory, no one could tell him anything about them, because the Japanese had destroyed all records. There were no books either that he could consult. So almost the first thing he did was to undertake a trip of the southern group of islands. The administration then owned no ships, so the next time the regular ship *Maharaja* came to Port Blair, she was taken off from her scheduled trip to the mainland, and off went Ghosh and his party, comprising the heads of all departments.

Ghosh found it a fascinating experience. "Car Nicobar was all right," he said, because they had seen ships before. But as soon as the ship was sighted in the waters surrounding Kondal, which lies between Little and Great Nicobar, up went the Union Jack! Ghosh asked the village headman, "Why have you put up the Union Jack?" He replied, "We always put up the Union Jack when a ship comes."

Ghosh: "Don't you know that the British have nothing to do with India any longer?"

Headman: "No. Nobody told us. We didn't know."

Ghosh: "Don't you know that India has been independent for the last two years?"

Headman: "No."

Ghosh: "Do you know that there has been a war?"

Headman: "Yes."

Ghosh: "Do you know that it is over? Do you know who has won?"

Headman: "No. We don't."

Ghosh: "When did you see a ship last?"

Headman: "Many years ago. But we don't remember when."

Ghosh says that the last time the *Maharaja* had paid a visit to Kondal was in 1937, which was 12 years before his visit. Nobody had bothered to find out whether those who lived in Kondal were dead or alive.

However, the chief commissioner and the village headman exchanged flags. The Union Jack was handed over to Ghosh, who gave the Indian tricolour to the headman, with instructions to hoist it when the next ship visited them.

The Nicobari cruise lasted ten days. In March 1950 Ghosh undertook another cruise, this time of all the inhabited islands. They went to some of the islands which had not been visited for the past 20 years! In some places, people hid themselves when the ship was sighted, coming out of hiding only when satisfied that those on board the ship intended to do them no harm.

Ghosh was chief commissioner for four years. It was during his regime that perhaps the last organized raid by the Jarawas took place. This was on 22 July 1952, and the objective, according to the official report, was to attack a woman when she was alone. The woman was killed, and the Jarawas disappeared before any action could be taken by the Bush Police. Earlier, in October 1948, it had been the other way round. Three Jarawas had been captured by a party of forest officials while the Jarawas were fishing. According to the official report:

> They were brought to Port Blair, and kept in the bungalow of a senior Forest Officer and kindly treated in the hope that they might respond to this treatment and go back as messengers of goodwill to their people. The result appeared to be satisfactory. But this was only a ruse on the part of the captured men; and ten days after their capture they escaped at night in the jungle.

Just before the arrival of Ghosh, the government of India had set up an advisory council which was "to be associated with the Chief Commissioner of the Andaman and Nicobar Islands in the discharge of his administrative function". Apart from the chief commissioner, five other members would comprise the council; the first council was to start functioning with effect from 1 April 1949, and a new council was to be nominated every March. When Ghosh was asked about it, he said: "Yes, there was a Council, which met occasionally, but really at the time what the Chief Commissioner said was done."

But, said Ghosh, what was of great concern to him all through his four years' stay in the Andaman islands was that they were "wide open to anybody". He narrated what can be described now as an anecdote. There was a young Parsi police-officer (an ex-naval commander) who, in sheer sport, said that he was prepared to take a wager that with the help of only six other able-bodied men he would be able to capture Port Blair and overrun the island. Ghosh first agreed to take him on, but then said: "I got cold feet. I got frightened. Supposing in that sporting experiment somebody got killed, I would be in trouble. So the experiment was never tried."

He, however, did take up the matter officially, suggesting to the powers-that-be that our armed forces have a "presence" in the islands. He was able to persuade General K M Cariappa, the then commander-in-chief, and also other service chiefs, and the matter was seized of the cabinet. But Prime Minister Jawaharlal Nehru turned it down, saying: "No. We have got no enemies. Who is going to attack us?" Are we not lucky that this state of euphoria ended soon in our country? Else one shudders to think what might have happened, or not happened, during the Bangladesh war with Pakistan in 1971. How successfully our navy was able to blockade the enemy's naval fleet! None dare enter the Bay of Bengal, which has become virtually our "lake", thanks mainly to the islands!

Ghosh narrated another interesting episode which took place when he was there. One day ten Chinese were captured; they had come to catch fish. They were duly taken into custody. But Ghosh felt that the government of India should take this particular opportunity to make some display of strength. So he sent a signal to request that some Indian naval vessal be sent to Port Blair. A mine-sweeper was diverted. That was all very well but, to their horror, it was discovered that there was absolutely no furnace oil in Port Blair to refuel the ship. So the mine-sweeper was stuck there for over a month until the regular passenger service ship, the *Maharaja*, brought oil in barrels from Calcutta!

During the chief commissionership of A K Ghosh over 2,000 Bengali refugees were resettled in the islands. "What was the state of affairs otherwise?" I asked him. "We were exporting timber . . . and a small amount of coconuts, but everything else had to come from the mainland," he said. "Rice, cooking oils, vegetables. In fact, for food, the Andamans depended entirely on import," he added. This was not so in the Nicobars, which were self-sufficient, except that, of late, they too had started eating rice. "I discouraged the Nicobarese from importing and eating rice," said Ghosh.

"Medical facilities were good", he continued, "particularly in Port Blair. Malaria had been controlled. What is more, all medical services were free. As against that, education was terrible. Only one school in the entire area, and the standard of teaching, very poor." But, Ghosh went on to say, things had improved by the time he left.

There was very little crime in the Andamans. In the Nicobars, in the four years that he was chief commissioner, there was only one incident—and that was of theft. Car Nicobar had no jail, so the man had to be brought to Port Blair and lodged in the jail there.

Chowra was still practising its own code of justice. One day, he remembered, he was told that the heads of two people had been chopped off, because they were considered bad people. They had been warned to change their ways, but had not. So the village council met and decided that they be beheaded, which they were. Ghosh, as chief commissioner, did nothing. "It was their law and method of meeting justice," he said.

Some of the earlier chief commissioners had talked at some length about the state of immorality among the "locals". When he was chief commissioner, the position, according to Ghosh, was:

In my time there is no doubt that there was a great deal of imbalance among the two sexes. Leaving out the children and the old men, the ratio was 4 men to 1 woman. At one stage, it had come down to 6 to 1. But there was no more immorality there than anywhere else in India. As a matter of fact, one result of this shortage of female population was that women were much more free. If the husband ill-treated his wife or if she didn't get on with him, she just left him and found herself another husband. Divorce was very easy. You just went to the deputy commissioner and said that you wanted a divorce. And that was the end of it.

The shortage of women had also proved a blessing in a way. According to Ghosh: "Eligible women being few, you had very little choice. You just married whoever you could. So you had Hindus marrying Buddhists, Buddhists marrying Muslims, Muslims marrying Sikhs. Religion had become a purely personal affair. It was growing very rapidly into a very homogeneous society."

On the subject of social life and the "locals", Ghosh said:

It was like a small district town, because of the lack of communication with the outside world. There was only one ship coming once every three weeks. You were thrown very much on one another. The whole tone, really, depended on the chief commissioner and his wife. It was for them to see that there wasn't too much in-fighting between the people.

I am sorry to say that there was not very much mixing between the "locals" and the official class. The officials were practically all from the mainland. And the local people, they were mostly clerks and subordinates... [and] suffered terribly from an inferiority complex.

It was while Ghosh was chief commissioner in the islands that the first Indian expedition to establish some kind of contact with the Shompens of Great Nicobar was organized in 1951. The idea was not only to get to know them but also to get to know more about them. It was led by B S Chengapa, conservator of working plans in Port Blair.

The first time the world heard of the existence of the Shompens was in 1831, from Pastor Rosen, a Danish missionary. It does not seem as though he actually met or even saw any. It was 15 years later that Admiral Steen Bille made the first recorded visit to Great Nicobar and ran into some. Then, during the 1870s, M de Roepstorff, while assistant superintendent in charge of the penal settlement at Camorta, paid three visits, on one of which he was accompanied by Chief Commissioner Cadell. In 1901, as readers already know, C Boden Kloss paid an extended visit to Great Nicobar and saw a great deal of the Shompens. He wrote: "In general appearance, these men resembled the Nicobarese, but were of slightly darker complexion—muddy coloured—and physically of more slender build, and leaner; they wore cotton *kissats* and large wooden eardistenders". (There is a brief mention of the characteristics of the Shompens in the chapter on the Nicobars and the Nicobarese.) According to the report submitted by Chengapa:

The exploration party first came in contact with the Shompens in the Jubilee river. They were friendly.... Next, they came in contact with [those] living about 5 miles from the mouth of the Dagmar river. They were also friendly. . . . The third lot of [them] were found many miles in the interior of the Alexander river valley 12 or 14 miles up the main stream from its mouth and then about 2 miles up a branch stream on the south. They were wild and hostile.

Chengapa estimated their number, at the time of his visit, to be no more than 100. He wrote: "It is noteworthy that out of 13 children only 2 belong to the friendly group." He described those living near the Dagmar river as "sickly" and thought that they would die out completely in a few years. But those found elsewhere, especially the menfolk, were "fine specimens of human beings, every one with the appearance of an athlete . . . . They have a luxuriant growth of hair on their head, but none on their faces or body". That is so even now, because I met some during my visit to Great Nicobar in 1975.

Chengapa also described their habitat as "the crudest" possible. Their huts, he wrote, "are built on piles varying in height from 3 feet to about 7 or 8 feet, with a rough platform and a rough roof of palm leaf". And their staple diet was, and still is, the Pandanus. "They cook them in a well-made boat-shaped vessel of sheets of bark" and, said he, "they can make fire by striking dry sticks". To supplement their diet, he added, "they hunt pigs, catch fish and collect fresh water mussels". They were, and continue to be, very fond of chewing betel-nuts and betel leaves. As a result, their teeth are very black and dirty.

The Shompens know how to make a canoe. Their canoes are small, with outriggers, and take only two or three persons. They also, observed Chengapa, "make baskets of rattan and of palm spathe, and cloth from the inner bark of two species of Ficus . . . . They manufacture a javelin or dart with an iron head [which] is used for warfare or for hunting pigs".

According to Chengapa, they were also fond of gardening then (though there are no signs of any gardens now). They disliked clothing, because "both men and women go about naked except for a loin cloth made of bark worn by men, and a strip of cloth worn by women". It was worn in the same style as that of the Nicobarese "with a tail behind". Chengapa found the coastal Nicobarese, "though strong, robust and hefty . . . terribly frightened of the wild Shompens".

The chief commissioner, who succeeded A K Ghosh, was S N Moitra, also of the Indian Civil Service. Those who knew him remember him as an able officer, quiet but very shrewd.

It was during his regime that the first five-year plan was drawn up, in which islands figured, and he was responsible for carrying out the objectives laid in it. Apart from that, he was the first chief commissioner after independence who paid a great deal of attention to beautifying the city of Port Blair. He laid out the present Marina Park, which was eventually supposed to extend, on one side, right up to Corbyn Cove, the finest beach and bathing resort in the city. On the other side it would have extended upto Chatham Island. (That part of his plan is yet to materialize.)

It was also during Moitra's time that the first public bus service was started in the Andamans. He was also responsible for the administration buying *Cholunga*, their first ship, for inter-island traffic. He built new roads; he was able to get for the islands a hospital ship, the *Indus*, under the Colombo plan. And it was while he was there that an Indian president (Dr Rajendra Prasad) paid his first ever visited to the islands. (The next time an Indian president set foot on these islands was in the year 1976 when Fakhruddin Ali Ahmed paid an official visit.)

Moitra has been followed by a number of mediocre chief commissioners.

Until the reorganization of states took place in India, the Andaman and Nicobar islands had the status of a part D state, but with affect from 1 November 1956 they became a union territory. This elevation in status was followed by the formation of an advisory council, consisting of the local member of parliament—who, at the time, was nominated by the president of India—and four others, including K R Ganesh (to be elected later as member of parliament) and Bishop Richardson. It was set up to advise the chief commissioner. (Incidentally, Bishop Richardson was the first islander to be nominated to the Lok Sabha, our House of the people.)

At about the same time, the president of India promulgated the Andaman and Nicobar islands' Municipal Board Regulation, which came into force on 1 June 1957. Elections were held on 23 April 1958, and the Port Blair municipality was inaugurated on 15 August the same year. It had nine elected members and three nominated by the chief commissioner. The deputy commissioner of Port Blair, who was then the only deputy commissioner in the entire chain of islands, was the ex-officio chairman.

With effect from 1961-62, yet another advisory committee was constituted. This one was to be associated with the minister of home affairs and its main function was to advise him "on policy matters relating to the administration of the Islands". It consists of the chief commissioner, the member of parliament elected by the islands, senior vice-president of the Port Blair Municipal Board and five non-officials nominated by the central government. They generally commute to the capital every few months. But for the second meeting of the committee, Lal Bahadur Shastri, the then home minister, visited Port Blair to preside over its deliberations.

The opening of an air service between Calcutta and Port Blair by the Indian Airlines in 1963 was a distinct landmark in the annals of the islands. To begin with it was a weekly *Dakota* service, and used to run only from November to the end of April. Later, in 1966, it became a regular weekly service running all through the year. A while later, it was converted into a biweekly service. But all along, the planes had to stop in Rangoon, en route for refuelling. (With effect from 2 August 1977, a direct biweekly jet service has started; it takes only two hours to fly from Calcutta to Port Blair, whereas earlier it used to take about five hours.)

Another landmark was the opening of an All India Radio station at Port Blair on 2 June the same year. It was a significant event, for the people there are completely starved of entertainment. Barring one picture-house (known, interestingly enough, as Mountbatten Cinema), no entertainment was available in the Andamans. (The position is much the same even now, except that another picture-house has since been built.) The setting up of a broadcasting service was therefore hailed with a great deal of excitement. It turned out to be something of a disappointment, though, because the transmitter installed was only of the strength of 1 kw, which was totally inadequate. Even according to the most optimistic official estimates of All India Radio, the effective range of such a transmitter is only about 30 miles during the day and about 80 miles at night. That ruled out any listening in the northern group of islands, the terrain being mostly hilly there. And as we all know, the ground wave, i.e. the medium wave, is incapable of surmounting that kind of hurdle.

The southern group of islands were a little more lucky because water is a better carrier, and between Port Blair and most of the islands in the Nicobar group there are vast stretches of sea. I must confess, however, that during my travels in both the northern and southern group of islands I was never able to catch the Port Blair signal anywhere. Freak listening yes—we used to get occasional letters from Madras and Calcutta, and sometimes even from as far away as New Zealand.

Another problem which made broadcasting in Port Blair a frustrating exercise was the multiplicity of languages. Although the main language was, quite rightly, Hindi (in actual practice, it is what was known as Hindustani before independence), language groups had obviously to be provided some fare in their own languages. So some time everyday had to be allotted to regional languages, which included Bengali, Tamil, Malayalam and Telugu. The result was that when programmes in those languages were broadcast, the Hindi listeners would normally switch off their radios because, although everyone there understands Hindi few, if any, understand languages other than their mother-tongues.

Recently, in 1976, after 13 years of broadcasting in the islands, the strength of the transmitter has been stepped up but, unfortunately, only to the extent that All India Radio has now put up a 20 kw medium wave transmitter, the effective range of which, again according to optimistic AIR engineers, is 80 miles by day and 150 miles by night. The signal is still not strong enough to be heard in the northern group, and the problem of providing alternative programmes when regional language programmes are being broadcast still remains; this is because for some reason, instead of using the existing 1 kw transmitter for broadcasting some of the language programmes, it has been placed in cold storage. So the joke on the people of Port Blair vis-à-vis radio broadcasting has been compounded.

Another significant fact is that while every radio broadcast from the rest of the world can be heard in these islands—the quality of the reception being excellent—All India Radio cannot, megawatt transmitter near Calcutta notwithstanding.

Thanks to the resettlement of refugees, the population of the islands has grown steadily. According to the 1951 census, it was 30,1971. By 1961, when the next general census was taken, it had more than doubled —63,524. And according to the 1971 census, it was 115,133.

Earlier, resettlement took place in a somewhat haphazard manner. But in 1964 an inter-departmental team was constituted to draw up what was described as "an integrated resources development plan" for the islands. In the light of the recommendations made by this team, 339 families of migrants from the erstwhile province of East Pakistan were resettled in Betapur in Middle Andaman Island, after reclaiming 2,050 acres of land. Another batch, consisting of 100 families, also refugees from East Pakistan, was settled in Neil Island after 1,190 acres of land had been reclaimed.

But prior to the introduction of the "integrated resources development plan", the refugees—or migrants—settled in the three islands of Great Andaman—North Andaman, Middle Andaman and South Andaman—comprised 2,887 families from East Pakistan, 157 from Kerala, 43 from Tamil Nadu, 184 from Bihar, four from Mahe and five from Burma.

Unfortunately, Little Andaman Island, the home of the Ongés, has also not been able to escape this fate of what they consider as interlopers being foisted upon them. Till the spring of 1975, 353 families had already been inducted and 104 were on their way; the proposal then was to settle migrants from East Pakistan and Sri Lanka there. Two thousand and two hundred were expected.

Some resettlement has also taken place in the island of Katchal in the Nicobar group. Here, the main idea was to set up a rubber plantation on a 6,000 acre area and settle 1,200 repatriate families from Sri Lanka. But by April 1975, rubber had been planted in just 1,250 acres and only 12 repatriate families—all from Sri Lanka except one that came from Malaysia—had been resettled.

Some repatriated families from Burma—37 of them—have also been resettled in a rubber plantation, covering 500 acres, in South Andaman near Port Blair.

But what I once thought was one of the most exciting schemes of resettlement was the one in Great Nicobar. That was completely virgin soil. (In early 1967, when I visited that island, the total population consisted of one platoon of the Central Reserve Police and less than half a dozen officials belonging to the Marine Engineering Department.) Besides, it is, strategically, a very important island, being closer to Sumatra (Indonesia) than to any other land mass which forms a part of India. True, there are a few aborigines—the Shompens—on that island, but they are now so few that they have become an insignificant factor. So when it was announced that a decision had been taken to resettle a hundred families of ex-servicemen, all from the Punjab, the news was hailed with great excitement. It seemed such a sensible and wise project.

It began with the arrival of 66 families, all Sikhs barring one, in 1969. Their enthusiasm could not be contained; they said they were going to establish a *Naya* (new) *Punjab* there. Within months of their arrival they were growing maize, rice, vegetables and fruit. (Somehow the soil there is not conducive to growing wheat.) They had built themselves a Gurudwara. And, of course, had started to brew their own moonshine. More families continued to be inducted, to use inelegant officialese, so that when I visited them in 1975 the population of the island was 4,800. It comprised 238 families. They were 100 from the Punjab, 40 from Maharashtra, 45 from Tamil Nadu, 24 from Uttar Pradesh, 15 from Kerala, nine from Karnataka and five from Andhra Pradesh. In all 1,495 acres had been reclaimed for the purpose of agriculture, as well as for homesteads. Officially, "the general pattern of resettlement assistance for each of the family is 5 acres of cleared land suitable for paddy cultivation, 5 acres of forest land for plantation, one acre cleared land for homestead plot as well as rehabilitation assistance amounting to Rs. 19,750".

However, according to one of their leaders who preferred not to be named, their hopes soon turned to ashes. He gave two basic reasons for their disillusionment: to begin with, the government did not keep faith with them. They had made all kinds of promises, but what they actually got by way of land, even after having been there for so many years, was far short of what they had been promised. And then government with their muddled thinking did not realize that, for purposes of ploughing, tractors were of no use in a terrain where it rained nearly ten months in a year. (The tractors are rusting and little ploughing with their aid is ever done.) The cultivators, my informant told me, had, all these years, been begging the government day in and day out that what they needed were ploughing animals—bullocks and buffaloes. Till April 1975, they had not been given any. (The then chief development-cum-rehabilitation commissioner told me that they were soon to get some, and that the *I N S Magar* had been commissioned to transport them from the mainland. By now, it is understood, they have got some.)

Apart from that, the gentleman in question told me that although they were now living in Great Nicobar, they could not possibly sever all connections with their relatives and friends in the Punjab. There are always the obligatory visits for purposes of marriage, sickness and the death of a near and dear one. And each trip costs a fortune. This state of affairs is particularly aggravating because their incomes are very low. Not only are they unable to grow much, but marketing and transporting whatever they produce is also a problem.

They dare not go back because then they would lose face and they have the proverbial Punjabi pride. They had set out to accomplish something. And God willing, he said, they *shall*, come what may.

It is a shame that government have little appreciation of their problems. Why cannot it, for instance, provide them with at least one free sea passage every two years, as they do to every central government servant? Are they any the less valuable as far as the welfare of the country is concerned? They are all ex-servicemen and have been brought there for a definite objective—to man a distant island outpost of the country. Unlike other refugees, they have come not because of dire necessity but out of a sheer spirit of adventure and enterprise. Their everyday living is far more difficult, and full of many more problems than that of a government servant sitting in Port Blair, who is given free accommodation, $33\frac{1}{3}$ per cent of his salary as special allowance and a free passage to and fro to the mainland every two years. Government servants living in the Nicobars get even more! And yet these people—all ex-servicemen—get nothing. Another problem is commuting between Great Nicobar and Port Blair (if and when they want to visit the mainland, in an emergency), because sailings between the two are few and far between; and consequently, also, irregular mail and newspapers.

The problem will continue to plague them unless government adopt a more imaginative policy. In this day and age, it should not be beyond human ingenuity to find a solution. An obvious one would be a weekly helicopter service, which could hop from Port Blair to Car Nicobar to Camorta to Campbell Bay and back. It is undoubtedly an expensive proposition, but I would have thought that the happiness of these brave, voluntary expatriates would be of greater value than the extra expense involved in maintaining such a service.

Statistics compiled for the year 1976 by the Statistical Bureau of the Andaman and Nicobar administration indicate that the total number of families settled in the islands till the end of the year 1975 was 1,129; the land reclaimed was 3,981 hectares and that allotted 2,450 hectares.

The greatest asset of the Andaman and Nicobar islands is their forest wealth. Someone has described it as "literally a gold mine of timber wealth". Sir H G Champion, an international authority in forestry, has written: "The Forests in their pristine glory, if it is found anywhere in South East Asia, it is in Andaman Islands." And yet precious little has been done to exploit their vast potential. J C Varmah of the Indian Forest Service, who was conservator of forests in the islands for many years, has given this excuse: "Though floristically very rich, unfortunately the very variety of species growing has not so far made the forests economically so very attractive a venture." Lalthan Zama, another chief conservator of forests, explains away this lack of substantial achievement in the area of forestry thus: "Although the history of forestry dates back to 1883 in these islands, only about 21 per cent of the forest area could be brought under scientific management owing to locational disadvantages, inconveniences of distances, lack of communications and absence of other infrastructures." A sad commentary, after nearly 30 years of administration by independent India! In the same context, R Narayana, sometime cottage industries' officer, has written:

> In spite of large quantities of timber being available we have very few industries utilising them properly. Certain private enterprises have to some extent exploited these resources and have set up plywood and match splints. In addition to these a few saw mills and furniture workshops in small scale also exist and that is all which we can mention about industrial complex of this territory.... With the changing times and with the increase of forests extraction there is a great potentiality for starting small saw mills, pencil slat factories, match splint boxes, manufacturing units etc.

This was written by Narayana in 1971. Six years after, came the welcome news that a forest development corporation has since been formed. One hopes that it will do something to redress the decades of neglect that the islands, a "gold mine of timber wealth", have suffered before and after independence.

In Chatham Island, the Andamans can rightly boast of having one of the oldest saw-mills in the country, perhaps in Asia. But going round it one gets the impression that time has stood still for a hundred years!

There has been a match splint factory, thanks to a Swedish enterprise, which has been running for many years, and with a great deal of efficiency. But as the saying goes, one swallow does not make a summer. During the war, Cato, a Swede, was manager of the Western India Match Company, popularly known as WIMCO. According to Compton Mackenzie:

> Cato who ran the match factory was allowed to go free at first but they [the Japanese] could not stand his contempt for them and took him away to Ross Islands, where he was murdered; nobody had been able to find out exactly where and how.

WIMCO has been operating in these islands for many years. In addition to this, the Andaman Timber Industries have a plywood manufacturing factory in Bomboo Flats, a suburb of Port Blair. And that is about all of the much-talked-about industrial development in the islands.

Some timber is used for making furniture, but most of the furniture is made in government-owned workshops. It is hardly of any significance so far as the economy of the islands is concerned. An average person, unless he has some influence, can hardly acquire any. Every chief commissioner, and other senior officers, come back home with wagon-loads of exquisite furniture made of rare and the most valuable ornamental wood, like marble wood and *burr*, not to talk of the items made in a variety of *padauk* wood.

Port Blair has a cottage industries' officer, but hardly any cottage industry worth the name. It maintains an emporium in Port Blair where you find a few knick-knacks, most of them ugly, and nearly all mother-of-pearl items are manufactured in Calcutta and transported back to Port Blair. No wonder the prices are high. One of the cottage industries' officers has written: "Certain type of shells which can be used in making some decorative articles are also available. The local artisans are well trained in manufacturing attractive curios out of these shells." (A tall claim, because almost no facilities exist for imparting training.) He goes on to blame the local artisans for "lack of ambition". A normal bureaucratic practice.

Talking of small scale industries, there is a story of how a particular chief commissioner decided to set up a poultry farm to cater to the requirements of those living in Port Blair. It is said that the appetite of the chief commissioner and his family for chickens and eggs was so enormous that by the time their needs were met there was nothing left for anyone else. So it became a losing proposition. It was, therefore, decided to auction the hens and the cockerels! Who was the one who acquired them eventually? Well, the readers' guess is as good as mine.

The story of fruit orchards and vegetable gardens laid by the government is the same: they have proved of little economic advantage to the islands.

In the Nicobars, excellent mats are made out of coconut-palm leaf— some of them like dunlopillos; the Nicobarese are also very clever at making miniature canoes and various other articles out of coconut shells. But, here too, one cannot buy any—unless of course you happen to be a government official, or the guest of one.

In the Nicobars in particular, and now in the Andamans too, a lot of coconut is grown, but nothing made out of coir that has been turned out locally, is available. (I could get no coir fibre for even a mattress!)

The story about the neglect of wealth lying in the waters around these islands is just as depressing. In 1878, Sir Francis Day, after a visit to the islands, listed as many as 136 species of fish in the seas around them. Many more perhaps have been discovered since then. P M G Menon, till recently director of fisheries, writes about what the government has done: "In spite of the fact that this Territory has a vast fisheries potential, it has to be admitted that the resources are not properly exploited." He goes on to admit that "foreign vessels from far off countries like Taiwan are very often seen to operate in these waters". And, according to him, "from 1960 onwards as many as 48 foreign fishing vessels have been captured while fishing in [the islands'] waters". There is no record of those that have escaped detection or capture.

Writing on the subject, S M Krishnatry, chief commissioner, adds: "Tuna, shark, mackerel and various commercially important marine products such as shrimps, crabs, oysters, lobsters, etc., are available in plenty." (Krishnatry's personal contribution in this field is that he has had a prawn named after him—the *metapenaeus krishnatry*!) It is a great pity but the only sea-food available in these islands lies in the sea and hardly any on anybody's table.

Very little has been done as fas as rubber production is concerned. The government of Free India had to wait for a little less than two decades before the first rubber planting was done, because it was not until 1965-68 that the "targeted area of 203.82 hectares was planted". Tapping did not start until 1972, and in 1974-75, the year for which statistics are available, the total production was 14.25 tonnes! The project is still called the rubber research-cum-development station.

Shipping is one field where definite progress is in evidence. There was a time when one solitary ship, the *Maharaja*, carrying passengers to and from the mainland, had to be taken off her regular run when the chief commissioner, or anyone else of some importance, wanted to visit the other islands. Now, according to an officially inspired report, the shipping fleet in the year 1976 comprised:

M.V. *Andamans* and M.V. *State of Haryana*, usually put on the Madras-Port Blair and Calcutta-Port Blair routes, also calls at Visakhapatnam every quarter; M.V. *Shompen*, a specialised timber carrier, the only one of its kind in the Indian fleet; M.V. *Vishwa Anand*, a multi-purpose, general cargo ship carrying timber, foodstuff, heavy machinery, capital equipment, cement, elephants and other livestock: M.V. *Onge* usually put on the run between Port Blair and Nicobar group of islands; M.V. *Yamuna* and M.V. *Tarmugli*, the chief Commissioner's touring vessel; M.V. *Kondul*, M.V. *Teressa*, S.S. *Cholunga*, T.S.S. *Yerewa*, M.V. *Ganga*, and M.V. *Cheetal*, all put on inter-island ferry services.

This sounds very impressive, but there is no mention of what happens when one or more ships have to go to the dry docks in Calcutta for annual servicing. That is when all normal traffic ceases for weeks together. Many a time, due to trouble of one kind or another at the Calcutta port, people are held up in Calcutta for days, sometimes weeks. And the government has made no provision for passengers so stranded; they have to fend for themselves.

The same applies to passengers who arrive in Port Blair and find that there is no ship which can take them to the island of their destination. There is no rest-house, nor retiring room suites, nor even a restaurant near any of the jetties. The people have to ask friends to put them up, or live in a *dharamsala* or Gurudwara.

Cargo also has to lie sometimes for months together because there is either no ship or it has missed the connection.

(In this context, I still remember that a junior colleague of mine in All India Radio was stuck in Madras for nearly *six months* because no ship was able to visit that port and, at the time, government would not pay him to travel to Calcutta and take a ship from there!)

However, there has been progress in two fields—construction of jetties and roads. There are many places today where you can land comparatively easily. But Car Nicobar has still no jetty. To land there means getting into a motor-launch from the ship anchored midstream. Then, from the motor-launch, you get into a canoe and sit there trying to maintain a precarious balance, with your shoes soaking in sea water that has seeped into the canoe. The last few feet you have to wade in the sea before you touch the beach. But in Port Blair itself, in addition to the antediluvian wooden jetty at Chatham, constructed by the British when they first arrived in Port Blair, there are two proper landing jetties—a built-up one at Marine and a deep-sea wharf at Haddo. There is also a proper jetty at Camorta, where you can land just off the ship.

Ten years ago there were very few roads, except in Port Blair itself, though the so-called Grand Trunk Road—which aims at covering the entire distance from one end of Great Andaman to the other, with ferrying facilities to cross the straits separating the three islands—was already under construction. Now, according to official 1977 statistics, the position with regard to roads is:

Black topped	323.5 miles
Other types	14 miles
In progress	69 miles
Length of Andaman Trunk Road	142 miles

In the field of construction, those who deserve praise are men of the Military Engineering Service (MES) and the Border Road Organization of the Indian Army, known as *Yatrik*.

Five years ago, there was not even one furlong of properly built road in Great Nicobar. Today there are two trunk-roads—one from Campbell Bay to the tip of the west coast, which is 28.6 miles long, and the other to Pygmalion Point, the southernmost tip of India, which is 27.3 miles long. Besides that, MES and Yatrik have also built office buildings and living apartments for defence personnel all over the islands.

The Military Engineering Service has really done well by these islands. They have rebuilt and reinforced the air landing strip in Car Nicobar. It is so modern and perfect now that even a jumbo jet can land there. They have also constructed, with the help and assistance of the local administration and the Indian Navy, a deep-sea wharf, which is 1,200 feet long and has a draught of 30 feet. Half of it is specifically reserved for the use of naval vessels. But what has been the greatest boon to the citizens of Port Blair and its suburbs is the construction of the Dhanakari dam. There was a time, only less than six years ago, when Port Blair used to have a water famine during the non-monsoon months every year, despite the fact that the yearly rainfall there is nearly 100 inches. By building a dam across the Dhanakari *nullah,* the problem of water shortage has been solved for the foreseeable future. The dam is 3,430 feet in length, 993 feet high and has a storage capacity of 2,250 million litres. It was formally declared open on 30 October 1973.

At the turn of the century, Port Blair used to have a military garrison supplied from Rangoon. It had 140 British and 300 Indian troops and some local European volunteers. Till the outbreak of the second world war, the army was always present in Port Blair. As readers already know, just before the Japanese occupied the islands, the British garrison, as also its Indian counterpart, left never to return, except for a while after the British reoccupation of the islands. The position today is that two wings of our defence services—the army and the navy—are represented in the Andamans and Nicobars, and there is also some representation of the Indian Air Force at Car Nicobar. Interestingly enough, the Royal Air Force continued to use Car Nicobar for refuelling facilities, for many years even after independence, and some RAF personnel were also stationed there.

The Indian Navy has, in Port Blair, an establishment known as the *I N S Jarawa,* and in Camorta another one—the *I N S Kardip.* The naval base at Camorta provides logistic suport to the ships operating from there and acts as a forward operational base. The Indian Army, however, is a newcomer to Port Blair. Before their arrival, their duties were performed by a naval garrison.

The Indian Navy also has a naval hospital, the *I N S Dhanwantri,* at Port Blair. It not only caters to the needs of the armed services' personnel but also provides the necessary succour to sick and wounded civilians.

In the field of education there has been undoubted progress. There is even a regular government-run college in Port Blair, whereas there was none in the islands ten years ago. And literacy has gone up: 51.64 per cent among men and 31.11 per cent among women, according to the 1971 census. The trouble, however, is that the only employment generally open to the "locals" is that of clerks, or posts of equivalent rank in forestry and other departments of the government—or teaching in schools. So those who go in for higher education have to seek employment on the mainland though, understandably enough, like most islanders elsewhere, they hate to leave the islands. So there are hardly any "locals" in high government posts—perhaps an assistant secretary or two in the secretariat. In Car Nicobar I discovered that only one Nicobarese had achieved the rank of *tehsildar*! So, unless job opportunities are provided, increasing educational facilities, or raising their level, is of no value. And that can happen only if the officials from the mainland stop thinking of themselves as colonial rulers!

Medical facilities that obtain now are definitely much better than ever before. According to statistics published for the year 1976, there are 555 beds available altogether, the population per bed being 321, which is not bad at all. Certain specialized medical services are undoubtedly available too, but they do not appear to be either enough, or up-to-date, and are not always properly manned. It is, therefore, not rare for a patient to have to go to the mainland for treatment. Of course, with the naval hospital now, things are much better.

It is in the field of tourism that the government has been completely at sea all these years. It could not make up its mind about whether or not to allow tourists. Some obsolete regulations formulated by the British government stipulated that no foreigner be allowed to visit the islands. No one sat down to think why. Obviously, the British wanted no foreigner to see the "penal" settlement and find out how convicts were being treated. Our benign government said it was for "strategic" reasons that some of the hydrographic charts being used by the shipping services are still those made by the British admiralty! And fishermen from Taiwan, Malaysia, Singapore and other south-eastern countries come and go as and when they like Only occasionally, an odd one is caught by naval patrol boats. Recently, there was news of an entire island in the Nicobar group being occupied by Thai fishermen.

Since 1974, however, foreign tourists are being allowed. But there is neither a worthwhile place for them to stay in, nor are there other facilities. There is only one taxi stand in Port Blair.

When a batch of tourists is in Port Blair, all accommodation in the government-run tourist houses is commandeered for them. There are no hotels or paying-guest facilities. Besides, there is no seriously considered policy about who is to be allowed in, nor any well-defined criterion for giving permission to a foreign tourist. There is no agency in Delhi which does this. It is all left to the "discretion" of the chief commissioner in Port Blair, who might well be a paranoiac! If it happens to be an important white man, or even a third-rate politician, the red carpet is laid, and the chief commissioner and all the senior officers turn up at the airport to receive him and his entourage. Not only that, the chief commissioner gives him his ship to go anywhere he likes. And if it happens to be an unknown man or woman of lesser status, the chief commissioner sits on the request for months, and at the last moment says no!

The biggest joke, till recently, was the policy on prohibition of alcoholic drinks. A story has it that a particular chief commissioner, who was himself quite fond of the bottle, was waylaid one night by some hooligans. They had obviously not recognized his car, being in a state of inebriation. Instead of taking action against them, he decreed next morning that there be total prohibition in the territory—even though he had no legal powers to do so.

But who cares? Every chief commissioner in Port Blair fancies himself a tin-pot dictator. Being central government territory, it is not the chief commissioner but the parliament of India that has the authority to legislate on the subject. The irony was that, under the regulations then in force (prohibition has since been withdrawn), you could not buy a drink, but drinking was not an offence *per se*! Well, as a consequence the black market in liquor flourished. Every kind of drink, including Scotch whisky, was freely available. And, of course, as has happened elsewhere in the country, illicit distillation became a cottage industry.

The policy of the government in regard to the aborigines is quite ambivalent. Their professed aim so far has been to help them survive in their present state; yet, some of the actions taken by them are, evidently, not those that would help their survival.

The friendly aborigines of the Andaman islands were given the soubriquet *Great Andamanese* by Sir Richard Temple, who was chief commissioner and conducted general a census in 1901. He estimated that at the time of the British occupation they had numbered 3,500. (Some others place the figure at over 5,000.) By 1901, they had already been reduced to a mere 625. Now they are only 24—15 males and nine females, which include seven children. The government has confined them all to Strait Island, which has an area of 1.4 square miles. When I visited them in April 1975, there were only two eligible couples among them. Their headman is known as their raja.

These two dozen Great Andamanese continue to be friendly. The fact of the matter is that unless they feel like it, it is not possible to visit them, for there are no landing facilities. When the steamer gets there, she blows a couple of loud whistles. And if in the mood, they come in their canoes and take you ashore. Else you go back and try again. (I was warned about it before I left Port Blair.) However, they are quite willing to sing and dance for you—they still love it. Otherwise, except that they know how to fish and make a canoe, they seem to have lost all other aboriginal characteristics. Instead of allowing them to build and live in their own natural shelters, the government has provided them with ugly PWD-built accommodation. The administration also provides them with a ration of *dal* and rice, and encourages them to go about clothed.

The only non-Andamanese who keeps them company on this lonely island, which lies 30 miles north-west of Port Blair, is B P Soni, a social worker. Soni, when I spoke to him there, expressed great concern because, he said, he had discovered that they had taken to opium. And despite the remoteness of the island, they somehow managed to get it. Soni's conjecture was that, since they had the freedom of the seas and could go by canoe to any of the neighbouring islands, "wicked" traders from the bigger islands come and barter opium for coconuts and sea shells.

The Ongés, in terms of the 1971 census, number 112. When I first met them in 1967 on the open beach at Hut Bay in Little Andaman, they were merry and cheerful and obviously happy. At that time they had the run of the entire island and roamed around at will. Now, because of the settlement of some migrants there, they are becoming more and more obliged to concentrate in the Dugong Creek area, although in theory they still have four or five camping sites. They seldom—and perhaps never will—come now to the beach at Hut Bay, which they used to love. Hut Bay is now full of settlers and government officials with their living quarters, offices, a rest-house, a club and the like. The few Ongés that I could meet during my last visit in 1975, I was told, had been brought there to be shown off to some important visitor. They looked sullen and sulky and were cooking *dal* and rice to eat. I missed their cheerfulness, their gay abandon. It was such a contrast to what I had seen earlier, when they had sung and danced and laughed! It was the beginning of the end.

In the name of so-called progress, here was an example of man's inhumanity. One could hear the death knell. The Andaman group has 204 islands; surely one could have been left to them to roam and wander all over as they pleased. Besides, why did the government not think of letting the Great Andamanese also come and settle here, and thus reunite them because, after all, many a millennium past, they were the same people. This is their belief and is in accord with their legends.

The Jarawas, after more than two centuries of hostility, have shown some signs of friendliness in the recent past, the credit for which must go to the deputy superintendent of police, Bakhtawar Singh, who heads the Bush Police. It all started with three Jarawa boys who, in 1968, strayed across into a village called Kadamtalla in Middle Andaman Island. They had then been captured by the men of the Bush Police and brought to Port Blair, where they were kept for a month and sent back loaded with gifts. Thereafter, gift-dropping in the area where they presumably lived was intensified. T N Pandit, superintending anthropologist of the Anthropological Survey of India, who was associated with most of the gift-dropping missions, thinks that their visits to that area helped them "gain some very useful experience and knowledge with regard to the Jarawas' reaction to gift-dropping work and their preference or otherwise for the various kinds of gifts dropped". Pandit continued:

> On 18 February 1974, a gift-dropping party led by a head constable reported seeing a large group of Jarawas in Foul Bay area. The Jarawas seemed to make friendly gestures and had dropped their bows and arrows on the ground. They seemed to desire more gifts. One of them even jumped into the water and swam across to the police party in their dinghy, stayed in the dinghy for a while and then swam back to his group.

This was unprecedented. Gift-dropping was therefore continued under the personal supervision of Bakhtawar Singh, who went there on board the *MV Kondul*, and anchored in the sea off the west coast. It had been reported that in a nearby place on shore, called Chotaliagang, there was a camp of 50 Jarawas. Bakhtawar Singh tells the story:

I stayed there and continued the mission. I used to go personally. I went for survey on the 3rd of April, and again on the 4th of April, and dropped gifts in their huts. I found the gifts dropped earlier lying there. [Obviously, they were out at the time.] I went again on the 5th of April, landed, and made my first contact that day with the Jarawas, who received me and other members of my party in a friendly manner. From then onwards, I have been going there, not only alone but with others also.

Since then there have been many more visits, and not only by Bakhtawar Singh—in fact one of the visitors was the former king of the Belgians. However, my impression at the time of my visit was, and still is, that the peace established was somewhat tenuous. (In May 1977, it was reported that a party of Jarawas had killed five Bengali settlers while they were fast asleep in their dinghy; the boat had apparently drifted into Jarawa territory by accident.)

The Jarawas are quite unpredictable. Much will, therefore, depend on how the administration handles them, even after genuine and durable contracts have been established.

The Anthropological Survey of India estimates the number of Jarawas at anything between 250 to 300; some others think they are as many as over 500. If they are as many, the only reason for their survival is that they have been left very much to their own devices and have had very little contact with our kind of *homo sapiens*.

If anything, the Sentinelese have kept even more to themselves. They just refuse to befriend. A recent attempt by a visiting party from Port Blair resulted in one of the members being shot at and wounded by an arrow. According to the Anthropological Survey of India, they number somewhere between 100 and 150—the sole inhabitants of North Sentinel Island, which lies south-west of Port Blair and has an area of about 47 square miles.

The Shompens, the only aborigines in the Nicobar group of islands, live in Great Nicobar. Their number, again according to the Anthropological Survey of India estimate, is also between 100 and 150. (In 1866, they were about 300 to 400, whereas according to the 1971 census, they were only 92.) By and large they have also lived in complete isolation in the past. Of late, however, some of them have been seen visiting Campbell Bay, where most of the settlers live. I saw and met some of them. I noticed that we have taught them how to smoke tobacco, and made attempts to put them into clothes. Amusingly enough, although they put them on when given, they never take them off. So the garments disintegrate on their bodies. Personally, I do not envisage any future for them.

The Nicobarese are in a different class altogether. (They are not classified as aborigines, but as tribals.) They have taken to amenities that are provided by civilization, but they have been selective about them; they have adopted them to their life style and environment. They are taking to education and have already become quite adept at sports like football, volleyball and the like. There is no doubt that given time, education and opportunities, they would know how to fend for themselves. Chief Commissioner Har Mander Singh summed up the situation when he said:

> These people have tried to preserve their old values. They have an institution of tribal leaders. They have a sense of cooperation as exists in other tribes also and, on this structure of tribal unity, have come modern ideas, which they have combined with their traditional values.

The only event of political importance that has happened since independence is that, in the 1971 general election to the Lok Sabha, it was decided that thenceforward the Andaman and Nicobar islands would be represented by an elected member and not a nominated one, as had been the practice till then. K R Ganesh, who stood on the Congress ticket, was elected with an overwhelming majority. Incidentally, Ganesh is a true "local" in the sense that one of his grandparents was a convict. Apart from that, in the real local cosmopolitan tradition, one was from Andhra and the other from Tamil Nadu. The tradition has continued and his brothers and sisters are married to persons who come originally from different states. (Ganesh, who for some years was a deputy minister and then a minister of state in Indira Gandhi's government, is no longer a member of parliament, having lost his seat in the 1977 election.)

His first great test insofar as representing the views of his constituents, namely the people of the Andaman and Nicobar islands, came when a couple of *Netajiphiles*—if I may be permitted to coin that expression—raised in the Lok Sabha, on 22 August 1969, the question of the name of the islands being changed to *Shahid* (martyr) and *Swaraj* (freedom) *Islands*, because Subhas Chandra Bose was supposed to have set up his administration there. Reacting very sharply to the suggestion, Ganesh said:

> While it is true that the Andaman and Nicobar Islands were declared the seat of the Provisional Government of Netaji Subhas Chandra Bose, as I have to be true to the people whom I represent, I must state that during that period three-fourths of the island was completely annihilated by the Japanese fascists. There is no house in Andaman and Nicobar Islands which has not suffered the scar of the second world war. Hundreds of local people were thrown into jails, thousands were decimated and thousands were thrown into the seas.... As far as we are concerned, we were completely annihilated, completely destroyed, the entire population of the island was destroyed by the fascists during that very period when the Provisional Government was functioning there.

When asked by Samar Guha whether this happened before or after Netaji, Ganesh replied categorically: "My answer is—before, during and afterwards." He went on to say: "We have a soul in the islands. We do not want the name of our islands to be changed. We have a soul." He repeated:

> Our history did not start in 1943. Our history started earlier, in 1857. We are the progeny of some of the convicts of the revolutionaries of the 1857 Revolution.... The name of the Andamans is in our soul. The tribes of Andamans are known with this name. We do not want to give up our soul. We will not be having any name if it is changed.... Our name cannot be allowed to be changed. We are opposed to a change in the name.... We are not going to allow you to do this. Our name cannot be changed by you.

And as far as records show, the issue has never since been raised. The question one would like to ask is that, although the penal settlement at Port Blair was undoubtedly an unmitigated evil, and designed by an alien government to punish those who did not conform to the political pattern outlined by them for the governance of this country as an imperial power, has any good come out of it? Yes, as the saying goes, out of every evil cometh some good. What is of utmost significance to the country is that it is in these tiny islands that the birth of true Indian cosmopolitanism has taken place. As K R Ganesh put it:

> The Hindustani-speaking people of the Andamans are of the utmost importance because they were evolved in the islands itself. They are the result of the capacity of the human beings to adjust to a new environment and build something there. A large number of convicts came from the north and the south of undivided India, constituting Pathans, Punjabis, Sindhis, Baluchis, Tamils, Telugus, Bengalis and people from Maharashtra and Madhya Pradesh. [These] large number of people were speaking different languages. [They] were made to adjust to a new and hostile surrounding, because... the surroundings of the Andamans at that time were very hostile—rainfall was very heavy, and there were heavy and dense forests with swamps and mosquitoes which took heavy toll of the life of convicts.... And they had no way to escape. They were inaccessible so far as the rest of the country was concerned. And when these very convicts were given a little more sympathetic and humane treatment, they tried to adjust themselves and build a new life. There was a large scale intermixing and intermarrying between convicts and free people. As a result of that, a new community slowly evolved, which today has the stamp of a small national group, which speaks a common language, which is Hindustani. A community which has its own cultural forms, which have been evolved in the islands itself. It has completely

eliminated caste from its social system; and to them religion is a very personal matter. These people have developed a cosmopolitan outlook. They are completely free from any prejudice. Such people, naturally enough, show some intelligence, some ingenuity, and a capacity to adjust to their surroundings and to their environment and the people who live with them.

When asked what, in his opinion, the islanders had gained since independence, he said that the biggest gain in his view was "in terms of consciousness, in terms of the islands being integrated with the mainstream of Indian life". Ganesh also talked about there having been "no dearth of money" as far as the Andaman and Nicobar islands were concerned. He said that "the plan expenditure on the Andaman and Nicobar islands stood only next to Nagaland and Kashmir".

But of the future, it is very tempting to say that everything lies in the lap of the gods. In this case, however, the gods are the government. Because, one member of parliament and a variety of advisory bodies notwithstanding, it is the government personified in the chief commissioner who is the only ruler on the islands.

It is for the constitutional experts to decide what set-up the islands should have, for nothing could be more unsatisfactory than the present one. The chief commissioner and all senior officials are sent from the mainland. And one can hardly blame them if they display little interest in the welfare of the local people. They have no stake in the lives of the local people, or their future. Uncharitable though it may sound, the poor islanders find a change in the official set-up, but it is only a change from *white* imperialism to *brown* imperialism.

As one wag put it: every chief commissioner spends his first year in the island in having a grand tour of all his "domain"—he owns a personal ship now; the next year he spends in getting himself some super furniture made; and the third year, which is also the final year, because the normal term is three years, he spends in getting ready to depart. It is sad, for most of the officials have set themselves up as absolute despots, and nothing matters except their own well-being. Nothing moves when the chief commissioner is away from his headquarters, which happens frequently. No one dare take any decision, lest it offend the big satrap. Every official belonging to the administration takes his cue from *CC*, as he is described in hushed tones.

The atmosphere is that of an Indian native state before independence. If you do not toe the line, you have had it. One chief commissioner even went to the extent of committing contempt of the Calcutta high court because the high court ruling did not conform to what *he* wanted to decree. The people, the local ones, are the ones who suffer. In any case, to this day there has been no social mixing between the rulers and the ruled. It would be unfair to generalize, however; some officers are more civilized, but then the difference is only one of degree. The evil is in-built and ingrained in the system obtaining there. The style may change, but the pattern remains.

The islands are not only enchanting, but abound in manifold wealth of every description, including natural resources and minerals. If oil can be struck off the shore of Sumatra, which is only a few miles away from Great Nicobar Island, there surely must be some below the waters lapping the coastline of some of these islands. Nothing has so far been done in this direction. It is understood that now some oil exploration is taking place.

It has been reported recently that, because of the discovery of mineral resources on the seabed in the Bay of Bengal, the government of India proposes at the next session of the United Nations conference on the law of the seas that India's control over the continental shelf be extended beyond the present limit of 200 miles, so that it extends to the outer edge of the margin where it reaches deep ocean floor. If that is agreed to, India is likely to earn an annual income of 300 million US dollars, because the seas around the islands of Andaman and Nicobar are supposed to be one of the four areas of the world which contain extensive deposits of manganese nodules. In fact thick sediments, which have been piling up for more than 35 million years perhaps, have already been discovered in the Bay of Bengal. This is also an indication of oil deposits.

As already stated, a vast undersea valley, 600 miles long, 25 miles wide, and surrounded by towering mountain peaks, lies buried one to three miles under the sea. No one can tell what mineral wealth lies in this valley!

If spices of every kind can be grown in Malaysia and Indonesia, they certainly can in the Andamans and Nicobars. The sea in full of fish; this can be canned and exported. There was a time when pearl oysters were known to exist in the Andaman Sea. Where have they gone? One can go on *ad infinitum*. We have not even tried to export bird's-nests, which are considered such a delight all over the world.

A glorious future awaits tourism, but it needs serious thinking and planning, so that it does not become the curse it has in some other countries. But we must at least make a start by providing the tourists with elementary facilities. Of late, however, one hears that a beach hotel, with separate self-contained huts, providing all the necessary facilities, is being planned. Similarly, the construction of a hotel in the town is reported to have started already. And the existing tourist bungalow has also added a special wing, with eight air-conditioned suites. As of today, though, with all the fabulous marine flora and fauna in the Andaman Sea, Port Blair does not possess even one single boat with a glass bottom, so that you can have a glimpse of what lies below in those blue and emerald green waters.

There has been some talk of making Great Nicobar a duty-free port. However, none of the other islands, where the Nicobarese live, should be touched. As it is, Car Nicobar is a small island and much too crowded. As

Ganesh put it: "The Nicobarese population is increasing and they need more land . . . . Car Nicobar is a very crowded island." Talking about the island of Chowra, he says: "Chowra [has] a population of 4,000 or more, with less than one square mile area." But as far as Great Nicobar Island is concerned, it is an excellent idea. Even there one has to be careful in choosing which part of the island can house all the paraphernalia of a duty-free port. It is the most logical thing to have because anyone with perception can see that, with Hongkong's future so uncertain and Singapore so crowded, Great Nicobar is *the place*, situated as it is on the trade routes of India, Burma, the entire Far East and South-east Asia. Besides, it is understood that the Indians living abroad have displayed great enthusiasm for a project of this kind, offering to provide all the foreign exchange required for the purpose. But, before anything of the kind is done, as Ganesh put it: "We must prepare a blueprint for the development of the islands and an infrastructure which should be in terms of its geography, in terms of its natural wealth, and in terms of its unique and enchanting beauty."

The time is now. For tomorrow may be too late.

Bibliography

BOOKS

Barker, F A
  Modern Prison System in India. London: Macmillan, 1944.
Brown, A R Radcliffe
  The Andaman Islanders. London: Cambridge University Press, 1922.
Buckland, C E
  Dictionary of Indian Biography. London: Sonnenschein and Co., 1906.
Chak, B L
  Green Islands in the Sea. New Delhi: Publications Division, Ministry of Information and Broadcasting, 1967.
Cipriani, Lidio
  The Andaman Islanders. London: Weidenfield and Nicolson, 1966.
Clifton, V M
  Pilgrims to the Isles of Penance. London: John Lang, 1911.
Collier, Basil
  A Short History of the Second World War. London: Fontana, 1970.

The War in the Far East. London: Heinemann, 1969.
Craddock, Sir Reginald
  The Dilemma of India. London: Constable and Co., 1929.
Crantz, David
  The Ancient and Modern History of the Brethren: a Succinct Narrative of the Protestant Church of the Brethren, now Translated into English. London: W and A Strahan, 1780.
Frederikes, Master Caesar
  Eighteen Years' Indian Observations. In *Purchas, his Pilgrims*, vol. 1. London: W Stansby, 1625.
Ghose, Shanker
  Political Ideas and Movements in India. New Delhi: Allied Publishers, 1975.
Ghosh, K C
  The Roll of Honour. Calcutta: Vodya Bharti, 1955.
Golant, William
  The Long Afternoon: British India 1601-1947. New Delhi: Vikas Publishing House, 1975; London: H Hamilton, 1975.
Gopal, Ram
  Indian Muslims—A Political History. Bombay: Asia Publishing House, 1964.
Griffiths, Sir Percival
  To Guard my People: The History of Indian Police. London: Benn, 1972.
Gupta, Manmathnath
  History of the Indian Revolutionary Movement. Bombay: Somaiya Publications, 1972.
Hayshida, Tatsuo
  Netaji Subhas Chandra Bose: His Great Struggle and Martyrdom. Bombay: Allied Publishers, 1970.
Hunter, Sir W W
  The Earl of Mayo. In *Rulers of India* series. London: Smith, Elder and Co., 1875.
  The Indian Musalmans. Calcutta: Comrade Publishers, 1945.
Hussain, S Yusuf
  Pen Pictures of the Andaman and Nicobar Islands, Port Blair. Port Blair: published by the author, 1954.
Johnston, Sir Henry, etc.
  The Living Races of Mankind by eminent specialists, including Sir Henry Johnston, R Lydekkor, Dr A H Keane, H N Hutchinson, A H Savage London, Dr R W Shufeldt, Professor Longford. London: Huchinson and Co., 1965.
Kirby, S Woodburn
  History of the Second World War. In *The War Against Japan*, vols. II and IV. HMSO, 1958 (reprinted in 1972).
Kloss, C Boden
  In the Andamans and Nicobars. London: John Murray, 1903.
Leigh, W H
  Voyages and Travels—an Account of Visit to Nicobars and Other Islands of the Indian Seas. London: P P, 1839.
Mackenzie, Sir Compton
  All Over the Place. London: Chatto Windus, 1948.
  My Life and Times: Octave Nine (1946-1953). London: Chatto Windus, 1970.
MacMunn, Sir George
  Turmoil and Tragedy in India in 1914 and After. London: Jarrolds, 1935.
Malgonkar, Manohar
  A Bend in the Ganges. London: H Hamilton, 1964.
Man, Edward Horace
  The Nicobar Islands. London: Guildford, Billing and Sons, 1933.

Mason, Philip
  A Matter of Honour: an Account of the Indian Army, its Officers and Men. London: Jonathan Cape, 1974.
Mathur, L P
  History of the Andaman and Nicobar Islands (1756-1966). Delhi: Sterling Publishers, 1969.
Mathur, Kaushal Kumar
  Nicobar Islands New Delhi: National Book Trust, 1967.
Mouat, Fredric John
  Adventures and Researches Among the Andaman Islands. London: P P, 1963.
Portman, M V
  A History of Our Relations with the Andamanese, vols. I and II. Calcutta: Office of the Superintendant of Government Printing.
Savarkar, V D
  The Story of my Transportation for Life (a Biography of Black Days in the Andamans). (Translated from the original in Marathi by V N Naik.) Bombay: Sadbhakti Publications, 1950.
  Echo from Andaman. Bombay: Gogate Printing Co., 1924.
Sen, Prabhat Kumar
  Land and People of the Andamans. Calcutta: Post-Graduate Book Mart, 1962.
Smyth, Sir John
  The Story of the Victoria Cross. London: F Muller, 1963.
Stewart, Major Rupert (compilation)
  The Book of the Victoria Cross. London: Hugh Rees, 1916.
Suba Singh
  Diwan Singh Kalepani (Gurmukhi). Patiala: Punjabi University.
Sykes, Sir Percy M
  History of Exploration. London: Routledge and Kegan Paul, 1950.
Thanesvri, Maulana Mohammad Jafar
  Kalapani (Urdu). Lahore: Abdul Aziz.
Toye, Hugh
  The Springing Tiger. London: Cassell, 1959.
Turner, C H
  Notes on the Andaman Islands from the Existing Information (1897). Rangoon: 1897.
Vaidya, Suresh
  Islands of the Mangold Sun. London: Robert Hale, 1960.
Whitehead, George
  In Nicobar Islands London: Seeley, Service and Co., 1924.
Williams, J H
  The Spotted Deer. London: Hart-Davis, 1957.

UNPUBLISHED WORKS, OFFICIAL PUBLICATIONS AND ARTICLES IN NEWSPAPERS AND JOURNALS

Unpublished records in the custody of the National Archives of India.
Unpublished records in the Historical Section, Ministry for Defence, Government of India.
Unpublished records in the India Office Library and Records, Foreign and Commonwealth Office, London.
Unpublished records in Rigsarkivet, Copenhagen.

Bibliography

Annual reports of the Andaman and Nicobar administration from 1864 onwards (except when the islands were under Japanese occupation).
The various five-year plans—reports published by the Planning Commission.
The Andaman and Nicobar Information, a periodical journal giving information about developmental activities in the islands.
Census Report, Andamans and Nicobars, 1901, by Sir Richard Temple, Bart.
Census Report, Andamans and Nicobars, 1911, by R F Lowis.
Census Report, Andamans and Nicobars, 1921, by R F Lowis.
Census Report, Andamans and Nicobars, 1931, by C J Bonington.
Census Report, Andamans and Nicobars, 1951, by A K Ghose.
Census Report, Andamans and Nicobars, 1961, by S K Sharma.
Report of the Indian Law Commission, 1837.
Reports of the Committee on Prison Discipline—1838, 1864, 1876-77, 1888.
Report of the Indian Jails Committee, 1919-20.
Annual reviews of jail operations by the Government of India, published in the *Gazette of India*, from 1857 onwards.
A note on the Administration of the Andaman and Nicobar islands, submitted by the Government of India to the Indian Statutory Commission, 1930, part 1, vol. 5, pp. 361-402.
Proceedings of the Council of the Governor-General of India, 1912, and 1914.
Proceedings of the Indian Legislative Assembly, 1921, 1922, 1926, 1933, 1935 and 1936.
Proceedings of the Council of States, 1921.
Proceedings of the Lok Sabha, 1969.

Bengal—Past and Present
"Letters Edifiantes on Bengal: Translated by H Hosten," January-June 1911, vol. 7, pp. 142-62.

Calcutta Review
"Summary of Papers Relating to Nicobar Islands," October 1870, pp. 266-70.

Geographical Magazine
H de Roepstorff: "Nicobar Islands." 1875, vol. 2, pp. 44-47.
H S Montgomerie: "Nicobar Islands," 1922, vol. 59, pp. 36-50.
H de Reopstorff: "Inland Tribe of Great Nicobar," 1878, vol. 5, pp. 39-44.

Imperial Gazetteers of India, Provincial Series
"Andaman and Nicobar Islands," compiled by Major W S Molesworth, 1909.
Colonel Wedgwood: "Hell on Earth," originally published in the *Daily Telegraph*, London, and reproduced in the *Searchlight*, Patna, 6 February 1921.

Indian Antiquary
Richard Temple: "Papers Relating to the Settlement in the Andaman Islands in the 18th Century," January-December 1819.

Indian Forester
T P Aiyar: "The Andamans—Their Geology from an Easy Chair," 1917, vol. 53, pp. 269-75.
Bonington: "With the Aborigines of the Andamans," 1931, vol 57, pp. 264-67.

Journal of Indian History
"The Danes in India," 1934, vol. 13, pp. 312-29.

Journal of the East India Association
"Andaman Penal Settlement," 1914, pp. 159-81.

Bibliography

Journal of the Indian Geological Survey
R D Oldham: "Notes on the Geology of the Andaman Islands," 1855, vol. 18, pp. 135.
F V Hothstetter: "Contribution to the Geological and Physical Geography of the Nicobar Islands," 1869, vol. 2, pp. 59-63.
J R Mallet: "Volcanoes of Barren Island and Narion," 1895, vol. 21, p. 36; 1895, vol. 28, pp. 22-23 and pp. 34-38.
G H Tipper: "Geology of Andaman and Nicobar," 1911, vol. 35, part IV, pp. 1-19.

Journal of the Royal Anthropological Institute of Great Britain and Ireland
W L Distant: "Inhabitants of Car Nicobar," 1874, vol. 3, pp. 2-7.
Hyde Clarke: "Notes on the Language of the Andamanese," 1874, vol. 3, pp. 467-68.
G E Dodson: "On the Andamanese and Andaman," 1877, vol. 6, pp. 209-14.
E H Man: "Andaman Islands," 1878, vol. 7, pp. 105-09.
E H Man: "Ornaments and Implements of Andamans," 1878, vol. 7, pp. 451-69.
A H Rivers and Lane Fox-Pitt: "Observations of Man's Collection of Andaman and Nicobarese Objects," 1878, vol. 7, pp. 434-51.
V Ball: "On Nicobarese Ideograph," 1881, vol. 10, pp. 103-08.
E H Man: "On Andaman and Nicobarese Objects," 1882, pp. 268-94.
Thomas Allen: "Andamanese Bone Necklaces," 1882, vol. 2, pp. 295-310.
E H Man: "On the Aboriginal Inhabitants of Andaman Islands," 1883, vol. 12, pp. 69-116.
Sir W H Flower: "On Affinities of Natives of Andamans," 1885, vol. 9, pp. 108-35; vol. 14, pp. 115-20.
E H Man: "Andaman Islands and their Inhabitants," 1885, vol. 14, pp. 253-72.
E H Man: "Nicobar Islands with Special Reference to Tribes of Great Nicobar," 1886, vol. 15, pp. 428-51.
E H Man: "Nicobar Islander," 1889, vol. 18, pp. 351-94.
E H Man: "Nicobar Pottery," 1894, vol. 23, pp. 21-27.
E H Man: "Nicobar Islander's Certain Deformations," 1894, vol. 23, pp. 232-40.
M V Portman: "Notes on Andamanese," 1896, vol. 25, pp. 361-71.
V Solomon: "Extracts from Diaries kept in Car Nicobar During 1895-1901," 1902, vol. 32, pp. 202-38.

Journal of the Royal Asiatic Society
"Andamanese Music and Musical Instruments," 1818, vol. 20, pp. 181-218.

Journal of the Royal Asiatic Society of Bengal
V Ball: "Notes on the Geology of Port Blair," 1870, vol. 163, pp. 231-39.
W S Kurs: "A Sketch on the Vegetation of Nicobar Islands," 1876, vol. 205, pp. 105-64.
Lieutenant-Colonel Prain: "On the Flora of Narcondam and Barren Islands," 1893, vol 325, pp. 39-87.

Journal of the Royal Geographical Society
F J Mouat: "Narrative of an Expedition to the Andaman Islands in 1856-62," vol. 32, pp. 169-260.
E H Man and Richard Temple: "Notes on Two Maps of the Andaman Islands," 1880, vol. 50, pp. 255-59.
M V Portman: "Exploration and Survey of Little Andaman," 1888, vol. 10, pp. 567-76.

Local Gazetteer
"The Andaman and Nicobar Islands," Calcutta: Office of the Superintendant of Government Printing, 1908.

Modern Review
"Andaman and Nicobar Islands," 1941, vol. 15, pp. 648-49.

National Geographic
Raghubir Singh: "The Last Andaman Islanders," July 1975, vol. 148, no. 1, pp. 66-91.

Scottish Geography Magazine
Colonel T Cadell: "Andaman and Andamanese," 1889, vol. 5, pp. 57-73.

Society Arts
Sir Richard Temple: "Penal Settlement at Andamans," 1898, vol. 49, pp. 292-305.
Sir Richard Temple: "Round about Andaman and Nicobar," 1899, vol. 48, pp. 105-25.
M L Ferrar: "New Penal Settlement in Andamans," 1931, vol. 80, pp. 48-61.

Supplement Andaman and Nicobar Gazette
A L Butler, November 1897.

Tropical Agriculture
"Coconut Industry in Andaman," 1932, vol. 79, pp. 349-52.

Vanya Jati (published by the Bhartiya Adim Jati Sangh, New Delhi)
Dr B K Chatterjee: "Onges of Little Andaman," 1953, vol. 1, pp. 86-92.
Dr B K Chaterji and G D Kumar: "Hunting and Fishing Appliances of the Onges of Little Andaman and their Affinities with the Negrito Race," July 1954, vol. 2, pp. 75-78.
Dr N D Majumdar: "Aboriginal People of the Andaman and Nicobar Islands," October 1958, vol. 3, pp. 149-51.

Index

Aberdeen, battle of, 78; incident near Muslim mosque in, 240

Achin Head (Sumatra), 10, 11, 23

Advisory council, formation and functions of, 288; setting up of, 284

Addison, Brigadier H J L, commander of troops fighting the Japanese, 270

Ahmad, Fakhruddin Ali, visit to the Andamans, 288

Ahmed, Sayed, Wahabi movement and, 183-84

Aka-Bea-da tribe, relations with the British, 25; *see also Andamanese*

Alexandra river, 10; valley of, 287

Alipore conspiracy case, 190

Alvi, Major Mansoor Ali, officer of the Indian National Army, 250

Andaman and Nicobar islands, as territory of free India, 56, 288; climate of, 18; flag hoisted at, 280-81; forest wealth of, 292-93; geodetic survey around, 18-19; liberation of, 247; notion of the state of "immorality" among the "locals" of, 285-86; plan expenditure on, 304; proposal to change the name of, 302-03; rainfall of, 12; sea-food of, 19; social life in, 286; status of a part D state, 288; varieties of fish around, 19

Andaman and Nicobar islands' Municipal Board Regulation, promulgation of, 288

Andaman Committee, 30, 143; appointment of, 50; investigations by and report of, 50-51

Andaman Club, 270

314 Index

Andaman Homes, 82; conditions under M V Portman, 138; escapes from, 128-29; establishment of, 125; Ford's policy on, 130-32; Homfray's opinion about, 133-34; policy on, 125; Tytler's policy on, 125, 127

Andaman islands, aborigines of, 299; account of Allied air attacks in, 262-63; air service between Calcutta and, 288; as territory of Free India, 56, 288; atrocities committed in, 275-77; bird's-nests in, 16-17; Blair's survey of, 3; British colonization of, 3, 56; coral reefs around, 16; cosmopolitan character of the population of, 281; fauna of, 16-18; first British occupation of, 21-28; first survey of, 29; forest flora of, 13-15; Ghadar party's role in, 208-10; highest peak in, 10; history of the Japanese administration in, 239-42; horror stories about, 275-77; Japanese air-raids on, 235-36; Japanese occupation of, 56; landscape of, 10; *lingua franca* of, 281-82; location and geographical features of, 8-10; Marco Polo's reference to, 2-3; marine zoology of, 16; medical facilities in, 285; number of families settled in, 292; origin and name of, 3-4; palm-trees of, 15-16; political prisoners in, 192-204; population during the British reoccupation and the Japanese reoccupation, 273; Ptolemy's reference to, 1-3; public bus service starting in, 288; rainfall in, 12; reference to Tanjore Inscriptions, 3; resettlement of refugees in, 290-92; road development in, 288; scheme for the colonization and development of, 179; second British occupation of, 56; strategic importance of, 233-34; Thanesvri's 18 years' sojourn in, 184-86; timber classification in the forests of, 14; travellers' accounts of, 2-3; volcanic crater in, 9

Andaman *Miniseibu*, establishment of, 243; objectives of, 243-44; staff of, 243

Andaman Sea, 305; Japanese shipping activity in, 264

Andaman timber, 14, 293-94; export of, 285

Andamanese, absence of bickering among, 126; Andaman Committee's encounter with, 52-55; Blair's encounters with, 23-24; canoes of, 64-65; Colebrook's account of, 29-30; complexion of, 60; dancing and singing of, 30, 62-63; decimation by syphilis of, 136; diet of, 30; dietary habits of, 61; fishing by, 61, 65; Ford's policy on, 131; free love among, 137; funeral and burial customs of, 61-62; habits of, 59; hair styles of, 60; hunting and fishing by, 61; huts of, 33-34, 63; ignorance about making fire, 62; indifference of, 127; introduction of the dog to, 133; lack of inhibitions among women, 126; language of, 30, 65; legend about, 7, 58; marriage ceremony of, 60; natural foods of, 139; navigating skills of, 64; the near extinction of, 137-38, 140-41; 1901 census of, 63; opium addiction among, 137; outsiders' encounters with, 23-24, 31-35, 39, 45-46; physical features of, 59; pottery of, 61; racial origin of, 57-58; reaction to insult, 127; relations with british, 25; religion of, 63-64; sexual life of, 59-60; syphilis scourge among, 136-37; taming of, 124-41; tattoo practice among, 60-61; tribal divisions and subdivisions of, 58-59; village layout of, 63; visit to Calcutta by, 127; weapons of, 34; *see also Jarawa tribe; Aka-Bea-da tribe*

Andamanese jungle, 276

Anderson, Captain R, report of, 198

Annual administrative report (1947-48) of the islands, features of, 280-82

Anti-Comintern Pact, signing of, 230

Arioto, difference between Eremtaga and, 59; *see also Andamanese*

Asian "co-prosperity", 245

Attlee, Clement, 214

Aurobindo, Sri, 190

Austin, H Godwin, 140, 157

Azad Hind Fauj, 247

Bagchi, Pushkar, 238; charges against, 240-41; Mackenzie on, 276

Bal, Lokenath, involvement in Chittagong armoury raid, 213

Banerji, Surendranath, 193

Banerji, Upendra Nath, 198

Bangkok Conference, 242-45; resolution of, 243

Baratang Island, 9, 22

Barry, tortuous career of, 210-11

Barwell, Major-General C A, chief commissioner, 135-38

Bay of Bengal, 284; naval activity in, 235-36; *see also Andaman and Nicobar islands*

Bengalee, comment on political prisoners' conditions in, 193-95

Bhagat Singh, imprisonment of, 210-11;

involvement in Lahore conspiracy case, 214-15; trial of, 216
Bhantus, deportation to the Andamans of, 181, 280-81
Bhargava, J L, on penal settlement, 175
Bhattacharya, Upendra, involvement in the Chittagong armoury raid, 213
Bird, Major A, charges against, 240-41; Japanese maltreatment of, 241; torture of, 276
Blair, Lieutenant Archibald, 3, 9, 16, 275; Andaman Committee's tribute to, 51; contacts with the aborigines, 23-24; first visit and report on Bay islands, 21-24; further visits to Bay islands, 24-27; on hostile attitude of the Andamanese, 55
Bose, Rash Bihari, *de jure* president of the Indian Independence League, 243; exile of, 243
Bose, Subhas Chandra, 243, 272, 302; broadcast over Rangoon Radio, 251-52; disappearance of, 247-48; Philip Mason's assessment of, 252; public speech in Andamans by, 249-50; role of, 247; tug of war between the Japanese and the representatives of, 257; visit to the Andamans of, 248-49
Briton and *Runnymede*, twin shipwrecks of, 35-40
British East India Company, 3; Blair's survey of Bay islands and, 21-24; colonization of the Andamans by, 24-25; move to abolish the settlement at Port Cornwallis, 28; on penal settlement proposal, 47-48
Brown, A Radcliffe, 62, 70
Browning, Lieutenant-Colonel H A, on condition of political prisoners, 195
Buchanan, Sir Walter J, 21, 171
Bucho, Colonel, 238
Burma, Japanese invasion of, 233-34
Burmese Association, resolution of general council of, 218-19
Burmese transportees, statistics on, 218
Burr wood, 14
Busch and Steen Bille, 6
Bush Police, establishment of, 164

Cadell, Major T, 138, 140, 149
Cairo conference, 261
Camorta, naval base at, 297
Camorta penal settlement, 102-03
Campbell Bay, 301
Cape Negrais (Burma), 8, 11

Captain Wimberley's expedition, 149
Car Nicobar Island, 5; British reoccupation of, 273; coconut tree legend about, 10-11; conditions of, 274; Japanese occupation and Richardson's account about happenings in, 266-68; Mackenzie's comment on, 277; Nicobarese name for, 89; *see also Chowra Island; Nicobarese*
Cariappa, K M, 284
Cellular Jail, 192, 195; construction of, 120-21; description of, 169-70; genesis of, 118; discipline in, 119; protests by political prisoners in, 196-204
Central Legislative Assembly, adjournment motion in relation to hunger strike in, 225-26; penal settlement issue in, 174, 179-80, 212-13; resolution of, 227
Chakrabarti, Ambika, involvement in Chittagong armoury raid, 213
Chamberlain, Neville, 231-32
Chatham Island, 27, 50, 168, 288; Blair's sojourn in, 25; Japanese navy on, 237; saw-mills in, 293
Chaudhuri, Captain B, attitude towards prisoners, 226; task of force-feeding taken up by, 226-27
Chaudhuri, D K Lahiri, 224
Chengapa, on Great Nicobar, 286-87
Chiang Kai-shek, attitude of, 261
Chowra Island, 98, 278; canoes made in, 99; claypots of, 99; importance to Nicobarese of, 98-99; population of, 306; witch-doctors of, 11, 99-100; *see also Car Nicobar Island; Nicobarese*
Christian evangelists, success of, 281
Churchill, Winston, 262
Cinema-houses, building of, 289
Cinque Island, 9
Cipriani, Lidio, 68-69; study on Andamanese, 58
Chittagong armoury raid, account of, 213-14, 224
Coco Island, 41, 42, 44
Colebrook, Lieutenant Robert-Hyde, 22; Jarawa vocabulary compiled by, 154; on Andamanese, 29-30; reference to Jarawas, 153-54
Colebrook Passage, 139
Colombo Plan, 288
Congress Working Committee, appeal to political prisoners to abandon hunger strike, 227
Convicts, Sir Stamford Raffle's approach to, 74-75; release and pardon of, 275

Cooperative movement, 282
Corbyn, Reverend H, 124; Andaman Home and, 125, 126, 128, 130, 155; policy differences between Lieutenant-Colonel R C Tytler and, 127; policy differences between Major Barnet Ford and, 128-29
Cornwallis, Lord, 3; briefing to Lieutenant Blair, 21
Cosgrave, W A, attitude towards prisoners of, 226; haughty nature of, 219-20; role of, 226-27
Cottage industries, in the islands, 293-94
Craddock, Sir Reginald, 168, 209; interview with political prisoners, 199; recommendations of, 201
Craddock Report, 168-71
Craik, Sir Henry, 224; on penal settlement, 174-75, 212; visit to Andamans, 179, 221

Dagmar river, 10, 287
Dakota service, beginning of, 288
Dampier, Captain Alexander, visit to Nicobars, 4
Danish East India Company, 5
Das, Lala Ram Saran, on penal settlement, 174, 212
Day, Sir Francis, on fisheries, 294
de Roepstorff, H, 140; translation of Nicobarese folk-tale, 106; visit to Great Nicobar, 286
Desai, Bhulabhai, hunger strike by prisoners and, 225-26
Diwan Singh, Dr, 242, 244-45, 271-72; arrest and inhuman treatment of, 246-47; prosecution of, 250; torture of, 249-50; role of, 236, 238-40, 249
Dollfuss, Engelbert, assassination of, 230
Douglas, Lieutenant-Colonel M W, 172, 198, 202
Duff Cooper, Lady Diana, 236
Duncan Passage, 9
Dutt, Batukeshwar, 216
Dutt, Kalpana, 214
Dutt, Ulaskar, cruel treatment meted out to, 196

Earl of Mayo, assassination of, 186
East Bengali refugees, resettlement of, 285, 292-94
Educational progress, 297
Edwina Mountbatten, 275
Emily, shipwreck of, 43-44
Falconer, Captain, 256

Fauré and Taillandiers, first attempt to convert the Nicobarese by, 5
Female population, shortage of, 285-86
Ferrar, Lieutenant-Colonel M L, 178; Preface
Fisheries, talk about developing, 294
Flat Island, 253
Flying Fish, shipwreck of, 41-43
Ford, Major Barnet, 128-32, 155
Forestry, lack of substantial achievement in, 292-93
Forest development corporation, formation of, 293
Franco, Generelissimo, leadership of, 230
Fredrick, Captain, early landings on the shores of the Andamans, 4
Frederike, Master Caesar, early observations of Andaman islands, 3
French East India Company, 5

Gandhi, Mahatma, 213, 214, 251-52; visit to Andamans, 227
Ganesh, K R, 288; on Andaman and Nicobar problems and development of the islands, 302-06
Ghadar, journal of the Ghadar party, 207
Ghadar leaders, ill-treatment of, 210-11
Ghadar movement, beginnings of, 210
Ghadar party, aim of, 206-07; birth of, 207; formation of, 207; headquarters of, 207; German support to, 208; role of, 209-10
Ghosh A K, 276; role of, 282-88
Ghosh, Barindra Kumar, petitions submitted by, 199-200
Ghosh, Ganesh, 212, 220; involvement in the Chittagong armoury raid, 213
Ghosh, Jiten, Indian revolutionary transported to the Andamans, 218
Gidney, Lieutenant-Colonel Sir Henry, 178, 180
Gunseisho, establishment of, 241
Gommeli, John Francis, 5
Government of India Act of 1935, 225
Government of India Resolution on penal settlement, 175-76
Great Andaman islands, 8-10
Great Nicobar, 283, 305-06; aborigines of, 101-02; canoes from, 287; rivers of, 10
Grieg, Major, 256
Guha, Samar, 303

H M I S Ramdas, attack at, 235

Index

H M I S *Sophie Marie*, loss of, 235
Haig, Sir Harry, 217; on penal settlement, 179
Hans Raj, Raizada, 221-22, 227
Harding, Lord, bomb thrown on, 242
Hari, Babu Ram, editor of *Swarajya* sent as political prisoner to Andamans, 188
Haughton, captain J C, superintendent of Port Blair penal settlement, 79-80
Havelock Island, 259
Heathcote, Lieutenant J A, as member of the Andaman Committee, 50, 55
Helfer, Dr (Russian geologist), fatal encounter with the Andamanese, 35
Henry, Captain, concern for Andamanese population, 134, 137-38; dictionary of Andamanese lauguages by, 138
Hewett, Sir J P, role in sending political prisoners to the Andamans, 188
Hindenburg, President Von, death of, 230
Hindi Association, 207
Hindu and Muslim population of Andamans, 282
Hindustan Socialist Republican party, 215
Hindustan Times, comment on Andaman happenings in, 271-73
Hiroshima, bombed, 260
Hitler, Adolph, 230-32
Homfray, J M, 128, 130-32; on Andaman Homes, 133-34
Homfray Strait, 139
Hope-Simpson, J, 201-03
Hopkinson, Captain Henry, recommendations for a penal settlement, 46-47
Hoti Lal, editor of *Swarajya* sent as prisoner to the Andamans, 188, 193, 199
Hudson, Colonel Christopher, 253, 255
Humayun Abdulali, 17
Hume, A O, 12, 17
Hussain, Khan Bahadur Khalifa Syed, 172

I N S *Dhanwantri*, naval hospital, 297
I N S *Jarawa*, 297
I N S *Kardip*, 297
Inam-ul-Majid, allegations against, 282; as chief commissioner of the islands, 275; reasons for transfer of, 280; role of, 280-82
India Command's Joint Planning staff, on capture and retention of Port Blair settlement, 260-61
Indian Armed Forces, account of performance during second world war, 235-36

Indian Association of Pacific Coast, formation of, 207
Indians immigrating to Canada, restrictions on entry of, 207-08
Indian Independence League, 207; birth of, 242-43
Indian independence movement, 247
Indian Jails Committee, appointment of, 171; members of, 171-72; recommendations of, 172-74
Indian National Army, birth of, 242
Indian National Congress, resolution for the release of Savarkar brothers, 212
Indian National party, formation of, 208
Indian Navy, role of, 297
Indian revolutionaries, first conference of, 207; see also Political prisoners
Industrial development in the Andamans, talk about, 292-94
Integrated resources development plan, introduction of, 290-91
International Pro-Indian Committee, activities and formation of, 209
Interview Island, 22, 54
Iqbal, Lieutenant Mohammed, 250
Ishikava, the Japanese admiral, 248
I' Tsing, early Chinese traveller, 2, 4

Jails Committee, formation of, 211
Japanese atrocities, account of, 269-72
Japanese surrender ceremony, 270-71
Japanese war criminals, 273; trial of, 275
Jarawas, 66, 134, 142; British encounters with, 153-56, first recorded reference to, 153-54; hair styles of, 60; kitchen-middens of, 154; punitive expeditions against, 159-64; raid by, 283-84; recent signs of friendliness by, 300-01; relations with British, 25
Jenkins, J L, report of visit to Port Blair, 167-68
Jetties, progress in the construction of, 296
Jinnah, M A, plea on behalf of prisoners, 226
John Lawrence Island, twin shipwrecks on, 35-40

Kakori conspiracy case, account of, 213-14
Kapur, Ladha Ram, Indian editor transported to the Andamans, 189-90
Katchal Island, resettlement of refugees in, 290
Kaur, Kesar, torture of, 247

Khan, Arfat Ahmed, account of visit to the Andamans, 269-70
Khan, Mohammed Yamin, visit to Andamans, 221; report of, 221-22
Khulna conspiracy case, 190
Kirti Lehar movement, 234-35
Kitchen-middens, evidence of, 64, 68; excavations of, 58; of the Jarawas' 154
Kloss, C Boden, 1, 9, 18; visit to Great Nicobar, 286
Koenig, Dr I G, account of Car Nicobar, 5
Koma Gata Maru episode, 208, 242
Kurile islands, 233
Kurz, Sulpiz, study of Andaman flora by, 14
Kyd, Captain Alexander, 26-27, 102
Kyd Island, 135, 139

Labyrinth islands, 8
Ladha Ram, hunger strike by, 197
Lady Nugent, shipwreck of, 44-45
Lahiri, Ashutosh, torture of, 210
Lahore conspiracy case, 210, 213-16
Lajpat Rai, Lala, death of, 215; protest against the Simon Commission, 215
Landfall islands, 8, 35
Language problem, 289
Little Andaman Island, 9, 32; area of, 67; Ongé tribe of, 67; resettlement of refugees in, 290
Little Nicobar, 283
Loganathan, Lieutenant-Colonel E G, 272; mission of, 250-51
Lowis, R F, 1911 census by, 160
Lukas, Sir Percy, 197-98, 201

McCarthy, Denis, leader of intelligence operation, 252-54
Mackenzie, Compton, on Car Nicobar, 277; visit to Great Nicobar, 278; visit to Port Blair, 275
MacMunn, Lieutenant-General Sir George and Moplah revolt, 177
Mahavir Singh, death of, 217
Malcolm, Sir John, on Andamanese, 35
Man, Edward Horace, 97, 140; colonization of Nicobars by, 56, 88; in charge of the Andaman Homes, 135
Manicktala (Alipore) conspiracy case, 196-97
Manipur revolt, 186-87
Marco Polo, 2-4
Marine products, 294-95

Mason, Philip, account of, 234-35; assessment of Subhas Chandra Bose, 252
Match company (WIMCO), 293
Medical facilities, 297-98
Megapode (Australian bird), description by Boden Kloss, 18
Menon, P M G, on fisheries, 294
Merk, W R H, proposal of, 166-67
Middle Andaman Island, 8, 172, 253, 300; destruction of, 233; refugee resettlement at, 290
Middle Strait, 139
Military Engineering service (MES), role of, 296
Mineral resources, discovery of, 305
Minto, Lord, 191
Minto-Morley reforms, 199-200
Moplah revolt, background of, 176-80
Morgan, D L, leader of punitive expedition against Jarawas, 161-62
Mouat Dr Fredrick J, 9, 59, 142; as head of the Andaman Committee, 50, 55; on the Andamans, 30
Mount Haughton, 242
Mount Thuillier, 10
Moutbatten, Rear-Admiral Lord Louis, visit to the Andamans, 274-75
Mountbatten Cinema, 289
Muddiman, Sir Alexander, visit to the Andamans, 175, 177-78, 213
Mukherji, Noni Gopal, hunger strike by, 117
Mushtaq Ali, on the arrival of Subhas Bose in the Andamans, 249
Mussolini, Benito, 230, 232
Mutiny of 1857, 104

Nancowry harbour, 5-6, 11, 102-03
Narayana, R, on lack of achievement in forestry, 293
Narcondam Island, 9
Nasik conspiracy case, 191-92
Nasim, Mohammed, shot by the Japanese, 240
National Union of Bombay, demands of, 211
Nawab Ali, torture of, 271
Nehru, Jawaharlal, 284; appeal to, abandon hunger strike, 227
Nehru, Motilal, 215
Neil Island, refugee resettlement of, 290
Nicobar islands, 9; areas and features of, 10; birds of, 17-18; British colonization of, 6-7, 88; British control over, 6; coco-

nuts in, 294: Danish colonization of, 5-6; early explorers' reference to, 4-5; fauna of, 17-18; forest flora of, 15; Japanese occupation of, 7; marine zoology of, 17; missionary pioneers in, 4-6; origin of the name of, 3; ornithological studies of, 17; palm-trees of, 15; penal settlement in, 102-03; populated islands of, 11, 102; rainfall of, 12; reference to Tanjore Inscriptions in, 3; timber of, 15; *see also Nicobarese*

Nicobarese, characteristics of, 301-02; canoes of, 94; coconut uses by, 93; customs of, 281; conversion to Christianity of, 89; "devil-murder" custom of, 97-98; dwellings of, 91; exorcism of evil spirits among, 91-92; feasts of, 92-93; folk-tale of, 104-06; foods of, 92-94; funeral and burial customs and feasts of, 94-97; legends of, 7; main item of diet of, 15; marriage and divorce among, 90; miniature canoe-making by, 294; naming of children among, 90; Pandanus diet of, 93; Pandanus legend among, 93-94; patriarchal system of, 94; population of, 306; pre-natal customs of, 89-90; religion of, 92; spirit-scarers (*kareau*) of, 91; *see also Car Nicobar Island, Chowra Island and Great Nicobar Island*

Nippon government, attitude of, 247-48, 251

North Andaman Island, 8; refugee resettlement in, 290

North Sentinel Island, 155, 156, 301

Odoric, Friar, description of the people of the Andamans, 3-4

Oil exploration, 305

Ongés, *Akar-Bale* legend of, 71-72; bows and arrows of, 71; British befriending of, 149-51; eating orgies of, 69; canoe-making by, 71; decorations on bodies of, 60-61; diet of, 69; encounters with the British, 143-44, 146, 148-51; family tradition of, 70; hair style of, 60; honey-gathering by, 69-70; ignorance of making fire, 68; language of, 67; legend of the cataclysm about, 67; Lieutenant Much's expedition against, 144-49; marriage ceremony of, 70; number of, 294-300; occupation of, 69; pet animals of, 68; pottery of, 68; puberty ceremonial of, 70-71; religion of, 70; sexual life of, 70; shelters and huts of, 68; singing and dancing of, 71; pipe-smoking of, 69; syphilis scourge among, 150; water provision for, 70; Wimberley expedition against, 149

Padauk tree, features of, 14

Panay Hanay cooperative stores, set up in the Nicobar islands, 282

Parmanand, role of, 209-10, 221

Patel, Vithalbhai, 215

Patterson, N K, 270, 275; on the abolition of the penal settlement, 273-74

Peace Treaty at Versailles, 229-30

Peace Committee, 241, 244; establishment of, 239

Pearl Harbour, 233

Penal settlement, 303; abolition of, 273; at Camorta, 102-03; proposal for, 46-48; Andaman Committee's recommendation of, 50-55

Penal system, punitive aspects of, 170

Playflair, Dr G R, as member of the Andaman Committee, 50, 55

Political prisoners, accounts of inhuman treatment of, 188-204; bomb-making conspiracy among, 198; complaints of, 222-23; Craddock's interview with and report of, 198-204; death of, 211; demands of, 202, 211, 223-24; demands accepted, 217-18; hunger strike by, 197-98, 211; number of strikes by, 225-26; numbers of, 211, 221; official communique on, 225-26; quality of food supplied to, 220-21; repatriation of, 228, 273-74; terms of, 198; treatment of, 210-11; torture of, 246-50

Ponti, Nicolo 3

Port Blair, Andaman Committee's recommendations on, 51, 55; bombardment of, 257; condition of the population at, 274; first British settlement at, 25-26; features of, 22, 24, 51; installation of All India Radio station at, 289; Japanese occupation of, 233-34; living conditions in, 251; naming of, 51, 55; raid at, 235; Thanesvri's account of, 185-86

Port Blair penal settlement, 73-74; attempts at escape by prisoners in, 76,78; convicts' conspiracy in, 76-77; convicts' plight in, 76; copper token currency of, 80; Craddock's report on, 168-71; cyclone in, 80; Jenkin's report on, 167-68; Mohammed Yamin's report on, 220-28; trouble with Andamanese in, 75-82; under Haughton, 79-80; under Dr Walker, 73-79; under Tytler, 80-82

Port Campbell, 22, 139-48
Port Cornwallis, 50; establishment of settlement in, 26-27; health hazards in, 27-28; abolition of settlement at, 28
Portman, M V, 126, 130, 140, 154-59; assault on, 141; as in charge of the Andaman Homes, 138; on British-Andamanese relations, 25; study on Andamanese, 59-60, 63, 66, 150-52
Port Mouat, 128, 155
Prasad, Dr Rajendra, visit to the Andamans, 288
Prince of Wales Island, 23
Prohibition, policy on, 298-99
Provisional Indian Government, installation ceremony of, 247-48
Prithvi Singh, hunger strike by, 211
Prothroe, Colonel M, chief commissioner, 186
Ptolemy, 1-3
Public Safety Bill, 215
Puluga, anthropomorphic deity, 7, 64
Pygmalion Point, 10

Quebec conference, 261

Raddich, Surgeon, death after sickness in unhealthy climate, 28
Raffles, Sir Stamford, proposal on the treatment of convicts, 74-75, 108
Rajendra I (Chola king of South India), military expedition to the Nicobars, 4
Rajguru, involvement in the Saunders murder, 215-16
Rama Rakha, death of, 211
Rani of Nancowry, achievement of, 103
Refugees, problems of the resettlement of, 290-91
Rempang Island, 264
Reorganization of states in India, status of Andaman and Nicobar islands until, 228
Resettlement Scheme, 290-92
Richardson, Bishop John, 89, 90, 92, 103, 278, 288; account of Car Nicobar and Japanese occupation, 266-68
Ritchie, John, recommendation on Bay islands, 20-21; Ritchie's Archipelago, 9
Roads, progress in the construction of, 296-97
Rome-Berlin Axis, 230
Rose, Sir Alec, *Lonely Lady* cruise, 14
Rosen, Pastor, Danish missionary, first reference to Shompens, 286

Roosevelt, 262
Ross Island, 74, 248, 257, 270, 293; Andaman Home at, 125; Japanese Navy swooping on, 235-37
Roy, B P Singh, sportsman, 227
Roy, Indu Bhushan, suicide by, 196
Roy, Dr Niranjan, 220
Rubber production, little progress in, 295
Rutland Island, 9, 141, 155

Sahay, Vijay Shankar, study on Nicobarese by, 99-100
Saddle Peak, 50
Salomon, A J, 265, 270, 271, 275; on the condition of the population of Port Blair, 274; signing of documents by, 271
Sarup Ram, accomplice of the Japanese, 241
Satyamurthi, S, adjournment motion in the Central Legislative Assembly by, 225
Saudagar, Mohammad, account of Andamans by, 257-59
Saunders, J P, 215
Savarkar, Ganesh Vinayak, involvement in the Nasik conspiracy case, 191-92
Savarkar, Vinayak Damodar, flight to Paris, 192; on demands of the political prisoners, 202; on Indu Bhushan Roy's suicide, 196; petitions submitted by, 199-200; story of transportation for life, 192; transportation to the Andamans, 191
Scott, Bob, assistant commissioner at Car Nicobar, 252
Sedition Committee and *Swarajya* case, 189
Sen, Nirmal, involvement in the Chittagong armoury raid, 213
Sentinelese, 66; *see also Andamanese*
Shah, Habib, 253, 254; death of, 255
Shastri, Lal Bahadur, visit to Port Blair, 288
Shipping, little work in the field of, 295
Shompens, 101-02; diet of, 287; exploration party to, 287; fondness for betel-nuts and betel leaves, 287; gardening, canoe-making and basket-making activities of, 287; number of, 301; habitat described as the "crudest," 287; *see also Nicobarese*
Shuddhi movement, launching of, 212
Simon, Sir John, 214
Simon Commission, 214-15; protest against, 215
Singh, Bakhshish, involvement in intelligence operation, 255, 256

Index

Singh, Gurdit, involvement in *Koma Gata Maru* episode, 208
Singh, Har Mander, on Nicobarese, 302
Singh, Havildar Gyan, 253
Singh, Mohan, 243, 247
Singh, Sardar Gurmukh, 220
Sinha, Bejoy Kumar, 220
Sohan Singh, hunger strike by, 211
Solomon, Vedappan, importance in converting the Car Nicobarese to Christianity, 89, 103
South Andaman Island, 244; Japanese landing in, 239; resettlement of refugees in, 290
South Reef Island, 54
South Sentinel Island, 16
Smyth, J W, inspection of Cellular Jail, 220
Srinivasan, officer of the Indian National Army, 250
Stewart, Major-General Donald, 134, 155, 186
Strait Island, 137, 299
Suba Singh, officer of the Indian National Army, 249, 250
Sullivan, Michael, on horror stories about the Andamans, 275-76
Sumatra-Burma chain, hypothesis on, 11-12
Swarajya, place in the history of Indian journalism, 189; case against editors of, 188-89

Tagore, Rabindranath, appeal to abandon hunger strike by, 227
Temple, Sir Richard, 63, 159
Tanjore Inscriptions, 3-4
Ten Degree Channel, 9
Teressa Island, 44, 45
Thanesvri, Maulana Mohammad Jafar, 228; transportation of, 184; release of, 186; launching of *Shuddhi* movement by, 212
Tharwardy rebellion, account of, 218-25

Thorne, J A, involvement in hunger strike by political prisoners, 225
Tikendrajit, Senapati, Manipur revolt started by, 186-87
Tiwari, Dudhnath, life with Andamanese, 78
Tomola, Andamanese ancestral chief, 7
Tonjoghe plant, immunizing effect of, 69-70
Tourism, future of, 305; progress of, 298
Toye, Hugh, on public meeting addressed by Subhas Bose in the Andamans, 249-50
Tuson, F E, in charge of Andaman Homes, 134-35
Tytler, Colonel R B, as superintendent of Port Blair penal settlement, 80-82; policy on Andaman Homes, 125, 127

United Nations conference on the law of the seas, 305
United States, genesis of the conspiracy in, 206-07
Usman, Baba Hari, involvement in throwing a bomb at Hardinge, 242

Varmah, J C, on Andaman forests, 292-93
Vincent, Sir William, 212; on penal settlement, 175
Viper Island, 135, 169
Viper Jail, 118, 122, 169

Wahab, Mohammad Abdul, Wahabi movement started by, 183-84
Wake and Guam, bombardment at, 233
Walker, Dr James Pattison, as superintendent of Port Blair penal settlement, 73-79
Water shortage, problem of, 207
Waterfall, Sir Francis, 236, 240, 254
Wavell, General, 234
Wavell, Lady, 275
Wavell, Lord, visit to the Andamans, 275
Wingfield, Lieutenant-Colonel M R G, commander of submarine, 256

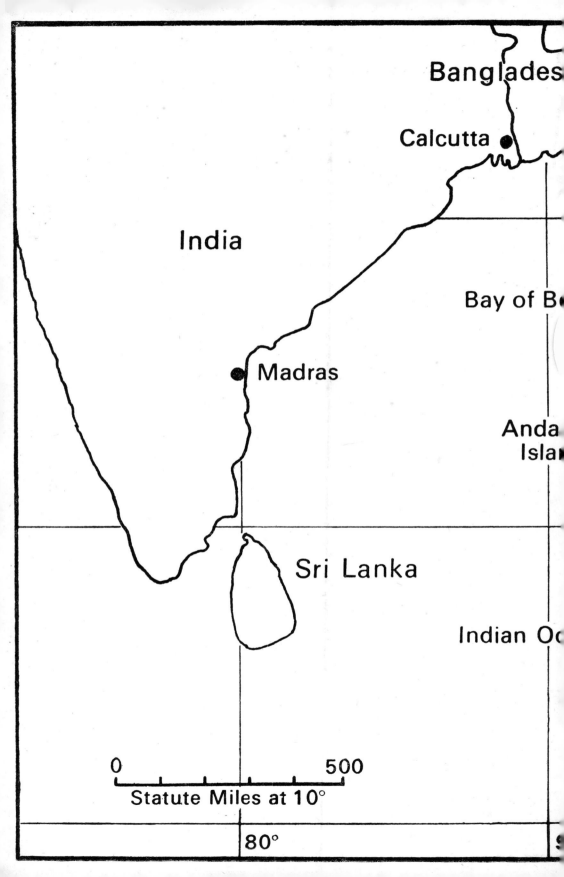